LDAP METADIRECTORY
PROVISIONING
METHODOLOGY

LDAP Metadirectory
Provisioning Methodology

a step by step method to implementing
LDAP based metadirectory provisioning
& identity management systems

By Marlin Pohlman Ph.D. E.I.

Writer's Showcase

New York Lincoln Shanghai

LDAP Metadirectory Provisioning Methodology
a step by step method to implementing LDAP based metadirectory provisioning & identity management systems

Writer's Showcase
an imprint of iUniverse, Inc.

For information address:
iUniverse, Inc.
2021 Pine Lake Road, Suite 100
Lincoln, NE 68512
www.iuniverse.com

ISBN: 0-595-26726-2 (pbk)
ISBN: 0-595-65619-6 (cloth)

Printed in the United States of America

Contents

Foreword

Over the past six years Directories have replaced application-specific lists and consolidated network information for thousands of companies. The reason for this growth is simple; changes made on a Directory server take effect for every directory-enabled application that uses this information. Network administrators along with human resources and data entry personnel are able to add a variety of information about a new user through a single interface only once, and immediately the user has a Unix account, an NT account, a mail address and aliases, membership in departmental mailing lists, access to a restricted Web server, and inclusion in job-specific restricted news groups. The new employee is also instantly included in the company's phone list, mail address book, and meeting calendar system. When the employee leaves, access can be disabled for all of these services with just a single operation. This is the value add of the directory to the enterprise, a single point of administration.

The technologies, companies and personalities that have emerged to support this movement include academicians, programmers, traditional DBA's as well as system integrators and software developers such as Netscape, Sun Microsystems, iPlanet, Critical Path, Critical Angle, Isocor, Lucent, Cisco, Innosoft, Oblix, Control Data, IBM and even Microsoft. The Directory Architect is one part programmer, one part DBA and one part system analyst with a solid knowledge of hardware and network topology, architecture, management and security issues. As this has been my field for over five years It has been my privilege to work with the best and brightest minds in each field. Implementations

I have participated in have spanned four continents and included such diverse technologies as DCOM and CORBA Object Directory Services using RFC2714, Directory based EDI and EFT solutions, Beowulf Cluster Systems which used LDAP directory servers as EPROM's, Wireless Directory centric Applications as well as traditional directory centric applications such as Single Sign on/PKI and Messaging and Mail systems.

As such I would like to give credit to the founders in this field which include Steve Kille, Tim Howes, Alexis Bor, Grodon Good, Wengyik Yeong, Jeff Hodges, Andy Coulbeck and Mark C. Smith who have created the body of knowledge from its humble beginnings as well as innovators such as Ian De Beer, Kevin Braunsdorf, Chris Guzman, Russell Brand and Fred King who designed and pushed directory systems beyond what many of us envisioned possible and crafted new uses for the emerging technology. I would also like to thank Seth Deutsch, Douglass Grey Stephens and Ian Fetterly for their contributions and support

This book is dedicated to Dr. Arvel Witte inspiration, mentor and uncle.

PART I

Fundamental Concepts

1
Introduction

In the last six years the term "directory" has become an integral part of network management. Directories offer network architects the opportunity to create repositories of information about network objects such as workstations, PDA's, printers, network appliances, and servers, and have that information available for use by multiple applications

Directories store information about objects. An object can be a variety of different things such as a person, an application, a unit of code or a printer. A lot of confusion exists between directories and databases, since both are used to store information, but in essence, directories are databases, but they are specialized types of databases that are designed for different purposes than conventional databases. Whereas conventional databases are designed for frequent updates, directories are designed to be read far more often than they are updated.

Since directories are read far more often than they are updated, directories are inherently scaleable. It is much less of an undertaking to replicate a directory out to several locations than it would be to replicate a database since updates to the directory are much less frequent. An example of this type of replication is a distributed database that is replicated out to several remote locations. Since the database is infrequently updated, replication out to these remote sites requires far less bandwidth than replicating a traditional database.

Directories have several other characteristics that distinguish them from traditional databases. Directories are usually less complex than databases since they don't need to support complex languages such as SQL. From a design perspective, databases are often designed to meet specific application needs whereas directories are designed to be flexible so that many different types of applications can read information stored in them

Several initiatives have attempted to create architectures for a directory service that allows the sharing of information between directories, as well as access to directory information via a standard suite of protocols. The first attempt at developing a standard directory protocol was X.500. While X.500 offered the functionality that network managers were looking for, it required a complex method of implementation that restricted its widespread adoption. Other initiatives included **QUIPU** a circa 1988 X.500 server with its database cached in memory, supporting chaining and replication using the ISODE protocol stack. **ros.gda** was a standalone database server based on API design from ISODE Consortium which improved QUIPU scalability. Later **D2** a circa 1993 X.500 directory server developed by ISODE Consortium and used C++, integrated LDAP responder and maintains support for DISP. In structure it was a similar database to ros.gda. and the introduced Tcl/Tk configuration tools DMC and DMD

The development of the x.500 standard was a significant achievement in database design. However the implementation was very complex and required significant computational resources. In order to overcome the complexities of X.500, while still providing the required functionality, the Internet Engineering Task Force (IETF) developed the Lightweight Directory Access Protocol, or LDAP.

Within traditional network structures a directory can be as simple as a list of MAC or IP address assignments, or as complex as a corporate directory containing physical office addresses, geographic office locations, and phone numbers. Traditionally, information about network objects such as users, devices, and applications has been stored in databases, spreadsheets, or even in paper files, leading to inefficient processes, redundant information, and an inability to share information between systems. With an LDAP directory, these limitations are eliminated. Network information about objects can be stored in the directory, associations between objects created, and information used to provision other applications.

2
LDAP History

Historically, X.500 the parent to the current line of LDAP servers was commissioned in 1988 by The CCITT (now the ITU-T) and developed by Marshall Rose and Martin Schoffstall. Its aim was to link up 15 companies and universities providing a replacement for the Internet, a white pages service that would return either the telephone numbers or X.400 O/R addresses of other project members. In 1986 the International Standards Organization (ISO) and the European Computer Manufacturers Association (ECMA) adopted the technology to provide name server service for Open Systems Interconnection (OSI) applications and initiated the formation of the Joint ISO/CCITT working group on Directories. Thus the OSI Directory Service (X.500) was born as an International Telecommunications Union (ITU) standard.

X.500 allowed each campus to have its own Directory system. The administrators at each site need only to keep their own site's data up to date. Users and applications access the only the local X.500 system. If the person being looked for was primarily assigned to the local site, their entry will be in the local X.500 system. If the person was primarily assigned to a remote site, then the local X.500 system will automatically contact the remote X.500 system at the remote site, and will retrieve the information from The Directory located at the remote site. The X.500 user agents switching between local and remote access is transparent to the user. If the X.500 access to the remote sites proves to be too slow, then the systems can be configured to automatically copy data to each other, and to regularly update the data. The system also provides security controls, to stop unauthorized users and applications from reading data from the Directory. X.500 had tremendous data capacity but lacked the ability to scale well requiring large memory intensive mainframes to host.

Several implementations of X.500 attempted to solve the memory problem and in 1990 Tim Howes, Mark Smith and Bryan Beecher, attempted to modify an instance of X.500 called Quipu to work on lower horsepower PC's and Macintoshes by modifying the underlying string encoding. (Quipu was an circa 1988 X.500 server with its database stored in memory, it supported chaining and proprietary replication and was developed in the UK using the ISODE protocol stack. Change log/LCUP agent and other enhancements were needed to make it a contender for a public directory service.) Finding the Open Systems Interconnection (OSI) infrastructure a fundamental limitation to the implementation of X.500 clients, Howes and Smith created "Directory Interface to X.500 Implemented Efficiently" (DIXIE) as a low-cost, simplified method by which TCP/IP based clients could access OSI Directory Service (X.500) without the overhead of the ISO protocols in 1991. This solution cited in RFC1249 was specific to their customized Quipu implementation of X.500. This was refined into LDAP.

LDAP was considered to be a lightweight protocol since it simplified the data model that is used to represent objects in the directory, and it used the lighter weight TCP/IP protocol suite, as opposed to DAP, which used the OSI protocol stack. LDAP allows data/objects in directories to be arranged in a hierarchical structure that can be tailored to an organization's specific needs. Using LDAP, an organization may map a directory structure such as a corporate phone book, to a hierarchical structure based on functional divisions, regions, or other boundaries. LDAP directories are arranged as trees, with the topmost node known as the root. Taking the example of a corporate phone book, the division may reside at the root level, followed by the specific region, then organizational units, then finally at the bottom of the tree, the individual.

LDAP was developed by the National Science Foundation under grant number NCR-9416667. The father of LDAP, Tim Howes along with Steve Kille, Wengyik Yeong, Bryan Beecher, Mark C. Smith and Colin Robbins developed the technology at the University of Michigan; Ann Arbor, as part of Tim's Ph.D. dissertation under Paul Killey, what is now known as the "slapd" server. Was first implemented in production by Mike Konopka with myself acting as Lead Architect for Netscape working under Roger Johnson, at Ford Systems Integration Center with Rob Singleton leading what was then the fledgling web group in Dearborn, MI.

The objects stored in the directory service can be anything that can be described through a set of attributes. Each object gets a set of attributes that describe the object's capabilities. For instance, a person object might have height, hair color, age, and sex attributes associated with it. Each person directory object would have values stored for each of their attributes.

In addition to storing and cataloguing objects, the directory service can provide search filters based upon different attributes. For example, one could use the directory service to search for all objects with age attributes that range from 20 to 25. The directory service would return a valid set of matching objects. This is often called reverse-lookup or content-based searching in many arenas.

3

LDAP Concepts

The enterprise is defined to mean all aspects of the computing environment—from the mainframe, to the server, to the desktop level.

However, from the perspective of directory server deployment, the enterprise also comprises the organization's resources and activities. The directory architect can understand resources to mean the people and Roles within the organization as well as the devices (printers, servers, and desktop systems) that the organization uses, and the applications that the end user run to support the organization (such as a web server or an accounting package). Further, the enterprise also encompasses the physical location(s) in which the organization resides. These differing locations can be separate buildings, cities, states or provinces, or even countries.

The directory architect should therefore consider the term the enterprise to mean the entire organization from the buildings that the client uses, to the software that the client runs, to the people that the client works with.

A directory service is a collection of software that an enterprise uses to store information about itself. Sometimes, but not always, directory services are based on a client-server architecture. Therefore, a directory service generally consists of at least one directory server and one or more directory clients.

An object in the real world can be modeled as one or more directory entries. Each directory entry is an object that has a set of characteristics describing the information carried by the object. These characteristics are implemented as attributes of the entry. For example, a User object might have attributes that define the first name, last name, employee ID, phone number, and other data associated with that user. Each of these attributes is common to all instances of the User class; however, the specific values of at least some of these attributes will be different so that different users can be identified.

The set of attributes that an entry has is determined by the *object class* of that entry. The object class defines which attributes must be included (for example, values must be specified for them) and which attributes may be included for a given entry (for example, they are defined in the schema but do not have to be instantiated). The complete set of object classes and attributes for a directory is defined as the *schema* of the directory.

Each attribute has a specific data type that may have restrictions qualifying the values of that data type (such as a string with alphanumeric characters only). This is called the *syntax* of the attribute. In addition, a predefined set of matching rules is defined for each entry to specify whether this attribute is considered a match for a search. (For example, given a string, ignore the case of each character in the string and see whether this attribute's value equals the value that is being searched for.) Attributes may also be multivalued, but they do not have to be. Finally, all attributes have object identifiers that uniquely define them. These are *ASN.1 identifiers*.

Directories have five important characteristics:

- The storage of information is optimized so that it can be read much more frequently than it is written.
- Information is stored in a *hierarchical* fashion.

- Information in a directory is *attribute-based.*

- Directories provide a *unified namespace* for all resources for which they contain information.

- Directories can efficiently distribute information in a distributed system through replication.

The first characteristic means that directories are very good at performing high-volume search operations (such as searching an address book), but not good at performing operations that require frequent writing (such as navigating a reservation system).

The second and third characteristics are linked. The second characteristics inferred that the information infrastructure is based on parent-child relationships. Containment, not inheritance, is the driving factor of a good directory design. The third point refers to the fact that the directory is comprised of a set of objects. Each of the objects has a set of attributes that contain the information. Thus, the information is spread through the attributes of the objects that form the infrastructure of the directory.

The fourth characteristic is very important. It means that common information can be located and shared by different directory clients because each application can use the same method of referencing an object. A unified namespace enables network elements and services to be seamlessly integrated with other types of information, such as users, applications, and servers.

The final characteristic is critical for building an information infrastructure. The directory server has the capability to control what information gets distributed when and to what other nodes in the system.

It is important to remember that the lightweight directory access protocol does not define what database is used to support the protocol or how replication is accomplished.

The basic function of a directory service is to allow employees to store information about the enterprise so that it later can be retrieved either by directly searching for that information or by searching for related but more easily remembered information, such as a name.

While some may disagree with the comparison the well known TCP/IP based Domain Name System (DNS) service that stores only two types of information, names and IP addresses, was the first example of a limited directory service. A true directory service is used to store virtually unlimited types of information. For example, a true directory service can be thought of as an electronic telephone book in that it almost always contains personal contact information such as a person's name, telephone number, mail address, office number, and so forth. But a directory server goes beyond this usage by allowing the enterprise to store other types of information such as:

• physical device information

• private employment information such as salary, government identification numbers, home addresses and phone numbers, pay grade, and so forth

• contracts or accounts information, such as the name of the client, final delivery date, bidding information, contract number, and milestone due dates

A traditional directory service provides a means for locating and identifying users and available resources in a distributed system. Directory services also provide the foundation for adding, modifying, removing, renaming, and managing system components without disrupting the services provided by other system components. Today's directory services are used to do the following:

1. Store information about system components in a distributed manner. The directory is replicated among several servers so

that a user or service needing access to the directory can query a local server for the information.

2. Support common searching needs, such as by attribute (for example, "Find the phone number for James Smith") and by classification (for example, "Find all color printers on the third floor").

3. Provide important information to enable single-user logon to services, resources, and applications.

4. Enable a location-independent point of administration and management. Note that administrative tools do not have to be centrally located and managed.

5. Replicate data to provide consistent access. Modifications made to any replica of the directory are propagated around the network so that any application accessing the directory anywhere sees consistent information after the change is propagatcd.

A directory service can be used to store and retrieve much of this information. This is because of the following four main reasons:

1. A directory is a natural publishing medium, capable of supporting a high number of reads as well as allowing arbitrary information to be stored and retrieved. Thus, there are no restrictions on the information itself; this provides inherent extensibility for accommodating additional as well as new information.

2. Directories are the *de facto* standard for containing user information and other types of information, and directory-enabled network applications require user, network, and other types of resource information to be integrated. The advantage is that information about network resources, elements, and services are not only colocated, but they are represented as equal

objects that have a common representation. This enables the different applications that want to use and share this information to access a single repository. This greatly simplifies the design of the overall system.

3. Directories facilitate finding information without knowing the complete path or name of the object that has that information. A directory service is more than a naming service, such as DNS. A directory service enables both the searching and the retrieval of named information.

4. A directory can also be used to point to other systems that contain information; this provides a single place where applications can go to find information.

LDAP

LDAP provides these services in the form of a robust, scalable TCP/IP based directory service that allows users to store all of the enterprise's information in a single, network-accessible repository.

Essential LDAP terms:

- SLAPD: Stand-Alone LDAP Daemon is part of the original University of Michigan implementation of the LDAP suite. The SLAPD assumes the basic functions of the x.500 DSA. SLAPD is an LDAP server than runs on many platforms and can be used to host a directory service instance.

- SLURPD: Stand-Alone LDAP Update Replication Daemon: SLURPD is responsible for distributing changed made to the master SLAPD database out to the various SLAPD replicas. It frees SLAPD from having to worry that some replicas may be down or unreachable. SLAPD and SLURP usually communicate through a changelog

- CLDAP: Connectionless LDAP defined in RFC 1798. CLDAP provides services for UDP (User Datagram Protocols) rather than TCP due to the fact that UDP has less fewer overheads than TCP connections

- Change log: is a flat file used to record changes in the SLAPD

- LDIF: LDAP Data Interchange Format used to describe a directory and directory entries in text format. LDIF is a text file format and all directory data is stored using the UTF-8 encoding of Unicode

LDAP is now an Internet standard for directory services that run over TCP/IP. One or more LDAP servers contain the data that make up the LDAP directory tree. An LDAP client connects to an LDAP server and submits a query to request information or submits information to be updated. If access rights for the client are granted, the server responds with an answer or possibly with a referral to another LDAP server where the client can have the query serviced.

There are several ways to look at LDAP. It is:

- A data retrieval protocol—used directly as an application server to retrieve information from a directory. For example, an LDAP server can contain a list of personnel contact information, like a white pages phone book.

- An application service protocol—used by different applications to retrieve the information they require. For example, a user creates a query to be sent to a search engine, the query is matched against an LDAP server, and this points to the place where the actual data is located. Another example of this use would be a DNS server that structures its records internally in an LDAP hierarchy.

- An interapplication data exchange interface—used by one application to exchange data with another, or as a gateway between two incompatible applications. For example, a Peoplesoft data-base can store a record into an LDAP server so that it can be retrieved by an iPlanet Mail Server client. In this sense, it can be used as a simple interface for creating vendor-neutral database queries.

- A system service protocol—used by an operating system to com-municate information between its different resources or compo-nents. For example, In a Single Sign On environment an LDAP server can contain the access rights of user accounts that are ref-erenced by the login system, the filesystem, and the application execution environment.

The LDAP information model defines the kind of data that is put into the directory

The LDAP information model defines the basic unit of information in the directory as an entry. This is a collection of information about an object. This can be a real object, such as a person, a binary object or any system component. The entry is made up of more fundamental elements known as attributes. Each attribute has a type and one or more values.

The LDAP naming model defines how the data is organized in the direc-tory and how applications refer to directory data.

The naming model specifies that entries are arranged in an inverted tree structure. The naming model identifies how users refer to a partic-ular entry within that structure. The structure is similar to a file system with three key differences.

a. In the LDAP model the root entry is conceptual rather than an entry data can be placed into *(Ex. dc=com, dc=coradon)*

b. In the LDAP model, every node contains data and any node can be a container. This contrasts with the file system where any given node is a file or a sub directory, but not both. *(Ex. dc=com, dc=coradon, o=People may contain attribute values as well as an ou=Employee sub branch)*

c.   In the LDAP model, names are order backward relative to file system names. E.g. Names are constructed branch to root rather than root to branch as in file systems *(Ex. dc=com, dc=coradon, o=People has com as the root directory component)*

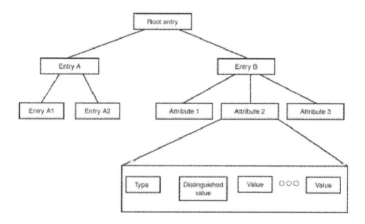

In a directory distinguished values are used to compute relative distinguished names (RDNs) and fully qualified distinguished names (FQDNs). The FQDN for an entry is built by taking the FQDN of its parent entry and appending the RDN specified in the entry. Thus, the FQDN at any level is the set of RDNs that together specify a path from the root of the DIT to that particular directory entry.

The directory database consists of one or more directory entries mapped in memory as a b-tree hash. Entries are structured to form a hierarchical tree of information. Each entry in the database is identified by a unique distinguished name (DN). The distinguished name is a string representation of the location of the entry in the directory tree and corresponds to a memory address in the slapd memory cache. Each entry can also have one or more attributes that further describe the entry.

The LDAP functional model defines how users and applications access and update the information in the directory

Nine basic functions are defined in the LDAP protocol. During analysis the classification of business process to a resulting function is essential to load estimates, which take place later in the architecture. The nine functions can be broken down into three taxonomies which have equivalent demands on the slapd relative to one another. These are as follows.

- Interrogation Operations (Cheapest)

    Search, compare (cheapest)

- Update Operations (Most Expensive)

    Add, delete, modify, and modify RDN (most Expensive)

- Authentication and Control Operations

    Bind, unbind, abandon (most hazardous)

Two LDAP Interrogation Operations allow LDAP clients to search and retrieve individual data entries.

Search—Used to search and retrieve entries

Compare—Boolean search where an entry referenced by RDN, an attribute name and a value returns an affirmative or negative response based on comparison of the attribute value (data). This is the least expensive operation in both memory and CPU usage

There are four LDAP update operations that enable manipulation of data.

Add—Used to create new directory entries; accepts two parameters: the RDN of the entry to be created and a set of attributes and attribute values

Delete—used to remove an entry from the directory; It has a single parameter the RDN of the entry.

Modify RDN—is used to rename and/or move entries in the directory. It has four parameters: The RDN of the entry to be moved/renamed, The new RDN for the entry, an optional argument giving the new parent of the entry and the delete-old-RDN flag. Since this is actually an aggregate command it is the most expensive in memory and CPU time and should be used sparingly.

There are two LDAP authentication operations and one control operation.

Bind—used by the client to authenticate itself to the directory using RDN and a set of credentials

Unbind—used to terminate any outstanding LDAP operations and disconnect

Abandon—used when the client is no longer interested in the results of a previously initiated operation. When the server receives an abandon request the server terminates processing of the operation. Unfortunately meta directory spawned join agents and x.500 Directory user Agents will be unaware of the terminate request and may continue to cycle for some time, hence the Hazard warning

Extended Operation—This is not a common LDAP operation but may be invoked providing the slapd has the appropriate plug in deamon. Any time a client whishes to use the directory extended operation take another look at the business case and analysis rational before proceeding. Most likely the operation belongs in a relational structure or piece of code.

The LDAP security model defines how information in the directory can be protected from unauthorized access

The security process on a standard connection is:

1. Open connection (Client >> Server)
1. Bind Operation (Client >> Server)
2. Results of Bind Operation (Server >> Client)
3. Search Operation (Client >> Server)
4. Results of Search Operation (Server >> Client)
5. Unbind Operation (Client >> Server)
6. Close Connection (Server >> Client)

As a message oriented protocol the LDAP client constructs LDAP messages containing a request and sends them to the server. The Server processes the requests and sends the results back to the Client. The Protocol permits the client to issue multiple requests to the server at once. The Client generates a unique massage ID for each request which is returned as a tag with the corresponding results.

Syntax

LDAP Call
Ldap://<hostname:port#>/<base
DN>?<attributes>?<scope>?<search filter>

LDAP Referral
ref: ldap://realserver.coradon.com/ou=people,o=coradon.com

Where:
        Referral ::=SEQUENCE OF LDAPURL—one or more
        LDAPURL ::=LDAPString—limited to characters permitted in
        URLs

TYPES OF METADIRECTORY PRODUCTS

• LDAP Access Routers (Commonly called Directory Access Routers)

- LDAP Trigger Proxy Servers (also referred to as Virtual Directories)

- LDAP Join Engine Servers (Commonly referred to as Metadirectory Servers)

A Metadirectory is simply an extension of an LDAP based directory service. By analogy a Meta directory is to a LDAP directory what a Datawarehouse is to a Relational Directory. It is an aggregate of systems supported by metadata designed to populate and maintain a unified Directory Service and provide links to data contained in external repositories. A Metadirectory can also be viewed as a progressive return to x.500 Directory User Agents where distributed data is presented in a homogeneous format as opposed to a referral list.

Until recently, the basic problem has not been finding and deploying directory services, but rather that enterprises are using too many directory services at once. Most of these directories are bundled as proprietary databases within an application and not as LDAP aware systems. For example, email systems are traditionally heavy users of directory services. As the many different types of proprietary email systems have spread throughout the enterprise, so too have their accompanying proprietary directory services. These directory services all stored the same types of information: user names, mail addresses, host information, mailbox information, passwords, and so forth.

The problem is that these different directories (some of which were proprietary, some of which were built around standards-based directory services) could not readily share data between themselves and LDAP aware systems. Thus if a user had a mailbox in two different email systems, that user's information usually had to be managed in two different directories. The result is increased costs in both personnel as well as hardware because user information is managed in multiple locations.

Multiple databases serving common directory needs are known as the n+1 directory problem, and it has long been a logistical and financial problem, as well as a security hazard for the enterprise.

The concept of a metadirectory service was invented to solve the n+1 directory problem. The idea is to provide a single, centralized repository of directory information that any application can access. However, the implementation of a metadirectory service faced some important difficulties. The most serious of these was the question of how the many disparate applications used in the enterprise were supposed to access the directory. The directory would have to be network based, but how can the data be abstracted for that access? LDAP, the protocol abstraction of choice with its single mastered referral model was simply not up to the task in its current (v.3) incarnation

There were other contenders for the protocol. One of these is the X. 500 ISO standard. X. 500 has several advantages that make it attractive for solving the n+1 directory problem. It offers an open communications protocol called the Directory Access Protocol (DAP) that any application can use to access the directory. It also offers an extensible information framework that allows the directory to store virtually any kind of information. Finally, X. 500 offers a remarkably robust directory solution that could be scaled to millions of users.

Unfortunately, X. 500 also had several limitations. Among these is a dependency on a communications layer that is not the Internet standard TCP/IP protocol, and complicated requirements for directory naming conventions. The result was a directory strategy that offers the scalability and robustness required by a global directory service but which suffers from expensive administrative costs.

The concept of the Metadirectory was invented to preserve the best qualities offered by X.500 in an LDAP context while reducing the administrative costs associated with X. 500 and abstracting the protocol layers to a single Lightweight Directory Access Protocol (LDAP).

LDAP provides an open directory access protocol running over TCP/IP. It retains the X.500 data model and it is scalable to a global size and millions of entries for a modest investment in hardware and network infrastructure. The result of a successful metadirectory deployment is a global directory solution that is affordable enough to be used by small organizations, but which also can be scaled to support the largest of enterprises.

x.500 & Metadirectories

During my work at Ford Motor Co. Alexis Bor former x.500 chair and CEO of Directory works stated over dinner that while in the short term LDAP (RFC 1777 at the time) would surpass x.500 in popularity, the IT community would recreate the functionality of x.500 incrementally as the protocol progressed. Six years later I find that his words still ring in my mind every time a new product emerges on the market or a new system is implemented and the functionality in the 88, 93 x.500 structures is recreated in TCP.

The first attempt to define a global, open standardized directory was the X.500 Directory Services Standard, which was promulgated by a combined technical sub-committee of ISO/CCITT. (CCITT has been renamed the ITU.) Initially driven by the need of the world's telephone companies to provide a directory service for the e-mail standard, X.400, it was intended that the directory would automate the world-wide White and Yellow Page telephone directories. However, the ISO participants quickly realized that the standard would be applicable to a far-wider range of applications, particularly in the area of distributed applications running over various lower architectures. As a result, the standard took more than a decade to develop. There are three official versions—1988, 1993, and 1997—representing increasing complexity. But that complexity has resulted in a standard that is very difficult to implement in an industrial-strength instantiation.X.500 is the name given to a series of standards developed by the ISO/ITU-T that specify how information can be stored and accessed in a global directory service. The X.500 specification proposes basic definitions to represent Person and Application. DEN will assume an X.500-based model of Person and Application to use in developing the representation of network elements and services and their binding to users and applications. Metadirectories borrow heavily from x.500 concepts thus it is important to understand some basic x.500 concepts

ASCE Association Control Service Element

The ACSE application-layer associations are logical connections, which enable an application system such as a library system to request an association to another application system, as well as to request the closure of an association. An association is established between two systems when they are connected, login procedures are performed, and they are ready to exchange application messages. In requesting an association the origin tells the target system which application context it is going to use. ACSE is also used to support the transparent exchange of security credentials.

ROSE Remote Operation Service Element

ROSE is a request/reply protocol intended for interactive applications. It is thex.500 analogue to a Remote Procedure Call in that it may be used to define procedures that can be executed remotely.

DSA Directory System Agent

The directory system agent provides the actual directory service and implements the service side of directory operations. This is functional analogue of the slapd daemon

DUA Directory User Agent

The directory user agent represents the client side of the directory service. The DUA represents the user in accessing the information in the directory. This is functional analogue of a Virtual Directory or Directory Proxy.

Chaining

Chaining means that the DSAs interact directly with one another through the DSP. Requests for information are forwarded from one DSA to another transparently of the DUA or end user who originated the query. In this manner, a query may be progressively forwarded by a number of DSAs creating a "chain" of DSAs involved in responding to the query. Results are collected and evaluated at each DSA in the chain and are forwarded back through the chain of DSAs to the DUA where the query originated.

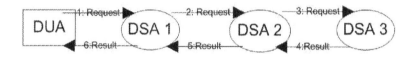

Referrals

Referrals operate by requiring the DUA to progressively contact each DSA involved to satisfy a query individually. Each contacted DSA returns as many of the results as it is able to evaluate

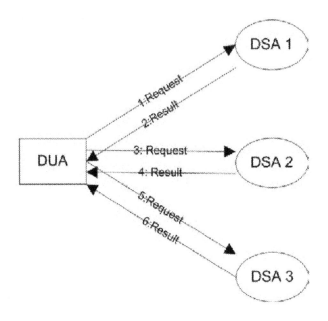

Multicasting

Multicasting is a special case of chaining in that the operation is forwarded to multiple DSAs in parallel. This is not normally time critical and does not require each DSA be contacted simultaneously. It is analogous to broadcasting a query out to multiple DSA's in the expectation that one or more will be able to satisfy the information request.

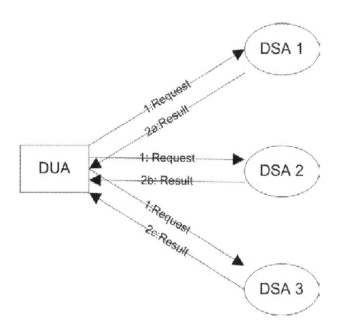

LDAP has four key advantages over DAP. First, it runs directly over TCP/IP (or other reliable transport, in theory), eliminating much of the connection set-up and packet-handling overhead of the OSI session and presentation layers required by DAP. In addition, the near universal availability of TCP/IP implementations means that LDAP can run on most systems "out of the box."

Second, LDAP simplifies the X.500 functional model in two ways. It leaves out the read and list operations, emulating them via the search operation. It also leaves out some of the more esoteric and less-often-used service controls and security features of full X.500 (e.g., the ability to sign operations). This simplifies LDAP implementations.

Third, though X.500 and LDAP both describe and encode protocol elements using ASN.1 and BER, LDAP uses string encodings for distinguished names and data elements. X.500 uses a complex and highly-structured encoding even for simple data elements; LDAP data elements are string types. This encoding is a big win for distinguished names, which have considerable structure leading to encoding/decoding complexity and size. LDAP relegates the knowledge of a value's syntax to the application program rather than lower-level protocol routines.

Finally, LDAP frees clients from the burden of chasing referrals. The LDAP server is responsible for chasing down any referrals returned by X.500, returning either results or errors to the client. Clients assume a single connection model in which X.500 appears as a single logical directory.

The Lightweight Directory Access Protocol provides a low-overhead method of accessing the X.500 directory. It runs directly over TCP, and makes several simplifications to full X.500 DAP, leaving out many of the lesser-used features. LDAP uses primitive string encodings for most data elements, making it more efficient and easier to implement than DAP.

Metadirectories and virtual directories replicate most if not all this functionality within a directory enabled network.

4
LDAP Applications

Conventionally, directories have been implemented for two reasons: as repositories for user and device definitions within a workgroup (e.g., NOS); or to provide address look-up in a collaborative application (e.g., E-mail and others). This has led to a diversity of directories within enterprises and the well-known frustrations of directory synchronization. Four accelerating business demands increase the pressure for an effective enterprise directory strategy:

1. Internally, the need to control access to information by internal and external users demands more efficient control of user rights, profiles and permissions

2. Internally, the need to govern network performance based on business rules (i.e., policy-based networking);

3. Externally, the exposure of infrastructure to common business partners. Addressing requirements are increasingly crossing enterprise boundaries. Not only do many corporate users now routinely access facilities outside the enterprise, but enterprises increasingly would like to provide access to people or functions from outside Beyond such requirements, extranet implementations require the management of additional sets of users that are not even part of the enterprise owning the system.

4. Externally, exposing the enterprise's infrastructure to customers. The creation of E-commerce systems requires recognition and tracking of users and customers. E-commerce is becoming a critical business driver for directory services, and while in part it is independent of the enterprise's internal needs for directory facilities, in practice it cannot easily be separated.

Rather than reacting to requirements as they arise, enterprises should start creating a decision framework directed toward clearly stated goals, prioritizing the objectives described above and showing how the full range of requirements can eventually be accommodated. Failure to plan proactively will lead to higher long-term costs and reduced flexibility in managing access to information resources. Such corporate standardization initiatives are fraught with problems, and must be undertaken with due regard for local needs and business imperatives; this issue, however, will not go away.

Two implementation paths are available: extending a workgroup user repository (from NOS or E-mail system) with additional data to form a fully-fledged directory system, or implementing an independent directory solution that will subsequently absorb existing facilities. Not surprisingly, those vendors, which have traditionally provided the former capabilities would have enterprises, take that path; other directory vendors would have enterprises take the latter. Even if enterprises choose to implement a directory solution starting from the NOS directory it is advisable to treat the directory strategy as an independent issue. The fundamentals are a clear analysis of requirements and a flexible architecture to support requirements over the medium term independent of product choices.

While it has been the practice of many directory experts to divide products into NOS directories, messaging directories, Internet directories the line between messaging directories and Internet directories has become blurred in many enterprise and carrier deployments. As such scale not usage is used to create an artificial distinction

Based on this analysis all commercial directory servers on the market can be divided into three functional segments:

- NOS Directories

- Enterprise Directories

- Carrier Directories

1. NOS Directories—these are directories designed to support the operation of the overall network environment. NOS directories are bundled with the network operating system, at no additional cost. NOS Directories are designed to support the operation of the network environment.

2. Enterprise Directories—these are directories that are designed to work as central data repositories for all corporate information, supporting multiple company applications. Enterprise Directories are designed to work as central data repositories for all corporate information, supporting multiple company applications.

3. Carrier Directories—these are directories, optimized for use by Service Providers. Designed to support a large number of users, carrier directories are used by Telcos, ASPs, CLECs, ILECs, Wireless Providers, ISPs and Portals. Carrier Directories are designed to support a large number of users, and are optimized for use by Service Providers.

Businesses seek directory services to help ensure that partners, employees, and customers have access to the correct resources—and only the correct resources—such as a firm allowing its suppliers to interact only with the purchasing department's orderings application or a customer being able to access only his purchasing history.

As dependence on directories grows, the challenge facing the enterprise is to create a directory-guided IT structure that meets the mission-critical requirements of scalability, availability, and reliability. While the lightweight directory access protocol (LDAP) facilitates intra- and inter-network communication, many LDAP directories crumble under the heavy-lifting demands of enterprise-scale business applications. For example, if the Web user directory fails at an e-Commerce firm, users cannot access the site and the company loses business. Moreover, for any firm, if the enterprise directory fails, employees cannot access e-mail, shared files, or applications that use the directory for authentication, such as human resources (HR) or Enterprise Resource Planning (ERP), resulting in lost productivity. Because a directory is, in effect, a highly specialized database, several prominent database suppliers are adapting their technologies for directory use. By creating a directory based on time-tested databases, these suppliers seek to provide directories with high transactional capabilities, full fail over fault tolerance, and multi-threaded processing capabilities. Suppliers' database experience allows them to extend the directory's use beyond user management and into the heart of carrier- and enterprise-class directory deployments.

Messaging, Collaboration & Groupware Analysis: While the common interpretation of this phase is inter and extra corporate email policies and access methods, This often is expanded to include the crystallization of internal business request, approval & reporting process within a collaboration environment

Portal Products: This encompasses the internet and extranet information portal solutions provided by the project. Often is a systems integration effort driven primarily by the directory and content sources. While the diagram, shows it as a peer process to the relational data services component it can easily fall under the relational data services architecture if the delivery of information is a key commodity of the enterprise.

Application Servers: If present; This component may either serve the portal component or often replaces the component entirely. It provides common services and application templates for existing code structures and will include the Transaction Processing, Queing and legacy integration efforts within an enterprise.

<u>Business Intelligence Services:</u> This component is a hybrid of application and relational data dependencies. It may take the form of Standalone Business Objects (DCOM, SOAP or CORBA), Stored Procedures, On line analytical processing components, Datamining techniques (Chi Squared, Neural Nets, Rule Engines) Modular database packages (such as Oracle modules), and Transaction Queing where logic is added to the data in route.

<u>Relational Data Services:</u> This encompasses all relational (SQL, OQL or Matrix based) data repositories within the enterprise and is often associated with a Database Analyst (DBA). The aggregate of these data sources if often referred to as a data warehouse

<u>Business Intelligence Services:</u> This component is a hybrid of application and relational data dependencies. It may take the form of Standalone Business Objects (DCOM, SOAP or CORBA), Stored Procedures, On line analytical processing components, Datamining techniques (Chi Squared, Neural Nets, Rule Engines) Modular database packages (such as Oracle modules), and Transaction Queing where logic is added to the data in route

<u>Electronic Data Interchange Services:</u> If present; these services permit the electronic transfer of funds and purchase requests between companies and with the federal government. These systems may be a s simple as HR Electronic Funds Transfer systems or could encompass a mature EDIINT Electronic Funds Transfer Mechanism.

<u>Enterprise Resource Planning Packages</u>: If present; these systems implement a series of industry and accounting best practices for the internal business structure which may be augmented by elements designed in the business intelligence phase. They are treated as separate systems in this model.

<u>Supply Chain Planning Packages</u>: If present; these systems implement a series of industry and accounting best practices regulating the delivery and procurement of product which may be augmented by elements designed in Phase 4.2B. They are treated as separate systems in this model.

ROI provides a cost/benefit calculation model and a case study. Using this cost analysis a company may realize five times return on enterprise directory investment. The conclusion reached is that "IT managers can demonstrate the value of, and the return on, an enterprise directory project by quantifying the short-term benefits in terms of dollars, and defining the long-term benefits in terms of strategic initiatives. Those savings will come only through the hard work and significant resource commitments that directory projects require, which includes dealing with dirty directory data and internal politics, both of which can derail directory projects. It's more difficult to measure the long-term benefits, but they're equally important. Over the long term, the directory will become an essential part of the enterprise computing infrastructure, providing the foundation for a variety of applications and services. E-commerce, extranet, and other distributed applications will not scale without a solid directory foundation.

5

Basic IT Architectural Principals

A IT architecture is a roadmap that provides detail sufficient to guide ongoing network planning, design, and implementation. Having developed an IT architecture, an organization will then have in place a framework for more informed decision making, including appropriate investments in network technologies, products, and services.

Most enterprises choose to develop a IT architecture that describes a target (i.e., future state) network set three to five years into the future. Because it always represents the desired future state of the system, the architecture gives network managers a goal that guides their ongoing implementation activities.

The most important elements of an architecture, and often the first components to be developed, are the "technology positions." Each technology position puts a "stake in the ground" in an area (and only in those areas) where organizations must decide which of multiple competing technology alternatives are appropriate. The intent is to help an enterprise understand any tradeoffs well enough to recommend what is best for them among the most feasible alternatives.

Templates, another major component of a network architecture, are models that show the distribution of functionality and the logical or physical relationships between architectural components. Templates typically illustrate the network topology, showing how the various technology positions are applied to different size sites or types of environments (e.g., large, medium, or small facilities; remote branch offices; WAN backbone; or inter-enterprise communications). Like "blueprints," templates guide network or system design. However, unlike network designs topology templates provide only approximations of the amount of bandwidth or switching capacity likely to be required. Since an architecture describes a 3-to-5-year future network, bandwidth needs will necessarily be imprecise. In general, network topology templates show order-of-magnitude bandwidth requirements (e.g., 10 Mbps Ethernet vs. Fast Ethernet, or 56 Kbps vs. T1 vs. T3 circuits). Other types of templates may be developed to show how protocols are layered on an end-to-end basis across the network. The primary value of a template is showing how all of the technology positions work together.

IT architecture *principles* represent the highest level of guidance for IT planning and decision-making. Principles are derived from business goals and corporate values, and they provide the primary linkage between business strategies and network technology strategies. Principles are generally simple statements of an organization's beliefs about how it wants to use networking over the long term. Technical Positions and Templates for an enterprise's network architecture should not be created in a vacuum; they must be based on an enterprise's particular type of business, corporate or organizational culture, and business goals. An organization that skips the step of developing its own architecture principles runs the risk that its network will not be "in sync" with its business. Thus principles represent the foundation for a IT architecture.

Principles are applicable not only to directories, but also to any type of information technology (IT) architecture. Principles summarize an enterprise's basic philosophies regarding how technology should be applied toward achieving business goals. These principles provide a linkage between business strategy and technology strategy, and thus between line management and technology management. Principles play a key role in developing any IT architecture. They can formalize a commitment by upper management to make investments in the IT infrastructure. Because many aspects of an IT architecture specification will likely be "enabling" in nature, it is often impossible to justify recommendations based purely on cost/benefit or ROI analyses. In this case, the IT or network manager may appeal to the higher order of direction offered by the IT principles.

Development of principles is usually the first step in the process of creating an enterprise directory architecture (although their place in the process is easiest to explain last). Technical Positions are then based on these principles. The last step is to create system Templates that show how the Technical Positions are applied to specific enterprise network environments and sites.

Development of an initial directory architecture is usually a 3-to-4-month process that begins with interviews and collection of information about the current and planned state of the network, as well as future business plans likely to impact network requirements. The good news is that collection of quantitative information about network traffic volumes is generally not needed—qualitative information is much more important. The "bad" news is that business unit (non-technical) managers must be interviewed to determine the likely future direction of the business; the challenge is translating these business requirements into future network requirements that must be satisfied by the architecture. However, involvement with business unit managers also helps to assure "buy-in" when the new architecture is unveiled; their support is needed for implementation.

After initial directory architecture development, the challenge is to keep it up to date. Because the architecture should represent the state of the network at least 3 years in the future, architecture maintenance is never really completed. It's like "painting a house"—as soon as one finish, it's time to start all over again. At a minimum, organizations should "refresh" their network architecture plans on an annual basis, with 6-month reviews often recommended. As long as vendors keep developing new network products and services, the work of architecture maintenance is never done.

Often developers will attempt to bake all the services an infrastructure will require into a single application or component. The tendency to over engineer a product or solution is not new, but it should be discouraged by any architect. A Metadirectory is a single component as is the directories it enhances and applications it supports. In the following section we will try to offer an explanation as to why the directories and metadirectory should be treated as separate sections of the architecture.

Monolithic Applications are:

- old fashioned
- easy to visualize
- easy to deploy at first
- a single point of failure
- hard to expand
- rife with proprietary protocols

Perhaps the term "monolithic" is unfair. It makes it sound like we are referring to Stonehenge. In fact we are discussing technology far beyond the ken of Neolithic pre-Celts. Back in the ancient days of the mid nineteen nineties, most applications executed on a single machine. Any attempt to distribute the system was managed by breaking up the application into a series of client-server processes through which a transaction streamed. Some load balancing was achieved by providing local copies of databases which were replicated and synchronized on a regular basis. Additional mechanisms included custom efforts to build what today we refer to as application servers. High availability was achieved by using slow expensive fault tolerant computers, and by having complex fail-over mechanisms. In those dark days, that was the best that could be hoped for without going to extraordinary means, but today we can do better. We will see the new approach.

Distributed Systems need to be:

- more available
- more scalable
- more maintainable

Distributed systems solve certain kinds of problems. one will use distributed systems to maintain a competitive advantage. Having many dispersed but parallel servers makes a service continually available. Dividing the task between many machines makes it possible to get it done in less time. Spreading your application and infrastructure across many machines prevents having to make the kinds of optimizations that can only be done by clever and laborious hand coding. It also makes it easy to reuse your code and components for similar applications.

Good component characteristics include:

- properties
- operations
- events
- ubiquitously deployable
- shareable
- distributable
- automation
- self-containment

- self-description
- trans-locatability

There are many features that a good component architecture should have. These features can also be used to identify the differences between objects and components. These features and characteristics are going to be described over the next few slides.

An operation is essentially a method of a component. It performs an action on the client's behalf. The client calls an operation, passing in zero or more parameters and expects zero or more return parameters. An operation can read and modify the properties of the component and can trigger events.

A property is a single definition of a behavioral aspect of a component. A property is the component equivalent to an object's attributes. A property is different from an attribute in that a property has the ability to describe an entire behavioral aspect of the component's operation where an attribute of an object is merely a store for the stateful data of the object. Attributes can, but don't have to, define entire constraints or operational characteristics. For example, suppose one were developing a paint component that could draw on the screen based on user input. A property of the paint component might be the style of the brush. The style is a property because one could define not only the color of the brush, but one could define the width, structure, shading, dottedness, etc. A single property can wholly define this aspect of the component, whereas in an object, an attribute can only store a single value of the property list.

Components should also export the events that they can generate. Events are asynchronous notifications of "happenings" within the component. For instance, a web server component might generate an event when a new user session begins or ends. Clients that are interested in receiving notification of component events would register their interest and would be notified upon their occurrence. Only the component is capable of generating its events.

A component should operate independent:

- of hardware

- of the underlying operating system

- of its application server

A component should be capable of being installed and executed on any system independent of that system's operating system, hardware, other system software, etc. A component architecture that supports a high degree of ubiquitous deployment allows developers to make decisions about the services that their components will provide without having to take environment limitations or constraints into account. Component developers will no longer have to concern themselves about the network protocols, system services, or other proprietary system issues that can affect the design or implementation of a component. This saves developers time during the development of components and integration.

Infrastructure services are those services that are generally required by all enterprise systems. Infrastructure services include transaction services, directory services, security management, concurrent access management (multithreading), persistence management, resource pooling, administration interfaces, load balancing, and fault tolerance. By providing an architecture that allows component developers to code only the business logic needed for their components, the development time for complicated component architecture is greatly decreased. Also, the source code for a single component will be less convoluted with code used to implement infrastructure services such as transactions or security. After all, why should a component developer have to understand the nuances of security roles and load balancing when all they want to develop is a component that performs mathematical computations?

They shouldn't. A good component architecture will provide a strict interface between the component and its execution environment so that application server providers can automate the injection of infrastructure services.

Standard infrastructure services include:

- directory services
- distributed transaction management
- security management
- concurrent access management
- persistence management
- resource pooling (ex: database connections)
- administration interface
- load balancing
- fault tolerance

The metadirectory is one such infrastructure service that touches each of these functions.

In general, metadirectory products are targeted at the problem of managing overlapping information contained in multiple directories and are required to implement multiple directories to support different platforms, applications and usage models. Therefore, companies turn to metadirectory products as a key solution for creating a manageable environment for heterogeneous directories and application databases. Unfortunately the term "metadirectory" is applied to a variety of products that, in fact, provide different levels of functionality. For the purpose of this book we define "metadirectory products" as providing:

1. Multidirectional synchronization between directories, databases and other types of user information stores. This is the traditional view of metadirectory products.

2. Providing a unified view of the information they are synchronizing, allowing applications (and, potentially, users) to access one directoryb(the metadirectory) for all pertinent information, instead of accessing multiple applications.

3. Providing a united view of information contained in multiple directories or databases While some products only provide a unified view many of these products do not provide synchronization as a core capability. Products in this space that only provide a unified view are termed "virtual directories."

4. Some metadirectory products are actually middleware infrastructures that enable organizations to drive their synchronization needs and create their own virtual view of directory and database contents. Most enterprises deploy metadirectory products first for the purposes of synchronization, and optionally to provide a unified view of their disparate information.

Metadirectory products that offer multidirectional synchronization between directories and a unified view of the information they are synchronizing are mainstream metadirectory products. Products that only offer a united view of information contained in multiple directories or are actually middleware infrastructures are niche products. As in the case of all niche products and are termed "virtual directories.", Not to be dismissed out of hand companies should consider the value of the specialized functions they provide. Metadirectory products typically do not support password synchronization between directories, nor do they necessarily provide strong administration interfaces. Thus, metadirectory products are frequently combined with other products (e.g., password synchronization, enterprise user management products and provisioning applications) to form a more comprehensive solution. In the simplest terms, metadirectory products provide a core rules-based and/or policy-based synchronization engine that can be exploited by an administrator or by other products.

Metadirectories facilitate the Persona-Based Computing: Persona-Based Computing is a driver for a Full-Service Directory Persona-Based Computing: is centered around building highly tailored computer applications that provide the most personal and productive level of service to users.

Each persona equates to a different user profile performing a particular transaction. What varies is the kind of access permitted, the type of network capacity being used, the type of computer device being used, and the amount of prior information available to help better profile the user—and thereby provide the most productive and friendly experience between the enterprise and the client.

At many points in the implementation there are systems that contain information about the devices, applications, and people attached to the network in the form of a directory. From an internal perspective, each person allowed on the network might have information about his or her name, location, access rights, etc., in 10, 20, or 30 directories—e.g., e-mail, firewall, financial applications, to name just a few. Some individuals can also have various ways of accessing the network—at home, at work, and on the road. And they may also be accessing with a different type of device—PC, laptop, or PDA. Each access requires different information about the individual, but our research clearly shows that few of the information points are linked so that the user profile can be shared.

The goal of the metadirectory is not just consolidation of objects from each individual department and technology platform, but also to collect event information about each object, and then describe how to act on this new information. This single image, combined with event information, enables every data object in the metadirectory to be secured, monitored, controlled, and automated. The meta directory therefore should do the following:

- Provide an easily created, updated, and managed central repository of data and events that is globally available to users and applications that need it.

- Provide a high level of security using both authentication and policy enforcement—where policy resides in the directory and the implementation of the policy is divided between the directory and the systems deployed within the enterprise—while leveraging delegated authority features.

- Offer configuration flexibility for centralized organization, region-based organization, and fully distributed organizations—and yet still enable flexible access by users that fall outside these parameters through sup-port of dynamic caching.

- Deliver a rich relationship manager that can find any object, group data objects based on (multiple) arbitrary hierarchies, and group objects into collections. The collections are then used to significantly lower the cost of managing and administering the directory since the relationships are created automatically. Objects are manipulated based on membership in any collection or hierarchy.

Selecting a Metadirectory Product

To select a metadirectory product, enterprises should first determine

1. which directory (or, in some cases, directories) is most strategic

2. the directories (or other authentication sources that need to be synchronized,

3. what the synchronization flow will look like

When new employees are added, should they be added to the human resources directory and then populated to other directories, or should they be added first to the e-mail directory and populated from there? Defining the data sources that need to be synchronized and the flow of synchronization allows an enterprise to evaluate the connectors and connector technology provided by metadirectory products. Provisioning systems do much to simplify this process at the point of entry but only metadirectory systems address this issue in pre-populated systems. The reason for determining which directory is strategic the metadirectory valuation process should start with products offered by the strategic directory vendor and then extend out from there.

The often-neglected architecture phase of the directory services component is often the source of frustration and massive remediation efforts of most fortune 50 companies. This springs from the simplistic notion of most IT managers that they can simply purchase a directory or meta directory product off the shelf and with a minimum of forethought simply install the software with defaults intact and expect the software to hum along quietly serving millions of queries per second collocated with other services on what is often an already overloaded environment. This is a fallacy.

Organic, unplanned growth is the primary cause of directory and metadirectory failure

---

As in other systems the physical structure and logical network connections of a Meta directory are interdependent on the data structures expressed in the directory itself. In is the objective of this book to illustrate in graphic detail the level of interdependencies that exist in a directory and Meta directory architecture engagement and how such an effort resides in the overall Enterprise Datacenter Architecture.

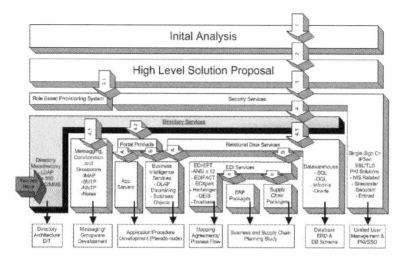

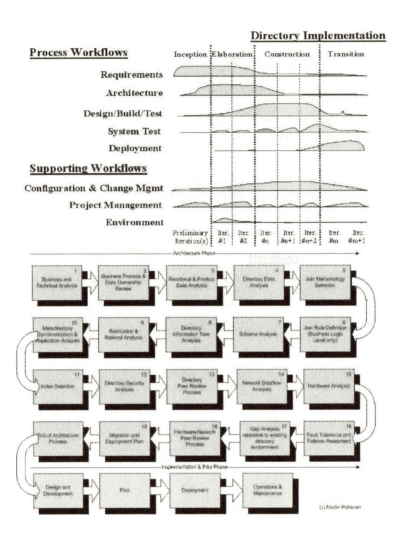

The diagrams listed above show the typical Metadirectory/Directory Architecture Analysis process and the position of that process in relation to the overall Enterprise Datacenter Architecture. The purpose of this primer is to set the framework and expectations for a successful Directory or Metadirectory Architecture engagement. In the framework of a typical Enterprise Datacenter Analysis.

It is important to remember that each layer in Diagram A creates a series of dependencies for the next deeper layer. Diagram B resolves the dependencies in a methodical way. Diagram B illustrates how each preceding step lays the groundwork for the step, which must follow.

Phase 1: The Initial Analysis: This details business objectives and goals of the project

Phase 2: High Level Solution Proposal: This process breaks down the Initial Analysis into a series of deliverables and milestones for the project. It is often accompanied by a proposed budget

Phase 3: Security Services Analysis/Architecture: This process defines the security requirements and methodologies, which will be used in the project. It includes any security packages and security services, which will police every aspect of the enterprise listed beneath the service in the model

Phase 4: Directory Services Analysis/Architecture
  Step 1: Business Process and Technical Analysis
   Step 2: Ownership Analysis
   Step 3: Relational Data Analysis:
   Step 4: Directory Data Analysis
   Step 5: Join Methodology Selection
   Step 5: Join Rule Definition (Business Logic Level only)
   Step 6: Schema Analysis
   Step 7: Directory Information Tree Analysis
   Step 8: Replication & Referral Analysis
   Step 9: Metadirectory Synchronization & Replication Analysis
   Step 10: Index Selection
   Step 11: Directory Security Analysis
   Step 12: Directory Peer Review Process

Step 13: Network Dataflow Analysis

Step 14: Hardware Analysis

Step 15: Fault Tolerance and Failover Assesment

Step 16: Gap Analysis relative to existing directory environment

Step 17: Hardware/Network Peer Review Process

Step 18: Migration and Deployment Plan

Step 19: End of Directory Architecture Process

PART II

Directory Powered Systems

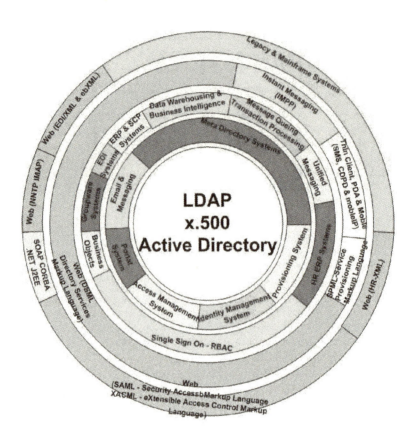

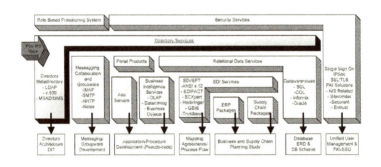

6
Provisioning

While a centralized metadirectory provides the framework for the provisioning of some of these resources, it does not provide the following functionality:

Translating business requirements (like hiring a contractor) to the specific IT tasks and configurations necessary to realize this need (like what exactly does the contractor need to do his job).

Creating a synchronized definition of the IT "workflow" necessary to realize the business need. For example, it is impossible to install the contractor's software before a computer is made available.

Maintaining a coordinated business view of corporate resources allocated. For example, when the contractor's job is finished, how can the company "deprovision" all the allocated services and make sure it recovers all the resources. In a complex and fast moving business environment

A typical large enterprise will have several different types of systems, many installations of those systems, numerous types of information stored on those systems, and will need to manage access to the information and to the systems themselves. A typical 25,000-user company has over 87 million permissions assigned. Each of these permissions must be properly managed to ensure that information is adequately protected.

Sometimes a better solution for managing information and system access is to employ an approach that leaves user privilege information at the native system level where it naturally resides and provides a mechanism by which it can be manipulated centrally. One such approach would be to create a memory index of this information for real-time retrieval and update as needed. This allows for the management of disparate user account data across multiple systems from a single point. Provisioning enables companies to automate the routine operations of setting up employees. Instead of maintaining multiple phone number databases, PC hardware, and all other employee tools, Provisioning provides a single platform for automating the requisition and provision of those tools. The software provides employees with instant access to the tools they need in order to successfully achieve their jobs.

Provisioning is a concept that drives automation, especially in terms of providing fulfillment to customers of service providers. Provisioning essentially boils down to the concept of using changes to a directory object to signal changes in applications that rely on that data.

Provisioning software also tracks changes to an employee's IT resources and the business reason for each change, creating a history for each employee that helps with IT resource audits and chargebacks. If an employee leaves the company, their access rights can be automatically rescinded and resources archived or reassigned as appropriate.

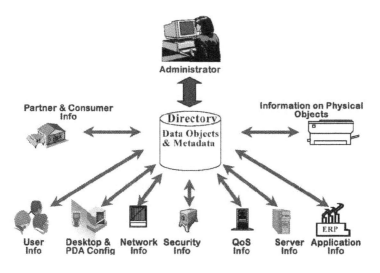

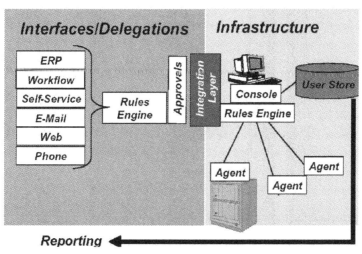

A directory significantly lowers the cost of administering multiple systems, and it also improves accuracy, control, and access to administrative systems. Although there is tremendous benefit in reducing the time and cost associated with the management of each individual system, managing just an individual system falls far short of controlling all of the issues associated with provisioning a user, a group of users, or even a business unit. Provisioning delivers a competitive edge because technology is finally responsive to the needs of the business. Simply Adding a new user into a system configuration list does not ensure that the user will gain access to that service. Figure 2 provides an example of all of the systems that are interconnected to provide a basic service and therefore requires that all system administrators be coordinated to ensure that the service is enabled.

User provisioning automates many of the traditionally manual processes and procedures required to manage users access to resources across the enterprise.
Workflow is the process of automating the business rules and approval process required to grant users access to an organization's resources. Combining the two allows an organization to automatically and quickly grant or deny access to users with a minimal of manual intervention or manual approvals

Provisioning is an emerging directory-guided IT solution that automates the deployment of IT resources and services based on business requirements. Provisioning solutions automate many provisioning activities by operating directly on enterprise directory data to enable IT services across systems, organizations, and geographies.

Current provisioning systems target large-scale system environments, such as those found in telecommunications companies and Internet Service Providers (ISPs). These high-end provisioning systems automate the processes of adding, changing, and/or terminating phone and Web services for millions of customers. An emerging class of Provisioning systems performs a similar task, but these systems are designed to automate such services within an enterprise. This focus on the enterprise also drives changes in several other areas. For example, by leveraging an enterprise-level directory, the Provisioning solution greatly reduces the need for custom integration of applications, systems, and devices deployed across the enterprise. The Provisioning solution also has the potential to manage a broader range of processes across organizations, geographies, and companies and can even integrate processes that manage physical assets that fall outside, but are related to, the IT infrastructure. In addition, a Provisioning solution will address the needs of not only the IT organization, but also business managers. Line-of-business (LOB) managers will be able to make requests using familiar business terms on the Provisioning system; and, in response, the system will sequence the tasks needed to accomplish those requests, reporting any problems discovered. Provisioning systems will be instrumental in helping companies respond more quickly and efficiently to the challenges posed by the Internet. In response to proliferation of the Internet, many enterprises must now reorganize the way they do business. Provisioning can help by significantly reducing the time it takes for the enterprise to change its physical IT infrastructure and associated systems. It will also forecast how long a requested change will take to implement and deliver alerts when a critical-path project slips—or when resource allocation problems exist. Perhaps most important, Provisioning will manage the provisioning processes that include the assets of business partners and directory.

Authorization solutions control what users can see and do in a system, which is a "must have" solution as companies expose more resources to more people.

Provisioning can be defined as an extension of Authorization. Authorization and provisioning are a natural combination as provisioning solutions create user accounts and rules while authorization solutions enforce the rules.

Provisioning systems, however, are a critical infrastructure component for business-to-business relationship management. This is because at a time when employees can work for a partner one day and a competitor the next, the integrity of the partnership depends on quickly reflecting an employees changed status in his or her own business as well as across resources owned by partners.

Account provisioning automates a company's ability to create, enable, disable, and delete user accounts in back-end systems. Using a provisioning solution, a company can model its desired business process for managing changes to user information and synchronize this process into the appropriate back-end systems. The benefits of rapid, smooth account provisioning range from increased productivity, as new employees are quickly connected to the resources they need, to improved security, as departing employees are consistently and promptly blocked from access.

Though the enterprise directory is the skeleton that makes Provisioning possible, an Provisioning solution needs significant muscle to deliver its benefits. The Provisioning application must:

- Utilize profiles that generalize both typical users and typical service requests;
- Translate business requirements to their IT profile;
- Provide a mechanism to control the provisioning process;
- Establish the tasks required to implement the business change;
- Manage the complexity of inter-related requirements;
- Track the critical path of provisioning efforts;
- Maintain historical information so that changes made to the IT infrastructure can be traced back to the business issue that caused them

CAPABILITIES OF POLICY-BASED PROVISIONING SYSTEMS

A policy-based provisioning system provides a control mechanism for populating user authorities into access controlled, heterogeneous resources. The provisioning system interacts directly with users and with two external types of systems: identity sources and access control mechanisms.

- Identity systems: deliver authoritative information about the users that need accounts. The provisioning system communicates directly with access control systems to create accounts, supply user information and passwords and define the entitlements of the account.

- Access control mechanisms: In reverse, local administrative changes made to an access control system are captured and reported to the provisioning system for evaluation against policy and reaction.

THE IDENTITY MANAGEMENT ELEMENTS OF THE ACCESS ECOSYSTEM

The role of the identity management system is to provide an authoritative store for information about users. Such components of the ecosystem are a collection of special purpose and legacy systems that have emerged independently throughout an organization. Common to them all is their authoritative information about some set of users with access rights. Frequently, employee information can be found in multiple HR systems accumulated through merger and acquisition activity. Business partner users are often located in directories or databases within each major business area, while customers may be found in a commerce area. Contractors tend to be difficult to locate. Often these contractors are best maintained using the provisioning system as the authoritative source of their identity information.

Many organizations contain efforts to create a consolidated source for authoritative identity information. Frequently, the goal of this effort is to establish an enterprise-wide user store to support user white pages. In the conduct of these projects, a directory is often envisioned as the ideal store because of its ease of distribution, fast access, and hierarchical organization. In order to establish a single physical or virtual identity store, it is necessary to link together the contents of the many existing identity stores. However, the existing stores are not eliminated, as there are usually many procedures in place to maintain them, and there are significant issues regarding data ownership to be overcome. Many organizations look to meta-directory technologies to solve this problem.

The meta-directory solutions can be an important part of the glue to establish an accurate, enterprise-wide identity store. These solutions are generic environments that can be programmed to maintain synchronicity between data elements in different instances and type of data stores. The meta-directory is a developmental tool that requires specific customizations to the specific data stores and data structures in the organization. Once in place, these systems perform their functions at the data layer of the architecture. They generally have no user interface and do not interact with users. It is helpful to provide two examples of common applications of meta-directories for identity synchronization.

Example 1: Multiple data sources each with an element that is authoritative

In this example, an organization is creating an enterprise identity store, but the challenge is that fields about an individual user are mastered from various other authoritative systems. For example, it is desired that the user's mobile phone number and cost center are maintained with the user information in the enterprise directory. In this example, an in-house telephony group maintains the user's mobile numbers in its database, and the user's cost centers are maintained by the HR system. The meta-directory can be used to monitor these specific entries in their authoritative stores. If the values change, the meta-directory will automatically update the enterprise directory with the new information.

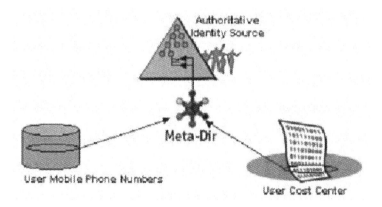

Example 2: Multiple divisional directories to be kept accurate

In this example, the enterprise is creating a virtual enterprise directory of user information. The challenge in this case is that multiple departments within the organization maintain their own stores of information for the users in their division. Each division desires to have a directory with all user information, but the information must be maintained in their divisional store. The meta-directory can be utilized here to update sets of users' data between multiple sources on change.

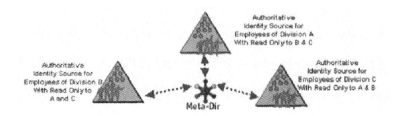

PRIMARY SERVICES

A Policy Based Provisioning System has five primary services:
1. Policy Management
2. Access Request Management
3. Access Rights Reconciliation
4. Auditing and Reporting
5. Password Self-Service

- Policy Management: provides a proactive method to assign, monitor and revoke entitlements for users. The policy engine allows users to be defined as members of groups, including roles. Policies define sets of entitlements to resources for these groups of users. Change to information about a user is evaluated to determine if it alters group membership. If there is an effect, policies are reviewed and changes to entitlements are put in place automatically and immediately. Likewise, a change in the definition of the set of resources in a policy may also trigger a change in entitlements.

- Access Request Management—Each entitlement defined with the entitlement engine may be associated with a workflow to gather approvals and collect information prior to granting the entitlement. To allow the system to adapt to changes in an organization, The entitlement engine supports the use of special fields such as 'supervisor' and 'resource owner' that are automatically resolved to individual or group addresses at the time of the request. Tasks can be escalated to other persons or groups if they are not completed in a defined time period. The entitlement engine may also collect information during this process. Tasks within an the entitlement engine workflow may follow branches based on data retrieved from the LDAP directory or from a user. The system can also be told to gather specific information from users who have unique knowledge. The owner of a resource is often in a unique position to add specific parameters about an account while it is being provisioned.

- Access Rights Reconciliation—The entitlement engine provides a closed-loop environment. Not only does the entitlement engine push entitlement changes to a managed resource, the entitlement engine also detects changes made by local administrators to a resource in order to determine if it complies with policies. The entitlement engine uses a real-time feedback mechanism to capture changes made by local administrators; the changes are then compared with policies.

- Auditing and Reporting: All requests, approvals and changes are time-stamped and recorded by the entitlement engine into a persistent database in a structured format. Reports can be generated over the Web for common tasks such as listing the accounts of an individual or listing the accounts on a resource. In addition, reporting tools are provided to allow a variety of reports to be generated for support of security audits or other purposes. Common database reporting tools can be used to create custom views of the data needed by an organization.

- Password Self-Service: Due to the central knowledge that the entitlement engine provisioning system maintains over all managed resources, the entitlement engine provides the ability for users to directly reset their passwords in one, or synchronize across all, of their accounts. Further, the entitlement engine is aware of the passwords rules for all the resources that it manages. In addition to checking the validity of a requested password change, The entitlement engine can be told to enforce additional password rules across the managed resources.

The entitlement engine can be told to react to a detected local change in one of three ways:

1. Suspend the changed account
2. Rollback the change to its previous configuration
3. Accept the change

The entitlement engine can also retrieve all the accounts within a resource in bulk. This capability is powerful in resolving a resource under the entitlement engine when all existing accounts need to be assigned to existing users and checked against policies.

While each Agent may be custom-created for the resource it manages. Each Agent within a provisioning system supports the same primary commands. At the heart of the provisioning system is a collection of features required to:

- Create Account

- Delete Account

- Suspend Account

- Restore Account

- Change Account

- Reconcile

- Change Password

As the number of people accessing applications and data increases, attempting to track who has access to what becomes ever more complex. The process of managing these access rights can function as a business enabler or business roadblock Unfortunately, most enterprises are discovering that their existing paper-based procedures, requiring intensive manual involvement, are roadblocks.

The key descriptor of existing access rights management processes is "separate"—separate people, separate steps, separate technologies, and separate directories for each system or resource. Different departments have varying procedures and processes while the physical process for setting up permissions for each application varies widely, employing different permissions, conventions, and application programming interfaces (APIs) for provisioning. The end result is that the activities to provision users require a large number of steps that cross the entire enterprise and may even cross enterprise boundaries. Not surprisingly, companies are seeking ways of automating and managing the provisioning process.

A provisioning systems role engine

- Should create a single control point that can administer setup, teardown, and reconciliation of access rights across disparate systems and software.

- It should be capable of functioning across a variety of operating systems, applications and networking platforms; including intranets and extranets, email, payroll, security systems, directories, and HR systems.

- It should use intelligent software agents that interface with managed applications and other systems resources (such as other procurement and groupware systems) and advanced workflow to automatically establish business resource access privileges and rights for employees, business partners, vendors, and contractors.

- a provisioning systems role engine should provide provisioning management.

- To initiate account setup, the administrator would select from defined access rights based on roles. The product then reconciles employee status information from HR databases with access privilege data from each platform. It then identifies and communicates with a pre-defined hierarchy of managers authorized to approve access. A provisioning systems role engine submits an electronic request form to the appropriate manager and if this manager is unavailable, the product notifies the next approver in the hierarchy. If multiple approvals are required, the product routes the request in proper sequence.

Acting as a trusted virtual administrator, provisioning systems role engines agents should translate requests and process configurations to the various systems they connect to via compressed and encrypted communication. The product should provide automated reconciliation of user account information to determine ideal state vs. actual state. Once access rights are established, users can then take advantage of self-service to change and maintain their own passwords. A provisioning systems role engine delivers an enterprise-wide reporting system featuring predefined reports as well as the capability for creating custom reports

POLICY BASED PROVISIONING SYSTEMS:

Policy-based engines allow defined groups of users to automatically receive certain entitlements to selected controlled resources. One approach to doing this is Role-Based Access Control (RBAC). This approach associates the entitlements to a role within an organization; users are then assigned to the roles. Any change to a user, a role definition or a resource may cause an automatic change to privileges depending on the defined policies of the organization. Policies are an effective method for automation because organizational policies, including roles, are redefined much less frequently than users and systems come and go. Delegation of authority allows the decision processes of provisioning to be made by the people with the best knowledge of the situation. For example, a business partner has the best knowledge of changes in their population and should make these changes directly to the system. In another example, the owner of a resource may be able to supply detailed parameters for a new account on their system and can inform the provisioning system of these details. Because provisioning systems create user accounts, set authentication credentials and handle user information, they must be treated as trusted systems. Trust is created by procedures for handling information but also must be incorporated into the design of the provisioning system and the environment on which it is installed for operation.

The Provisioning ecosystem is a complex of products working together to solve the challenges of accurate user access control of protected resources. The solutions in this ecosystem include:

- Identity stores containing user information
- Provisioning engines evaluating user privileges against organizational rules
- Access control systems gating a user's access at the time they are attempting to use a protected resource.

Alone, these solutions are important pieces of a security environment but when working together, they form a system that allows privileges to be maintained quickly, accurately and proactively.

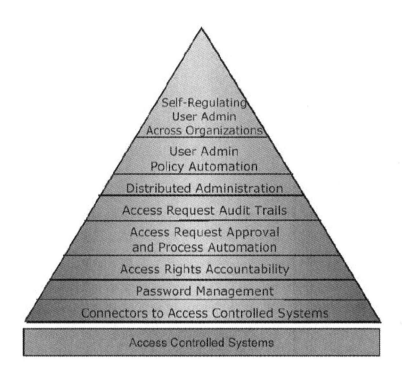

CONNECTORS TO ACCESS CONTROLLED SYSTEMS

In order to automate provisioning, it is necessary for the system to communicate securely with each target system being managed. If the connector does not exist, then an administrator must still make the required changes. The connectors, or agents, are the key mechanisms that translate the commands of the provisioning system into the proprietary language understood by the managed resources. Further, the richness of the language used is important. Managed systems (SAP, for example) support the definition of hundreds of parameters describing user access. The connector must support the needs of the managed system and the needs of the organization in creating or changing accounts. Finally, the communication between the provisioning system and the managed system must be secure. The link must be encrypted so no one can "listen" and steal passwords. The link must also allow authentication of the source so that a new command cannot be injected into the system to create an inappropriate account.

PASSWORD MANAGEMENT

Password management is the ability to control password quality and change passwords throughout an environment. As companies deploy more and more systems that contain access controls, the number of passwords required to be remembered by each user increases. This increase poses a risk to the organization as more users have a tendency to write down the many secrets in order to keep track of them, as well as the increased load on the help desk to reset forgotten passwords. About 40% of helpdesk activity is related to resetting forgotten passwords. With each call costing nearly $30 dollars to execute and a typical user calling three times each year, reducing this cost has significant payback. Password management systems allow users to self-service their own accounts. Users visit a web-based system, authorize themselves, then may reset or synchronize their passwords on all their accounts. Further, the passwords they select can be evaluated against rules on their formation to ensure uniform conformance with organizational password policies.

ACCESS RIGHTS ACCOUNTABILITY

Orphan accounts are those valid accounts found on most systems that cannot be associated with a true user. These types of accounts pose one of the most serious threats to corporate security because, when used inappropriately, cannot be detected as a traditional cyber attack. The inappropriate use of these orphan accounts is a case of an electronic imposter. They aren't detected because the accounts are perfectly valid. The key to the control of orphan accounts is to associate every account with a true user, which may be an employee, contractor, business partner or customer. When the users' status with the organization changes, their access rights must change too. The ability to control orphan accounts requires that the provisioning system links together account information with authoritative information on the users themselves. Authoritative user identity information is typically found in HR and various databases and directories containing information on users in other businesses. Orphan account control includes finding these accounts on an ongoing and rapid basis, then reacting to them in an automated fashion by generating a report to security personnel or automatically suspending the account.

ACCESS REQUEST APPROVAL AND PROCESS AUTOMATION

If meta-directory implementers want their solutions to be used for provisioning, they will need to custom craft the scripts and connectors for this task-at least until any standard way of expressing provisioning information is enabled. In addition, most meta-directory providers will have to move into new territory by network-enabling and encrypting communications links between a provisioned resource and the meta-directory. To compete effectively, many meta-directories will also need to introduce the kind of turnkey business logic, user interfaces, rule-based engines, and workflow capabilities that are evolving with today's provisioning systems. Most of today's meta-directories don't come close without major modification.

Enterprise provisioning systems go a long way toward addressing internal issues. Outside an enterprise, however, complications will arise because different vendors with different architectures already supply provisioning solutions. And even more solutions can be expected to enter the marketplace. Even if an industry, say the auto industry, decides to handle provisioning within a trading hub (and requires partners to implement a backend system), the odds of all partners converging on a single vendor and architect are low.

Provisioning solves the challenge of handling employee management by effectively streamlining and automating information technology (IT) activities associated with employee movement. This includes ensuring rapid productivity for new employees, efficient handling of employee movement and dealing with the IT ramifications of employee departures.

Access request approval automation is a key component in rapidly and accurately changing user access rights. The approval processes are a specialized form of workflow that determines, based on organizational policy, who needs to approve a requested change to access rights prior to its execution. Many organizations still rely on paper and e-mails forwarded in many different paths through the organization. These approaches can be very slow as the requests sit idle in an inbox or are rejected because they are missing key information. A complete provisioning workflow system automatically routes to the proper approvers, escalate to alternates if they sit too long and require information to be filled out before accepting the approval. This process automation can turn a process that takes typically nearly a week to one that takes minutes. Some organizations also require that information about accounts or background information is added to the request as it flows through the process. This is useful to hide unnecessary details from users in the request and approval process. This information may come from users involved in the process or they may be computed or extracted from other systems.

ACCESS REQUEST AUDIT TRAILS

Centralized audit trails of access requests are an important aspect of supporting independent audits of security practices and procedures in an organization. Security audits are part of every organization, whether conducted by internal auditors or external audits supporting formal bookkeeping. If record keeping is incomplete, inaccurate and stored in multiple locations, then these audits can be both time consuming and labor intensive. Audits are frequently very disruptive to business efforts, but are mandatory for the safe and secure operation. Among other things these teams look for orphan accounts or inappropriate access privileges that exist on important systems. The audits occur from once a month to once a week, depending on the organization. These audit trails capture all aspects of the administration of access rights, from requests with reason to changes and account details.

DISTRIBUTED ADMINISTRATION

Distributed administration allows the administrative tasks involved with provisioning, whether manual or automatic, to be distributed securely among various organizations. This is important for two reasons: accuracy and scale. It is wise to move the process of requesting and approving access changes close to the people that know if such resources are really needed by the individual. Further, this distribution allows the workload to be balanced across a large number of users rather than a single dedicated and centralized team. This becomes fundamental in large organizations and those with multiple business partners. To accomplish this, the system must support delegated administration and user authentication. Delegated administration allows the responsibilities for using and changing the system to be delegated down through an organization in a controlled manner. Delegating administrative tasks to request access for a user, approve a change, or define local policies can be assigned to individuals throughout an organization or its partner network. In this way, individuals that have the most accurate knowledge of users' needs can request or approve changes. Lower levels can define local policies for access rights assignment within the framework created by higher levels. A key aspect of delegated administration is filtering the information presented to an administrator on a "need to know" basis. Not only does this make the system more useable to the administrator, but it also prevents exposing information to personnel with no need to know. For example, external business partners may be administering their own users into a common supplier environment but each partner must remain invisible to the other partners. Authentication to the system becomes critical at this point. As far-flung individuals may make changes effecting access rights for others, it's critical that system security is maintained. Frequently these interfaces are accessible to users over the Internet that require stronger authentication approaches for these functions. In addition to username and password authentication, multifactor authentication support such as client-side PKI certificates, security tokens or biometrics must be provided.

This ultimate level of the hierarchy is the ability to provision across multiple organizations that contain user groups and shared services. In this environment, a change in a users status is automatically reflected in access rights inside the user's organization and into outside services offered by other organizations. As the provider of services to other organizations, user access rights are automatically established based on your security policies and the assertion of the users' authenticity provided by the sponsor or a third party.

User Administration Policy Automation is the business engine that evaluates and enforces business processes and rules for granting access. Role Based Access Control is one concept for granting users to access rights based on the assignment to a defined role in the organization. Rule based approaches can also be applied to determine the conditions for granting access rights or the characteristics of a user that should have access rights directly or by assigning them to a role.

Provisioning automates the creation of a new employee's "IT profile", defining and allocating the resources required by a new employee to do his or her job. These include computers, telephones, cell phones and pagers, as well as the related configurations, such as user names, passwords and access to network applications. When an employee leaves the company, a provisioning system ensures that the employee is "out of the system" immediately, by disabling access to precious IT resources, all in a structured and documented way

Provisioning eliminates the manual aspect of user access rights For example when an enterprise hires a new employee, Human Resources generally keeps employee data in a database, which is updated manually. IT departments also crease a user profile with an e-mail identification and rights to certain business applications, granted by the business. Often non-IT administrators set up user accounts, using independent methods, which are separate from the IT and system administrator's database. Different rights for each employee are stored throughout the organization, e.g., a technical position would require different rights than an employee in a HR department. By the time this is set up, a lot of productivity is lost. It can take weeks for a new employee to begin work for just this reason.

The automation is key to managing large numbers of users to disparate resources in order to assign, monitor and revoke entitlements for users. The business engine allows users to be defined as members of groups, including roles. Policies define levels of entitlements to sets of resources for these groups of users. Advance engines police changes to information about a user in order to determine if the change entails changes to group membership based on the defined policies. Likewise, a change in the definition of the set of resources in a policy may also trigger automated changes in entitlements.

Other key capabilities of these advanced provisioning policy engines include:

1. Mandatory and Optional Entitlements—Mandatory entitlements are always granted but optional entitlements are not automatically pro-

visioned. Optional entitlements may be requested by a user in the group and granted upon approval.

2. Pre-requisite Services—defines services that must be granted prior to creation of the access rights. For example, NT rights must be granted prior to privileges for user of Microsoft Exchange.

3. Entitlement Defaults and Constraints—each characteristic of an entitlement may be set to a default value, or its range can be constrained, depending on the level of the entitlement to be granted

ACCESS CONTROL ELEMENT OF THE ORGANIZATION

Frequently, Access control or Single Sign-On products are components of an organization's ecosystem. At its core, the access control element delivers a key access control mechanism to gate user access to web pages and URLs. The product is found in many intranet and extranet environments, but does not address the access control mechanisms found in non-web environment. Access control solutions are distinct from provisioning solutions, as they are access controls during a login session where the user interacts directly with these systems when attempting to access protected web-based resources. Provisioning components, on the other hand, are administrative systems that create and configure the accounts for each user in the web and non-web space. Access control and provisioning systems are commonly found working in combination for complex web environments that include backend systems housed in the enterprise.

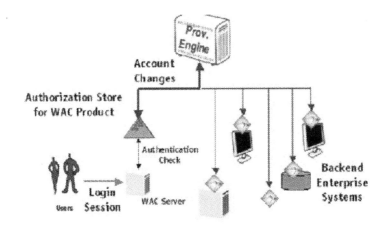

ACCESS CONTROL AND PROVISIONING

Access control solutions often provide administrative tools that overlap some aspect of a provisioning system. These administrative tools deliver the ability to manage user accounts, some on a delegated basis, but their scope is exclusively over the access control product. Most access control solutions utilize an LDAP directory as the store for web authorization data. In some cases, the administrative environment provided by the access control solutions is satisfactory to deliver provisioning, but this is only the case when the environment administered is limited to web applications. Once enterprise systems are part of the environment, an administrative solution that delivers common management of disparate systems is required.

ACCESS CONTROL AND IDENTITY MANAGEMENT

Access control elements can deliver an aspect of a user identity management environment. For business extranets, for example, the directory supporting the access control product may be the primary store of user information about the business partners. If the processes are in place to maintain accuracy of this information, then this directory may be one component of an organization's authoritative source of user information. access control products may assist in the management of this information through delegated administration environments. These allow users to update their own information over the web in a controlled manner. However, there are generally other, stronger sources of user identity available for employees, contractors and customers.

In conjunction with people and processes, provisioning systems form a core part of the enterprise security architecture. The provisioning system provides automated process enforcement of administration across all other user authentication and access control systems. This allows close and responsive coordination over who can get access to what information or system capability.

The problem addressed by provisioning and the provisioning ecosystem has evolved due to the piecemeal rollout of secure systems common throughout organizations over the last 10 years. None of these systems can be administered through a common environment, leading to islands of administration spread out through most organizations. Further, the policies and procedures for granting and revoking access privileges for users have also developed without an overall planning process. In parallel, islands of information about actual users have been created around Human Resource (HR) systems and business area partner directories. These are not able to be reconciled automatically against access rights on protected systems, resulting in a slow approval processes for access changes, large number of active accounts without valid users, and IT departments that are overloaded and slow to respond to access or revocation requests. These same groups frequently fail Service Level Agreements and security audits because they cannot keep up with the workload. As a result the provisioning system provides a clear ROI for large organizations. Among the core values of the provision solution are:

- Improve accuracy and reduce cost for user access rights creation and revocation for internal system and resources external to your organization

- Improve security and scaling of administrative staff by allowing workload to be divided among administrators with the accurate knowledge of user access needs

- Reduce security risk and audit costs by establishing a system-of-record for access changes and approvals

- Eliminate security threat of active accounts that have no valid owner or unapproved configurations

- Reduce help desk cost by converting password resets to a self-service activity

- Improve service quality through self-service of passwords changes and access requests

The values are produced by various key capabilities of the provisioning solutions. These are strategic solutions that provide comprehensive capabilities over the user administration problem; delivering value immediately and containing features to support administrative efforts, as they become more complex and far reaching. In addition to the architectural and technical characteristics of the solution, the features that the system provides must be evaluated. The capabilities can readily be arranged into a pyramid, the base of which is the most core-required capability of the provisioning solution. Having the foundation provided the lowest level, one can move up to higher, more powerful capabilities that build upon the lower levels of the foundation. The provisioning value pyramid reference model is shown.

At the center of this architecture is the provisioning system, which includes interfaces to identity information stores and to the access controls systems. The data within these systems is intelligently linked together using sets of rules that embody the policies of the organizations, which dictate who should receive what level of access under what conditions. Further, the rules control how the accounts are defined and who must approve of them. The policy-based provisioning system covers formation of User IDs, passwords and details of the authorities that a user receives on a specific.

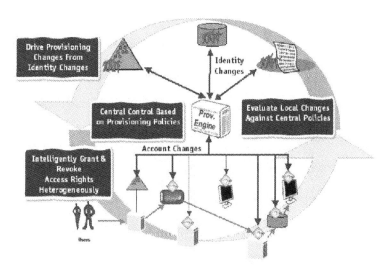

A key element of the architecture is its bi-directional and event-driven nature. A change made directly to an access control list of a managed system is reported up to the provisioning engine that compares the change against allowable policies. Violations can be reported to security staff and reacted to immediately. Similarly, a change in an identity source is reported to the provisioning system and, based on policies; accounts may be automatically created, suspended or restored. This new architecture provides a self-regulating environment. Once in place, users' accounts are vigilantly compared against identity and policy to ensure that the right people, and only the right people, have proper access levels into the right systems.

The big change is the migration to an e-business model, moving from inward-facing to global applications managing user access and provisioning is a tall order as enterprises become more heterogeneous and the number of users who need access grows.

As enterprises create virtual enterprises and create more collaboration with trading partners, this reinforces the need for an automated process to manage these resources spending on technology is moving out of the enterprise and toward using more managed services. Security is a pre-requisite to deliver transactions on the Internet. Companies are look-ing for ways to automate that process and achieve ROI (return on investment)."

five business drivers companies are facing when it comes to taking the leap into identity management:

- Business facilitators—Enterprises will need to have customers, business partners and the supply chain self-register in order to get to interactive sites and solutions and have access to what they need, Witty said;

- Cost reduction—Automated identity management solutions cut costs because fewer people are needed to run them and help desk calls are reduced;

- Improved service levels—Witty points out that internal service level agreements are shrinking, and before lone, the only way to support them is through automation;

- Security risk management—Keeping tabs on who has access to what is vital to securing enterprise data, networks and applica-tions;

- Regulatory compliance—Legislation like the Health Insurance Portability and Accountability Act (HIPAA) and the Gramm Leach Bliley Act (GLB) are forcing enterprises to standardize their management of users in many cases.

DISTRIBUTED ADMINISTRATION

Distributed administration allows the administrative tasks involved with provisioning, whether manual or automatic, to be distributed securely among various organizations. This is important for two reasons, first is accuracy and second is scale. It is wise to move the process of requesting and approving access changes close to the people that know if the resource is truly needed by the individual. Further, this distribution allows the workload to be balanced across a large number of users rather than a single dedicated and centralized team. This becomes fundamental in large organization and those with multiple business partners. Distribution should be performed all the way down to the individual level when desired for self-service or self-enrollment. To accomplish this, the system must support delegated administration and user authentication. Delegated administration allows the responsibilities for using and changing the system to be delegated down through an organization in a controlled manner.

Delegating administrative tasks to request access for a user, approve a change, or define local policies can be assigned to individuals throughout an organization or its partner network. In this way, individuals that have the most accurate knowledge of users needs can request or approve changes. Lower levels can define local policies for access rights assignment within the framework created by higher levels. A key aspect of delegated administration is filtering the information presented to an administrator on a need-to-know basis. Not only does this make the system more useable to the administrator but also it prevents exposing information to personnel without need-to-know. For example, external business partners may be administering their own users into a common supplier environment but each partner must remain invisible to the other partners.

Authentication to the system becomes critical at this point. As far-flung individuals may make changes effecting access rights for others, it's critical that the system security is maintained. Frequently these interfaces are accessible to users over the Internet and that requires stronger authentication approaches for these functions. In addition to username and password authentication, multifactor authentication support such as client-side PKI certificates, security tokens or biometrics may be needed

ROLE CHOICE

Alternatively, the choice of role could be based on the location of the user (by checking the IP address of his machine, for example). That could be severely limiting, however—although one might try tracking day, time and machine used for different roles then presents a default choice to the user based on those parameters.

Another approach could revolve around the way the person authenticates. Note that using different usernames isn't the same thing as using roles—this would be assuming different identities. The directory doesn't know that the different users are actually one person.

A third way would be to use multiple authentication methods perhaps a password plus a smart card. One of the methods would actually identify the user and be used to authenticate for any role, while the second would distinguish one role from another. I don't know of anyone actually using this method but it might be worth trying out.

None of these methods is truly dynamic. The only way for the user to change roles is to tell the system that the change should occur

In order to automate provisioning, it is necessary for the system to communicate securely with each target system being managed. If the connector does not exist, then an administrator must still make the required changes. The connectors, or agents, are the key mechanisms that translate the commands of the provisioning system into the proprietary language understood by the managed resources. The communication between the provisioning system and the managed system must be bi-directional, secure, and bandwidth efficient. Bi-directionality is critical to capturing changes made directly to the managed system and reporting the change to the provisioning system for evaluation and response.

- The link must be encrypted.

- The link must also allow authentication of the source so that a new command cannot be injected into the system by an imposter to create an inappropriate account.

- The managed resources are physically distributed across the corporate WAN or public Internet, bandwidth efficiency must be considered. These networks often have limited available capacity and are expensive, requiring the provisioning system to operation with as little overhead as possible.

When selecting a provisioning system one should evaluate.
1) Connector availability for all target systems that needs to be managed
2) Connector development tool availability for in-house or unsupported target systems
3) Capabilities of a connector must be specific and adequately fine grain to support your operations on the target managed system
4) Connector communications must be bi-directional to send efficiently changes from the managing system and to report changes made to the local resource.
5) Connector communications must be secured with encryption
6) Connector communications must be secured with authentication using in-house or included credentials
7) Connectors must protect authentication credentials used to logon to administrative privileges on managed systems
8) Connectors should operate on target resources that are available only over bandwidth constrained networks

9) Connectors should have the option to operate on remote resources without requiring installation on the remote target

10) Connector operation does not interfere with the day-to-day operation of the target resource, especially those with limited available processing capabilities

11) Connector should not hamper the rights of the local administrator or place limitations on the abilities of the managed resource

12) Ability to reach user self-service through the web without logging onto the network

13) Ability to establish interactive voice response for password reset functions

14) Challenge-Response system to authenticate a user with forgotten password by using shared secrets

15) Ability to implement password formation rules to enforce password strength across the organization

16) Ability to synchronize passwords for multiple systems to the same value to reduce number of different passwords to be remembered by the user

17) Delivery of success/failure status for password changes to requestor

18) Ability to securely deliver passwords to users for new accounts

19) Flexible mechanisms to connect to multiple data stores containing accurate information on valid users

20) Ability to load identity store information on scheduled bulk basis

21) Ability to detect and respond to identity store changes in near real-time

22) Ability to retrieve account information from target managed resources on scheduled basis both in bulk or in filtered subsets to preserve network bandwidth

23) Local administrators maintain rights to create, delete and change accounts directly on resources, these changes must be detected and reported in near real-time

24) Local administrator changes must be compared against a system-of-record of account states to determine if changes comply with approved authorities and policies

25) Ability to notify designated personnel of access rights changes made outside the provisioning system

26) Ability to compare account UserID with valid users to determine accounts without owners (orphans)

27) Ability to automatically suspend or delete a detected orphan account

28) Ability to automatically suspend or rollback a reconfigured account that violates policy

29) Ability to examine reports on orphan accounts

30) Ability to readily view the accounts associated with a users or a resource

31) Ability to assign discovered orphan accounts to a valid user

32) Web-based mechanism for requesting access to a system

33) Automatic approval routing to persons appropriate to system access requested and organizational structure

34) Review and approval mechanisms that offer a zero-footprint client

35) Ability to use defined organizational information to dynamically determine routing of approvals

36) Ability to delegate approval authority to another

37) Ability to escalate a request to an alternative approver if allotted time elapses

38) Ability for different personnel to view different levels of information based on their job duties

39) Ability to request information from approval participants to define account-specific information during the process

40) Ability to determine service instances where physical account should be created

41) Ability for the system to change account information in the managed resources of your specific organization.

42) Ability to request information from specific participants in the workflow process

43) Ability to request information from external functions, applications or data stores during the process.

44) Time-stamped records of every access change request, approval/denial, justification and change to a managed resource

45) Time-stamped record of every administrative and policy-driven changes to access rights

46) Time-stamped record of any encountered orphan accounts and bypasses of administrative systems

47) Convenient, flexible means to run reports showing audit trails for users, systems, administrators and time periods

48) Audit trail is maintained in a tamper-proof environment

49) Ability to define organizational structures based on access granting authorities of an organization

50) Ability to delegate each administrative tasks with fine-grain control (e.g. approval authority, user creation, workflow definition)

51) Ability to delegate administrative tasks to 'n'-levels of depth

52) Ability to access all delegated capabilities over the web with a zero-footprint client

53) Ability to create private, filtered views of information about users and available resources

54) Ability to incorporate Access Control solutions to include provisioning system within the SSO environment

55) Ability to incorporate user authentication approaches commensurate with internal security policies

56) Ability to distribute provisioning system components securely over WAN and Internet environments including crossing firewalls

57) Ability to associate access rights definition with a role within the organization

58) Ability to assign users to one or more roles

59) Ability to implicitly define subsets of access to be unavailable to a role

60) Ability to explicitly assign users with individual access rights

61) Ability to dynamically and automatically change access rights based on changes in user roles

62) Ability to define implicit access rights available to users in a role upon their request and approval

63) Ability to use defined organizational information to dynamically determine routing of approvals

64) Ability to detect, evaluate and respond to user authority changes made directly to a managed resource

65) Ability to report on roles, rights associated with roles, and users associated with roles

66) Ability to set designated times for changes in access rights or policies

67) Ability to create unique user IDs consistent with policies and not in current user or previous use by the organization

68) Ability to create user authorizations extending an existing account

69) Adherence to standards adopted by other organizations

70) Secure environment for transmitting access changes across the public internet

71) Protection of private user information through secure facilities and sound processes

72) Reports of user rights into external systems, sponsors of users and audit trails of access rights changes

73) Availability both as public infrastructure and private operation

74) Pricing based on value delivered

75) Entirely web-based to allow easy distributed administration on an unlimited scale

76) Integrated functionality that does not require duplicate data entry or manual synchronization of information shared for multiple functions

77) Ability for servers to be inexpensively configured for high availability operation, including disaster recovery

78) Ability for utilized data stores to be configured for high availability operation

79) Ability for provisioning system to maintain accuracy when local administrators maintain privileges to make changes to target resources

80) Ability to operate on a secure operating system environments such as Unix or mainframe

81) Ability to operate using secure web servers

82) Resilient communications design between distributed components to withstand network or target resource outages

83) Multi-layered security architecture for operation in a DMZ and for management of users and systems in untrusted environments

84) XML-based extensibility and interaction with external systems

85) Use of common and de facto standards for interfaces internal and external to the provisioning system

86) Integration of LDAP directory services as identity stores, access control system authorization stores and internal user account and policy stores

87) Inclusion of a persistent data store or repository for audit trails and system recovery

88) Ability to respond quickly to user interactions including report requests, access change requests, policy changes, password self-service

The policy engine should also support:

1. Mandatory and Optional Entitlements—optional entitlements are not automatically provisioned but may be requested by a user in the group

2. Pre-requisite Services—defines services that must be granted prior to creation of the access rights. For example, NT rights must be granted prior to Exchange

3. Entitlement Defaults and Constraints—each characteristic of an entitlement may be set to a default value, or its range can be constrained, depending on the capabilities of the entitlement to be granted

4. Creation of a single account with multiple authorities governed by different policies

5. Creation of user Ids using a set of consistent, user-defined algorithm What should you evaluate?

SELF-REGULATING USER ADMINISTRATION ACROSS ORGANIZATIONS

This ultimate level of the hierarchy is the ability to provision across multiple organizations that each contains user groups and shared services. In this environment, a change in a users status is automatically reflected in access rights inside the users' organization and into outside services offered by other organizations. As the provider of services to other organizations, user access rights are automatically established based on your security policies and the assertion of the users authenticity provided by the sponsor or a 3rd party.

XML PROVISIONING SOLUTIONS

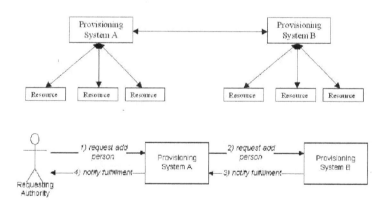

SPML

There are several areas of provisioning systems that would benefit from standardization. XRPM and ADPr both adequately address the business needs and possible benefits for establishing standardization in this space. Each initiative identified this need at opposite ends of the provisioning scenario. XRPM set out to define the set of standards required to facilitate interoperation and functioning at the Provisioning-System-to-Provisioning-System level. In contrast, ADPr set out to define the set of standards required to facilitate interoperation and functioning at the Provisioning-Systems-to-Managed-Resource level.

Service Provisioning Markup Language as stated SPML does not address the needs of end-to-end service definition in the context of order entry/order management and service delivery. SPML assumes a pre-existing trust model between participating provisioning service points and utilizes available security mechanisms for encryption and message integrity.

1. Request and response for specific provisioning requests (e. g., between two parties)

2. Query and exchange of available Provisioning Service Targets

3. Query and exchange of available Provisioning Service Target attributes and options

4. Query and exchange of available Provisioning Service Targets instance identities

5. Query and exchange of Provisioning Service Targets hierarchies

XRPM

eXtensible Resource Provisioning Management (XRPM) provides an initial set of use cases for the eXtensible Resource Provisioning Management, XRPM, Working Group. XRPM's objective is to provide an XML standard for the open interoperability between provisioning systems and resources in order for access rights to be provisioned.

EPP

Internet Engineering Task Force (IETF) Internet-Draft. Reference draft-ietf-provreg-epp-05.txt describes an application layer client-server protocol for the provisioning and management of objects stored in a shared central repository. Specified in XML, the protocol defines generic object management operations and an extensible framework that maps protocol operations to objects. This document includes a protocol specification, an object mapping template, and an XML media type registration. EPP is specified in XML Schema notation. EPP meets and exceeds the requirements for a generic registry registrar protocol as described in Generic Registry-Registrar Protocol Requirements. EPP content is identified by MIME media type (application/epp+xml). EPP is intended for use in diverse operating environments where transport and security requirements vary greatly as well as for use in a layered protocol environment. EPP was originally designed to provide a standard Internet domain name registration protocol for use between domain name registrars and domain name registries. This protocol provides a means of interaction between a registrar's applications and registry applications. It is expected that this protocol will have additional uses beyond domain name registration...EPP is an XML protocol that can be layered over multiple transport protocols. Protected using lower-layer security protocols, clients exchange identification, authentication, and option information, and then engage in a series of client-initiated command-response exchanges. All EPP commands are atomic (there is no partial success or partial failure) and idempotent (executing a command more than once has the same net effect on system state as successfully executing the command once). EPP provides four basic service elements: service discovery, commands, responses, and an extension framework that supports definition of managed objects and the relationship of protocol requests and responses to EPP objects.

ADPr

ADPr (Active Digital Profile) is an open XML-based schema designed to provide a vendor and platform-independent exchange of provisioning information to allocate and deploy applications, devices, systems, and service to employees, business partners, and customers. XML, short for Extensive Markup Language was designed especially for web documents. ADPr allows designers to create their own customized tags, enabling the definition, transmission, validation, and interpretation of data between applications and between organizations. ADPr allows multiple systems to exchange a complete set of provisioning information, including the action to be taken, the data required to perform the action, authentication and authorization information about the requester, the relationship between the systems, and any other context that defines the environment of the request.

PSML

PSML will provide the framework for standards-based interoperability in the provisioning market. Provisioning systems are an integral part of the identity and access management infrastructure for both large enterprises and trading communities. An XML-based framework for exchanging user, resource and service provisioning information. Provisioning Services Markup Language (PSML) is a specification for the automation of user or system access and entitlement rights to electronic services. Provisioning Services Markup Language (PSML) presents an end-to-end specification for the automation of user or system access and entitlement rights to electronic services. PSML provides the framework for standards-based interoperability in the provisioning market. In the past provisioning vendors and enterprise systems resource vendors use proprietary APIs and data models for security administration. In today's IT environment provisioning systems are an integral part of the identity and access management infrastructure for enterprises. The PSTC initiative removes a major obstacle to the deployment of effective account management strategies that span applications, platforms, and corporate boundaries. Through broad-based industry collaboration on the framework, it is now possible to achieve convergence on a single standard, which vendors can then leverage to deliver truly effective solutions to customer provisioning problems.

RETURN ON INVESTMENT:

Provisioning solutions show strong returns on investment in organizations with significant numbers of user accounts. The large number of user accounts is due to the combination of the number of users and the number of resources being managed. A user to a provisioning system is virtually any human being with privileges to an access controlled resource, including employees, contractors, business partners and customers. Because of the large number of users accounts, provisioning systems utilize automated policy-based engines and delegation of authority to increase productivity and decentralize the activities involved in provisioning while maintaining centralized control.

The center of any provisioning solution encompasses

- Automated user profiles;
- Access request management;
- Policy enforcement;
- Audit trails.

All of these solutions provide a tangible return on investment for organizations with large amounts of user accounts. The large amount of user accounts is increasing daily—not only from provisioning solutions deployed for internal employees but also as enterprises continue to expand the internal network out to partners and customers. A user is defined as anyone that uses an access-controlled application (this includes anyone who requires a password to use their computer).

The rules of the digital economy demand that enterprises extend network resources to and process access requests for partners, contractors, and customers. The value chain is rapidly evolving to the concept of the "virtual enterprise"—where lines are blurred, boundaries compromised, on-line collaboration is necessary, and digital transactions are fluid. In this volatile environment, enterprises struggle to walk the thin tightrope between securing their assets and ensuring that users get access to the resources they need to do their jobs.

Complexity and most importantly the expense associated with today's configured services. a typical ROI is often achieved in six to nine months. Provisioning also provides an additional layer of security by providing the automated means of de-Provisioning, or terminating mission critical access to former customers and/or employees. Provisioning solutions generally enable enterprises to seamlessly provision an array of multi-layered services and applications across an entire IT infrastructure in minutes. Current (2002-3) solutions are generally designed for multi-vendor technology networks that provide top-to-bottom access control over application, policies, services, VPN, wireless devices, e-mail accounts, and more.

Beyond the features that a provisioning system delivers to earn its return on investment, the provisioning system must also succeed in the complex, wide area operational environment of an enterprise. The provisioning system interfaces with a number of external systems and operates on a considerable amount of information distribute widely across the enterprise. Key operational success factors are provided below:

It must not interfere with the performance of the systems being managed and continue to operate without degradation when the managed system is temporarily inaccessible. Conversely, managed resources must be fully functional when the provisioning system is unavailable.

- It must be responsive to users interacting with the provisioning solution features for searches, reporting, approvals, self-service and auditing.

- It must load and maintain synchronization with user information from existing HR and other identity systems both statically and dynamically.

- It must load account and authorization information from existing operational systems without data entry

- It must detect and reconcile accounts created by, and/or changed by, other administrative systems (e.g. the local admin console provided with the managed resource).

- It must be configurable and scalable for large environments and high availability operations utilizing shared communication capacity on corporate WANs.

- It must provide end-to-end security over account changes.

- It is important that the features of the provisioning system are built upon architectures and deployed in an environment appropriate to the enterprise. Among the key requirements to evaluate:

7

Operations, Identity & Access Management

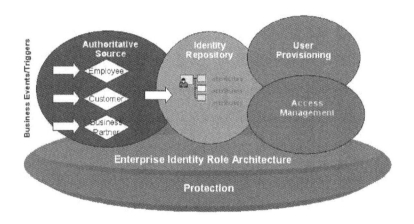

OPERATIONS MANAGEMENT

Operations management is about the way organizations produce goods and services. Everything you wear, eat, sit on, use, read or knock about on the sports field comes to you courtesy of the operations managers who organized its production. Operations management focuses on carefully managing the processes to produce and distribute products and services. Usually, small businesses don't talk about "operations management", but they carry out the activities that management schools typically associate with the phrase "operations management."

Major, overall activities often include product creation, development, production and distribution. (These activities are also associated with product and service management is usually in regard to one or more closely related product—that is, a product line. Operations management is in regard to all operations within the organization.) Related activities include managing purchases, inventory control, quality control, storage, logistics and evaluations. A great deal of focus is on efficiency and effectiveness of processes. Therefore, operations management often includes substantial measurement and analysis of internal processes. Ultimately, the nature of how operations management is carried out in an organization depends very much on the nature of products or services in the organization, for example, retail, manufacturing, wholesale, etc. This definition reflects the essential nature of Operations Management: it is a central activity in organizing things. Another way of looking at an operation is to consider it as a transformation process.

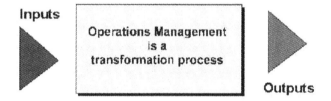

Operations are a transformation process: they convert a set of resources inputs into services and goods e.g. outputs. These resources may be raw materials, information, or the customer itself. These resources are transformed into the final goods or services by way of other 'transforming' resources—the facilities and staff of the operation.

Operations Management (or Production and Operations Management as it is sometimes referred to) involves a lot of different disciplines. The operations function may be located in any department. In university, for example, it may be located within a Business School or Engineering

School. In Industry, operations may be seen as the domain of logistics, production planning, or process control. Hence, operations interfaces with many different disciplines and many themes are developing which require the support of Operations Management. The following diagram provides a few examples.

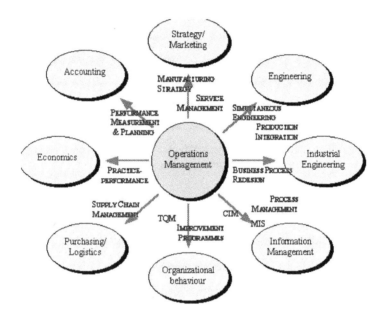

Operations management is about developing and managing value-adding processes, and supporting these through various tools, techniques and methods.

Metadirectory Management

The management of metadirectory contents and security can be centralized, distributed, or a combination of both. The metadirectory can be created so that changes to certain entries can be made only in the connected directory then imported into the metadirectory. Changes to other entries may be made only in the metadirectory and then propagated to the connected directory. Different people can manage different portions of the metadirectory. This level of control extends, not just to the entries themselves, but also to the individual attributes. Therefore, end users can manage parts of their own identity information telephone numbers or addresses, for example. The metadirectory does not impose any management model. It lets one create a directory whose management matches the realities of your organization, its security and access control requirements.

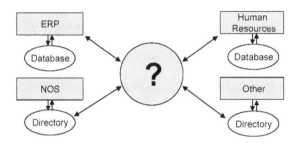

Connectivity A common operations management issue is connectivity to many forms of identity data. Connectivity requirements are simple: the more directory services, databases and applications to which identity management solutions can connect, the more value they can offer. Unknown data in one repository may be obtained from another. An identity management solution can connect to a given repository, if it is able to:

- Obtain information about what has changed in the repository.

- Add new objects to the repository.

- Delete objects from the repository.

- Change an existing object's attributes to different values.

To be a comprehensive solution, technologies should be able to connect to data in:

- Standards-based directory services via LDAP Version 3.

- Popular existing e-mail applications and non-LDAP directory services.

- Enterprise Resource Planning (ERP) applications.

- Databases via access methods such as SQL.

- Applications in which the only interface to identity information is through application programming interfaces (API) and no directory interface is available.

Failure Management

The ability to propagate a change to multiple repositories is a key requirement for identity flow management technologies. Any time an engine makes multiple updates, the opportunity exists for one or more of the updates to fail and for data in different repositories to become inconsistent. For example, if a person's title, salary and cost center are changed, but if the metadirectory is unable to update the user's title in applications, identity data will be left in a state of confusion. Typically, this means that an administrator must investigate the situation and make corrections.

Information Management Flow

Information management flow is the process of managing the flow of identity authentication and authorization information between repositories. Information management flow functionality must be able to:

- Detect changes to identity data and propagate updates to other repositories.

- Aggregate data from different repositories into metadirectories that contain a holistic view of identity data from across the enterprise.

Track related objects as they change their positions in directory trees and other repositories due to periodic reorganization.

Authentication and authorization

Authentication and authorization actually have very specific meanings, though the two processes are often confounded, and in practice are often not clearly distinguished. We will use the term "access management" to describe broader systems that may make use of both authentication and authorization services in order to control use of a networked resource.

Authentication is the process where a network user establishes a right to an identity in essence, the right to use a name. There are a large number of techniques that may be used to authenticate a user passwords, biometric techniques, smart cards, certificates. Note that names need not correspond to the usual names of individuals in the physical world. A user may have the rights to use more than one name: we view this as a central philosophical assumption in the cross-organizational environment. There is a scope or authority problem associated with names; in essence, when a user is authorized to use an identity this is a statement that some organization has accepted the user's right to that name. For authorization *within* an institution this issue often isn't important, and in some schemes a user may only have a single identity; for cross-organizational applications such as those of interest here, this relativistic character of identity is of critical importance. A user may have rights to use identities established by multiple organizations (such as universities and scholarly societies) and more than one identity may figure in an access management decision. Users may have to decide what identity to present to a resource: they may have access because they are a member of a specific university's community, or a member of a specific scholarly society, for example. Making these choices will be a considerable burden on users, much like trying to shop for the best discount rate on a service that offers varying discounts to different membership and affinity groups (corporate rate, senior citizen rate, weekly rate, government rate, etc.). A single, network-wide (not merely corporate wide) access management authority would simplify many processes by allowing rights assigned to an individual by different organizations to become attributes of a master name rather than having them embodied in different names authorized by different organizations; yet such a centralized identity system probably represents an unacceptable concentration of power, as well as being technically impractical at the scale the enterprise will ultimately need.

IDENTITY MANAGEMENT

Identity Management infrastructure solutions are comprised of several components including the enterprise directory services component, the user provisioning and workflow components and the privilege management components. Combining these components with the business goals creates a return greater than the sum of the parts. Without the foundation of an Identity Management infrastructure many of your strategic IT initiatives/goals are unattainable.

Our strategy for our clients is to implement an IDM solution with these key design principles:

- Simplicity: Reduce the current environment's complexity

- Consistency: Consolidate and integrate current/future services

- Easy of Use: Automate maintenance

- Data Integrity: Accurate and Timely user management

Privilege Management Infrastructure engines are security solutions for integrating single sign-on, user authentication/authorization/entitlements, and application personalization within HTTP environments. These products can integrate a number of standards-based user directories making it possible to manage a significant portion of your web access control components from a single console. Most security middleware engines are fully redundant, allowing for massive scalability and high availability.

A tiered approach to strong authentication can include a combination of:

- User ID and Password
- Challenge Response
- Hardware/Software Tokens
- Digital Certificates
- Biometrics

Strong authentication mechanisms combine multi-factor techniques to validate an individual's identity. The multiple aspects of one's identity may be dissociated, enhanced, or integrated online. A single person's identity embodies multiplicity. Cyberspace offers a niche for each of these specific facets of selfhood. Individuals often talk about how one can "deconstruct" themselves online. In different environments, individuals can divvy up and present their characteristics in packets of various sizes and content. Individuals can express, highlight, and develop specific interests and life experiences while setting aside others. Online communication tools even give individuals the choice about whether to permit how you look. The desire to remain anonymous reflects the need to eliminate those critical features of the users identity are not intended to display in that particular environment or group.

Compartmentalizing or dissociating various online identities like this can be an efficient, focused way to manage the multiplicities of individual identity. Role theory in social psychology speaks about how a successful life is an efficient juggling of the various tasks and positions individuals accumulate and develop William James wrote about how the normal mind operates in a "field" of consciousness in which one's awareness shifts among different hot spots of ideas, memories, and feelings. Cyberspace another manifestation of this maneuver. It gives the enterprise the opportunity to focus on and develop a particular aspect of corporate identity. It even affords the chance to express and explore facets of an individual's role and identity that is not expressed in face-to-face communications. Everyone in the CEO's in-person world may not know that he is a business consultant in an online persona. In an IT environment Network Identity is comprised of software, hardware, and services for managing the identity of users on the Internet or in a corporate network. The management of multiple versions of user identities across multiple applications makes the task even more daunting. Here are the building blocks of an identity management system:

Password reset relieves the management burden and costs of password-related support calls while enforcing strong password policies by enabling users to reset their own passwords and unlock their accounts without the aid of a help desk. Typically, a user accesses a password-reset application through a standard browser, desktop client or telephone (interactive voice response). Users are authenticated by a set of questions to which only they know the answers.

Password synchronization facilitates help desk operations, requiring users to know a single password across different systems, reducing the chance that they'll forget one or more passwords. However, unlike single sign-on (SSO) solutions, the user still has to enter an ID and password for each application. Synchronization products don't require the drastic changes to a company's existing IT infrastructure and cost that SSO or high-end access control management products require. The software typically resides on a server, and APIs link the software to databases, help desks and security frameworks.

Single sign-on can be considered a step up from password synchronization in that it lets a user log on once to a PC or network and access multiple applications and systems using a single password.

Identity management must enable safe, secure, efficient and personalized connections for a company's employees, patients and business partners, all of whom need to access a multitude of applications from a variety of connection points.

Goals of a successful identity management strategy

Management

- Establish authoritative source(s) for each identity
- Build identity based business processes
- Establish enterprise-wide identity data characteristics

Authentication

- validate that each user is who they say they are.
- Establish single identity authentication
- Enterprise-wide authentication process
- Leverage existing identity management solution
- Based on What you know (Password), Digital certificate (software token) or What you are (Biometrics)

Authorization

- validate that each user has been granted rights to access a resource.
- Establish enterprise-wide role based access controls
- Privilege or entitlement: a user capability to perform an operation, or access data.
- Privilege management: administration of all user privileges, by admins and applications.
- Fine-grained access control: the ability to control user access to objects within a page.
- Leverage business roles and job requirements
- Leverage on identity management and authentication solution(s)

Protection

- Focus on internet, network, hardware and application/software

- Secure identity solution from authoritative source to entitlement

The metadirectory provides a solution to the problem of identity management. Identity is the summary of information about people, applications, and resources scattered in directories and databases throughout most IT enterprises. Examples of identity data associated with people include names, mailboxes, salaries and job titles. Application identity information includes the network addresses where clients can find servers. It also includes lists of services that applications can provide. Network resources, such as printers, also have identity attributes their location and the printing capabilities they support.

The Identity Management Challenge

The diversity of identity data and the number of places where such data reside raise a number of management challenges:

- Not all identity data is kept in directories or exposed through a directory service interface such as Lightweight Directory Access Protocol (LDAP). For example, many systems only expose identity information through specialized application programming interfaces (APIs).

- Identity information frequently is duplicated in multiple places, and versions tend to drift out of synchronization over time if left unchecked.

- Typically, there is no single place where administrators and applications can access or manage an aggregated view (sometimes called a join) of an enterprise's identity information.

- The number of places where companies must manage identity data increases with each additional application and platform.

These challenges make it difficult for companies to implement comprehensive and integrated identity management solutions. Leaving an enterprise environment in this state increases cost and complexity.

Common Identity Management Scenarios

Most large companies are already starting to grapple with some form of identity management project. Common efforts include:

- Global address book applications. Synchronizing mailbox information between the different e-mail directories within a company enables users to locate other users and send them e-mail across differing systems.

- Hire/fire solutions. Propagating information about a newly hired employee such as title, role and access rights to all systems that require identity data enables speedy establishment of services. Systems also must perform the same processes quickly in reverse when employees leave to prevent breaches of security.

- E-commerce applications. Synchronizing enterprise identity information, such as digital certificates for suppliers and extranet users, is enabled with directories that reside outside of firewalls.

In the past, many companies have tried to create a single directory to hold all enterprise identity information. Most of these efforts failed for several simple reasons:

- Many applications cannot be modified easily to use directories.

- There are good reasons, such as various replication and security requirements, why some applications need to keep identity in their own formats.

- Political boundaries inhibit complete consolidation regardless of what is technically possible.

This suggests that identity data will continue to exist in many places, and companies need to find ways to make different directory services and application repositories work together. Assuming that there will be many identity repositories, solutions must provide:

- Management of identity flow between repositories.

- Mechanisms for maintaining data integrity throughout the identity management infrastructure.

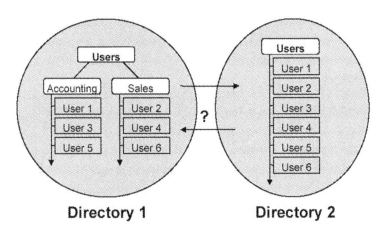

Directory 1   Directory 2

Related Object Tracking

When administrators deploy identity management solutions, they must be able to tell the identity management flow engine that John Smith, jsmith and smithj are all the same person. Then the engine must be able to track relationships as identity data is periodically reorganized. Solutions must not lose track of users simply because they change position in a directory tree structure moving from the IT department to the Sales group, for example.

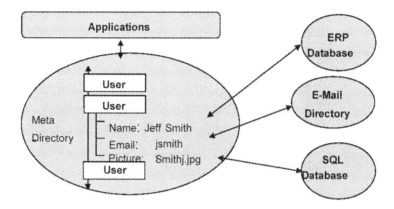

Data Aggregation in a Metadirectory

While identity information resides throughout most enterprises, directories that contain an aggregation of identity data from many other repositories can offer great value. The term *join* to represents an aggregated view of an enterprise's identity data.

With a metadirectory, applications can access a variety of information in one place, using a single access method and security model, instead of interacting with each of the source repositories. Metadirectories also maximize performance because data can be stored in indexed form. There is no need to fetch data from sources, which may reside across wide area network (WAN) connections, at runtime. To offer the greatest value, data aggregation capabilities must be able to:

- Gather and incorporate information from many sources including directories, databases and applications.

- Group related information together even though it may be stored in different ways in different places. For example, data about a user named John Smith might be stored under names such as John Smith, jsmith and smithj in different systems, as seen in above.

- Push changes back out to sources when users or applications make changes to the aggregated view. This means that metadirectories must be integrated with change event processing infrastructures.

Integrity Management: Integrity management is the process of ensuring that identity data does not become corrupt or out of synchronization between repositories as changes occur. Integrity management functionality must be able to:

- Maintain identity data ownership relationships.

- Act appropriately when failures occur.

- Maintain referential integrity within identity data.

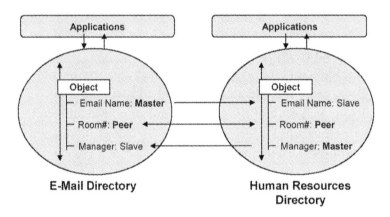

E-Mail Directory   Human Resources
                                       Directory

Data Ownership

An important aspect of enterprise identity management is recognizing ownership relationships that must be maintained between applications and data. For example, a person's mailbox name is owned by the e-mail system that hosts the mailbox. Within most companies, the HR system owns the data corresponding to whether or not a person is an active employee. With no enterprise identity management infrastructure in place, these ownership relationships are preserved by default because no other applications have the ability to access and update e-mail and HR data. With synchronization connectors and information flow management deployed, however, the situation changes. Consider a case in which mailbox information is being synchronized with the HR directory by a connector. The connector is not configured correctly, a user could change the mailbox attribute in the HR system and the connector would overwrite the mailbox value in the e-mail directory, causing tremendous confusion. Solving the problem is not as simple as just preventing changes from flowing backwards to the e-mail directory. The HR system may own information, such as the name of a person's manager, which must flow back to the e-mail directory. Other attributes, such as a person's office number, may have no clearly defined ownership and these should be data that anyone can update. As a solution requirement, administrators must be able to define and enforce ownership relationships at the attribute level. If a change is in accordance with the ownership rules, it is allowed to pass through, otherwise it is blocked or reversed. For example, if a person changed a mailbox attribute in the HR directory, the identity management solution would simply set the attribute back to the value contained in the e-mail directory.

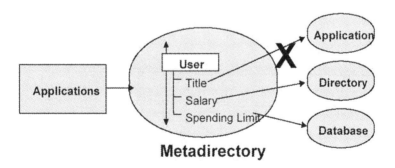

Metadirectory

Referential Integrity

In database systems, this challenge is usually addressed with transactions that ensure all updates occur successfully or are rolled back as a unit. Unfortunately, most directory services and application programming interfaces do not support transactions. This means that identity management solutions must find other ways such as using log-based, desired state mechanisms that continue to request changes until confirmed to ensure that all repositories eventually reflect changes. Another challenge that identity management solutions share with databases is maintaining referential integrity between repositories. Referential integrity refers to the need to maintain relationships between the values of related pieces of data in different locations. For example, identity management solutions must be able to ensure that a person's title listed in the human resources system is consistent with the person's spending limit in the procurement system. Databases solve this challenge by providing stored procedure and trigger features that enable administrators to execute a business rule each time a data value changes. Directory services do not provide similar features today. Therefore, identity management solutions must provide the capability to execute business rules, which will reject changes that do not meet referential integrity requirements.

Only a metadirectory solution addresses all these issues.

If Internet/intranet, proprietary e-mail, and other directories contain identity information about a limited number of individuals in a specific location, the metadirectory is capable of containing identity information about all individuals in all locations. The metadirectory lets the enterprise integrate any number of disparate identity repositories in virtually any format. Thus, the metadirectory becomes the object root of identity information within the enterprise. The metadirectory provides the rationalized and unified view of identity objects that consist of attributes from a variety of directories. This integration enables you to lower administrative costs, eliminate duplication, reduce discrepancies, and make the identity information widely available. The metadirectory is flexible enough to adapt itself to any enterprise's organization, structure, politics, and management styles; and dynamic enough to change as they change.

Data Sources

The metadirectory collects its identity information from the other connected directories and repositories in the enterprise. Nearly all e-mail, database, and other directory applications can export their contents in some form. The metadirectory can collect this data through file exchange, in an e-mail message, or through an on-line, protocol-driven transfer. The directory administrator or end user can add other metadirectory identity information.

Directory Content

Think of directories as containing identity information about people, such as e-mail addresses, but this is a limited view. The metadirectory can contain much more information about any real-world objects. Objects may be:

- Physical, such as people or computers;

- Conceptual, such as organizations or departments;

- Geographic, such as countries or cities;

- Digital, such as document files for on-line viewing.

The only requirement of the metadirectory is that these objects be organized in some sort of hierarchical structure. For example, a person might be described as part of a department that is part of an organization that is located in an Internet domain or a country. Or, in a multinational corporation, an employee might be part of a division located in a country that falls under the corporation in the organizational tree. A person is not necessarily the lowest level of the hierarchy. For example, a document or a portable computer belonging to that person might also be represented by a directory entry below the person entry in the tree.

Managing Changing Information

When identity information about a person (or other object) exists in one or more connected directories and one or more places in the meta-directory, the join engine maintains it. If changes are made in both the metadirectory and the connected directory, the objects will soon drift out of synchronization. The addition of a metadirectory allows one to determine not only where objects can be created or deleted, but also in which directory individual attributes of existing objects can be modified. Join engines are often scheduled to periodically compare the contents of the connected directory with the contents of the metadirectory. If the contents differ, the metadirectory synchronizes them. The connected directory and the metadirectory can differ in two ways:

- Objects may exist in one that do not exist in the other.

- Objects that exist in both may have different attribute values.

- Increased administration costs resulting from a distributed user population (i.e. customer, vendor, employee)

- Decreased user productivity and satisfaction due to multiple user ids

- Decreased security as a result of independent and inconsistent access management capabilities

- Decreased authentication strength resulting from application driven authentication requirements (e.g. Certificates)

Change events occur any time administrators; users or applications add, delete or modify a piece of identity data in a repository. Unmanaged, identity data changes quickly become disorganized. Identity management solutions therefore must provide features to detect changes, perform necessary data format translations and then update all repositories that should reflect the changes. For example, if an administrator adds a new employee to the human resources (HR) database, this change event needs to cause systems that the person will use to reflect the addition. The change is propagated to other directories and applications.

ACCESS MANAGEMENT

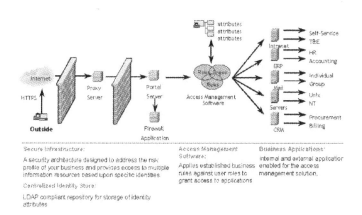

Secure Infrastructure:
A security architecture designed to address the risk profile of your business and provides access to multiple information resources based upon specific identities

Centralized Identity Store:
LDAP compliant repository for storage of identity attributes

Access Management Software:
Applies established business rules against user roles to grant access to applications

Business Applications:
Internal and external application enabled for the access management solution.

Cross-organizational access management for web-based resources has emerged as a topic of great interest among many information consuming institutions and information resource providers. These organizations wish, as precisely and as flexibly as possible, to enable access to particular networked resources to particular members of institutional consumer communities. Access should be simple for the user, should guarantee a large measure of privacy to the user, should not depend entirely on the user's location or network address but rather on the user's membership in appropriate communities, and should provide necessary management and demographic information to institutional consumer administrators and to resource providers.

A flexible and robust access management service is more than a technical architecture; it must also address a number of other difficult issues, including policy and infrastructure considerations, deployment of technology in an uncertain market and broad consensus and development of standards among key players.

Two technical infrastructure components are minimally required for an institutional access management system: the ability of a user to obtain an identity on the network, known as authentication; and the ability to correlate a user's identity with rights and permissions to use various services, called authorization.

Often these two services are combined in simple ways which blur their distinction, such as the unix implementation of file permission policy through group membership, "uids" and "gids." More robust and scalable authentication and authorization services may instead arise independently and be supported by special purpose systems rather than as side-effects of particular operating systems or other technologies.

As remote service providers create increasingly sophisticated services which are customized to individual users, they find they must implement independent user "registration" infrastructures: essentially building duplicate id, password, and user-profile systems for populations that are already part of well established and carefully maintained institutional id systems and directories at their "home" institutions. This is an unfortunate duplication of effort for the provider and annoyance to the user (who must login to each such service independently). Its underlying security model compounds its problems: still largely by IP source address or proxy web server.

Given these limitations in the existing approaches and the redundant efforts required, we have been investigating alternative architectures, which can leverage the existing authentication, and authorization databases at the local organization based on the following guidelines:

- It must be a real-world solution; that is, it must take into account the browsers and web servers currently in use, existing ID and directory systems and an average level of user expertise. Web server modifications must be as modular and as simple to maintain as possible.

- It should allow the retrieval of user attributes when specifically needed for the business of a service (for example, a user's fax number for a document delivery service), while otherwise protecting user information from illegal or inappropriate use. For example, student information is strongly protected in the U.S. by the "FERPA" legislation. The American Library Association has adopted a set of privacy guidelines as well, reflecting the public's heightened concerns that personal information will be collected and used without the individual's consent.

- It should protect any user "secrets." In particular, a user's password may never travel across the network in the clear.

- It should restrict access to services with the desired granularity. For example, some services may be provided to the entire Columbia University student and alumni population; others might be provided to all registered students in a particular set of departments; still others might be restricted to department heads and department administrators.

- It should be reasonably efficient, both in terms of Web server processing and in terms of network traffic.

- It should be as painless to manage and to scale as current technology permits.

In the descriptions of architecture models below, we use a few terms in specialized ways:

- Credentials refer to information needed to authenticate a user, most commonly a user id and a password; but other methods, such as a digital certificate or "smartcard" are possible.

- Third-party is a service provider outside of the local organization.

- Attribute is typically found in an institutional directory service. It is a characteristic of an individual user, which can be more precise (e.g., a name) or less precise (membership in an arbitrary group).

Most access management modules maintain a cache of user credentials and attributes so that it need not contact the authentication and directory systems for every user request. A user might request a document containing 20 restricted images; the institutional validation and directory systems will be contacted only once.

Public facilities also pose traditional problems in this model. User credentials are kept in the browser until the browser is closed or until the user logs out (typically by requesting a URL which asks the user to explicitly erase the stored password). In this model, user credentials do not expire, and there is no provision in the web protocol for the server to demand fresh credentials. Therefore, if the user does not remember to log out or exit the browser, the next user who sits down at the same workstation will inherit their credentials and capabilities. This model does not scale well. If more than one such web server exists in the enterprise, each must be modified to communicate with the corporate authentication and directory systems. Any change to corporate authentication or directory systems requires a change to all modified servers. If there is more than one corporate authentication or directory system in use, the server has no means of choosing which one to use. And this method cannot be scaled to access management between a corporation and a remote service provider. Each web server providing restricted services would need to support the authentication and directory systems of all subscribers to its services; this would rapidly become unmanageable.

Almost immediately, corporations require more than a single directory system: the corporate offices and certain financial institution already maintain independent directory systems, and wish to continue using them, but also wish to incorporate these existing systems into existing access management process. Therefore, one attempts a more scalable architecture by introducing a "broker" service to consolidate and generalize access management. This service often includes new Access Management Broker server and a new plug-in module for web servers.

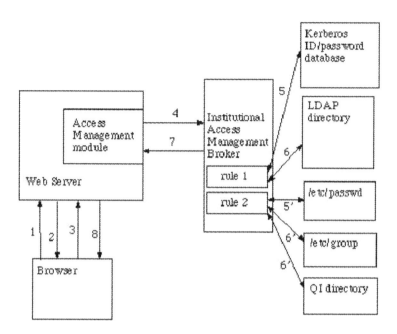

In this model, requirements for granting service are encoded, in advance, in sets of "rules." The Access Management Broker server uses a particular rule to decide which authentication and authorization components to use several and how to combine and interpret the information retrieved from them. The protocol between web server and broker server permits the web server to suggest a preferred rule.

A single transaction would then follow:

1. User requests a restricted service.

2. Web server asks browser for user credentials.

3. Browser prompts user for name and password, and resubmits the request with user credentials.

4. Web server's access management module sends to the broker: the user's credentials, the service desired by the user, and any user attributes it wishes sent back.

5. Broker determines which authentication and authorization rule to use based on the requesting host and the requested service. Broker passes user's credentials to the appropriate authentication system to check the credentials.

6. Broker uses the same rule to collect user attributes from the appropriate institutional directory system(s). It then determines, based on the user's attributes, whether the user is permitted to access the requested service.

7. Broker notifies the web server whether user is permitted to access to the service and also returns any permissible user attributes which may have been requested by the web server.

8. Web server provides access to the service.

This model has some advantages. Maintenance is much easier: Servers need only to talk to the broker through a single protocol; changes made to institutional ID or directory systems are reflected by changes in the broker software and nowhere else. The broker maintains a cache of credentials and attributes, preserving the performance of the previous model. A Broker server may request that a cache entry be considered stale beyond some interval, or it might request live verification every time for increased security at the expense of performance.

User privacy is also better protected in this model. The entire directory is abstracted to the presentation server by default. A Broker server must explicitly request any user attributes it requires for business (e.g., a fax number if the service to be performed requires fax to the user, or a cost center identification). Broker server rules can therefore implement useful access management policies.

Unfortunately, the above methods cannot be extended out of a corporation because the user name and password still move through the web server unencrypted. In a cross-corporate setting, that web server would be operated by a remote, or "third-party" service provider, i.e., a provider at another institution, commercial or otherwise. It was not acceptable to permit our user names and passwords to travel either across the Internet unencrypted or through a remote server managed by an outside organization. As a first attempt to solve this, we proposed to channel all requests for such third-party services through a proxy.

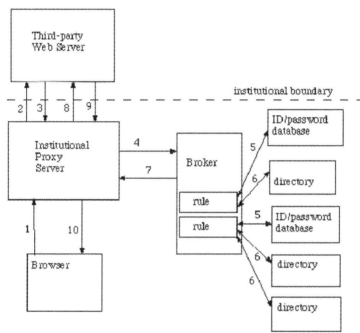

Cross-Corporate Access Management through enterprise Proxy

This interaction would work like this:

1. The user must have previously authenticated with the proxy in order to use it. These credentials are present in every request the user sends to the proxy and are kept in the proxy's cache.

2. User requests a restricted service through proxy.

3. Proxy forwards request for restricted service to third-party server.

4. Third-party server asks proxy for user credentials.

5. Proxy checks user credentials from cache with broker, including an identifier for the third-party and the name of the restricted service as additional parameters.

6. Broker validates user credentials as before.

7. Broker does authorization check as before.

8. Broker sends result back to proxy.

9. Proxy sends an institutional credential previously agreed upon with the service provider back to the third-party server along with the user's request for service.

10. Third-party server checks the institutional credential against a local table, verifies it, and allows proxy access to the service.

11. Proxy forwards service to user.

12. Future requests from the user for the same service must be intercepted by the proxy so that the institutional credential can be passed along to the third-party service provider with the request.

This architecture is relatively easy and only requires modifications only to the corporate proxy server. However it has the usual drawbacks associated with proxies: if the proxy does not handle all requests, the user is initially directed to the proxy through another resource at the user's institution. In this case, absolute URLs in documents returned from the third-party through the proxy must be rewritten to point back to the proxy; and relative URLs must be rewritten so that the proxy recognizes them as requests to forward. If the proxy handles all traffic, it will become a bottleneck.

There is no mechanism in this method for the third-party service provider to retrieve user attributes when required. We considered this a big disadvantage. And this method encourages service providers to allow access based on a fixed password, the institutional credential. While that seems to be the state of the art today, we prefer not to encourage its continued use. Fixed institutional passwords should be carefully guarded because they enable transactions to be performed on behalf of an entire institution; but the prevalent procedures for establishing and maintaining them with service providers is subject to many kinds of compromise.

Since many corporations are moving towards the use of proxies as gateways to third-party services, this model may be a natural first step for them.

Cross-Organizational Access Management via Cryptographic Module

Both the Netscape and the Microsoft Explorer browsers are able to incorporate cryptographic plug-in modules. Using a PKCS#11 module for the Netscape browser in Unix. This approach will work in a cross platform environment enabling the following apprach

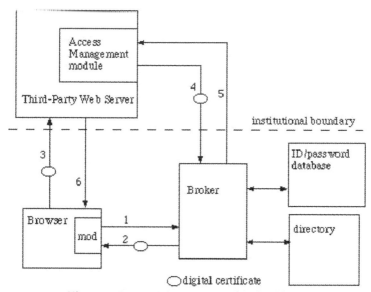

Figure 4. Access Management with Certificate

Before any services are requested, the user must activate the browser module. This is done in the browser by logging on to the module. The user is then prompted for a "PIN" and responds with an id, password and an identification of the local institutional access management broker.

1. The browser module, acting over a secure channel, contacts the broker and presents the user's credentials (id and password) and the preferred processing rule for the broker.

2. The broker validates the user, as described above, and then obtains or generates a temporary private key and a temporary digital certificate, which are returned back to the module. The certificate contains the address of the broker and an opaque identifier of the user, again temporary, and known only to the broker. This new certificate is then available within the browser for subsequent use with third-party services. In current browsers, the user must then explicitly select it, indicating a desire to be "known" by this identity.

3. In this diagram there is a server plug-in which handles the broker communication at remote, third-party providers. Third-party service providers use this server plug-in and use TLS (secure channel). The user's new certificate is sent to the third-party server during initialization of the TLS channel. The plug-in will use the certificate as the user's credentials rather than id and password.

4. Because the certificate contains the address of the broker, the third-party server can establish contact with that broker, send it the user's certificate, the class of service it plans to provide, and any further user attributes to be retrieved back for business purposes.

5. The broker can perform authentications as above and return authentication and any requested (and permitted) attributes back to the third-party.

6. The service is delivered to the user.

This architecture is the most secure and most flexible. Because the certificates are temporary, administrative problems usually associated with certificates are avoided: we do not need to establish a complex distribution system or invent special methods to accommodate people using more than one workstation; we do not need long-term revocation lists; and we do not need escrow and key recovery infrastructures. Because the browser module for all transactions installs a single certificate, certificate handling (installation, update, etc.) is automated.

The access management problem

Managing access to on-line information is a broad problem, which occurs in a wide range of different applications. Managers of on-line information wish to implement policies about who can access the information, under what terms and conditions.

Examples of areas where access management is needed due to legal issues include

- Digital libraries: Libraries often need to restrict access to parts of their collections for various reasons, including restrictions imposed by donors, concerns about privacy or obscenity, licensing arrangements, and other agreements with copyright owners.

- Electronic publications: The most common reason that publishers and other copyright owners wish to manage access is because they require payment for use of materials, but there are other reasons, such as preventing the spread of unapproved derivatives.

- Security, classification, and trade secrets: Governments sometimes classify information in order to control access for security

reasons. Commercial organizations use similar methods to protect confidential information and trade secrets.

- Medical records: Medical information is usually kept confidential, except to people who can demonstrate that they have a need
to know.

In publishing, the term "rights management" is often used, but this
term is very narrow in scope. The phrase "terms and conditions" is also
widely used. The term "access management", which this paper uses, is
a broad term that applies in all areas. Independent of terminology, it is
important to view access management from the perspective of the
manager of the information. In a digital library, information is
obtained from a variety of sources, for example by license from a publisher, or by a donation with restrictions on use. In drawing up its
access management policies, the library will reflect agreements with
publishers and other third parties. There may also be relevant laws that
must be embodied in the policies. However, with digital materials as
with physical items, the library is responsible for managing access to its
collections. The following diagram shows the general access model.

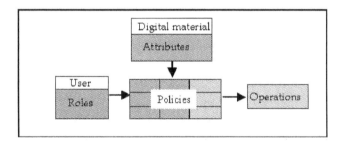

The central concept of the framework is that access is controlled by
policies. Each policy relates some group of users with some set of digital material and permits or denies certain types of operations on the
material. Policies require information about the users, which is provided in the form of roles, and about the digital material, which is pro-

vided in the form of attributes. A key feature of this model is that the evaluation of roles, attributes, and policies takes place dynamically. The association of a policy with a user and specific material does not occur until the user wishes to access the material. Many attributes are expressed as metadata, which is stored with the material in the repository, but attributes may be obtained in real-time, perhaps by executing a program. User roles are often established by authentication, which can take place at any time. Some other approaches to access management encode access policies with each item of material, so that each item is labeled with all the information that is required to manage access to it. Any policy change requires processing every item in the collection. In a large collection, this is a major task, prone to error. By keeping the policies separately, changes of policy can be reflected without alteration to the stored digital material. An alternative approach to access management is using secure containers of information. In this approach, all information about some digital item is encapsulated in an encrypted container this works well for directories and the encryption of directory data as opposed to implementing ACL's which add overhead to the directory. The container may include the digital material, its attributes, the policies, and the code necessary to enable the operations. The container can be stored in a directory, transmitted over a network in clear text, or even transferred to external media such as CD-ROM. The containers are used to enforce the access policies, including control over subsequent use.

As corporations implement networked information strategies which call for sharing and licensing access to information resources in the networked environment, authentication and access management have emerged as major issues which threaten to impede progress. While considerable work has been done over the last two decades on authentication within institutions and, more recently, in support of consumer-oriented electronic commerce on the Internet, a series of new technical and policy issues emerge in the cross-organizational authentication and access management context.

The Cross-Corporate Access Management Problem

The basic cross-organizational access management problem is exemplified by most licensing agreements for networked information resources today; it also arises in situations where institutions agree to share limited-access resources with other institutions as part of consortia or other resource sharing collaborations. In such an agreement, an institution, a university, a school, a public library, a corporation defines a user community, which has access to some network resource. This community is typically large, numbering perhaps in the tens of thousands of individuals, and membership may be volatile over time, reflecting for example the characteristics of a student body or company. The operator of the network resource, which may a web site, or a resource reached by a portal or transaction processor information retrieval protocol needs to decide whether users seeking access to the resource are actually members of the user community that the licensee institution defined as part of the license agreement. The issue here is not how the licensee defines the user community for example how a university might define students, staff members and faculty. It is assumed that the institution and the resource operator have reached some satisfactory resolution on this question. Rather, the issue is one of testing or verifying that individuals are really a member of this community according to pre-agreed criteria, of having the institution vouch for or credential the individuals in some way that the resource operator can understand. Such arrangements are often called "site" licenses, but this term is really inaccurate a better term is "group" license or "community" license, emphasizing that the key consideration is membership in some community, and that physical location is often not the key membership criteria. Progress in inter-organizational access management will benefit everyone. To the extent that resource operators and licensing institutions can agree on common methods for performing this authentication and access management function, it greatly facilitates both licensing and resource sharing by making it quick, easy and inexpensive to implement business arrangements. It benefits users by making their navigation through a network of resources provided by different operators more seamless and less cumbersome. The central challenge of cross-corporate access management is not to set up barriers to access; it is to facilitate access in a responsible fashion, recognizing the needs of all parties involved in the access arrangements technically, there are also a series of intertwined policy and management considerations which need to be considered. Group licenses may be subject to some additional constraints (for example concurrent user limits) rather than on transactional models where individual users may take actions to incur specific incremental costs back to the licensing institution over and above base community licensing costs. Any incremental cost transactional model will need to incorporate at least two additional features: a set of user constraints that become part of the attributes for each authenticated user and which are made available to the resource operator, and a means by which the resource operator can obtain permission for transactions by passing a query back to the licensing institution. This involves a much more complex trust, liability and business relationship between resource operator and licensing institution, as well as consideration of financial controls and a careful assessment of security threats.

Granularity and Extensibility

There is a need for fine-grained access control where institutions want to limit resource access to only individuals registered for a specific class; this arises in electronic reserves and distance education contexts, especially when a class may be offered to students at multiple institutions. Other variations are also possible: limiting access to law students, to faculty, to graduate students and faculty in physics. This sort of fine-grained access management is likely to be very complex, since there will be great variation from institution to institution in how groups of users are identified, named and specified. There is also some overlap between fine-grained authentication and demographic information that may be needed to generate management information.

- Most access to network information resources is not controlled on a fine-grained basis. There is a very real danger that by accommodating all of the needs for fine-grained access management into the basic access management mechanisms we will produce a system that is too complex and costly to see wide-spread implementation anytime soon.

- The information needed to support fine-grained access management probably needs to be kept within institutions for privacy reasons, and should be treated as attributes to an identity rather than expressed as additional identities. This also has implications for the locus of authorization decisions for fine-grained access management.

- The resources (such as electronic course reserves) that are subject to fine-grained access management will be within an institution, or within one of the institutions in a consortium of institutions that are collaborating closely through shared courses or similar projects. The case where an external commercial networked resource will be access controlled to members of a small group like a class will be rare.

In some cases, the presence of fine grained access management mechanisms may encourage irrational license economics. For example: there is an electronic journal that prices based on the number of people that have access, rather than on the number of people that actually use it. This would encourage a corporation to define a fine-grained group of authorized users to a portal in order to save money. Such an arrangement is complex and sets up barriers to access for the rest of the enterprise. It would probably make more sense to initially price access for the entire enterprise based on the approximate number of people who will actually use the portal, and then if it turns out a few more people are using it that were originally expected, negotiate a slightly higher revenue sharing agreement rather than defining a special access group.

Having summarized the many and sometimes conflicting requirements that an access management system must address, we now consider a number of actual schemes currently in use or under consideration and analyze how well they meet these requirements.

It's important to recognize that in solving real-world problems more than one approach may be relevant at a single institution; one might use one scheme for one class of users and a different scheme for another class. For example, an institution might choose to manage access for kiosks and public workstations by IP source address, and to use a credential scheme for other users. Indeed, virtually all of the major institutional systems that are currently being deployed combine multiple approaches. Also, note that approaches can be cascaded in a hierarchy; for example, a resource might be set up to first check whether a user could be validated by an IP source filtering approach but if the IP source address isn't valid for access, the resource might then apply a credential-based access management test.

At the most general level, there are three approaches—proxies, IP source filtering, and credential-based access management.

Basically, with IP filtering, the licensee institution guarantees to the resource operator that all traffic coming from a given set of IP addresses (perhaps all IP addresses on one or more networks) represent legitimate traffic on behalf of the licensee institution's user community. The resource operator then simply checks the source IP address of each incoming request.

In the case of a proxy, the licensee institution has deployed some sort of local authentication system, and users employ specific proxy machines to send traffic to the resource and receive responses back from that resource; the local authentication system (which is invisible to the resource operator, except that the resource operator knows that it is in place in order to guarantee that traffic coming from the proxy machines is legitimate) is used to control who can have access to the proxy machine. As a business matter, the resource operator may want to know something about how the local authentication system works in order to have confidence in the proxy, but this does not enter into the actual authentication which is performed operationally by the resource operator. The resource operator will most commonly identify the proxy machines by their IP addresses (or some variation such as reverse DNS lookup), and for this reason from the resource operator's point of view proxies are often just considered to be a special case of IP source address filtering—a resource operator who is set up to do IP source address filtering can accommodate a licensing institution employing proxies with essentially no additional work. However, proxies can actually be identified using either IP addresses or any credential-based cross-organizational authentication scheme (such as certificates). Because of this, and also because many of the policy and technical issues surrounding proxies at a higher level are quite distinct from those involved in IP source address filtering, we will treat proxies as a separate approach.

The third approach is credential-based. Here the user presents some form of credential—a user id and password, or a cryptographic certificate, for example—to the resource operator as evidence that he or she is a legitimate member of the user community. The resource operator then validates this credential with some trusted institutional server (or third party server operating under contract to the institution) before deciding whether to allow access. Note that there needs to be advance agreement (most likely as part of the license contract or resource sharing agreement) as to how the mutually trusted institutional servers or third parties (such as certificate authorities) are identified and authenticated themselves.

For completeness, it is worth noting that there is one other possibility: the resource operator assigns credentials to individual members of the licensee community (perhaps in cooperation with the licensee institution). This is what was done historically when small numbers of users needed access to a few specialized information resources. The trouble is that it does not scale manageably to large numbers of users or large numbers of resources, and particularly not to both. While it's reasonable for an institution to distribute one set of credentials to each member of its user community (for example, in conjunction with an internal authentication system) it's not reasonable to distribute hundreds of different credentials for different resources to each user, or to expect the users to manage them or to keep straight which credentials are for use with which resource. Thus, we will not consider this model further, other than to recognize that it may have its place for specialized resources that serve only a handful of users.

Proxies

Proxy based approaches simply shift the problem, since an institution will still have to deploy an internal authentication and access management system in order to control use of the proxy servers. However, it may be easier to implement an internal system than to implement a system that must be used by a wide range of resource providers; proxies modularize and compartmentalize the authentication problem. It is important to distinguish between two different kinds of services that are sometimes referred to as proxies. The first, which we will call mechanical proxies, are services which take make use of facilities designed directly into implementations of protocols such as HTTP. To use a web proxy server, one configures a browser to pass all HTTP requests not directly to the destination host, but instead to a proxy server, which intercepts these requests and when necessary retransmits them to the true destination host. In this case, the operation of the proxy should be invisible to the end user. The second type of proxy is an application-level proxy (historically, these have often been called "protocol translation systems" or "gateways"). An application level proxy functionally forwards requests where appropriate, but does not rely on protocol mechanisms. An example might be a directory proxy, where in order to reach an access-controlled directory based resource. In the web environment, a service such as the anonymizer (**www. anonymizer.com**) is a good example; here, one accesses the web page of the service and provides the URL of the remote resource one really wishes to access. The anonymizer service not only forwards requests on, but also dynamically re-writes each page coming back from the remote resource prior to presenting it to the end user, for example, replacing each URL in the retrieved page with a URL that accesses the anonymizer with a parameter of the actual remote page that is being requested. As the environment becomes more sophisticated, applications proxies become increasingly problematic: for example, an applications-level proxy generally will not handle pages that contain Java applets properly.

- Feasibility and Deployment: This is not entirely straightforward. Proxies introduce a considerable amount of overhead, and the institution will need to invest in the installation and operation of proxy servers. Some overhead may be mitigated by having the proxy server perform caching operations as well as access management, although this introduces a range of other responsibilities and problems. Also, proxy servers become mission critical systems; they need to be available and reliable, and to be sized so that they do not represent a performance bottleneck. Proxies and in particular application level proxies have scaling problems not only in terms of computational resources to support a large user community, but also in terms of configuration management and support as the number of resources available to the user community multiply. Each resource needs to be configured, and as resources change, configuration changes will be needed in the proxy. Integrating a local authentication system with a commercial proxy server may be challenging. Programming for an application level proxy can become quite complex. One useful distinction is the locus and complexity of decision making that the proxy must perform. At the simplest level, a proxy can just screen all potential users without regard to the resource that they want to access; essentially there's a single authorization to use the proxy, and through it all of the resources that it permits access to. At a more complex level, the proxy might consider both the user and the resource in order to make an authorization decision; at the most complex level, it may track in detail the user's interaction with various resources and make very specialized decisions about what requests it will and will not pass through to the resources.

- Authentication strength: obviously, this depends on the local authentication system. There is the danger of systemic compromise if the proxy server is successfully attacked (that is, the local authentication built into the proxy server is broken) or the proxy is misconfigured. A breach of the local authentication system is likely to be a very high visibility event which will receive rapid response from the licensing institution; a breach of the proxy may be more insidious and more difficult to detect. The communication between the proxy server and the resource can be very strongly secured and authenticated using certificates and session level encryption.

- Granularity and extensibility: in theory, anything is possible if enough work is done on the proxy server. For fine-grained access control, however, it's necessary for the proxy to consider who is trying to access what, rather than just having the proxy server authenticate members of the user community prior to any use of the proxy. It's not clear how hospitable commercial proxy software is to this kind of application, or how complex the institution-specific programming will have to be; the more complex it gets, the more likely there are going to be security vulnerabilities.

- Cross-Protocol Flexibility: Because the authentication mechanism used between proxy and user and between proxy and resource need not be the same, there's a particularly high level of cross-protocol flexibility. In the worst case, the proxy can use a very general authentication approach like source IP filtering to support protocols between the proxy and the resource, and can use specialized methods (even embedded within application proxy code) to authenticate users to the proxy server.

- Privacy: proxies can provide real anonymity of use if they are set up properly; the resource operator need not even get a source IP address for the end user. On the other hand, they provide a choke point for potential systematic institutional monitoring of what the user community is doing, which may be some cause for concern.

- Accountability: in general, proxies provide poor accountability, since they offer anonymous access. At best, some level of accountability can be provided by correlating local logs at the proxy (which is tied into the local authentication system) and monitoring at the resource. In theory it would be possible for the proxy to pass some pseudonym or identity to the resource, but it's not clear how this would be accomplished in a standard and interoperable fashion.

- Management data: just as a proxy is a choke point for monitoring, it is also a choke point for collecting management data, including demographically faceted data or individual data since it authenticates users and then sees all of their requests to resources. Of course, correlating this to applications-level events and terminology is hard. It is not clear how a proxy could pass demographic data along with requests to a resource to permit faceted statistics collection at the resource side.

It is hard to fully evaluate the proxy approach for two reasons. To some extent it just moves the authentication problem because it presupposes the existence of an institutional authentication system, and the problems of deploying such a system really need to be considered. Second because a proxy—particularly an applications level proxy—is a point at which custom programming can be inserted almost anything is possible, at least in theory, but it's hard to evaluate the implementation and maintenance cost of such a system, and the extent to which it demands custom interfaces to the resources themselves, as opposed to using completely standard interfaces.

Conclusions

Both proxies and credential-based authentication schemes are viable approaches. Proxies have the advantage of compartmentalizing and modularizing authentication issues within an institution. But they also place heavy responsibilities upon the licensee institution to operate proxy servers professionally and responsibly. Proxy servers will become a focal point for policy debates about privacy, accountability and the collection of management information; successful operation of a proxy server implies that the user community is prepared to trust the licensee institution to behave responsibly and to respect privacy. Similarly, resource operators have to trust the licensee institution to competently implement and operate a local authentication system; anomaly monitoring of aggregated traffic from a proxy server by a resource operator is very difficult, and the resource operator will have to largely rely on the institution to carry out a program of anomalous access monitoring. A cross-corporate authentication system based on a credential approach has the advantage of greater transparency. Administrators can have a higher level of confidence in the access management mechanisms, and a much greater ability to monitor anomalous access patterns. The downside is much greater complexity; issues of privacy, accountability and the collection of management statistics become a matter for discussion among a larger group of parties. Further, it seems that a credential system means that there has to be cross-corporate interdependency in order to avoid systemic compromise of the authentication system, as opposed to a simple relationship of trust recognized in a contract for the proxy approach.

One point that seems clear is that an institutional public key infrastructure may not extend directly to a cross-institutional one; it may be desirable to issue community members a set of pseudononymous certificates for presentation outside the institution as well as individually identified ones that are used within the institution in order to provide a privacy firewall while still maintaining some level of accountability.

IP source filtering does not seem to be a viable general solution, although it may be very useful for some niche applications, such as supporting public workstations or kiosks. It can be used more widely—indeed today it usually is the basic access management tool—but it definitely cannot support remote users flexibly in its basic form. Most real-world access management systems are going to have to employ multiple approaches, and IP source address filtering is likely to be one of them.

8

Single Sign On

Directories serve a variety of important functions within the IT infrastructure of an enterprise. One of the important functions of directories is to provide a common authentication and authorization mechanism for applications and systems. Having to supply the credentials only once is a critical ease-of-use feature, particularly in business environments where productivity depends on fast and efficient, yet secured access to corporate assets.

Single Sign-On

- Directory Integration
- Authentication Services
- Entitlement Services
- Affiliate Services

Single Sign On is defined as the ability of an entity to be authenticated once sufficiently to gain access to all authorized resources throughout one or more domains without additional authentication. Network resources are: printers, computers, routers, applications, files, directories, mailboxes, etc. all of which may be spread throughout a global enterprise on servers of various types running different/heterogeneous operating environments. Single Sign On eliminates the need to have users continuously authenticate themselves, providing a better user experience. Once a user is identified, their authentication credentials are passed with them, in a secure fashion, as they move about the resources they need for their tasks. SSO continues even if the users tasks take them to different security or Web domains. Having to supply the credentials only once is a critical ease-of-use feature, particularly in business environments where productivity depends on fast and efficient, yet secured, access to corporate assets.

With a single sign-on system, employees at an organization using the software can be authenticated and authorized to access certain services. Single sign-on can be considered a step up from password synchronization in that it lets a user log on once to a PC or network and access multiple applications and systems using a single password. Typically, products authenticate the user at logon and present the available applications on the desktop. When the user selects an app, the SSO agent presents the authentication credentials in the background. On the downside, SSO technology requires its own infrastructure, such as an authentication server, that verifies user identity and permission rights before granting access to the various systems. As a result, SSO solutions are typically more costly and difficult to deploy and manage than password synchronization solutions.

With the growth of e-business, organizations are wrestling with the challenge of managing secure access to information and applications scattered across a wide range of internal and external computing systems. Furthermore, they have to provide access to a growing number of users, both inside and outside the corporation, without diminishing security or exposing sensitive information. The management of multiple versions of user

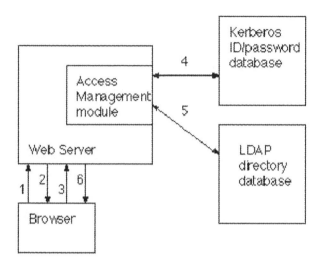

Web Access Management and Messaging Flow

A transaction in this scenario would proceed as follows:

1. User requests a service.

2. Web server asks browser for user credentials.

3. Browser prompts user for name and password, and submits the request with these user credentials.

4. Web server's access management module passes user's credentials to institutional validation system to check if the credentials are valid.

5. Web server's access management module collects user attributes from the directory. Based on the user's attributes it determines whether the user is permitted to access the requested service. For example, the user must be a member of a particular role.

6. Web server delivers the service.

This is an improvement over web authentication provided by a typical web server; it allows the server to leverage the existing infrastructure of the corporate identity system and directory. It assumes that there is a secure communication channel (TLS) between the browser and the web server.

PASSWORD BASED CREDENTIALS

Assume that institutions simply maintained databases of (pseudonymous or identified) user ids and passwords. Note carefully that the idea here is that a member of the enterprise user community has a single userid and password for access to all licensed resources, and not a separate userid and password for *each* licensed resource.

Using TLS-encrypted forms (which eliminates the problems of transmitting passwords in the clear), it would be fairly easily for a resource to ask for this userid and password securely; one could then have a special purpose protocol so that a resource could securely check whether the userid and password were valid by querying an enterprise userid/password database server. Note that TLS can set up an encrypted connection with a server certificate but no client-side certificate.

The special purpose userid/password checking protocol doesn't exist today, but is not hard to design or implement, and since it only needs to be implemented by the resource operator and by an enterprise server or two at each licensee institution, it might be much less problematic than making all licensee community users go through the complications of obtaining and installing certificates on their machines. Further, similar protocols for userid/password checking are already in use for validating users to terminal servers (i.e. TACACS, RADIUS); these might be used, or at least adapted.

Users are already familiar with user ids and passwords, including the need to keep passwords secure, to change them, and to pick them well (or at least they are more familiar with these issues than, for example, certificate use). Userids and passwords can be carried in the minds of people rather than being installed on specific machines the way that certificates are; this helps with kiosks, computer labs, libraries and other shared machine settings—assuming that one can teach the user to log off when he or she is finished, rather than just leaving the machine signed on. Probably the biggest problem with this approach—which is not shared with certificates—is that the resource operator obtains a set of globally valid credentials for the user, and has to be trusted to keep them secure. There are also some secondary problems—Trojan horse resources that capture user ids and passwords under false pretenses, for example, are a much more serious threat than they are in a certificate exchange environment.

Passwords and user ids carried over TLS encryption fare feasible and deployable. Assuming that a protocol such as SAML for verifying user ids and passwords with an enterprise server is standardized and deployed, the amount of work faced either by a licensee institution or a resource operator is quite manageable. Special desktop software is not required for web access; for other protocols, such as Telnet, an TLS-capable Telnet is needed. Z39.50 credentials are a particular problem because no Z39.50 interface to a service like TLS is currently defined. User ids and passwords are linked to people rather than network addresses of machines. One problem with userids and passwords is that they don't encourage seamless navigation among resources; each resource is going to explicitly annoy the user by asking for his or her userid and password on each visit.

While passwords represent relatively weak security, a system can be put in place to require them to be difficult to guess (by forcing the use of pass phrases rather than passwords, or avoiding use of words in a dictionary), and also insisting that they be changed frequently. The use of a TLS based transport removes the security problems of transmitting them in the clear. The protection provided by TLS will depend on whether US-only (long key) or international (short key) versions of TLS are supported by the user's browser. Userids and passwords are subject to systemic compromise from two perspectives; if the enterprise password verification server is compromised, new passwords would have to be issued to all members of the user community. Also, each resource operator now shares in the responsibility for keeping userids and passwords secure; if any resource operator's site is retaining user ids and passwords, and is compromised, this will compromise all other resource operators as well as the home institution (if the institution is using the same userid and password for internal and external authentication and authorization purposes).

Granularity and extensibility. An enterprise single sign on server will just verify that a particular userid/password combination is valid (it would also know what resource operator was asking). In situations where an access management decision needs to be made that goes beyond validity of the userid/password pair, the key question is the locus of that decision. The resource operator will either have to maintain a list of valid Ids (identities) or the password server will have to keep information about what resources a userid has access to. Or the institution would have to offer resource operators access to a user attribute database keyed on userid.

Cross-protocol flexibility: because passwords operate at a higher level of abstraction than protocols they are general. Telnet and Z39.50 support should be straightforward, assuming that there is encryption on the link over which the passwords are transmitted.

Privacy and accountability. The use of user ids and passwords transfers personal information directly to the resource operator. This information may be pseudononymous or identified; it will not be anonymous. To this extent, it undermines privacy but offers accountability. Management data faceted by demographic categories will be available from the resource operator only to the extent that the licensee institution

provides demographic data as a byproduct of userid/password validation. there is no opportunity for the licensee institution to collect statistical information directly, other than a count of how often userid/
password pairs are validated by the various resource operators.

Summary: to the extent that an enterprise password verification server
controls the export of individual and demographic information, passwords could work surprisingly well in a TLS-protected context. A primary benefit is that users are familiar with the model. There are
important missing pieces here, particularly the protocol to permit
resource operators to verify userid/password pairs with institutions that
issued them. Probably the greatest weakness of this approach is the
dependency on each resource operator to protect userid/password
pairs, and the danger of systemic compromise due to a security failure
on the part of a single resource operator.

By issuing different passwords and userids for different resources, it is
possible to reduce the interdependence among resource operators and
the dependence on each resource operator in maintaining security.
However, large numbers of passwords and userids are extremely
unfriendly and confusing for users, and probably impractical. For users
who only use a single machine (or who are willing to store a cookie file
in a network file system), and for resources that don't require high
security, it's certainly possible to store userids and passwords as cookies
on the user's machine (though many users have become "cookie-pho-
bic" due to the overly dire publicity surrounding cookies); once stored,
the user doesn't have to enter them at all, improving seamless cross-
resource navigation. This is the approach that is taken by many low-
security commercial services in the consumer marketplace today.

CHALLENGE AND RESPONSE

The process in which an entity requesting authentication is challenged
by and responds to an authentication authority. Each cycle of challenge

and its associated response is called a leg. The number of legs may vary depending upon the authentication mechanism used or the requirements of the authentication authority. Multiple legs are required to ensure that the authentication authority knows the entity and vice-versa. More legs provide stronger security. The Kerberos standard defines the type and number of challenge and response legs which it requires.

TOKENS AND TICKETS

A token granted by an authentication authority that grants the bearer permission to access an object or service. In Kerberos, this is the session ticket. In Windows NT, this is the security access token. Possession of a token/ticket by an entity is proof of its having been successfully authenticated. Such possession may preclude the holder from any future requirements for authentication usually for a defined time period. Thus tokens and their use make authentication a more efficient process by eliminating any unnecessary, secondary authentication attempts of an entity already deemed to be valid. Tokens which expire after a defined lifetime have another useful attribute: they force an entity, however valid, to be re-authenticated. This may detect an impostor at the end of the expiration period automatically and issue an alert.

SECURITY POLICY

A security policy defines an organization's top-level direction on information security, including principles for sharing data over the public Internet. The security policy should include statements on how the organization will segment data according to its sensitivity, parties requiring access, and the levels of control (including strength of authentication and encryption) required to match the levels of risk.

SINGLE SIGN-ON AND AUTHENTICATION

Single sign-on describes the concept of identifying an individual once, and then, having identified the individual, permitting access to controlled resources without further proof being required from the user. Single Sign On permits the user to move between domains without any further interaction on behalf of the user. In a complex environment, there will typically be resources that require more protection than others. For example, an organization may require simple 'UserID and 'Password' for access to some administration systems, but may require stronger controls or proof, such as smart card or biometrics, for financial transactions. Protection levels may be assigned to resources, which can indicate the required degree of authentication that is required.

AUTHENTICATION

Authentication is the process of validating the claimed identity of a named entity to a level of proof sufficient to gain the approval of an authentication authority. Proving that an entity is who it claims to be. The authentication authority stipulates in advance which information must be provided to do so. Windows 2000, a Kerberos KDC or Windows NT may each require different, predefined information about that entity when acting as authentication authorities A tiered approach to strong authentication can include a combination of:

- User ID and Password
- Challenge Response
- Hardware/Software Tokens
- Digital Certificates
- Biometrics
- Passwords

- Two factor tokens
- X.509 certificates
- Passwords over TLSSmart cards
- Forms-based Full CRL
- support OCSP
- support (Fall)
- Authentication Levels
- Method
- Chaining and "fallbacks"
- Custom methods
- Web-based single sign-on (SSO) across multiple Web domains
- SAML-based SSO and authorization between partner sites

Each Authentication method has an Authentication Authority. The Authentication Authority is the party responsible for authenticating a named entity. Acting as a proxy, it may request validation by another Authentication Authority in order to complete its own responsibilities. The act of authentication may be delegated by one Authentication Authority to another. When it does so, its own identity may be subject to authentication by that Authentication Authority; for example, a mail server which must decide who is allowed to read secured mail or mail attachments. In the case of delegation, the responsibility of authentication still remains with the original designated authority. For example, an administrator of a router is required to login in order to change the behavior of the router. The router may, in turn, delegate the authentication of this administrator to a remote domain controller. The user is the person requesting access to a resource. The identity of this person may be validated by a secret password, a smart card or a biometric attribute such as a fingerprint. Ensuring uniqueness of personage is a different challenge than that of computer systems or applications and hence requires different validation techniques. In Kerberos, a user principal defines the user. Any system participating in a network identified by a unique network address. In most cases but not all, this is an IP address. Since some computer systems have multiple IP addresses, they may possess multiple identities by which to be authenticated. This attribute can be useful in restricting access to some parts of a computer system. Systems are capable of falsely impersonating another system by substituting another network address which is not their own. Hence, they should be challenged to prove their true identity. In Kerberos, a host principal defines the system.

Authentication Roles

- Impersonation: The assumption by an authenticated entity of another valid identity. Thus, a single entity, such as a web server, can use a series of valid identities in order to service multiple users. This capability is useful to applications or proxies in order to act on behalf of another entity. A mail server is an example. Impersonation may be authorized or unauthorized.

- Trust relationship: A trust relationship exists between two domains when an entity authenticated by the authentication authority for the trusted domain is considered to be authenticated by the other domain. Thus, an entity authenticated by the trusted domain can access resources the other domain. The token (see above) possessed by the entity is used to control access to these domains.

- Duplication: The assignment by an authenticated entity of its own identity to another entity thereby allowing multiple entities to operate in parallel with a single identity. This is often used by processes/threads to duplicate themselves and assign their duties to their child processes/threads. Web service requires multiple, simultaneous processes all of which possess the same valid identity.

APPLICATIONS

From a Single Sign on perspective an application is any program which requires authentication of itself or requests authentication on behalf of other entities. In Kerberos, the application is defined by a service principal. For any security system to succeed, it has to be easy to use. In the case of application authentication, the single most important ease-of-use characteristic is that the user should not need to learn various ways of authentication or remember multiple passwords. Ideally, one authentication system would be sufficient. But for heterogeneous sites, multiple authentication mechanisms have to coexist. The problem of integrating multiple application authentication mechanisms, such as Kerberos [Neuman 94], RSA [Rivest 78], and Diffie-Hellman [Diffie 76, Taylor 88], is also referred to as the *integrated login*, or *unified login* problem. Even if users have to use multiple authentication mechanisms, they should not be forced to type multiple passwords. Furthermore, users should be able to use the new network identity without taking any further actions. The key here is in modular integration of the network authentication technologies with login and other system-entry services.

MODULAR DESIGN

Modular design and pluggability have become important for users who want ease of use. In the PC hardware arena, no one wants to set the interrupt vector numbers or resolve the addressing conflict between various devices. In the software arena, people also want to be able to replace components easily, for easy customization, maintenance, and upgrades. This separation will enable the number of decision components to be minimized and the economy-of-scale benefits gained. To do this, there needs to be an API between the enforcing and deciding components. At present, these APIs are proprietary (for example, MVS SAF—Security Authorization Facility), but there are signs that standardization will happen in the next few years. This is starting to happen in Java authentication and Authorization Service (JAAS) and Security Services Markup Language (S2ML), for example. Decision components need data to help them make their decisions. They need facts about the entity requesting access, and policies on when to grant access. These could be very simple—for example, a list of groups of which the user is a member, and a list of access rights for each group. Note that the enforcing component is a key part of the decision data, e.g. access to a database may be allowed through a specific transaction, but not directly via typed in SQL. Where it is not practicable to separate the decision component from the enforcing component, data sharing can attain better control. This could be done by sharing a data store between components, or possibly by populating an integrated component's data store from a master data store. To simplify the administration, it makes sense to group resources into sets of related items, and then to give access SAML based authentication software deserves special attention because authentication forms a very critical component of any secure computer system. The authentication infrastructure and its components may have to be modified or replaced, either because some deficiencies have been found in the current algorithms, or because sites want to enforce a different security policy than that provided by the system vendor. The replacement and modification should be done in such a way that these changes do not affect the user. The solution has to address not only how the applications use the new authentication mechanisms in a generic fashion, but also how the user will be authenticated by these mechanisms in a generic way.

SINGLE SIGN-ON ACROSS MULTIPLE DOMAINS

Today's most successful businesses have an Internet presence. This Web presence and its underlying infrastructure can be constructed in many ways. Optimal Web-enabled business infrastructures increasingly include the following elements to provide access to the resources required.

- A directory server that contains a combination of customer, employee, partner and possibly even supplier details.

- Security mechanisms (policy and enforcement tools) to make sure that each user of the site is authenticated and only gets the information to which they're entitled.

New business is built upon partnerships and the benefits those partnerships provide to customers. For traditional bricks and mortar companies, the business needs to drive traffic to the partner store with some sort of marketing incentive, for example a proof-of-purchase at one store giving a sizeable discount at a partner store. In an online partnership, the partners need to provide a simple way to move back and forth between corporate Web sites. But, to date, this has been hard to achieve since there is no standard way to pass user information securely between sites. Typically, users must register different identities with duplicated information at each site, which is enough to discourage them from taking full advantage of these partnerships. Also, the complexity and cost of setting up such customized systems has been an impediment to implementation by the partnering companies themselves. SAML (Security Assertion Markup Language) standard solves this problem. The SAML standard defines a new way to securely share information between separate corporate access and authorization systems. SAML allows companies using access and authorization systems to share trust between separate networks and without requiring the systems in those networks to share the underlying data.

When users are forced to use multiple passwords to access different resources, it results in an administrative nightmare, with a mass of helpdesk calls related to lost, stolen, or forgotten passwords, not to mention the security risk of individuals using the "sticky note password management scheme". SAML eliminates this problem by allowing any resource to share a single set of login credentials, meeting the requirements for corporate single sign-on (SSO). SAML eliminates the need to have users continuously authenticate themselves as they access different data. For the Web, this means users authenticate once and SAML, using secure cookies, will provide a single sign-on experience for the user. On the extranet, where business-to-business productivity depends on user ease-of-use, this capability is critical. SAML also provides multi-domain SSO, overcoming an industry drawback of Web-basedSSO—cookies are particular to a single Web domain. For many access products, this means that when users cross-domain boundaries (i.e., follows a link at sales.com to product.com) they must re-authenticate. SAML provides the ability for the new domain to securely query the original one via XML to retrieve and verify the user's credentials. SAML eliminates the need for the user to re-authenticate, providing a full cross-domain SSO environment. SAML strengthens the SSO model by incorporating the use of digitally signed credentials. Once a user has been identified, their credentials are passed with them securely—as they move about the resource they need for their tasks. The use of digital signatures, based on public-private key technology, creates a secure scalable SSO environment, which fully supports load sharing and fail-over over multiple Web servers and validators.

SAML

SAML, the Security Assertion Markup Language, is used to setup single sign-on between physically separate authorization systems. SAML is based on an industry-adopted standard, which means that all vendors' products should interoperate. SAML provides an interoperable mechanism for passing credentials and other related information between Web sites that each have their own authentication and authorization system. The traditional way of handling Web-based single sign-on is using Web server cookies. But cookies are an incomplete solution, current day security mechanisms prevent these cookies from being transmitted between sites. Since cookies cannot be used, another mechanism is needed. This mechanism must be able to work with the browsers and Web servers of today and must be able to provide a secure mechanism for communicating credentials and related user information between partner sites.

Supporting SAML technologies
• SOAP
• SAML assertions

Simple Object Access Protocol (SOAP) SOAP is a protocol that is used to exchange structured information between different web based systems and/or applications. SOAP basically provides a way to structure how separate systems are going to exchange information. The underlying transport used to pass the SOAP "messages" can include HTTP, asynchronous messaging and SMTP. SOAP over HTTP provides an effective means to access application services secured behind a firewall. It removes the need to open RPC ports across the firewall. However, by its very nature, it gives direct programmatic access to these services through a standard HTTP based interface. It is vitally important that the calling user's identity can be authenticated and access to the service authorized. SOAP therefore needs a mechanism to pass and authenticate a user's credentials across platforms; in such a way that the user's identity can be mapped back to the native security services of the accessed platform. Future SOAP standards will need to be supported as they are developed. Various asynchronous messaging Bidders have also proposed the use of SOAP over HTTP to pass messages across the Internet. It is therefore expected that SOAP messages might be passed within other SOAP messages. Each SOAP layer would need to correctly contain the appropriate security identity, for example the internal layer passing the credentials of the user accessing the SOAP service, the outer layer passing credentials between messaging hubs. Firewall technology may need to be enhanced to enable access to SOAP services based on Name Assertion entity. The current functionality of enabling or disabling based solely on port number may not be flexible enough. In order to address the inherent insecurity or SOAP, several messaging initiatives are underway. It is expected that once standardization is complete, a definitive mechanism can be provided by all vendors. In the mean time, it is important to provide security to all resources (web or otherwise) that a SOAP message may request. Through the integration of Meta-Directory to "illuminate" these resources and custom Policy Server agents, a reasonable modicum of security can be created within a heavy SOAP environment. In practice SOAP has primarily been designed to use HTTP as its transport mechanism. Thus, two different systems that are talking SOAP to each other can send structured messages over HTTP (using TLS if desired). The SAML standard requires that the separate systems in a SAML-based relationship, communicate using SOAP.

SAML assertions SAML allows for one system to assert characteristics of an entity. These assertions can be in the form:—This user is "Jon Smith".—This user is a member of the group Engineering.—This user has GOLD status. These assertions are how the SAML systems tell each other about a given user that is going from one site to the next. Assertions are passed between SAML aware systems using SOAP in a well-defined structure.

For each SAML relationship partners agree on what attributes are going to be shared. This data can then be used to make authorization decisions. For security reasons all attributes received from a partner are qualified by the name of the partner. Thus even if two partners are presenting the same attribute to you they will not be able to be confused. In order to take advantage of SAML, links that are pointing to a partner's site must be modified to the SAML specification. A standard redirect such as

http://www.securesite.com/pagetogoto.html

would be modified to:

https://saml.securesite.com/saml-out/securesite.com?TARGET=http://www.securesite.com/pagetogoto.html

The SAML partner link will redirect the user to the SAML server on an TLS connection and the actual target link is passed as a parameter. It is up to the SAML server to redirect the user to the next stage. When configuring a SAML partner the servers must exchange some information to set up the relationship

SAML-based SSO and Authorization Between Partner Sites

The Security Assertion Markup Language, SAML, is an XML-based standard for sharing user information and security credentials between otherwise unconnected Web sites, regardless of the authorization products used by either partner. SAML allows on-line business partners to further strengthen business relationships amongst each other and their constituencies by allowing them to securely share authentication and authorization information across corporate boundaries that have separate user databases and authorization policies in an industry-approved secure manner. SAML enables a seamless user experience for navigating between multiple Web sites across corporate boundaries. Users can now experience Web single sign-on with the transparent transfer of security credentials and user information (e.g., this user is "Jon Smith"; this user is a member of the group, Suppliers; this user has GOLD status) across affiliated sites. This eliminates the need for users to actively participate in the re-authentication process or to be pre-registered.

What does SAML provide?

SAML has been designed such that it gives partnering organizations the following features and benefits:

- Enables the exchange of authentication and authorization information between sites that have separate user databases and authorization policies in a coherent/uniform manner.

- Supports the distribution of additional information (for example, group information, credit card information, etc.) about the user to partnering sites by using pre-specified structures in the SOAP message. Includes the ability for the vendor to include proprietary information. In order for that proprietary vendor information to be useful, both sides of the exchange must know what to do with it.

- Defines the security mechanisms to protect the information that is to be passed between sites. These include: protecting the conversations between SAML servers using TLS, preventing replay attacks, preventing SAML memory stores from growing without bound (some types of denial of service attacks), and preventing third-party theft attacks

How does SAML work?

Shown below is the basic architecture required for a SAML-compliant site and how such a site interacts with another SAML compliant site. The graphic illustrates how each Web site that wishes to take advantage of SAML needs a SAML service as part of its architecture. The steps shown are as follows:

The user authenticates to Site1's Web system and browses through the system. 2 The user clicks on a link that takes her to Site2. The browser is first transparently forwarded to Site1's SAML service. This SAML service adds a partner ID and handle to the link, so that Site2 can identify the session as having originated from Site1.

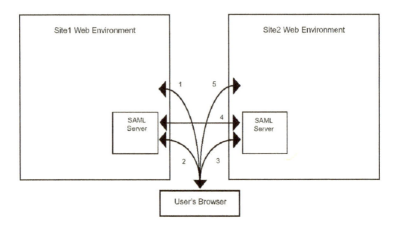

In a given environment that there will be a separate Web server and SAML server(s), or the SAML service could be combined with a Web server, or there may be no traditional Web server at all. In the latter case a company might be using an EJB server or some other software to handle their Web environment. 3 The browser is now redirected to Site2's SAML service, which retrieves the initial link and the additional information. The partner ID tells Site2 how to contact Site1 and the handle tells Site2 how to ask for the information for this connection. 4 Site2's SAML service calls back to Site1's SAML service directly (using the partner ID), and using the handle created in Step 2, retrieves the identity of the user and any additional information that is available from Site1. 5 Site2's authorization solution then decides whether or not it will let the user access the information. Note: The information added in step 2, is a binary piece of data that is fixed in size. The information passed between Site1 and Site2 in step 4, is XML encoded using SOAP and layered on top of HTTPS (i.e. HTTP over TLS). Figure 1 shows that a small service is required on all partnering sites. This service is typically:

A separate server dedicated to dealing with the SAML communications of the system. Several separate servers handling the incoming and outgoing SAML communications Another entity combined with another server (like a Web server). It is important to note that when the system is using SAML to communicate between separate networks, the SAML server that is initiating the interaction, the "from" site (e.g. Site1 in our example), creates the SAML information and stores it locally. The memory store, and the SAML exchange itself could be attacked. The SAML standard specifies how to counter the potential vulnerabilities as follows:

- The meta tags that refer to the current connection must have a limited lifetime. That is, they "expire" if not used quickly.

- Tags may only be used once. This and the above requirements protect against replay attacks and prevent SAML servers being subject to some types of denial of service attacks. • A SAML server should only give information about a user trying to access resources to the site for which the handle was generated. Thus if Site1 generates a handle for Site2 and Site3 queries Site1 for the information, Site1 should not pass the information to Site3. This prevents a third site from being able to access the SAML assertions that are meant to go to a legitimate partner site.

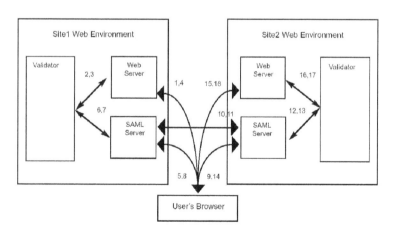

SAML also helps companies and administrators manage delegation. Most authorization products, including SAML, provide the ability to delegate the management of users and policies. In principle, this is a good feature to make available, because it allows the senior security officer to:

- Delegate the management of resources to the group of people who are dealing with that information on a daily basis (Web managers, etc.).

- Delegate management of access policy to particular groups of people within the organization with the appropriate credentials. For example, engineering might have their own Web site that only they can see. The administration of the policy for access to that Web site might be delegated to the engineering manager who might in turn delegate that to her assistant.

- SAML provides a solution to the cross-domain delegation management problem. Instead of this traditional type of delegation, each company sets up their own user database and establishes a SAML-based relationship with each of its partners.

To do this, the partners must:

1. Agree on the standard information to be stored, which requires that they exchange some role information.

2. Add their partners' roles into their user directory.

3. Define the policy they wish to apply locally for their partners using these agreed-upon roles. Now, when the SAML information is transferred, the system will be configured to pass the relevant attributes. These attributes will put that user in the desired partner-role, using a SAML assertion. In this way, partners get access to the company's information based on the roles that were established for that partner.

SAML may well prove to be a cornerstone in the network computing industry. Its ability to glue together separate networks and separate systems makes it a very important piece of the puzzle for the following reasons:

- Improved user experiences and business relationships: SAML provides a secure way to allow users to navigate between multiple Web sites across organizations. This allows users of multiple Web authorization products to give users a much better Web experience by providing seamless ways of crossing the traditional corporate and domain boundaries. This inter-connection of corporate sites makes business relationships in the electronic world easier to implement. Once the barriers to implementation are removed, relationships are easier to develop in a traditional sense.

- Solid security architecture: Security is not an after-thought with SAML; it is an integral part of the SAML specification. This means that each step of the solution defines the security mechanisms required to support that step.

SAML SERVER

The SAML Server sends and receives security "assertions" about users that have been authenticated when moving between sites in a federated environment. When an authenticated user proceeds to, or comes from, a partner's Web site, the SAML server transmits/accepts user information and authentication credentials to extend single sign-on across sites.

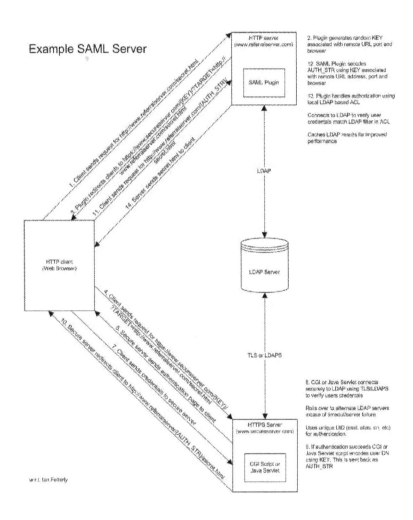

The user experience is further heightened through role-based authorization, which provides access based on a users relationship to an organization, and single sign-on (SSO), which reduces the users need to continually reauthenticate themselves. The SAML server is the gateway to SSO between partner Web systems with a separate authorization system. It handles the logistics of accepting users from partner sites and storing the required user information into a directory server and of sending users to partner sites and creating and sending the required assertions.

Common Responsibilities

- Receive SAML requests from partners
- Authenticate partner's certificate
- Create a user record in LDAP to store all received assertions
- Clean out users records that have expired
- Pass incoming users off to the correct URL
- Send outgoing SAML users to the correct partner SAML URL
- Gather personalization data from a SAML user's LDAP entry and create the required assertions for the partner
- Create a pointer for partner to request information for this user
- Ensure that only the correct partner can get the information pointed to by the pointer
- Expire internal cache for stale pointers that never get acted upon
- Authenticate SAML partners every step of the way

Common Features

- All SAML related communications over TLS
- Handles both incoming and outgoing SAML connections separately
- Allows specification of access policy for users going in either direction
- Fully integrated with SAML personalization system
- Self maintaining (all cleanup process automated)

- Separate component from the other components to allow for flexible deployment

- Export to file configuration of parameters needed by partner

- Can be used for partnerships for different companies

- Can be used to SSO for separated internal organizations (e.g. recently acquired offices that have their own separate network)

- Can be used as a kind of delegated administration configuration for partners

Personalized User Experience

A typical SAML server incorporates features to enhance your users' online experience by enabling the ability to personalize the users Web experience. Administrators can often specify what user, role or resource information to return to the application when an access request is made, allowing dynamic Web engines to customize the content.

ROLE-BASED AUTHORIZATION

Role-based access allows you to create polices based on information stored in user profiles. For example, your business partners could automatically be entered into the 'Gold' role if online transactions with your company total a minimum of $100,000 in one month. However, they enter the 'Platinum' role if the total exceeds $1,000,000, which might include access to deeper discounts and exclusive marketing programs. The degree of protection afforded to any communication between an entity and an authentication authority during the authentication process. All legs of a challenge and response cycle should be afforded strong protection while the authentication process is under way. Authorisation is divided into two parts the enforcing function and the deciding function. For example, if a user tries to read a file, the file system is the enforcing function. It is the entity that actually provides the physical access. In the case of MVS, the deciding function is RACF, and the file system will ask RACF if the user can have access. In the case of Unix, the file system does the deciding itself by looking at the user's membership of groups, and the file's access rights from each group. It is the intention to separate these components wherever possible and practicable.

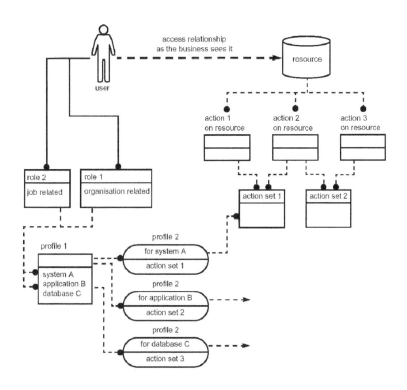

POLICY SERVER

The Policy Repository is the data store for user profiles, resource information and the associated policy data needed for the Single Sign On system. To reduce management overhead, the policy repository should interface with existing corporate user data rather than create an independent user list. An LDAP compliant directory server is ideal for both minimizing copies of user data and integrating with PKI (Public Key Infrastructure) solutions. The Policy Server is the process that accepts and evaluates policy queries on behalf of SSO/SAML enabled applications. When a query is received, the policy server accesses the required policy information from the repository, interprets the policy logic and current conditions, and returns the decisions to the application. The policy administration system configures all aspects of the SSO system, including:

- Create, manage and view authorization policy

- Manage resources, users, groups and attribute-based roles

- Define and manage delegated administration

- Manage authentication and encryption requirements

- Audit and reporting of policy changes

Native Password Management: In addition to password authentication, The policy server also provides the ability to define strong password policies, significantly increasing the security of password-based authentication. Almost all policy servers support native password management capabilities including password strength characteristics, expiry policies, and account lockout based on suspicious behavior. The server should allow the administrator to define the following strength policies on setting and maintaining passwords:

- Password length—Minimum and/or maximum

- Required characters—Alpha, numeric and/or special

- User name match—Must not contain the user's first or last name, or User ID

- Dictionary match—Must not contain dictionary words

- Password history—Must not match users last 'X' number of passwords

Scalability and performance

When a great deal of dependency is placed upon infrastructure components it is clearly important that resilience is built in. The enterprise should have a number of policy servers located at strategic points around the country. It is possible to configure how traffic is managed across replicated systems. Load balancing and fallover is supported between policy servers, Web agents and directories.

COMMON DIRECTORY

The directory is shared with other security functions and hence it provides a common point of definition of people's access rights. The Single Sign On system should be integrated with a single logical directory, replicated for resilience, to hold details about all employees and contractors. This directory can also be used to hold information on suppliers and customers the directory is structured as a tree. At the top is the enterprise, and, below that, namespaces for employees, roles and applications. It is very straightforward to add branches to hold other objects, such as customers. Users are assigned membership of groups. These groups are currently designed to represent various roles within an application, but, over time, they can be generalized to represent job-related roles. These roles will then be associated with several applications. Each application is often associated with a container object, and that object has a set of containers within it to represent the various policies defined in the directory. This direct association of policies and directory containers will make it clear what the security requirements are for any resource. The groups of users will be put into these containers and hence users will be linked to a policy and thus given access to a resource. This model is general, and can be defined in terms of LDAP queries for applications that can work directly with a directory. It also makes it easy to export the details of users with access to an application as a flat file, for import into other systems. The user object can be used to hold other security related data, e.g. for storing information to support legacy single sign-on.

SSO Product Selection Criteria

Companies should use the following selection criteria when evaluating SSO products.

1. Multiple Authentication Types—All SSO products support passwords, of course. But some will support additional authentication types, such as biometrics, digital certificates, tokens or smart cards.

2. Authentication Method—The method differs from the type by representing the underlying authentication architecture. How well does the product handle the registration, suspension, revocation and sharing of credentials?

3. Quality of Administration—In the case of employee SSO, the emphasis is placed on easy-to-use administrative console, intuitive commands and integration with user data repositories already in existence (e.g., human resources databases). Web SSO products are evaluated similarly, with the added point of distributed, subordinate administration—allowing multiple administrators to manage subsets of the user population.

4. Breadth of Supported Applications—How diverse are the supported target applications and platforms?

5. Granular Access Management—The Administrative console should permit the administrator to control authorization not only to certain applications, but also under certain conditions. SSO products are heavily weighed on this point.

6. Robust Architecture—How fault-tolerant and efficient is the underlying architecture of the product itself? How well does it scale to loads and to geographic distances?

7. Use of Directory Services—To what extent does the product rely on directories, compounded with the ability of that directory to be used for other purposes simultaneously?

8. End User Ease of Use—For employee SSO, this refers mainly to the familiar desktop experience and the elimination of normal log-in interruptions. For Web SSO users, this refers to the degree to which the user's desktop browser is modified in any way.

9. Vision—Also known as product road map, which vendor projects the most visionary use for its products during the next five years?

10. Desktop Security—Applicable only to employee SSO products. The client software required for employee SSO should have additional value, such as screen locking, encrypted credential or script storage, etc.

PASSWORD SYNCHRONIZATION

On the periphery of sign-on options is password synchronization. Instead of single sign-on, these products touch the target applications to force identical credentials across various platforms. Instead of creating only one sign-on event, password synchronization products produce a single password that a user re-enters with each log-in. So, instead of remembering multiple passwords, the user needs to keep track of only one. The shortcoming of password synchronization is that it relies on the lowest common denominator of password policies. For example, if the mainframe application has a six-digit maximum password length, and the NT domain has no maximum, the synchronized password must conform to the six-digit maximum. This makes enforcing a robust password policy tricky. In the past, these products have been much less expensive to purchase; today, prices are competitive with employee-SSO solutions.

THE FUTURE OF SSO

Public key infrastructures (PKIs) are thought to have all the functions of employee- and Web-based SSO. While this, in fact, is currently true, advancements in PKI integration could make SSO products obsolete in the next three years. In this event companies would be advised to focus on PKI implementation and integration. In that case, a user would present a certificate seamlessly to each authorization mechanism inline between the user and the target application. The firewalls, routers, switches and access control software all would check the validity and authorizations associated with the certificate on the fly. Finally, upon reaching its target, the application itself would call a directory to authenticate the user, and then dynamically permit access to appropriate resources. In addition, directories and LDAP integration could centralize all user credentials so that SSO could become a byproduct of the directory itself.

9

Role Based Access Control

In order for authoritative information to be maintained, access control needs to be imposed for privileges to read, write, search, or compare. Access control can be done on a subtree, entry, or attribute type and granted to individuals, groups, or "self" (which allows an authenticated user to access this or her own entry). This scheme provides a great deal of flexibility. For example, an administrator may want to only allow people in a human resources group to change the title or manager attributes, allow administrative assistants to change office location and pager number information for just their department, and allow individuals to modify their own home phone number, license plate, and so on. As such the access control model included in RFC 2820 U13 is intrinsically a role based security. As such an administrator is able to delegate policy administration for specific subtrees to other users. This allows for the partitioning of the entire directory tree for policy administration, but still allows a single policy to be defined for the entire tree, independent of partitioning among multiple physical servers.

First and foremost, the role based access solution needs to work at a practical level. From the user's perspective, it should facilitate access, minimizing redundant authentication interactions and providing a single-sign on, user-friendly view of the array of available networked information resources. It needs to scale; it must be feasible for institutions to deploy and manage for large and dynamic populations of community members. It needs to be sufficiently robust and simple so that user support issues are tractable; for example, a forgotten password should not be an intractable problem. It needs to be affordable.

From the resource operator viewpoint, a viable access management system should not require a vast amount of ongoing production and maintenance. Configuration to add a new licensing institution should be simple, and ongoing maintenance of that configuration should not call for large amounts of information to be interchanged between resource operator and licensing institution on an ongoing basis (such as file updates). Software parameter changes—not new software—should be necessary to add additional institutions. There should be a clean, simple, and well-defined (standard) interface between resource operator and licensing institution. A systems or network failure at one institution should not degrade a resource operator's service to other licensing institutions.

Practical solutions are inextricably linked to the installed base of software. Ideally, all of the software needed to implement a role based access solution should be available either commercially or as free software. Good solutions will leverage off of the installed technology base, and also current investments in upgrading that technology base: they should not be specific to libraries or even to higher education if possible, at a mechanism level (though libraries or higher educational institutions may use these mechanisms in conjunction with policies that vary from those common in the corporate or consumer markets). Most importantly, the software support that end users require should be available in common packages—such as web browsers—that are already part of the installed base. Any solution that requires custom specialized software to be installed on every potential user's desktop machine starts with a severe handicap. Similarly, any solution requiring specialized hardware, such as biometric systems or smart card readers, is certainly not going to be feasible on a cross-enterprise basis, and while it might imaginably be workable within an institution's internal authentication system, some other technique would be needed to convey cross-organizational access management data. Few resource providers will be willing to limit access to users equipped with such specialized facilities.

POLICY BASED MANAGEMENT SERVICES

A typical large enterprise will have several different types of systems, many installations of those systems, numerous types of information stored on those systems, and will need to manage access to the information and to the systems themselves. It has been estimated that a typical 25,000-user company has over 87 million permissions assigned. Each of these permissions must be properly managed to ensure that information is adequately protected.

Policy Based Access Management Services

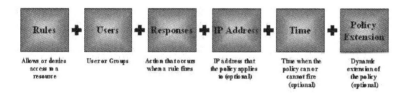

- Restrict access by user, role, groups, dynamic groups, or exclusions

- Fine grained access control at the file, page or object level

- Can allow access based on location and time

- Active Rules dynamically access external data in real time

Any solution also needs to reflect current realities; in particular, it must be able to recognize the need for a user community member to access a resource both independent of his or her physical location (for example, a user must be able to connect to the internet via a commercial ISP, a mobile IP link, or a cable television internet connection from home), and also the need for people to access resources by virtue of their location (for example, access may be granted to anyone who is physically present in a library, whether or not they are actually members of the licensee community).

The Policy Server manages the access control policies established by an administrator. These policies define which resources are protected and which users or user groups are allowed access to resources. Using policies, the implementer can set time constraints on resource availability and IP address constraints on the client attempting access.

A policy protects resources by explicitly allowing or denying users access to resources. It specifies the resources that are protected, the users or groups that have access to these resources, and the delivery method of those resources to authorized users. If a user is denied access to a resource, the policy also determines how that user is treated. When the implementer constructs a policy, they can include multiple rule-response pairs and bind them to individuals, user groups, or an entire user directory. The implementer can also configure multiple policies to protect the same resources against different sets of users, adding responses that enable the application to further refine the content shown to the user. One of the configuration options of a policy is a time restriction. If the implementer specify a time restriction for a policy and a rule in that policy also contains a time restriction, the policy fires during the times when both restrictions overlap. For example, if a policy can only fire between 9:00AM and 5:00PM and the rule can only fire Monday through Friday, the policy can only fire between 9:00AM and 5:00PM, Monday through Friday. If a policy does not fire, the rule will not fire. In addition to supporting static rules, the implementer can configure an *active policy*. An active policy authorizes users based on dynamic data obtained from external business logic.

A *resource* is any object that a user may attempt to access or any privilege that a user may attempt to get. A *realm* is a collection of resources grouped together according to security requirements. All resources in a realm are protected by the same Agent. You associate realms with policy domains; policy domains can contain one or more realms. To configure realms, think of the organization of your environment's resources as a directory structure of the resources that reside on your server. You need to determine which sections of the directory have common users and resources. Each realm can require a different authentication method to gain access. A rule defines a set of actions and responses for the resource it protects. For example, if a collection of CGI scripts are protected by a rule in a realm, one group of users is allowed access to the scripts, while another group of users is denied access and redirected to another site in the company's network. A *rule* is comprised of a realm, a resource, an action, and optionally, a time constraint, as shown in the following diagram:

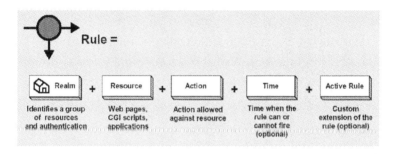

By default, a rule allows access to a resource; however, an implementer can create a rule to deny access to a resource. A deny access rule should always take precedence over an allow access rule. This ability to create allow and deny access rules enables you to configure two different policies for resources in the same realm but for different users. One policy allows certain users access, while the other denies a different group of users access.

A *policy domain* is a logical set of resources grouped together from an administrative perspective. For example, a corporate intranet may be implemented across five Web servers that support the Marketing and Finance divisions of a company. These divisions can be partitioned into a *marketing* policy domain and a *finance* policy domain. Policy domains make the administration of a site much easier because independent administrators can be assigned policy management responsibilities for different domains based on their job function. As users or resources change, the administrator knows how to properly update the policy for the domain. After establishing policy domains, you then associate resources, rules, and responses with each domain.

POLICY DOMAIN SIGN-ON

A policy domain is a logical grouping of resources associated with one or more user directories. In addition, policy domains require one or more administrator accounts that can make changes to the objects within the policy domain. Policy domains contain realms, rules, responses, and policies. The resources in a policy domain can be grouped in one or more realms. A realm is a set of resources with a common security (authentication) requirement. Access to resources is controlled by rules, which are associated with the realm that contains the resource. Besides acting as a container for domain objects, policy domains also connect to user directories. RBAC systems authenticate users based on the requirements of the realm in which the target resource resides

Within the enterprise components may act as independent domains in the sense that an end-user has to identify and authenticate himself independently to each of the domains with which he wishes to interact. The end user interacts initially with a Primary Domain to establish a session with that primary domain. This is termed the Primary Policy Domain Sign-On

To invoke the services of a secondary domain an end user is required to perform a Secondary Domain Sign-on. This normally requires the end user to supply a further set of user credentials applicable to that secondary domain. An end user has to conduct a separate sign-on dialogue with each secondary domain that the end user requires to use. The secondary domain session is typically an operating system or application shell within an environment representative of the end user. From a management perspective this legacy approach requires independent management of each domain and the use of multiple user account management interfaces. Considerations of both usability and security give rise to a need to co-ordinate and where possible integrate user sign-on functions and user account management functions for the multitude of different domains now found within an enterprise. A service that provides such co-ordination and integration provides cost benefits to an enterprise through reduction in the time taken by users in sign-on operations to individual domains, including reducing the possibility of sign-on operations failing

- improved security through the reduced need for a user to handle and remember multiple sets of authentication information.

- reduction in the time taken, and improved response, by system administrators in adding and removing users to the system or modifying their access rights.

- improved security through the enhanced ability of system administrators to maintain the integrity of user account

- configuration including the ability to inhibit or remove an individual user's access to all system resources in a coordinated and consistent manner.

In the domain sign-on approach, the system is required to collect from the user as, part of the primary sign-on, all the identification and user credential information necessary to support the authentication of the user to each of the secondary domains that the user may potentially require to interact with. The information supplied by the user is then used by domain sign-on services within the primary domain to support the authentication of the end user to each of the secondary domains with which the user actually requests to interact.

From a management perspective the single sign-on model provides a single user account management interface through which all the component domains may be managed in a coordinated and synchronized manner.

Significant security aspects of the domain Sign-On model require the secondary domains have to trust the primary domain to:

- correctly assert the identity and authentication credentials of the end user,

- protect the authentication credentials used to verify the end user identity to the secondary domain from unauthorized use.

The authentication credentials have to be protected when transferred between the primary and secondary domains against threats arising from interception or eavesdropping leading to possible masquerade attacks

DELEGATED ADMINISTRATION

Delegated Administration Services provide an intuitive and flexible way to build and manage a complex directory. Delegated Administration extends a Single sign on Registration Services by adding two-tiered management of an LDAP user directory. Additionally, RBAC server provides event-driven workflow for pre-process and post-process administration and registration events. Shared workflow libraries can be developed and customized to support the workflow functionality required. Libraries can evaluate a pre-process request and govern whether to accept or reject it. If accepted, the request is carried out. If rejected, the request is not being carried out and a pre-process request is returned. After a RBAC server request is successfully processed, workflow libraries evaluate the post-process request and take any action as dictated by the business process and return success or fail status to the RBAC server application. RBAC server user roles offer a flexible way to assign capabilities to a user. Roles are groups in a directory that are associated with RBAC server policies. The role represents a selection of privileged operations. By applying the role to a user or a service, the principal can perform the operations. For example, by confining certain privileges to an Employee role or a Manager role and applying the role to a user, the user's accessibility is confined to the privileges granted it by the role.

Linking groups to policies allows you to control access to protected resources without having to move individual users into and out of RBAC server policies. User roles are groups in an LDAP directory. The groups are identified by a custom attribute. You can configure a policy in a RBAC server to authorize users in a specific LDAP group, for example, cn=Buyer. When you create an organization or add a user to an organization, RBAC server searches for groups with the cn attribute in the RBAC server End User Policy Domain. The roles are listed in the template. From the displayed list, administrators can assign the roles to users, which creates a *group_of_unique_names* entry under the organization in the LDAP directory. In this example the cn of the *group_of_unique_names* entry matches the cn defined in the policy, which links groups to a RBAC server policies, as shown below.

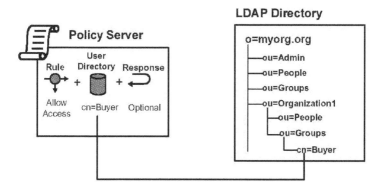

RBAC server stores user information in an LDAP user directory. The implementer must configure a connection to an existing directory or create a new instance of an LDAP directory. When configuring the connection, the implementer must specify an administrator with sufficient privileges in the ACL to modify the LDAP directory. In most access control products the RBAC server policy domains logically group together administrator resources and self-registration resources to simplify administrative tasks. The implementer can specify multiple user directories in a policy domain.

The issue of privilege management is one of the most critical aspects for business. Users require access to information, but each user must be authenticated and then authorized based on their privileges before gaining access. A RBAC server can meet the requirements for building and managing secure user-based Web sites and portals. The privilege management model for Web resources often varies across servers, Web application servers, operating systems, and development tools. Consequently, the administration of one server can differ from the administration of another, and the privilege management capabilities offered by these various servers and tools can differ. These differences can lead to administrative problems as well as an inconsistent security framework. The privilege management model for multi-tier applications can delegate user privileges differently for each tier. This implementation would allow users of one client to perform tasks that users of other clients could not. A RBAC server's ability to deliver user privilege information to applications makes it an excellent access control solution for applications based on a three- or four-tier distributed architecture.

As user populations for portals, extranets, and intranets increase, delivering and securing content in heterogeneous environments can be done many different ways, depending on the platforms, operating systems, Servers and applications in use. Administering these more complex environments is often more costly and time consuming than administering single-platform environments. As a result, the quality of Web site security is sometimes lower in heterogeneous environments.

A centralized approach to security management provides the following advantages:

- Applying the same security policy to each application eliminates the need to write complex code to manage security in each application.

- The time and cost to develop and maintain multiple security systems is reduced, making it comparable with developing and maintaining only one security system.

- Customers, business partners, and employees accessing the network all have their security privileges managed through a RBAC server whether they access the corporate network locally or remotely through the Internet or a private network.

Implementing a comprehensive security system is a challenge for both the architect and the enterprise. A role based infrastructure presents unique challenges in approach and implementation. While the objective of a secure infrastructure may seem self-explanatory, one must have a solid definition for secure. In the context of this exercise, "secure," indicates freedom from the majority of perpetrated system penetration attempts both internal and external. As systems will never be entirely secure, the goal of the security consultant is to make penetration cost prohibitive. Cost cited in terms of time or processing power. In order to satisfy these criteria, a sensitivity audit must be executed against the data to be guarded. In example, financial and personal data requires a higher level of security than inventory of an inexpensive item.

One of the base concepts of delegated administration is that a name or identity has attributes associated with it. These may be demographic in nature or they may capture permissions to use resources. Attributes may be bound closely to a name (for example, in a certificate payload) or they may be stored in a directory or other demographic database under a key corresponding to the name. Attributes may change over time; for example, from semester to semester the set of courses that a given identity is associated with may well change. Just because some system on a network has knowledge of a name does not necessarily imply that it has access to attributes associated with that name. There is a fine line between rights to names (authentication) and attributes; for some purposes, simply knowing that a user has a right to a name from a given authorizing authority may itself represent sufficient information (an implicit attribute, if one wishes) that can support access management decisions.

Authorization is the process of determining whether an identity (plus a set of attributes associated with that identity) is permitted to perform some action, such as accessing a resource. Note that permission to perform an action does not guarantee that the action can be performed; for example, a common practice in cross-organizational licensing is to further limit access to a maximum number of concurrent users from among an authorized user community.

Note that using delegated administration authentication and authorization decisions can be made at different points, by different organizations.

Some libraries are establishing consortia which involve reciprocal borrowing and user-initiated interlibrary loan services; in a real sense these consortia are developing what amounts to a union or distributed shared patron file. One can view this as moving beyond just common role based access to a system of shared access to a common directory structure for user attributes, and a common definition of user attributes among the consortium members. This is an example of a situation where very rich attributes are available to each participant in the consortium as they make authorization decisions; interlibrary loan and reciprocal borrowing represent a much richer and more detailed set of actions than would be typical of a networked information resource.

OBJECT ORIENTED DATABASES

Object-oriented databases suffer from logical data dependence, in that, users must know the object structure in order to pose queries on deeply nested structures. Directory technology addresses this challenge by abstracting the location and structure of data from the requesting party.

Logical data independence is the independence of an application program, or user process, from the underlying data type's growth or change in representation. To relate this to a database system, this means that, regardless of the changes made to the underlying schema, the existing written programs or users' ad hoc queries should still function as if no changes were made. This concept of data independence is a very powerful and necessary one, since this makes the querying of databases more manageable. Object-oriented databases suffer from this logical data dependence, in that, users must know the object structure in order to pose queries on deeply nested structures. Directory technology addresses this challenge by abstracting the location and structure of data from the requesting party. Directories provide a way to name, manage, and access collections of attribute-value pairs and the location of data within a repository.

Object-oriented implementation techniques rely on the public interface on a object type/class to collect all the permissible operations/methods needed by all potential users. Thus, methods placed in the public interface are available to all potential users regardless of their intended responsibilities within the object-oriented system/application. As a result there is no way to prevent access by a user to a method in the public interface programmatically. Adopting a user-role based security approach to public interface design leads to a strategy that restricts access to the public interface on a role-by-role basis, where different user roles would have access to specific and limited subsets of public interfaces based on their enterprise responsibilities. Such a scheme finely tunes the security policy and is an important first step to minimizing misuse and corruption.

Accommodating disjoint security realms is a challenge for administrators who have to maintain duplicate data sets and for users who need to recall multiple pass phrases, yet joining security realms together can expose one realm to the weakness of the other. In addition, the current approach of granting access via general access control lists empowers technical support staff with extreme policy authority. These two challenges can be overcome only by addressing the system holistically rather than provincially, as has been the traditional approach.

Role Based Access Control is an authorization strategy in which an entity's permission to access and manipulate targeted resources are determined by the entity's role or function within an organizational context. Role based access controls principal motivation is to streamline security policy administration. Under RBAC, many discrete authorizations can be aggregated within a defined role. One or many roles may be assigned or attributed to individuals. Roles may be constructed or attributed hierarchically, so that one role may be constructed of several other roles, even further streamlining administrative overhead.

A distinction is made between authentication (verifying that you are who you pretend to be) and authorization (what it is that you are allowed to do). There is also a mission driven distinction between access rights (here used as a synonym of authorization) and access control: ensuring that the rights are not violated. A key requirement is that the policies of the enterprise must be properly represented in the electronic infrastructure, in a method more comprehensive than the assignment of access rights in arbitrarily groupings to servers which may or may not host unrelated applications and data. Key to this approach is the application of directories, public key infrastructure and single sign on technology

In RBAC user roles, system policies and profiles are defined in a directory hierarchy. Once a role has been defined, privileges can be established assigning both implicit and explicit denial permission methods, thereby insuring the roles of the users dictate the application's functionality at runtime.

From a technical aspect Generic security classes and exception handling for dynamic role-based behavior are required to facilitate this system. However, prior to addressing the technical challenges two critical factors for the enterprise are management buy-in and a commitment to the division of authority.

The role based administration approach requires management to decentralize the granting of access rights into two distinct individuals, system and resource-management. To accomplish this, management must establish a comprehensive system access policy. As these policies are established the natural resistance of the enterprise must be factored in the creation of the management structure so central to this concept. To counter management apprehension attention must be turned to the present state of affairs, notably the central administration of access control by technical staff removed from the management process. This creates a technocracy that is counter to the best interests and management structure of the enterprise.

The primary advantage on this approach is the separation of authority and responsibility in to two functions. The system administrator who is responsible for the assignment of application access to roles defined by management and the resource-management administrator who assigns individuals roles within the organization.

With Role Based Access Control, each user is associated with a set of roles and each role is associated with a set of operations which a user acting in that role may perform. The power of role based public key as an access control mechanism is the concept that an operation may theoretically be anything. This is contrasted to other access control mechanisms where bits or labels are associated with information blocks. These bits or labels indicate relatively simple operations, such as, read or write, which can be performed on an information block.

This approach address the need to exert greater negative control over system applications and data. As threats to the enterprise become common, the need for a comprehensive security system becomes evident.

Prior to role based access control, businesses and consumers have been limited to only a fraction of potential capabilities of electronic messaging and Internet-based technologies. That tiny fraction has delivered significant advances in speed, effectiveness and economy but truly astounding leaps forward remain outside our reach. Businesses and consumers are reluctant to advance much further until pivotal issues of identity, confidentiality, privacy, trust and authority are satisfactorily answered.

There are five fundamental elements to secure electronic commerce:

1. Integrity—verification that the information in a message or file has not been modified.

2. Authentication—assurance as to the identity of the originator of a message or file.

3. Non-repudiation—undeniable proof of participation by both originator and recipient of a message or file.

4. Confidentiality—the privacy of information, so no one but the intended recipient may read the contents of a message or file.

5. Availability—ensuring the information is not denied to authorized requesters.

CORBA and DCOM/SOAP/dot Net are potential implementations of RBAC, though it is not clear to what extent these will be used from desktop machines in the future. There are also a set of issues involving authentication in conjunction with JAVA applets and systems like Authenticode or PICS, which are not well understood at this point. Many of the authentication and authorization problems in this area deal with a user's machine making decisions about what applets it is willing to accept and to execute, and what authorizations it is willing to assign them; these are similar to questions about document authenticity and integrity and are out of scope for this paper. The other set of problems center around an applet making decisions about a *user's* rights; while technology and standards in this area are still in flux, most of the current approaches seem to assume some kind of certificate infrastructure. This is an area where more work is clearly needed.

PKI

Public key encryption involves negotiating a shared key using public key technology to encrypt all transmissions between two parties. The management of these shared keys is critical to enterprise security and has been a major challenge for security companies wanting to offer interoperability.

PKI provides four elements which enable electronic commerce and set the foundation for secure transactions.

- Digital signatures

- Integrity

- Authentication

- Non-repudiation

Integrity proves that a sent document hasn't been tampered with. Authentication ensures that only those allowed to speak to each other actually do. Digital signatures are meant to put a digital signature on each electronic document, allowing senders to sign off on them. And finally, non-repudiation eliminates the opportunity for someone to refute the content of a transmission.

PKI provides a high degree of confidence that:

- Private Keys are kept secure

- Specific Public Keys are truly linked to specific Private Keys

- The party holding a Public/Private Key pair is who the party purports to be.

Integrity proves that a sent document hasn't been tampered with. Authentication ensures that only those allowed to speak to each other actually do. Digital signatures are meant to put a digital signature on each electronic document, allowing senders to sign off on them. And finally, non-repudiation eliminates the opportunity for someone to refute the content of a transmission.

In a credential based approach, the user interacts directly with resources on the net rather than working through an enterprisely-provided proxy intermediary. The key problems here are:

- What are the credentials that the user presents to the resource?

- how are these credentials presented securely?

- how are the credentials validated with the issuing institution?

For a credential based approach to scale, all of these activities need to take place in a standardized fashion. The most commonly discussed credentials are X.509 certificates, which are attractive because browsers and servers already have some support for them (designed to enable electronic commerce) and because other software components needed for an X.509 public key infrastructure are already becoming available on the marketplace. However, many other forms of credentials are possible, including userids and passwords, one time passwords, and the like. Indeed, it's useful to differentiate between application-level credentials—where the collection of the credential and its validation is packaged into the application itself, such a obtaining and checking a userid and password—and credentials which are built into protocol mechanisms, such as the use of certificates with HTTP and SSL. The protocol based mechanisms are more general and often require less work to implement on the part of the resource operator, but are less familiar to end users, calling for a larger investment in infrastructure and user education. Credentials can be confusing to analyze because they can potentially carry both authentication and attribute information together, or they can be used purely (or almost purely) for authentication.

.X.509 certificate based credentials, an essential part of PKI, are substantially more complex than passwords, but offer a number of advantages. In essence, an X.509 certificate (plus the private key that goes with the certificate) gives a machine credentials that support its right to make use of a name, and allows this assertion to be verified by checking with a certificate authority (which might be operated by the licensee institution, or operated by a third party under contract to the licensee institution). X.509 certificates include expiration dates, and certificate authorities can also provide revocation lists to invalidate certificates prior to their expiration date (though checking such lists can involve substantial overhead, and not all systems supporting certificates currently check revocation lists.) X.509 certificates and corresponding private keys are messy to distribute (much more so than, for example, a starter single use password for a local authentication system), and complicated for users to install, particularly in cases where the certificate needs to be installed in multiple machines owned by a single user. Backup and recovery needs to be considered carefully lest a user lose his or her certificates permanently as the result They are highly intractable in cases where users share machines, such as public workstations. X.509 certificates can contain demographic data (though there are standardization problems here about how to encode them in the certificate payload) which could be used for resource-operator based statistics gathering or fine-grained authorization decisions.

In contrast to passwords, there is already a well defined protocol/process which can be used to validate an X.509 certificate-based credential that has been presented to a resource operator.

Note that an X.509 certificate based credential does not consist of simply the certificate itself, but rather a complex object that includes the certificate and is signed with the (secret) private key corresponding to the certificate; since this is computed anew each time a credential is needed, X.509 based certificates do not share the password-approach problem that security depends on each resource operator carefully protecting the user's credentials.

Userids and passwords are application level constructs; they can be designed into an application using any protocol, assuming only that the connection can be encrypted. The exchange of X.509 certificates is a lower level, protocol-integrated operation and does not rely on encryption. Thus, there is work involved in extending the use of X.509 certificates to work with protocols other than HTTP, such as Telnet. (Z39.50 already contains facilities for certificate exchange). There is also still a need for an SSL-type service to encrypt the connection where confidentiality is desired; SSL can also handle many aspects of certificate exchange without the need for upper level protocol engineering, if it is available (though the application—if not the applications-level protocol—still needs to know something about certificates). One advantage of certificates is that they are more flexible than most other mechanisms; they can be used for signing electronic mail messages, for example (though generally a separate key is used for signing). And much of the current work on new protocols and services—for example in the Java environment—seems to be based on certificate models.

The issues involving privacy, accountability and management data change little from the password scenario already discussed. One point worth noting that if the user has several certificates—for example, an identified one for use with an internal enterprise authentication and authorization system and a pseudononymous one for use with external services—he or she must select the correct certificate for presentation in order to maintain privacy.

Proxy/Credential Hybrid Schemes
There are several interesting and confusing schemes that after much discussion the initial reviews of the paper recognized are really hybrids of the proxy and credential approaches. In these schemes, the user contacts an applications proxy in order to gain access to the resource. The proxy authenticates the user, checks his or her authorization, and then prepares and submits a set of credentials to the resource. After the user's connection to the resource is established through these creden-

tials, the proxy steps out of the way (via an HTTP redirect) and the user interacts directly with the resource. This has several useful results. It greatly reduces the overhead generated by use of a proxy, and minimizes the resource requirements for the proxy machines. It reduces some of the privacy concerns related to the proxy. And it means that short lived rather than long-lived credentials (something perhaps more akin to a Kerberos ticket, philosophically, though it may be embodied in a certificate based credential) can be sent to the resource operator; further, it may avoid the need to store these short-term credentials locally on the end user's machine. This approach is covered in the Single Sign On chapter under SAML

SECURITY STANDARDS IN INFORMATION TECHNOLOGY

Further, using ISO (International Standards Organization) requirements the following security levels are identified:

- Level 0—no signature, no encryption, open e mail
- Level 1—signed e-mail message, file transfer or web authentication request
- Level 2—signed and encrypted message or file transfer
- Level 3—notarization by a 3rd party CA, signed and encrypted message or file transfer
- Level 4—Military/Defense security protocols
- Level 5—Hardware-based signatures and encryption

The implementation of the ISO security requirements required for international distribution of a secure, trusted commerce platform requires a stable infrastructure. The following components have been identified as vital components in a stable structure:

- network components

- messaging servers
- policy servers
- secure web clients and servers
- directory and database repositories
- security-enabled messaging clients
- a PKI (Public Key Infrastructure) comprised of multiple Certificate Authorities (CAs)

Of the seven listed components, the interaction of the last two items form the foundation for many of the activities required of electronic commerce. The activities of the certificate management system include, but are not limited to, the following:

- user identity validation
- public and private key pair generation
- certificate generation and signing
- managing certificates in a directory
- performing certificate revocation and publish certificate revocation lists (CRLs)
- key and certificate distribution
- managing CA (Certificate Authorities) certificates and cross-certificate pairs

The messaging client interface enables the above certificate management operations by facilitating:

- the retrieval public certificates from the directories via LDAP (Lightweight Directory Access Protocol) or DAP (Directory Access Protocol)

- the encryption of message body contents with public keys stored in the certificates

- the signing of messages with private keys

- the submission of signed and/or encrypted messages to the SMTP or X.400 messaging servers

- the retrieval of signed and/or encrypted messages from the message stores

- the decryption of message contents using recipient's private key

- the verification of signatures using sender's public certificate and key

- The combination of certificate management systems and the messaging client interface enable a secure commerce system.

Role Based Access Control provides the following strategic advantages to companies implementing standards based electronic commerce (EC) infrastructures over the internet.

- Provides a migration path from traditional EDI (Electronic Data Interchange) to standards-based EC

- Immediately broadens the range of trading partners companies can do electronic business with—by creating a security infrastructure which runs over the Internet, companies can expand secure EC relationships with virtually any trading partner.

- Radically shortened value chain in business communications—secure EC leverages network speed to most business transactions, removing the paper trail bottleneck.

- Non-repudiation (digital signatures) brings companies a more secure and reliable communication resolution vehicle than existing paper trails—for example order processing discrepancies between buyers and sellers are virtually eliminated.

- Third-party trust elevates the integrity bar of business transactions—by relying on trusted third-party Certificate Authorities, companies have more confidence that their new trading partners share the same integrity.

- Authentication confirms identity of transaction participants—this feature virtually eliminates discrepancies and reduces the cost of transaction validation through follow-up phone calls, fax messages, mailings, etc.

- Reliable security dramatically speeds the process flow of most transactions between two organizations, allowing electronic media to replace the paper-based systems.

- Static, dynamic or attribute responses returned to apps

Techniques to implement role based access controls within a corporation.

- Source IP filtering isn't subject to systemic compromise, and doesn't come with export control restrictions.

- Granularity and Extensibility: To the extent that membership in specific groups can be linked unambiguously to specific network addresses (for example, in an office, a dorm room, or a computer lab) fine grained access is feasible. Such direct linkage is often not the case, however; students in a class may share use of a computer lab, or need to use public workstations in a library.

- Cross-Protocol Flexibility. Since all protocols of interest run on top of IP, source IP address based access control is quite universal.

- Privacy Considerations: To the extent that source IP addresses can be linked to individuals (for example, personal workstations in offices) there are some privacy issues. And certainly source IP addresses are correlated to demographics, if the resource provider is willing to invest in understanding the campus network architecture. Access in a source IP filtering authentication environment is probably somewhere between anonymous and pseudononymous, with some ability to move from pseudononymous to identified access in individual cases if the resource provider is willing to go to the trouble to do so (this is the case of personal workstations used primarily by a single individual).

- Accountability: There is limited accountability—at the level of machines rather than people—which mirrors the privacy situation. One has relatively good accountability for individually-owned personal workstations and relatively poor accountability for everything else; for a large, shared machine one gets accountability to the machine level, and then has to work with the administrator of that machine to identify a specific user or users. If dynamic IP address assignment is used (as is often the case for laptops in public areas, for example), then accountability is particularly weak.

- Management Data: An enterprise can collect some usage data at a highly aggregated level that is not well correlated to application-level constructs through a border router, or get aggregated usage data from the resource operator. Demographic data can be obtained to the extent there is correlation between IP address blocks and demographics (for example, there might be a campus subnet for a medical school); this demographic data will be sketchy and imperfect at best, and some differentiations (such as students as opposed to faculty) will be very hard to extract. Individual level usage data will be possible only in the case where there are personal workstations, and all work by an individual is done on that workstation.

Summary: IP source address based access management tracks the activities of machines rather than people. To the extent that there's a very close correlation between the two, it works reasonably well. Unfortunately, the correlation has never been that good and many trends (such as the move from enterprise modem banks to purchase of commercial dial up access to the internet) continue to weaken this correlation. IP source address access management may work particularly well for fixed-location, enterprise managed public terminals, such a public workstations in libraries or computer labs.

10

eMail, Groupware & Unified messaging

One-To-One electronic messaging (email between people) and one-to-many (broadcast, news publishing or email to groups) have been features of host-based systems for many years; the explosion of local-area PC networks has seen the introduction of many new email systems.

A viable directory based email management system must meet an evolving and very demanding set of requirements imposed by several different constituencies, including IT, upper management, and end users.

- Interoperability: Any email management system must work with existing infrastructure, and provide a single, central point of control and reporting. For most companies, it must work in heterogeneous, geographically distributed environments. Moreover, the system must be capable of scaling to meet demand, and adapting to new technologies.

- Minimal impact: The system must not introduce any new risks, additional latency, or new resource requirements. For many companies, management systems that require high levels of integration with installed mail servers present unacceptable risks.

- Visibility: Current system health and resource usage information needs to be close at hand. Email administrators need real-time information to get immediate status on incoming load, characteristics, and system health. But usage analysis and trend information is equally important for capacity planning, budgeting, and policy enforcement.

- Protection: Any solution deployed needs to protect the organizations' email assets. The system needs to be able to detect threats, preferably in real-time, and mitigate them without email administrator intervention. This should be the condition whether the threat is a virus outbreak or a denial of service attack.

- Reliability: The objective of any email management system must be to maximize resource availability, and mitigate the impact of failure or service interruptions.

Directories enable the efficient management of email and messaging systems

Electronic mail, or email has been around for over two decades. In 1982, the ARPANET email proposals were published as RFC 821 (transmission protocol) and RFC 822 (message format). Two years later, CCITT drafted its X.400 recommendation, which was later taken over as the basis for OSI's MOTIS. In 1988, CCITT modified X.400 to align it with MOTIS. MOTIS was supposed to be the representing application of OSI, a system that was to be all things to all people. After a decade of competition, email system based on RFC 822 are widely used, whereas those based on X.400 have disappeared. The reason for RFC 822's success is not that it is so good, but that few functioning X.400 implementations exist

X.400

The basic service of X400 electronic mail provides the notification of message not given. When a message cannot be given to a recipient an opinion of not given is generated and turned over to the transmitter

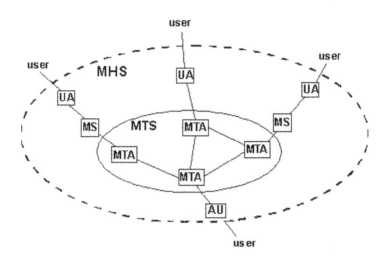

The System of Electronic mail operates in absence of point-to-point connection between the Originator and the Recipient of a message. The MHS heart is the Message Transfer System (MTS) It is a service of general purpose communications, independent of the applications, and implementing store-and-forward service. It is composed of message transfer agents (MTA) which cooperate to relay the messages until their destinations. The MTS operates independently of the type of interchange required by the application and it is transparent compared to the nature of the contents of the message. An MHS direct user reaches MHS services through an User Agent (UA)—it is an application which interacts with the MTS to subject and receive the messages.

- P1: protocol used for the communication from MTA to MTA. It can be compared with the address writen on the envelope containing your letter and which allows to carry out the sorting and the routing of the mail.

- P2: protocol of interpersonal electronic mail. Used between two UA, it can be compared to the standards of letters presentation.

- P3: access protocol to the MTS. Used for the communication enters MTA and MS or between MTA and an UA.

- P7: protocol used between MTA and an UA who is not directly connected to a MTA. In fact it is very similar to P3, except a service of storage intervenes (using Message Store)—apart from the MTA and the UA.

The main variants of X.400 are:

- X.400/1984—published only by the CCITT (which is now named ITU-T)

- X.400/1988—a complete rewrite of the standards, published jointly by ISO and X.400

- A number of updates to the standards, sometimes called X.400/ 1993, but not published as a joint set.

X.400 systems have always relied on directories in the form of X.500 directories to provide routing, access control and identity management features.

SMTP

To transfer mail reliably and efficiently, the Simple Mail Transfer Protocol (SMTP) defines mechanisms for relaying mail between networks on the Internet.

Simple Mail Transfer Protocol (SMTP), documented in RFC 821 is the Internet's standard host-to-host mail transport protocol and operates over TCP port 25. SMTP uses asymmetric request-response protocol developed in the 1980s, The protocol is designed to be interpreted by both computer or a human. The server provides a clear set of commands is well-documented in RFC 821. From a user viewpoint, the replies always take text form starting with a three-digit code identifying the result of the operation with a continuation character to indicate another lines following, and human readable text

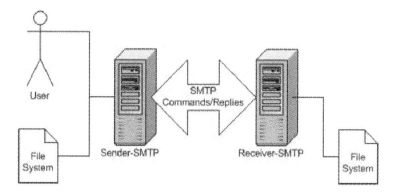

If mail delivery fails, sendmail (the most important SMTP implementation) will queue mail messages and retry delivery later. However, a terminate algorithm is used, and no mechanism exists to poll all Internet hosts for mail. SMTP does not provide any mailbox facility, or any special features beyond mail transport. A better-connected host can be designated as a DNS mail exchanger, then arrange for a relay scheme. There are two main configurations to enable relays. One is to configure POP mailboxes and a POP server on the exchange host, and let all users use POP-enabled mail clients. The other possibility is to arrange for a periodic SMTP mail transfer from the exchange host to another, local SMTP exchange host which has been queuing all the outbound mail.

The SMTP design is based on the following model of communication:

- The user sends a mail request,

- The sender-SMTP establishes a two-way transmission channel to a receiver-SMTP. (The receiver-SMTP may be either the ultimate destination or an intermediate.)

- SMTP commands are then generated by the sender-SMTP and sent to the receiver-SMTP.

- In the response phase SMTP replies are sent from the receiver-SMTP to the sender-SMTP in response to the commands.

- Once the transmission channel is established, the SMTP-sender sends a MAIL command indicating the sender of the mail.

- If the SMTP-receiver can accept mail it responds with an OK reply. The SMTP-sender then sends a RCPT command identifying a recipient of the mail. If the SMTP-receiver can accept mail for that recipient it responds with an affirmative; if not, it responds with a reply rejecting that recipient (but not the whole mail transaction).

The SMTP-sender and SMTP-receiver may negotiate several recipients. When the recipients have been negotiated the SMTP-sender sends the mail data, terminating. If the SMTP-receiver successfully processes the mail data it responds with an OK reply. The SMTP provides mechanisms for the transmission of mail; directly from the sending user's host to the receiving user's host when the two host are connected to the same transport service, or via one or more relay SMTP-servers when the source and destination hosts are not connected to the same transport service.

- RFC 1327 specifies mapping between X.400 and SMTP based Internet mail

- RFC 1328 specifies downgrading from X.400/88 to X.400/84

- RFC 1405 gives a mapping between X.400 and Mail-11 (DECnet)

- RFC 1494, 1495 and 1496 specify mappings between X.400 and Internet mail when MIME is factored into the game

- RFC 1465 specifies a routing documentation format for X.400 networks

- RFC 1502 gives recommendations on how to do extended character sets in X.400

- RFC 1506 is a tutorial on RFC 1327

- RFC 1615 and RFC 1616 talk about how and why to deploy X.400/88

- RFC 1648 interface definition between the Postmaster convention to X.400 networks

- RFC 1649 gives operational requirements for the GO-MHS community (open X.400 on the Internet)

- RFC 1685 specifies how to write O/R names

SMTP systems may utilize directories for profile and routing.

MIME

To allow messages to be more than just plain text, the Multipurpose Internet Mail Extensions (MIME) standard "extends" the format of messages to allow for audio, video, international character sets, and multi-part messages. Most Internet messages are stored in MIME format.

The Multipurpose Internet Mail Extension (MIME) protocol was developed to define a method of moving multimedia files through existing email gateways. The default protocol for standard text messages is defined in RFC 822, and is widely used on the Internet. These messages are sent via SMTP, defined in RFC 821. Both of these have limitations when it comes to sending larger, multimedia files.

RFC 821/822 mail systems do very well for text messages sent in US-ASCII that fall within the limitation of 1000 characters or less per line. However, for international character sets, or image files, this system simply won't work. Another limitation is the possible loss of information when a message is transferred between X.400 and RFC 822 hosts.

This is clearly unacceptable, especially since the message may be relayed forward to another X.400 host which would know how to handle the non-textual information.

However, since the RFC 821/822 mail systems pervade the Internet, a compatible solution needed to be found. MIME provides a nice extension to RFC 822 messages. It is intended to coexist with RFC 822 standards, rather than replace them. It does this by adding five new headers that follow the same format and content rules as those defined in RFC 822. It is important to note that LDAP entries my be expressed as MIME types

POP MAIL

A POP3 mail client uses POP3 to retrieve mail and uses SMTP to send MIME-formatted mail. Post Office Protocol version 3 (POP3) via (port 110) permits workstations to dynamically access a mail drop on a server host (TCP/IP). The Post Office Protocol, version 3 (POP3) is the most commonly used protocol used for retrieving email messages on the Internet. The technical specifications can be found in RFC 1225. Each POP3 session consists of three stages: authorization, transaction, and update. A session is a structured conversation between the POP3 server and the client user agent (UA), more commonly referred to as an email program. In each stage, POP3 commands are sent from the client UA to the POP3 server, and the server sends a reply code of +OK or -ERR back to the client. Both reply codes may be followed by a text string providing more information about the reply.

In POP3 mail is taken from the mail server and handled on your local machine (where your POP mail program is located) any messages that have been downloaded by POP are accessible on the users local workstation when you are not connected to the server. POP makes periodic connections to the e-mail server and transfers messages and then disconnects. It can easily filter and redistribute the users email, since it has to read it all coming in anyway. And since it makes a local copy, users can save all y mail onto floppies or other storage directly. Most POP email programs are already set up to delete your email off the server once the transfer is completed. That means that the users local machine is the only place that your email exists. Unless the user chooses to back up email every day, they could lose all your email if something happens to their local machine.

POP mail systems rely on directories for access and identity management. In addition POP mail systems may use directories for encryption and certificate management. POP servers leverage directory data to manage alias and disk quota information on most major sendmail variants

IMAP MAIL

An IMAP mail client uses IMAP to retrieve mail and uses SMTP to send MIME-formatted mail. The Internet Message Access Protocol (IMAP) defined in RFC 1730 uses port 143 and was designed as a superset of POP3, and enhances both message retrieval and management. The Internet Message Access Protocol (IMAP) is a more recently developed email protocol and it attempts to solve some of the problems raised by POP. It also consists of a mail server, which stores email, for users to access with client programs. The difference is that IMAP assumes you will keep your email on the server, and makes it easy to only download the specific messages you want to see at that time. It allows you to create separate folders for storing messages on the server. You can then access those folders and your "inbox" from several different machines, each running an IMAP client program. From all of them you will see the same set of folders and same messages in the inbox.

With IMAP, mail stays on the server—but it can be either kept on the server or saved your local machine, and "feels" as if the user handling it on their local machine. Since everything takes place on the email server, they can access there email the same way from multiple locations. With IMAP a user can make local copies that can be accessed when they are not connected. Because the IMAP email program needs to maintain a connection to the email server, and messages never get downloaded to the local computer, there is no "off-line" mode. This could cause problems for people who want to do their reading and composition while they are disconnected from the network (on a laptop computer on a plane for example). Since email remains on the email server, if the users are used to a POP email program taking your messages off the email server, the buildup of email on the server may take you by surprise. Deletions take place on a centralized machine, and are reflected in your email listing, so you always know exactly what email exists at any given time and can easily remove unwanted messages. Multiple mailboxes can be created to sort and categorize your mail.

LDAP directories are an essential part of all IMAP deployment. All server based systems leverage the directory for identity management and encryption. IMAP4 permits manipulation of remote message folders, called "mailboxes", in a way that is functionally equivalent to local mailboxes. Directories facilitate this feature. IMAP4 also provides the capability for an offline client to resynchronize with the server. IMAP4 includes operations for creating, deleting, and renaming mailboxes; checking for new messages; permanently removing messages; setting and clearing flags; RFC 822 and MIME parsing; searching; and selective fetching of message attributes, texts.

GROUPWARE

Organizations are increasingly recognizing the importance of managing what they consider their most valuable asset: Knowledge. This work is a contribution towards that end, proposing a system for representing, recording, using, retrieving, and managing individual and group knowledge: a group memory system. It has always been true that a significant part of an organization's knowledge resides in the minds of the people that make it up. However, in the current organizational environment, where downsizing, reengineering, restructuring and high rates of organizational turnover are common, enterprises are beginning to find that it is easy to loose a vital element of their intellectual property: corporate knowledge. Put simply, organizations are beginning to recognize that they can suffer a failure of their collective corporate memory.

Groupware is technology designed to facilitate the work of groups. This technology may be used to communicate, cooperate, coordinate, solve problems, compete, or negotiate. While traditional technologies like the telephone qualify as groupware, the term is ordinarily used to refer to a specific class of technologies relying on modern computer networks, such as email, newsgroups, videophones, or chat.

Groupware technologies are typically categorized along two primary dimensions:

1. whether users of the groupware are working together at the same time ("realtime" or "synchronous" groupware) or different times ("asynchronous" groupware), and

2. whether users are working together in the same place ("colocated" or "face-to-face") or in different places ("non-colocated" or "distance").

The purpose of groupware is to manage knowledge within a company and is a departure from traditional "database" or "messaging" products. A groupware platform provides a structure in which to integrate and relate information from existing sources, while changing the way that people share and use that knowledge.

Modern groupware products are designed from the very start for global use, since its users areblikely to be anywhere in the world. When people use technology to communicate, various types of information are communicated through many channels, both implicitly and explicitly.

Types of awareness information vary from awareness of documents, projects, and tasks to awareness of the location and activities of co-workers. Telepointers, office snapshots, video glances, document/ project tracking, and background noise are some of the various forms of providing awareness, which have been used to date. In creating support for awareness, considerations include: what information to provide, how to provide it, how to give users control of the information, reciprocity, privacy, and interruptions.

Traditional database systems have become the backbone of most corporate information systems. They are designed to manage the tabular information generated by business operations such as order processing, inventory control, and payroll management. These applications are *data-centric;* that is, they are designed to organize information by breaking it into its most basic elements; only sorting and querying these data elements to support specific decisions gain knowledge and information. What they cannot do, however, is embed knowledge in the information itself, or relate it to particular individuals or activities. Furthermore, they are *transaction-oriented,* and built to reflect the most current state of the data. They are generally not good at reflecting the changing states of information over time. If they are distributed, they require a single-system image so that if a number is debited in one place, disconnected users debit it everywhere in a single transaction; in this sense they cannot easily support access.

Traditional electronic mail and messaging systems, on the other hand, are designed for the efficient transmission of messages from one place in an organization to another. They can handle either simple or complex information, and they can deliver it to specific individuals or applications. However, they generally have no facility for capturing or tracking that information; they simply fulfill their destiny of reliable delivery, much as a telephone system reliably transmits from end-to-end without caring whether there are people or modems communicating with each other.

For most organizations, it is extremely important that robust and scalable strategies for both databases and messaging be developed. In addition, it is important for any organization that values knowledge as a corporate asset to develop a strategy for managing and disseminating that knowledge.

Store-and-forward email messaging is necessary but not sufficient for groupware systems. When used as a method of database synchronization, a unidirectional message route is not robust. Their needs to be a connection-oriented, bi-directional, method of document sharing for groupware systems to function.

BI-DIRECTIONAL SYNCHRONIZATION IN OBJECT ORIENTED GROUPWARE SYSTEMS

An object oriented message replication facility means that databases on different servers are automatically synchronized, and change conflicts resolved in much the same way as a directory change log, As in LDAP this paradigm scales easily from two to thousands of replicas of a database. The combination of true replication with an object store—where documents and application design elements are self-contained message objects releases workgroups from constraints of time and geography.

Replication is the process of re synchronizing the contents of one database replica with another database replica. Core replication functions in a groupware object system make it possible for both client and server programs to initiate database replication. Replication can be between a local computer and a server computer or between two servers. Replication can be unidirectional or bi-directional. An edit in one replica will permit the use of replication to merge the edits into another replica of the same database. Replication resolves the most difficult problem that arises in a distributed, real-time groupware product: how to keep multiple copies of databases synchronized while multiple users and programs work on them.

Sending	Sharing	Replication
	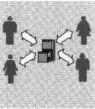	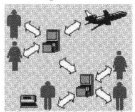
Electronic Mail	Document Database	Full or selective synchronised Database Replicas

Three models for communication: one-to-one messaging, sharing a common database, and distributed documents in replicated databases throughout the world. Groupware servers can often be configured to communicate with one another in a peer-to-peer, hub-and-spoke, or even purely ad hoc topology. Due to the flexible nature of modern object oriented groupware systems, topology planning can often be independent of application or information strategy planning, thus simplifying deployment within a large organization. Flexibility, as always, is the key to long-term management.

CSCW

Because of the peer nature of most groupware architecture, interconnection of servers to other servers or users to servers is treated identically, which is why it's so easy and natural for permitted mobile users to use a modem to connect their computers "into the system". Groupware is designed from the ground-up for occasionally connected communications, whether the entity communicating is a user or another server.

CSCW or "Computer-Supported Cooperative Work" is the study of how people work together using computer technology. Typical applications include email, awareness and notification systems, videoconferencing, chat systems, multi-player games, and real-time shared applications (such as collaborative writing or drawing).

Relevant to the question of criteria is that of the stakeholders in the evaluation: to whom does the evaluation and the system matter? Who has the power to decide what happens to the system? Relevant stakeholders might include:

- Systems developers, whose concern will be with functionality, efficacy and usability

- Individual users, whose concern will be with efficacy, usability, and effects on individuals

- Middle management (the ones with the checkbooks), concerned with efficacy, individual effects and organizational effects

- Top management (the strategists), concerned with organizational effects, standards and effects on society (maybe!)

- Employee representatives (such as trade unions), concerned with individual effects, group effects and usability

- Outside parties (governments, the public, standards bodies), concerned with standards, individual effects and the effects on society

CSCW includes many computer science notions and technologies including HCI, networks, multimedia, object oriented concepts, virtual reality, and artificial intelligence. These are not the only technologies used in Groupware applications; the most appropriate technology is used for specific cooperative communication tasks. Several technologies may be used in the collaboration process.

Video Conferencing Server

Video Conferencing Servers, a CSCW application, provides an extensible platform for real-time online conferencing. A user can schedule and conduct online conferences with live audio and video, and you can offer additional features such as whiteboard drawings, chat, application sharing, and file transfer. Users can structure online conferences by reserving conference resources, inviting conference participants, and setting the properties for each conference. Conferences can be public or private and can accommodate two or more attendees. The centralized reservation system allows users to schedule and join conferences from the calendar. Video Conferencing Servers provides powerful tools for real-time collaboration between coworkers in large and small companies. The majority of video conferencing servers are based on T.120 protocols and IP multicast protocols. Directories act as intermediaries posting availability and protocol between participants

Data Conferencing Servers

Data Conferencing Servers, another CSCW application, are a conferencing technology that provides multiple collaboration tools, including multiparty application sharing, chat, whiteboard drawings, and file transfer. These features are often based on the T.120 International Telecommunications Union—Telecommunication Standardization Sector (ITU-T) Recommendation for Multimedia Conferencing. Data Conferencing Servers creates a data conferencing environment that optimizes conference performance and network resources, and provides a bridge for participants on remote sites and across firewalls. Directories again act as intermediaries posting resource location and data format between participating systems

KNOWLEDGE MANAGEMENT

A global enterprise vision (or group memory view) is a representation of what matters to people at different levels and positions at the organization. The knowledge management will provide a group memory overview of employee's capabilities, project experiences, and essential knowledge areas of expertise. Integrated because it uses a shared representation, meaning, and visualization of the organization: organizational structure, past and current projects and the related business processes, and people involved. The knowledge management will act as an environment where different people (at the individual and group level) with different interests and skills will manage heterogeneous and distributed knowledge embedded in business process activities. The enterprise vision addressed in this paper is composed of five enterprise dimensions: organizational (group) structure, competence management, business processes, project experiences, and knowledge sources, including data, information and physical resources. Advances in information technologies and directories and emerging trends in knowledge management and organizational memories, are enhancing the ability of users to communicate and coordinate among business processes. In order to categories and classify such organizational knowledge for future reuse, appropriate tools must be developed. The practical result of this research work is the design and implementation of a group memory system to manage heterogeneous and distributed knowledge embedded in business process activities.

The main difference between a traditional database management system and a system that can be cited as knowledge-based is an additional inference layer that must be incorporated. The directory facilitates this role; the directory assists specific corporate activities in the competence management context. Such inference layer will assist semi-automatically a systematic categorization and classification of individual and group competencies including their levels of granularity. Underlying this hierarchy of competencies and the related project experiences, competence gaps can be identified within the organization.

UNIFIED MESSAGING

Unified Messenger, including voice mail domains, addressing, client and server operations, and telephony concepts. Today the internet, e-mail, voice mail, and fax are established as strategic, enabling technologies at companies large and small. As a result, users are receiving both a larger volume and more types of messages However, each kind of message typically requires its own access medium (telephone, personal computer, or fax device) and support structure (capital equipment, management tools, and service procedures). The task of retrieving, prioritizing, and storing messages can be inconvenient, complex, and time-consuming, even though messaging should enhance and streamline the communications process. Unified Messenger enables everyone to view, listen to, send, store, and retrieve all their messages from one mailbox (the "unified mailbox") with whatever access tool is the most convenient at any particular time: telephone, desktop computer, portable computer, or fax device. With Unified Messenger, organizations can simplify communications administration, maintain accurate messaging directories, and reduce communication costs.

Voice

A Unified Messenger voice mail domain is a group of Unified Messenger voice servers that share the same set of properties. The servers in a voice mail domain can be seen as a single, "virtual" server for that domain. This virtual voice server allows any Unified Messenger subscribers in the domain to call in using the telephone user interface, access their mailboxes, and retrieve their messages. Also, the virtual voice server can call the telephone of any subscriber who runs Unified Messenger PC client applications to play back voice messages. Any changes made to a voice mail domain's properties are updated and replicated automatically to all voice servers in the domain. Voice mail domains provide the ability to store and retrieve properties that belong to a set of servers working together to give integrated call answering.

The voice server is a gateway between the LAN (data) and the telephone network (voice). It provides the following functions:

- Call management. Provides an interface between the voice cards and the Unified Messenger telephony applications.

- Messaging. Provides communication between SMTP and the Unified Messenger applications.

- User Profile. Provides access to the data associated with individual subscribers, such as numeric address and spoken name.

- Text-to-speech. The voice server includes a speech synthesis device that allows subscribers to hear their e-mail messages over the telephone. This feature is also used for name confirmation, when a recorded name is not available.

- Multilingual Translation: This identifies the language of e-mail messages and translates them in that language.

PBX

The telephone switch (PBX) transfers calls from within the enterprise or from the outside telephone network (PSTN) to the Unified Messenger voice server. Using PBX integration, the voice server receives information about calls as they are routed, such as:

- Who the call was originally intended for (called party).

- Who placed the call (calling party).

- What caused the call to be directed to the voice server (for example, there was no answer or the telephone was busy).

FAX

The fax server is a component to which the voice server delegates all functionality related to sending and receiving faxes. Unified Messenger systems, in conjunction with a compatible fax server, offers the following fax features:

- Fax messages can be received and stored in a subscriber's mailbox.

- Subscribers can send fax messages and e-mail messages to fax devices for printing.

- A copy of a subscriber's Inbox listing can be faxed to a fax device through the telephone user interface.

11

Portal Systems & Application Servers

A portal creates a single access point for

- Employees (intranet)

- Partners (extranet)

- Customers (Internet)

- Portals deliver:

- An integrated web-top environment from isolated programs and information silos

- Automated identification and distribution of content relevant to the user

- A personalized interface for each user based on their role in the organization

Portals Drive ROI

- Leverage human capital

- Act on accurate information

- Find what you're looking for with personalized view

- Increased revenue

- Easy for partners and customers to do business

- All information needed, 24-hours-day
- Cost effective control
- Consolidate multiple apps, multiple websites
- Manage fewer environments
- Distribute worldwide
- Leverage your existing and future IT investments

The costs are usually divided as:

- Server license(s)
- End User licenses
- Support Fees
- Consulting & Customization Costs

In addition to other situation-specific criteria, users must evaluate any independent on its:
1) financial viability
2) global sales/support
3) ability to maintain deep/broad application integration facilities
4) integration with application servers
5) contextual collaboration and community services rollout
6) strength of role and process management facilities
7) price

In general licenses for a single server can range from 25K-100K. Costs for end user licenses can vary depending on how many you are buying and what kind of discounting they are willing to give you—we have seen from $25 per end user up to $400 per end user for the portal packages that are out there. At $100 per end user and 5000 users you have a 500K software cost.

Any architect should expect to spend at least as much on consulting as is spend on software. In some cases it is 2-5x the software price. The amount of consulting/customization an implementation needs depends on how much out of the box functionality the client can live with and how many "portlets" have to be custom built.

There is convergence between the pure-play portal solutions and the application servers, where the pure-plays are trying to provide more flexibilty and the application servers are trying to provide more functionality out of the box. We will address both as scparate technologies knowing that a substantial functional overlap exists.

PORTAL SERVERS

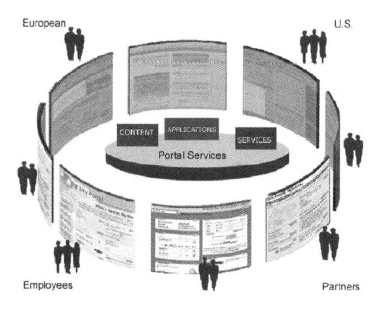

There has always been a clear division between public and private networks. A public network, like the Internet, is a large collection of unrelated peers that exchange information more or less freely with each

other. People with access to the public network may or may not have anything in common, and any given person on that network may only communicate with a small fraction of the network's potential users.
A private network, on the other hand, is comprised of computers usually owned by a single organization that share specific information with each other. These users are assured that they are going to be the only ones accessing this network, and that information sent between them will be only seen by others in the enterprise. The typical corporate Local Area Network (LAN) or Wide Area Network (WAN) is one such example of a private network. The line between a private and a public network has always been drawn at the gateway router, where a company installs a firewall to keep intruders using the public network out of the private network, or keep their own internal users from perusing the public network.

A virtual private network (VPN) is a way to simulate a private network over a public network. A portal server creates a VPN in a way that blurs the line between a public and a private network in a more secure way. A portal server users create a virtually secure, private session over a public network such as the Internet.

A portal is a community-based web site that securely holds a collection of data related to different topics, including such things as news and stock quotes, applications, and services. The available data content may be customized by the user that has write permission to change providers, display of data, and links to other allowable web sites from those available. Services can include the use of provider applications and utilities; for example email and file management and storage facilities. A corporate portal is a personalized web page that brings together data and productivity tools relevant to corporate users. Corporate users can include employees, vendors, marketing partners, customers, and allied business users From a corporate portal, customers can purchase a product in a secure e-business transacting environment. Likewise, vendors can provide product to the corporation.

Content Infrastructure is Critical to Portals

- Content Infrastructure drives successful portals

- Extend content contribution without loss of control

- Deliver relevant, timely content

- Reuse content across all initiatives with best of breed architecture

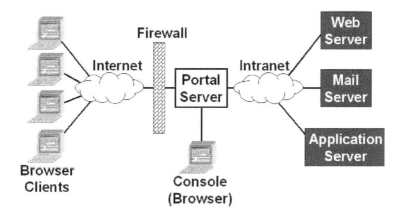

A Portal Server enables remote users to securely access their organization's network and its services over the Internet. Additionally, it gives your organization a secure Internet portal, providing access to content, applications, and data to any targeted audience—employees, business partners, or the general public.

A Portal Server system includes the following features:

- Cost-effective, efficient and secure access to internal corporate information, personal email, productivity applications, and internal web sites.

- Leverage to the Internet and Internet service providers (ISPs) to reduce costs.

- Simplification of remote access for end users.

- Selective authentication scheme from one of six included modules

- Customization of authentication via pluggable modules.

- Independent software interfaces for users and administrators.

- Local or remote administration through a web-based console from either Internet Explorer or Netscape browsers.

- Controlled user access to corporate resources at any level of granularity.

Most Portal Server gateways provide the interface and security barrier between the remote user sessions originating from the Internet and the corporate intranet.

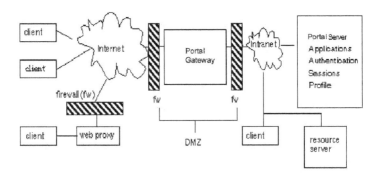

A major part of implementing a Portal Server platform involves organizing users and applications into a hierarchy. Through the structure, an administrator can be designated to manage gateways and servers, control access to the site's intranet, design the portal page, and determine the look and feel of users' desktops.

Most Portal Server software on the market has two main components:
The gateway component of the Portal Server product
The server component of the Portal Server product

For security reasons, the recommended installation is to put the gateway component of the Portal Server product on a computer separate from the server component. The server component and gateway component can, however, be installed on the same computer if chosen

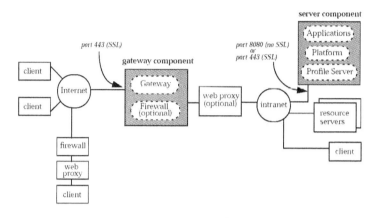

The gateway component

The gateway component of the Portal Server product contains the following components: the encrypting proxy (eproxy), and the optional firewall. By default, the gateway is configured to listen for client traffic from the Internet on port 443. The gateway component of a Portal Server product uses the transport layer security secure socket layer protocol (TLS-TLS) to communicate with a browser, and can be configured to use TLS to communicate with the server component.

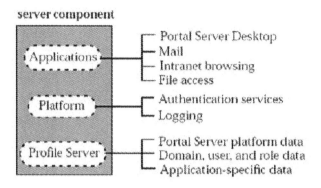

The Server component

The server component of the Portal Server product contains a profile server, the platform, and the applications. (If you are using multiple server components, only one server in the installation group contains the profile server.) The profile server stores the majority of the Portal Server platform, user, and application-specific data. The platform includes services such as authentication and logging. The applications include desktop, mail, intranet browsing, and file access. The server component of the Portal Server product is configured to listen for traffic (non-TLS) from the gateway component of the Portal Server product on port 8080 by default; it can be configured to listen for TLS traffic from the gateway component on port 443.

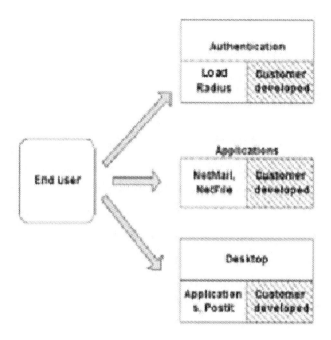

Portal Server can be extended in several ways,

Business Specific

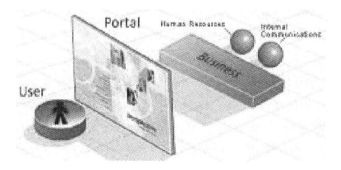

Functional Portal:A portal delivering applications for a single corporate function

(e.g., HR, Finance)
Benefit: To improve the effectiveness and efficiency of the function

The consumer portal, also called Internet portals, addresses the needs of an even wider user base than the enterprise portal. Consumer portals can be divided into two types: vertical and horizontal. Vertical portals are sites that focus on a subset of the Internet market. These are portals that cater to users with a common interest, for example, a portal for users interested in travel. Though the user base is large, the site's focus and content is limited. Horizontal portals, often called mega portals, are large-scale sites that bring together a wide range of unrelated information. Many of these sites provide their own applications as well as links to other sites. Yahoo.com is an example of a horizontal portal. The horizontal portal has similar technology and infrastructure requirements as a vertical portal. It is only distinguished from the vertical portal by the size of the user base and the scope of content.

Functional Solution:A web application for a single corporate process (e.g., new hire, travel, time and attendance, recruitment etc)
Benefit: To improve the effectiveness and efficiency of a particular process

Enterprise Specific

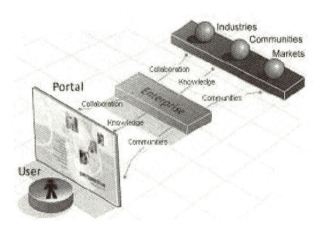

Enterprise Portal: A multifunctional, enterprise portal which creates a personalized work environment for employees, that can be accessed any time, from any place.

Benefit: One environment, e-culture, mind share, new way of working.

An enterprise portal is one that aggregates business applications and information to match specific needs of its user population. An enterprise portal can be internally focused if the users are employees, or externally focused if the users are primarily partners and customers. An example of an enterprise portal that is externally focused is Coradon.com, whose site includes information about the company's products and services. An enterprise portal's main purpose is to address the needs of the business, its customers, and its partners. This type of site focuses on the extranet and internet user, who may be registered or anonymous. Personalization, user registration, and anonymous user support are just some of the features that make a portal capable of handling a variety of users with a wide range of business needs. The enterprise portal can also provide access to intranet users, making a variety of internal resources available. For example, a company's employees can access corporate information appropriate to internal personnel only. Enterprise portals also offer links to partner sites and related industry sites, also referred to as affiliate sites, that extend the usefulness of a portal. Even the functions of enterprise portals are expanding as the integration of data and applications increase.

Thin Portals: An enterprise portal to deliver global corporate communications and linkages to existing Intranet and Internet applications or sites

Benefit: To provide one channel for communications and facilitate searching for and accessing information

Portals, extranets, and intranets need to address the expanding and diverse user base and the ways these users access information. To do this, portals need to consider the following issues when implementing e-commerce infrastructure:

- Securing content: To increase business, sites need to allow users access without exposing themselves to security risks. Secure authentication and authorization must be available, which includes the ability to apply more strict security measures to sensitive resources.

- Managing users, entitlements, and granular access control reliably and cost effectively: Access must be based on entitlements, permitting different levels of access to different users; keeping the administration of user profiles efficient for entitlement-based access control is critical.

- Customizing the user experience: Users across the Internet economy want a positive experience when accessing information or engaging in a transaction. In addition to feeling that transactions are secure, users want to traverse different areas of a site without having to re-enter credentials each time, to visit sites related to their original destination, and to view content relevant to their needs. A successful e-business site must address these needs and find ways to distinguish themselves from their competition to retain user loyalty.

- Scaling for large and small numbers of users and handling data traffic Providing comprehensive capabilities to respond quickly to user requests even during high-peak traffic is important. If response is slow, users will go to other sites where they can get their information more quickly. In addition, a site needs to integrate legacy and new applications together.

- Integrating existing systems together with new Web-based methods of doing business Being able to deploy e-business across heterogeneous hardware and software environments is necessary. Existing user directories may also need to be integrated.

- Providing a seamless integration between portal and affiliate Visitors to a portal site should be able to link easily to related businesses. Establishing relationships should result in increased visibility and revenues for both the portal and the affiliate.

Session Management

Sessions are a general mechanism which server side connections can use to both store and retrieve information on the client side of the connection. The addition of a simple, persistent, client-side state significantly extends the capabilities of Web-based client/server applications. A server, when returning an HTTP object to a client, may also send a piece of state information which the client will store.

Included in that state object is a description of the session credentials for which that state is valid. Any future HTTP requests made by the client which fall in that range will include a transmittal of the current value of the state object from the client back to the server.

There are two main types of sessions:
• User session
• Application session

A user session is associated with a user. An application session is associated with an application without the context of a user. The session type (user or application) property in a session is used to distinguish a user session from an application session. A session is created when a user or an application authenticates itself successfully. The authentication service creates a new session in the Portal Server through a private interface provided by the Session Service.

APPLICATION SERVERS

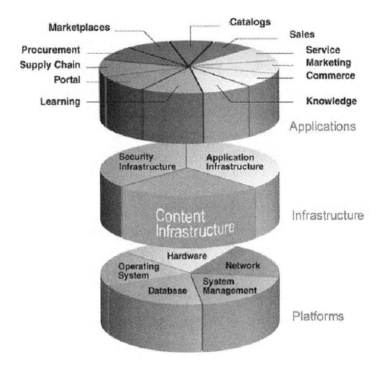

An Application Server is the middleware between enterprise data sources and the clients that access those data sources. Business code is stored and processed on the Application Server rather than on clients. An application is deployed and managed in a single location, and the application is accessible to large numbers of heterogeneous clients. Applications on an application server run in a distributed, multitiered environment. This means that an enterprise system might consist of several application along with multiple database servers and web servers. The application code can then be distributed among the application servers.

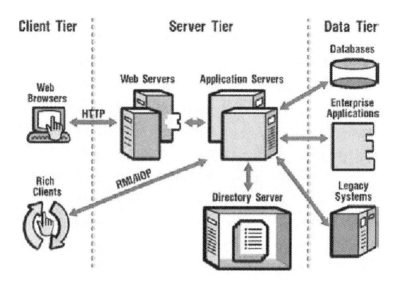

Overall, the machines and software involved are divided into three tiers:

- a client tier, represented by web browsers or rich clients.

- a server tier, represented by a web server and an application server.

- a data tier, represented by relational databases or other back-end data sources.

The application server handles requests by running the appropriate application code (and accessing data sources if needed). The application server then returns the results to the web server, which in turn forwards the reply back to the client.

An application server Provides a single E-Commerce platform to build business-to-business, business-to-employee and business-to-consumer e-commerce solutions andenables rapid development of enterprise applications through the use of

- a multi-tier application model.

- core services for building high-performance, scalable, transactional applications.

- standardized application development tools.

The result of this approach is

- Faster time-to-production

- Higher functionality web solutions

- No resources wasted modifying existing enterprise applications

- Enhanced management and performance of enterprise system services

An application model is a *conceptual* division of an application into functional components.
it divides an application into multiple layers

- presentation

- business logic layer

- data and legacy access

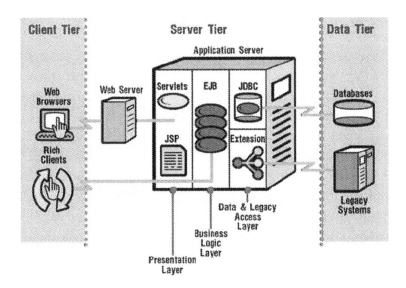

The application server is the "workhorse" enterprise software that provides application infrastructure for modern business systems. Application servers evolved from the need to support applications that share data and resources with other systems, and generate dynamic information for Web pages and other user interfaces. They introduced into server-side architecture, a new layer of functions and services between Web servers and underlying applications and databases

Presentation Layer

The Presentation Layer separates the key elements of application presentation and management from application business logic. Delivering the user-interface—defining the terms on which the user can interact with the application. By abstracting the presentation layer the developer is able to give the portal or application a common look and feel and common navigation across the enterprise

Business Logic Layer

The Business Layer contains the application's business logic independent of the user interface, including distributed components, running in the application server environment. The majority of application servers on the market support the J2EE framework as the preferred business logic abstraction layer. Within the J2EE framework these components are usually represented by Enterprise JavaBeans. Java Beans or EJBs provide scalable, portable, server-side components for interacting with any kind of client. Developers can focus on the business purpose of the objects and methods. EJB container handles the underlying infrastructure services, such multi-threading, load balancing, clustering, object life cycle, transactions, security, messaging, and persistence. The portability of the J2EE architecture enables EJBs written in Java to be deployed on any platform and operating system supporting Java.

There are three major types of enterprise beans defined in EJB 2.0:
• Session Beans are business process objects that act as verbs that perform actions, such as transferring funds between two bank accounts, performing purchase order approval routing, or calculating the price of an order.
• Entity Beans are data objects that act as nouns and usually represent real-life objects, such as bank accounts, purchase orders, employees, companies, and vendors. Entity beans are in-memory objects that physically map to data stored in underlying relational databases or legacy systems. Persistence can be manually performed by the developer (bean-managed persistence) or by the application Server (container managed persistence). Typically, session beans "call" entity beans to achieve their desired actions, such as a purchase order approval router (session bean) that deals with purchase orders (entity beans).
• Message-Driven Beans are messaging objects that are designed to receive and route messages from clients to other Enterprise Java Beans.

For example, a logging service can receive logging messages and "call" a session bean to perform the actual logging.

Data and legacy access Layer

The application server works within the framework of existing access controls for both LDAP and relational database management systems. A user or application must log into the database before gaining access to the data. Developers can write applications so that users enter login information only once and the application saves the information in a session object. Thereafter, the application uses the initial login information to log into different databases, as needed, in the background without requiring additional user input. An Application Server shields back-end data by acting as a secure gatekeeper between the web server and the directory or relational database system.

COMPONENTS COMMON TO PORTALS AND APPLICATION SERVERS

Portal platforms are products that are used to integrate unstructured content, business intelligence, and applications into a single corporate and e-business portal solution. Portal platforms therefore come with a set of portal services, that support all these types of content as well as other critical components that integrate with your corporate infrastructure.

Portal services are effectively components of a portal or application server that together make up the services a portal has to offer. For example a content categorization service, a search service, a publish service, a security service, a directory service etc. Portal Services commonly provided by an application server include

- Common Development Kit
- Thread Management

- Failure Recovery
- Session Management
- Security

Common Development Kit

Portal platforms should provide support for a portal development kit to connect to all types of content, support for and integration with web application servers, support for web services to dynamically integrate content into portals without forcing corporations to develop non-portable portal adaptors that are proprietary to a single portal platform. In addition, portal platforms are the single "horizontal" portal that other content specific portals should plug into.

Thread Management

An application server supports the multi-threading capabilities of the host operating system. An application can optimize performance by processing requests on multiple threads, which maximizes CPU resource utilization. Application developers automatically take advantage of multi-threading in their applications. In addition, developers can run database operations such as queries, inserts, updates, deletes, and so on, asynchronously. Asynchronous operations allow an application to do other work while a time-consuming operation, such as a large query, runs in the background.

An application server assigns threads from a dynamic thread pool. As such System administrators can use the Application Server to specify settings for multi-threading, such as the following:

- minimum and maximum number of threads to handle all requests
- minimum and maximum number of threads to handle asynchronous database requests.

Components commonly found is a thread management subsystem include

- Thread Manager: provides the dynamic pool from which threads are assigned.

- Queue Manager: manages the list of pending requests and monitors whether the maximum queue length, or "high watermark," has been exceeded.

- Request Logging: stores information about requests in a back-end database. By default, this service is off.

Failure Recovery

An application server enables the developer to distribute all or part of an application across multiple servers. As a result, if one server goes down, the other servers can continue to handle requests. An application server also minimizes downtime by providing automatic application restarting. Developers need not be concerned with building recovery and scalability features into their application. The application inherits these features simply by being hosted on the runtime environment.

Session Management

As a result of this approach the application server maintains integrity of shared state and session data. State is maintained and replicated in a distributed user-session information and distributed application-state information. Information is maintained as long as more than one application server installation is running in a cluster with the server that crashed. Most application servers provide a number of classes and interfaces that application developers can use to maintain state and user session information. State and session information is stored on each server in a distributed environment. For example, an application can display a login screen, prompt users to enter their user name and password, then save this information in a session object. Thereafter, the application uses this same information to log in to multiple databases without prompting the user to type it in again. Similarly, in an online shopping application, a session object can store a list of products selected for purchase (such as quantity, price, and so on) and persistent variables (such as running order totals). State and session management is especially important for applications that have complex, multi-step operations. In an environment where application logic is partitioned across different servers, system administrators can use

Security

Most application servers provide secure web server communication and supports TLS-TLS, HTTPS, and HTTP challenge-response authentication. Event logging and tracking enables detection of, and protection against, unauthorized access.

APPLICATION AND PORTAL CLUSTERS

An application or portal cluster is two or more application or portal servers connected by a reliable network
A cluster provides:

- Synchronization of session and state data

- High availability through failure recovery

- Application scalability

Policy	Advantage	Disadvantage
Round robin	Simplest; least overhead	No intelligence
Weighted round robin	Accounts for different types of machines	Limited intelligence. Ignores dynamic conditions
Server response time	Accounts for network delays	Ignores differences in per-component response
Component response time (the default)	Accounts for network delays and individual components	Slightly more overhead needed to maintain
Application Server Based	Finest possible control	Difficult to configure; measuring and broadcasting the info affects performance

12

EDI and Financial Services

As Internet business continues to grow, the mechanisms surrounding commerce are starting to change. Currently, Internet commerce follows a simple two-party model. There is a buyer and a seller, and payment is handled over traditional channels. This model inhibits the growth of business-to-business e-commerce. In the real world, commerce is a complex process, with intermediaries providing products and services, which facilitate the transaction, and minimize the risks involved. As more and more products and services are sold online, organizations will expect these associated services to be delivered online as well. New entrants into this services market are threatening the profits of the traditional intermediaries in commercial exchange.

The goal of Electronic Commerce is do conduct business faster, better and cheaper and the appropriate technology should be used for the level of readiness of a "trading partner". EDI advocates can claim that there methods are superior because business is conducted without human intervention for the lowest possible cost of processing. EC advocates can claim that they can reach the greatest number of trading partners with fast secure exchange of business documents.

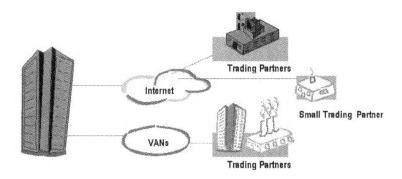

Electronic Commerce generally refers to "doing business electronically" and increasingly to business conducted via the internet. Companies are learning to work better, faster and cheaper by using Electronic Commerce to reach new customers and shorten the Supply Chain. Consumers usually see electronic commerce as a web site where shopping and purchasing can occur "online". Business users of Electronic Commerce strive to move business documents once printed on paper via electronic networks. In a manufacturing and distribution environment where goods are made and shipped "just in time" there is no place for paper and mail exchange of purchase orders, invoices and payments. Electronic Commerce refers to the such documents when they are sent by fax, email or any variety of methods which are electronic but are usually read by someone before being data-entered into a computer. The exchange of highly standardized business documents that can be sent from computer to computer with human intervention is called Electronic Data Interchange.

EDI

One of the more commonly accepted definitions of Electronic Data Interchange, or EDI, has been "the computer-to-computer transfer of information in a structured, pre-determined format." Traditionally, the focus of EDI activity has been on the replacement of pre-defined business forms, such as purchase orders and invoices, with similarly defined electronic forms.

In it's simplest form, EDI is the electronic exchange of information between two business concerns (referred to in the EDI world as trading partners), in a specific predetermined format. The exchange occurs in basic units called messages, or transaction sets, which typically relate to standard business documents, such as Purchase Orders and Customer Invoices. Over time the business community has arrived at series of standardized transaction formats to cover a wide range of business communication needs.

Each transaction set has an extensive set of data elements required for that business document, with specified formats and sequences for each data element. The various data elements are built up into segments, or logically related groups of data, such as vendor address (which would be made up of data elements for street, city, state, zip code, and country).

All of the related segments for a transaction are then grouped together, and are preceded by a transaction header and followed by a transaction trailer record. If the transaction contains more than one transaction (many purchase orders sent to one vendor) several transaction groups would be preceded by another type of record, referred to as a functional group header, and would be followed by a function group trailer.

EDI standards were first developed on an industry-by-industry basis in the 1970s. The Banking industry developed its NACHA standards while the Transportation and other industries worked on industry specific standards. These pioneers in standard setting soon realized that there was a need to have cross industry standards so that documents such as purchase orders and invoices could be sent from any one company to another, regardless of industry. In 1979 Accredited Standards Committee X12 was founded to be the cross-industry standards development organization accredited by the American National Standards Institute. It is often referred to as ANSI ASC X12. Membership in ASC X12 is composed of over500 companies, government agencies and non-profit corporations

In the late 1980s and early 1990s, electronic commerce, specifically Electronic Data Interchange (EDI), emerged as a powerful tool to help corporations reduce the costs of business processes. In the latter half of the 1990s, a new paradigm emerged: Internet commerce, based on interoperable, Internet-specific EDI standards.

Traditional Document Exchange

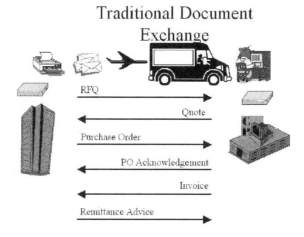

RFQ

Quote

Purchase Order

PO Acknowledgement

Invoice

Remittance Advice

EDI - X12 / EDIFACT

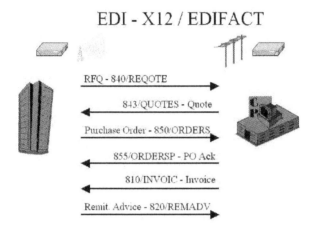

RFQ - 840/REQOTE

843/QUOTES - Quote

Purchase Order - 850/ORDERS

855/ORDERSP - PO Ack

810/INVOIC - Invoice

Remit. Advice - 820/REMADV

Electronic Data Interchange (EDI) is the exchange of routine business transactions in a computer-based format, covering such traditional applications as, purchasing, acknowledgments, shipping and receiving, invoices, payments, and financial reporting. EDI transaction set standards are often first used as a replacement for repetitive paper-based business communications (such as purchase orders or claim forms). The goal of EDI is to pass and process information without human involvement (unlike fax and E-mail).

EDI Files

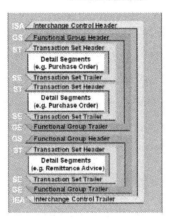

EDI Interchanges

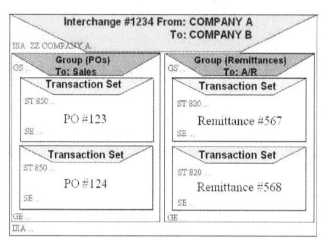

EDI is the exchange, among organizational entities, of computer processable data in a standard format. This standard format is not a computer "language", and there is no "incompatibility" between it and any user's computer software and operating system. Use of an EDI standard is somewhat analogous to the use of International Morse Code for radio communications. One electronic standard can similarly be used across multiple languages. Users of EDI need to translate information to or from their internal computer systems into the EDI standard that is used for transmission to and from other entities.

EDI is also used as a substitute for other types of contacts such as phone calls, fax, and face-to-face discussions. Consider the example of a hospital that needs to know if a patient is eligible for medical services. Without EDI, an administrator would make a phone call. With EDI, the administrator can send an eligibility inquiry via computer and receive a response. Additionally, an insurer may choose to update its providers with eligibility information on a periodic basis. The automated trading of information can streamline an existing process to the benefit of both parties.

In order to avoid the difficulties and expenses that would be incurred if each institution were to impose its own proprietary formats on every institution with which it transacts business, national standards for EDI were developed.

One of the first places that EDI was traditionally implemented was in the purchasing operations of a business. Before the implementation of EDI, a purchasing system would allow buyers to review their material requirements, and then create purchase orders, which would be printed out and mailed. The supplier would receive the purchase order, and manually enter it into their customer shipping system. The material would be shipped, and an invoice would be printed, which would then be mailed back to the supplier.

Even if the purchased materials were shipped and received on the same day the purchase order was received, the cycle time could be as much as a week, depending on the speed of the mail and the backlog at the supplier's order entry system. With the introduction of EDI, this process changed dramatically. Purchasing agents would still review their material requirements and create their purchase orders. But instead of printing them out and mailing them, the purchase orders would be transmitted directly to the suppliers over an electronic network.

On the supplier's end, the transaction would be automatically received and posted. This new process could allow the shipment of material on the same day the purchase order was sent. As an added bonus, suppliers could send their shipping documentation electronically to the buyer in the form of a shipment notification, providing the buyer with accurate receiving documents prior to the actual arrival of the material. And the supplier gained an additional advantage as well, since now the invoice could be sent directly to the customer's accounts payable system, speeding payment to the supplier.

EDI is a process that can touch many parts of a business. It is crucial to get involvement of all affected parties within the business. Also it is equally important to develop a good working relationship with the individuals and groups that will be affected within the new trading partner's organization.

It is important to remember that EDI implementation will eliminate paper documents that have probably been the single most visible focus of many jobs. Removing that paper will generate a considerable degree of insecurity. It must be replaced with the confidence that "the system" has the paper, all the time, every time. Extended involvement of the user community in requirements definition, pilot projects, testing, and parallel testing is vital, and should be a high priority consideration for the EDI coordinator.

The changes in the computer technology environment and the increasingly integral role information technology now plays in today's manufacturing, distribution and service environments, along with changes in business philosophy and practices, have changed the definition of Electronic Data Interchange. The definition must now be more encompassing than merely the rapid transmission of electronic documents.

EDI must now be viewed as "an enabling technology that provides for the exchange of critical data between computer applications supporting the process of business partners by using agreed-to, standardized, data formats". EDI is no longer merely a way to transmit documents. It is a means to dynamically move data between companies that will be used by computer systems to order raw materials, schedule production, schedule and track transportation, and replenish stock.

To address the security issue, the Internet Engineering Task Force (IETF) formed the Electronic Data Interchange-Internet Integration (EDIINT) Work Group. The original Internet Request For Comment (RFC) on EDI and plain Multipurpose Internet Mail Extensions (MIME) were authored by David Crocker. RFC 1767 was a good foundation, but it did not address security or implementation guidelines. The EDIINT Work Group built on this foundation and established the Requirements for Interoperable, Secure EDI. The formal

Internet-draft for MIME-based Secure EDI specifies the Internet standards needed to securely exchange EDI documents using MIME and public key cryptography. For important information about how leading software vendors are conducting interoperability tests for MIME-based secure EDI.

Benefits of EDI

To remain competitive in today's global economy, businesses are being forced to re-evaluate the way the do business with their customers and their vendors. The focus of these relationships has moved relentlessly towards greater speed through shorter transaction cycles.

At the same time, however, there is a growing emphasis on flexibility, in being able to respond quickly to changes in consumer preference and demand. These two factors, together with the necessity of delivering high quality products to gain and maintain customer loyalty, while keeping rigidly controlling and/or reducing costs, define the significant challenge of business in the future.

With the dramatic increases in price/performance of computer technology, the impact of some of the drawbacks that led to limited implementation of EDI are being is being reduced. What used to require mainframe power (and specially conditioned environments) can now be handled on computers that fit conveniently on or under the desk, and can operate in the office, warehouse, or production floor.

There is a similar revolution going on in the software industry. The elapsed time from conception to deployment of new software is being dramatically reduced through such the implementation of object-oriented software design, increasingly powerful 4GL development tools, and rapid application development techniques. Software developers can now produce packages that can run on a variety of hardware platforms, allowing them concentrate on delivering greater functionality and flexibility to their core packages, rather than spending precious development time and dollars on customization for a specific platform.

The general benefits of using EDI are derived from the use of computer processing and information networks to streamline and enhance business activities conducted with external parties. EDI can:

1. Eliminate the cost of paper, voice, or mail handling

    *   No data re-entry required by receiver

    *   No postage or courier charges

    *   Handle large volumes of messages without an increase in staffing

2. Expedite the speed of communication

    *   A single message can be simultaneously routed to multiple parties

    *   Receiver's actions can be automatic for some messages

    *   Messages can be sent/received at any time

    *   Information moving between computers moves more rapidly, and with little or no human intervention.

    *   Sending an electronic message across the country takes minutes or less.

    *   Mailing the same document will usually take a minimum of one day.

    *   Courier services can reduce the time (while substantially increasing the cost) but at best can shorten the cycle to hours.

    *   Facsimile transmissions work well for small documents, but for several hundred pages, it's not a feasible solution.

3. Expedite the accuracy of communication. Even when alternate means of document transfer are used they suffer from the major drawback of requiring re-entry into the customer order system, admitting the opportunity of keying errors. But information that passes directly between computers without having to be re-entered eliminates the chance of transcription error. There is almost no chance that the receiving computer will invert digits, or add an extra digit.

   - One-time data entry at the source

   - Reduced errors; improved error detection via automated edits

4. Improve overall management of information

   - Uniformly structured and defined messages conveyed to each party

5. Provide access to additional applications and services, such as:

   - Directories (e.g., trading partner ID)

   - Information bases (e.g., utilization information)

   - Electronic mailboxes (e.g., interpersonal communications)

6. Economics

The cost of sending an electronic document is not a great deal more than regular first class postage. Add to that the reductions in cost afforded by eliminating the re-keying of data, human handling, routing, and delivery. The net result is a substantial reduction in the cost of a transaction.

XML

XML (eXtensible Markup Language) is a simplified subset of the Standard Generalized Markup Language (SGML, ISO 8879) which provides a file format for representing data, a schema for describing data structure, and a mechanism for extending and annotating HTML with semantic information.

For a quarter-century, electronic data interchange standards for purchase orders and other documents have been the basis for electronic commerce between large businesses. But traditional EDIFACT & ANSI X12 EDI is likely to be replaced by a newer Web-oriented technology called Extensible Markup Language (XML). Among other things, XML is expected to make life easier for small companies to do business electronically.

One point of concern is whether XML, approved by the World Wide Web Consortium (W3C), will be backward-compatible with existing EDI technology. There are a lot of synergies between XML and EDI. XML is a language that can be used to write format-neutral documents containing structured data. The XML specification was approved as a W3C standard, and products are in production that will let companies process XML forms or database searches via the World Wide Web. DISA has joined with the government-funded CommerceNet Consortium to determine compatibility between XML and EDI.

XML/EDI provides a standard framework to exchange different types of data so that the information be it in a transaction, exchanged via an Application Program Interface (API), web automation, database portal, catalog, a workflow document or message can be searched, decoded, manipulated, and displayed consistently and correctly by first implementing EDI dictionaries and extending our vocabulary via on-line repositories to include our business language, rules and objects. Thus by combining XML and EDI we create a new powerful paradigm different from XML or EDI!

For example, the ANSI X12 EDI structure lets users program "if/then loops" in business logic. But this is something XML cannot yet do however loops in X12 are important, and XML does not yet solve that business problem. XML may prove fine for electronic catalogs, but not for more complex EDI processes in its current form.

With the introduction of XML the ANSI Standards Committee (ASC) X12, which coordinates EDI standards development under DISA, appears to be exiting the business of writing EDI standards. ASC is currently repositioning the X12 committee to incorporate EDI with all the other electronic commerce technologies, such as XML, Java and data mining. The ASC X12 committee is no longer going to be concerned about application-level syntax, opting to get out of the technology business and let technologists master the technology development.

Why XML?

Although these benefits for EDI are compelling actual acceptance and implementation of EDI is far less prevalent than might be expected, because for all the acknowledged benefits, the technological complexity of EDI presented a number of major stumbling blocks.

- **Expense:** Computers, especially mainframes, and their business application systems were complex and expensive. Primarily serving the peripheral functions of a business, they were not regarded as being fully integrated into all business activities. Traditionally, the mainframe-computing environment was viewed as an information repository. EDI required that information technology be extended beyond core functions. So while there were substantial savings to be gained from the use of EDI, the cost of re-designing and deploying software applications to integrate EDI into an existing portfolio of business applications was high enough to offset the anticipated advantages.

- **Networking Complexity:** The need for extensive telecommunications capability posed a second major barrier to widespread EDI implementation. Beyond the computer itself, a basic requirement of EDI is a means to transmit and receive information to and from a wide variety of customers or suppliers. This required a heavy investment in computer networks. Unlike the mail, to send electronic documents there must be a specific point-to-point electronic path for the document to take. So companies were either required to develop extensive, and expensive networks, or rely on intermittent point-to-point modem communication.

- **Alternatives:** Because of the technological complexity and cost of implementation, cheaper alternatives short-circuited widespread utilization of EDI. To gain some of the advantages of EDI without the high price of computer hardware, software and networks, many innovative alternatives were developed. Overnight courier service, facsimile machines, and the ability to give customers limited access to mainframes through dumb terminals provided comfortable, quick, and reasonably priced alternatives to inviting a major alteration of business environments.

Enterprises have a variety of motivations for wanting to get involved with XML. Many are desperate to get involved in e-commerce but have no idea how to get started, given their current technology. In industries that already have online marketplaces and portals springing into existence, XML is often the required admission ticket. Many firms view the advent of XML as the golden opportunity to automate processes from beginning to end, with the XML format as the central touchstone.

For EDI companies, the motivations emerge from some of the drawbacks to EDI itself. Most EDI traffic flows over VANs, which can be expensive. The open and free Internet beckons, and while EDI over the Internet is possible, it's not fun. In contrast, XML is a child of the Internet and seems a more natural format to use. EDI is also primarily a one-to-one technology, while Web-based marketplaces allow many-to-one connectivity. One goal for exploring XML is to broaden groups of trading partners to include those who don't use EDI.

As with the original adoption of EDI, one draw of XML is the fact that potential business partners may be using it. Another reason to master EDI/XML interoperability is so you can offer that connection as a service to others. Many of other companies are struggling with EDI's limitations due to such things as a lack of real-time information and EDI's point-to-point nature.

One advantage of XML is its utility in any-to-any connectivity; it can ensure that a given product will enable the enterprise to connect with everyone it anticipates needing to. There are also different dialects of EDI, and a company may want to offer based on different product requirements. For example, you might use one component to do EDI mapping and another to translate between XML and EDI. Another consideration here may be integration with existing systems. It's also advantageous to have data in XML format for supporting e-commerce and portal sites. Pure translation products may be wonderful, but if they can't take it to the Web.

It is important to remember that XML is a data format, not a protocol or an application. The argument is that XML, as a data format, isn't going to buy much by itself. What matters is the system—including transport, storage and transformation—that is built around it. For example, an application may receive a message for processing. That processing may include various stages such as validation and sequencing. One of these stages may involve translation between EDI and XML. Thus, the overall process is a much bigger picture that this translation must fit into. This is especially true when using EDI/XML transformation as part of an enterprise-class environment.

- Can the system handle the load?

- What if the enterprise is offering this connectivity as part of a service?

- Can the system scale to manage unpredictable volume?

• How does the EDI/XML platform behave as part of a system where security, reliability and fail-over require special technologies and strategies?

XML is slower than EDI. The messages must be larger—as much as 10 times larger—requiring greater bandwidth and more cycles to move and process. For those merely seeking any-to-any connectivity, this isn't a major barrier. But when you start thinking about handling enterprise-level volumes of transactions, you clearly have to explore the ramifications of moving to XML.

DIRECTORY ENABLED EDI AND CASH MANAGEMENT SERVICES

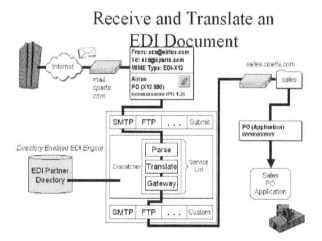

A directory enabled banking middleware product that provides a common security infrastructure to multiple applications by routing messages between identity services and back end systems. This infrastructure understands digital identities and how they can be used to help manage the risks involved in delivering commercial services online. The eCommerce engine reintermediates financial institutions into Internet business-to-business e-commerce, helping them by:

- Delivering payment and credit products such as factoring and online loans

- Helping to generate revenue from new commercial authorization services such as user validation, identification and warranty

- Offering informational services (such as address checking, Kite/Quality Mark confirmation and credit scoring services)

- Providing comprehensive security and risk management facilities

- Generating non reputable evidence tokens

- Providing common authorization services across applications, which avoids the cost and duplication of silo approaches

- Delivering extensibility which allows incremental deployment of new applications

- Reducing time to market for new applications using the platform

- Coordinating identity and application information for integration with Customer Relationship Management.

Transactional non-repudiation

Messages are routed to business services by a powerful, flexible, rules-based router. eCommerce engines are configured to use business services that implement logic or connections to existing systems. This separates business rules and entitlement policy from specific business logic, allowing dynamic management of business rules without changes to business function code.

Business to business electronic commerce is already significant. By 2003, business-to-business revenue is expected to top $1.4

trillion1—10% of total global sales to businesses will be conducted over the Internet. Currently the model for online business to business is a simple two party model. Vendors have focused on procurement and selling processes between two organizations. This is inhibiting the growth of electronic commerce. In the real world, business-to-business electronic commerce involves a number of organizations that provide products and services that facilitate the transaction and minimize the risks and exposures of each trading party. By bringing these services online, a larger volume of commercial transactions will be carried out electronically. These services present banks with a significant role in "oiling the wheels" of electronic commerce. By better understanding the activities of the customer across all banking services, banks will be able to tailor products and prices due to their understanding of the risk models that surround both the merchants and their customers.

Before any application issues are considered, a commercial infrastructure is required to resolve identity issues and provide a basis for a legal framework for these services. Establishing this infrastructure is a critical challenge for banks. Operating the identity infrastructure provides new revenue opportunities for those banks. The required infrastructure needs to allow for interoperability between banks without compromising the ability to deploy value added services. The infrastructure needs to be able to cope with multi party trading environments.

As more products and services become available across an open network, there are new sets of operational risks that the organization has to manage which are common across the whole range of products. Operational risk covers a number of areas, some of which are new because of the use of open networks in transactions and some of which already exist but change because of this new environment. To address these risks, a new approach to delivery technologies will be required. These are the issues that the directory based EDI platform seeks to address. Directory based EDI transaction managers provide a common security infrastructure, which can be used by multiple applications, and can make decisions on the basis of policy set centrally. This supports a workable risk model for commercial electronic commerce, one in which the bank is a key as a mediator.

The Internet is changing from a shop window to a trading floor. Where businesses once used the Internet to boost traditional advertising campaigns, they are now using it to keep up with competitors, hang on to existing customers by enhancing customer service, reduce the costs of the customer order and fulfillment processes and expand market coverage. In the USA, 78 % of e-procurement enabled enterprises are online, and more than a quarter of those attribute an increase in revenue to the application of interactive technologies. As more and more organizations conduct their business online, so more transactions and the services needed to support those transactions will correspondingly be required to move online. A company that makes use of the Internet or other open networks to sell their products and services will expect to be serviced by their bank in the same way.

The business-to-business electronic marketplace opens a wide range of opportunities to the bank and large, medium, and small businesses all offer growth markets for various financial services products. Opportunities for increased revenue exist both in current and new markets and nearly all services extend from the provision of basic cash management services.

Business customers will require banking services to help them conduct business in this new dynamic environment. However, existing 'paper based' or non electronic products are not suited to support electronic trade—they are not 'real time' and therefore can not support or easily be integrated into organizations who wish to conduct business online in real time. Off line services do not fit into an automated buying and selling process.

While inter corporate directory servers will allow a bank to strengthen links with its business customer, it is the other directory based products and services that support business-to-business transactions. Products and services such as financing receivables, financial reporting, reconciliation & control, factoring and trade services (such as Letters Of Credit, FX, Payments etc) must be moved online to support electronic trades in a global real time environment. Any bank which fails to offer these services in the electronic medium faces the risk of losing customers to those more forward thinking banks who have developed a range of products for the electronic marketplace.

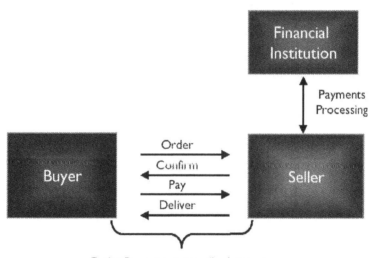

Order Processing over the Internet, disintermediation for the Financial Services Provider

The payment-processing role is not a fair reflection of the part that banks have in the real world as 'risk intermediaries' for business-to-business trading. Today's electronic solutions do not enable the bank to introduce value add electronic services further down the buying and selling value chains as they keep the purchasing cycle separate from the financial and reporting functions.

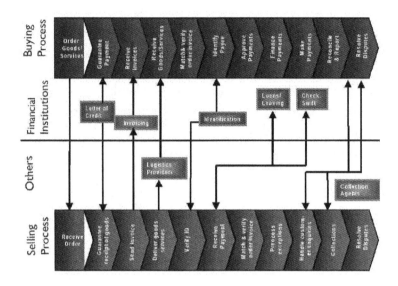

As more and more trades are executed online and as the value of those trades increases, so too will the demand for those services which will help organizations manage and underwrite the risk of transacting in the electronic medium. On the Internet, the tendency to trade with unknown business partners will therefore rise & trading with unknown parties will create new and increased risks (payment risk, credit risk, delivery risk, foreign exchange risk, operational risk). Many of those risks have a common requirement: the need to be able to identify parties involved in transactions and their entitlement to engage in a specific transaction. A bank is in prime position to offset these risks by offering commerce facilitation services (e.g. identity services & directory services). As demand for instant online commerce facilitation services across all industries, in both domestic and international markets, will be large, it will be vital to put in place an infrastructure, which can be used to deliver these services. Once a bank has an established relationship with a business they will be able to build on that relationship to provide other products and services, which are ideally suited to the electronic environment. Opportunities exist to increase market share and customer retention by providing on-line decision making and underwriting facilities.

Both banks and banking customers gain benefits from real-time, automated transactional products that support business-to-business trading. These services offer banks a significant role in "greasing the wheels" of electronic commerce.

- By understanding and using technologies to exploit the underlying risk profiles of business-to-business transactions, banks will be able to provide banking services at a reduced cost and with increased revenue.

- An identity infrastructure is required to support these initiatives. Banks can expect significant revenues from new products and services based on this identity infrastructure, beyond revenues from moving existing product sets to the Internet.

- By better understanding the activities of the customer across all banking services, banks will be able to tailor products and prices due to their understanding of the risk models that surround both the merchants and their customers.

The many benefits to be gained from offering online business banking services include:

- Cost reduction;

- Increased transaction revenue;

- Opportunities for new products and services

- Opportunities for increasing revenues through cross selling

Other business benefits include reduction of attrition, new customer acquisition (thus increase in market share), reduction of proprietary software and terminal costs and hence increased competitive edge etc.

Cost reduction

To process a payment through a bank branch costs approximately $1.93, while by computer the costs are a mere 19 cents. On an average payment of $1000, billers are likely to save as much as $19 per transaction if presented and paid electronically. As well as being cheaper than transactions conducted by ATM, teller or telephone, electronic services are more reliable, faster and capable of providing far more interactive & detailed information.

In comparison, most existing cash management services today are telephone based, paper based, and batch-oriented systems. Even for those business customers electronically connected to their banks with common directories, the majority of banks batch data to business

- The infrastructure required to support transactional banking offers the opportunity to develop new product lines.

- In the first place, banks will be able to generate revenue from identity services, both as an online check and with some bank backed warranty attached.

- Based on the identities issued, banks will be able to supply a range of informational products and services (such as confirmation of address and credit checks).

- Finally payment, credit and financing products can be offered through the infrastructure.

This approach, extending the underlying infrastructure, provides a strategy for the implementation of these transactional services: starting with revenue generating identity services and then building on that initial platform. The following sections look at two areas: validation services and facilitation products.

Validation services

The ability to validate a digital identity will not only be imperative for a bank to authenticate their customers and underpin the signing of transactions, but can be offered as a service in its own right, the bank can offer the identity services to its merchants as an outsourcing facility. This enables the merchant to manage the risk of dealing with their customers over the Internet as the bank can provide an identity warranty, which will guarantee the identity of the Merchant's customer.

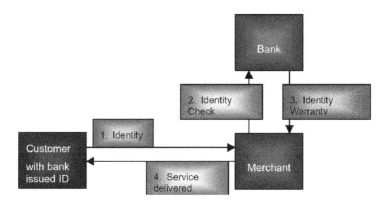

For the bank this has the added benefit of immediately deepening market presence and should offer significant opportunity to attract new customers. If a bank chooses to rely on other third parties for identity services, then the bank will not only risk greater disintermediation, but even more importantly, may lose ownership of that customer.

Banks can provide simple identity services with no liability taken, or choose to underwrite the transactions that rely on those services. The pricing model can reflect the liability assumed—with simple validation services being charged at a flat rate per validation (say $0.5) and warranty services being offered based on a percentage of the value of the commercial transaction. Banks have balance sheets that will allow significant differentiation from traditional online identity services—such as that offered by Verisign—where liability is capped below the value of many business-to-business transactions.

Facilitation services

Facilitation services build on the basic validation services described above. An increasing amount of businesses that wish to expand trade either domestically or internationally will seek the benefit of sophisticated and integrated financial management. It may not be economically viable for these organizations to hire a dedicated financial manager.

There is a wide range of outsourced services that a bank could offer to its business customers to help them expand and exploit the greater trade opportunities that Business to Business electronic commerce offers. One example of this is Accounts Receivables Outsourcing. Due to the rapid pace of Internet sales and sales growth, Accounts Receivable management has become a challenge for many large Internet sellers, and thus introduces an opportunity for financial institutions

Cash management services are the foundation of a bank's relationship with their customer and support the relationship for all the other services that a bank undertakes with that customer. It is these additional services, which offer a bigger margin, and hence opportunity for greater profits than cash management services alone.
Significant opportunities must therefore exist for a banking service which not only provides cash management, but the ability to process tax forms, electronic invoicing and bill payment services, online financing or loan underwriting as well as access to basic financial advice and other trade and business facilitation services.

The decision-making processes that support transactions are well established in the real world. They involve services, guarantees and facilities from a number of organizations—such as banks and credit reference agencies. However, offline services do not fit into an automated buying and selling process, and now these services are required to move online and be authorized in real time to support electronic trading.

Directory enabled EDI provides a foundation for online delivery of these mediation services by delivering a common security infrastructure, which allows secure integration between new or existing applications and the Internet. This enables organizations doing business in real time to better manage the risks that they undertake by allowing them to bring the real world decision-making processes online. A directory enabled EDI engine uses the directory as a repository of information about users, the roles to which they are assigned, and rights assigned to those roles to take decisions about the conditions required to access business services—a customer's entitlement. The product uses information about the method of user authentication, the types of transaction or service requested and the liability or cover that may be provided by third party financial institutions to take decisions on allowing access to business applications and placing conditions on that access.

New revenue streams—by being the first to market with a system that will provide additional benefits (shown below) to their clients, banks will not only retain their current clients but acquire new ones.

- Cost reduction through process automation—administration costs will be lower due to the full automation that real time services allow.

- Increased profit—by managing risk better the financial services company can offer better terms to sellers whilst ensuring that their risk of loss and therefore cost is considerably reduced.

- Reduced fraud—the bank reduces the risk of fraud occurring by being able to verify the identities of both the commercial customer and of their client.

- Improved image—the first banks to implement new systems will improve there image with clients by being forward thinking and recognizing technological advances especially where those clients are already using the Internet in their business.

- Increased customer satisfaction—the efficiency of the services will improve the clients' cash flow and reduce their costs. Occurrence of errors will be reduced to a minimum and disputes will be easily resolved.

As the Internet makes it easier for the parties to a transaction to communicate directly, traditional value-chains are repeatedly broken and re-formed. The disintermediation of previously mainstream financial institutions is one example of this. With more of the commercial cycle on-line, e-business transactions are increasingly multi-party, and the two-party model implemented by most e-commerce solutions is less and less appropriate: it does not offer the infrastructure services needed to underpin multi-party online transactions. As a result, a number of ebusiness models are evolving, as illustrated in the following diagrams. The first shows a 4 party mediated e-commerce scheme, where several parties to a transaction each complete their part of it in a more or less linear process.

N-corner model

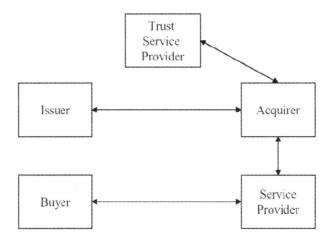

Directory Model

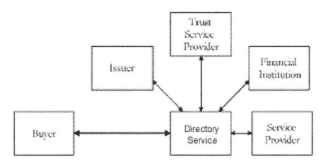

In this model, the owner of the portal is in a position to offer added value services to any of the other participants, while at the same time enforcing the basic logical steps through which the transaction must pass. These value-add services, in the first instance, will be built up on new authentication methods (such as smart cards and digital certificates) and existing business processes, such as risk management, transaction authorization, and so on. Examples of such value-add services are invoice discounting, volume purchase/procurement, and price comparison, warranties of identity and transaction and so on, depending on the nature of the Portal provider's core business and value-add proposition. This model is therefore a good starting point for organizations planning 'hosted' or Application Service Provider (ASP)-style implementations.

Banks, as the primary trusted intermediaries for commercial transactions today, are presented with a significant opportunity to undertake, adapt and extend this role in the electronic market. Banks already have a highly developed understanding of the commercial risk models, which apply to their commercial clients, and to their customers in turn. They also already play a role as trusted intermediaries. The challenge is to capitalize on these core skills for e-business. As a basis for these and future mediated services, banks will need to contribute to a commercial framework for identity, liability and legal services in the online environment. The Identrus consortium is one such initiative, bringing a number of banks together in a common framework of identity, liability and legal provisions. The aim of Identrus is to provide an infrastructure for secure, manageable inter-bank transactions.

Stage 1: 2-party, single user-group

Stage 1 shows a simple 2-party application, where a service provider (such as a bank) controls all the necessary components to deliver a service to the user. It assumes a single user-group, such as internal employees of a bank, or existing bank customers. The bank issues credentials (certificates) to the users, and uses those credentials as the basis for controlled access to services. In addition to access control, the credentials may also be used as the key to retrieve user-specific information (for example, from relationship management systems) and thereby to control the terms of business for a given transaction. Some banks already have online services, which they would like to deliver, but have not yet built up a user-base of smart card and certificate credentials. They may therefore need an initial rollout on the basis of User-ID/password authentication, followed by a switch to smart card/certificate-based authentication for the same application. One of the basic functions of a directory enabled EDI engine is to separate the authentication mechanism from the application, so that multiple phased or concurrent authentication mechanisms can be used to control access to services.

Stage 2: 3-party, shared CA

Service Provider

```
Shared
CA
```

*2 - Certificate
Status Check*

```
Directory
Server
```

User Group 1 — *1 - Certificate based authentication*

3 - 3-party Application → User Group 2

Stage 2 shows the inclusion of a second user group, but one whose credentials are still issued by the bank. A simple example of such an application would be secure email. Subsequent applications, such as e-procurement or invoice factoring, would enable the bank to mediating e-commerce transactions between two of its commercial customers. The two user groups might enjoy very different terms of business with the bank, but share a common means of identifying themselves and an interest in common three-party services. The portal server is used to deliver the application function itself—such as e-mail, or the bank's e-procurement service. Note that this may well mean that, in mediating e-commerce, the Bank may be changing the emphasis of its traditional commercial role. However, it should also be noted that the Bank is still seeking to capitalize on its core strengths—the fact that it is a trusted intermediary, and the fact that it can bring together shared interest groups in a commercial context.

Stage 3: 4-party, third-party CA

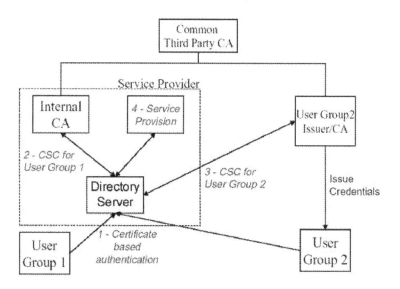

Stage 3 shows a simplified 4-party implementation. Here, the two user groups have credentials issued by separate institutions. The issuing institution for User Group 2 has been omitted for simplicity, but that institution and the service provider share a common third party CA. As far as the service provider is concerned, this means that the credentials of members of User Group 1 can be validated by reference to its own systems, while the validation of User Group 2's credentials will require reference to at least one other party. The portal server acts as the control point for these interactions, and ensures that the correct authentication and authorization processes map each user onto the appropriate set of services and terms of business.

Simultaneous Threat and Opportunity

As is evident from the layout of the portal-based model, banks and other financial institutions face the risk of disintermediation if they cannot support online transactions with a corresponding set of online services for identity, payment and credit services, risk management and other e-business enablers. To counter this threat, banks need to find ways of adding value, which capitalize on their core characteristics of trust and mediation. This trusted intermediary status applies to the bank's relationships with its suppliers, partners, customers and employees. A directory enabled EDI platform provides PKI-enabled portal services, which support these, trust relationships.

On the other hand, e-business presents banks with an opportunity because:
—Other potential intermediaries understand commercial risk and trust services no better than the banks;
—Where no organization acts as an intermediary, either one of the trading parties has to manage liability, risk and the legal aspects of the transaction, or these factors go unmanaged, greatly increasing the risk of conducting the transaction online.—Where the appropriate infrastructure is in place (as illustrated by the diagram and the Identrus ini-

tiative) there is the opportunity to increase market share by being able to accept, and act on, the credentials of users with whom there is no previous commercial relationship.

In the late 1980s and early 1990s, electronic commerce, specifically Electronic Data Interchange (EDI), emerged as a powerful tool to help corporations reduce the costs of business processes. Now, in the latter half of the 1990s, a new tool has emerged: Internet commerce, based on interoperable, Internet-specific EDI standards. Internet commerce has the potential to deliver huge productivity gains to its adopters because it is global, ubiquitous, and affordable. It is rapidly becoming a secure, reliable, and powerful enabler.

Across industry sectors, the same pattern is evident: retail, telecom, manufacturing, pharmaceuticals, utilities, public sector and so on—all recognize the need to bring all the right resources to bear in support of their core business, and to do so competitively, for sustained performance. In all these sectors, enterprises are recognizing that there is an urgent need to align their IT and service delivery efforts with the enormous power of the Internet. In the business-to-business banking market that urgency is now starting to generate both collaboration and competitive impetus. Collaboration takes place up to the point where institutions recognize that they have common aims:

Enterprises are facing the challenge of harnessing the Internet's high return-on-investment potential for existing and planned electronic-commerce (e-commerce) programs. A business document gateway product can help enterprises realize that potential—because of its unique flexibility it can handle simple file transfer processes, more sophisticated EDI-based processes, and the very complex processing requirements that arise in today's information system environments.

A directory enabled EDI engine allows companies to send and receive business transactions over both the Internet and existing EDI networks while providing extensive tracking and auditing capabilities as well. A directory enabled EDI engine also may have application integration tools designed for complex system integration needs. a directory enabled EDI engine provides the means to develop shared infrastructure services in support of these common aims. Where institutions see the opportunity for commercial advantage, competition takes over:

Directory enabled EDI allows banks to capitalize on these opportunities efficiently and sustainability. Businesses that want to start doing Internet-based electronic commerce face the fundamental challenge of finding a way to exchange business transactions and documents with other companies in their supply chains, as well as with resellers and customers. Existing systems do not adequately solve this problem. Legacy and enterprise resource planning (ERP) back-office systems do not extend beyond a company's boundaries. Existing EDI networks extend beyond company boundaries but because they do not use the Internet, they allow communication only with large trading partners and require transaction service fees. This situation makes it difficult for companies to deploy new intercompany business processes with existing systems alone.

Receive and Route an EDI Document

A directory enabled EDI engine is an Internet-based e-commerce messaging software solution that allows companies to conduct business-to-business electronic commerce, also called Internet commerce, over the Internet, extranets, and intranets. Built on Internet technologies, a directory enabled EDI engine addresses the messaging and application integration challenges that companies are facing with their existing e-commerce programs. It can provide secure and reliable communications through open, standards-compliant support of SMTP and S/MIME, FTP, HTTP, or TCP/IP APIs. To help ensure privacy and data integrity and nonrepudiation of receipt, a directory enabled EDI engine may employ certificates, encryption, authentication, digital signatures, or signed receipt notices. Other key features may include any-to-any mapping and translation capabilities, mailboxing, document level tracking, and a browser-based Java user interface.

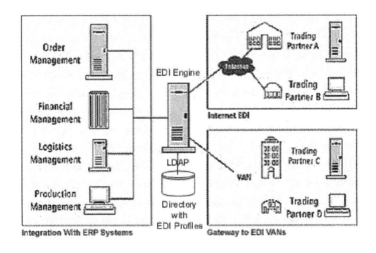

ebXML

The vision of ebXML is to create a single global electronic marketplace where enterprises of any size and in any geographical location can meet and conduct business with each other through the exchange of XML based messages. ebXML enables companies and individuals, to do electronic business with one another,

In order for enterprises to conduct electronic business with each other, they must first discover each other and the products and services they have to offer, a directory centric stage. They then must determine which business processes and documents are necessary to obtain those products and services; again this is a directory centric profile driven operation. After that, they need to determine how the exchange of information will take place and then agree on contractual terms and conditions. Once all of this is accomplished, they can then exchange information and products/services according to these agreements.

To facilitate this, ebXML provides an infrastructure for data communication interoperability, a semantic framework for commercial interoperability, and a mechanism that allows enterprises to find, establish a relationship, and conduct business with each other. Data communication interoperability is ensured by a standard message transport mechanism with a well-defined interface, packaging rules, and a predictable delivery model, as well as an interface to handle incoming and outgoing messages at either end.

Commercial interoperability is provided by means of a specification schema for defining business processes and a core components and context model for defining Business Documents. EbXML recommends a methodology and provides a set of worksheets and guidelines for creating those models. A business directory of business process and information models promotes business efficiency by encouraging reuse of business processes or parts of predefined business processes. In order for the actual conduct of business to take place, ebXML provides a shared directory where businesses can discover each other's business offering by means of partner profile information, a process for establishing an agreement to do business (Collaboration Protocol Agreement, or CPA), and a shared directory for company profiles, business-process-specifications, and relevant business messages.

13

Enterprise Resource Planning and Supply Chain Planning

The traditional, vertically integrated business model features complete end-to-end process control, but with high fixed costs. Under most "old economy" legacy systems, data processing is a relatively clumsy, manual operation. In the past, the higher costs of the vertically integrated model were outweighed by the control over information it provided. Directory based management tools offer new opportunities to economize through better access to information. Companies can operate more inexpensively and nimbly by using supply chain partners, outsourced service providers, joint ventures, and contract workers. Directory based business applications provide customers, suppliers, partners, employees, and executives in every part of the enterprise with secure, role-based access to critical information, regardless of their location or relationship to the company. With no software to maintain on the client, directory based solutions are also far more scalable than legacy systems. While enjoying the advantage of virtually instant return on their new systems, companies implementing web-based solutions also recognize their value for accommodating future growth. With opportunities for efficiency savings in the millions or billions of dollars, it is obvious why companies in all industries are stepping up their investments in directory technologies.

ENTERPRISE RESOURCE PLANNING

An ERP system is an integrated, online management system with modules for specific functions such as accounts receivable and payable, materials management, personnel benefits administration, inventory management, budgeting and the broad set of activities supported by multi-module application software that helps a manufacturer or other business manage the important parts of its business, including product planning, parts purchasing, maintaining inventories, interacting with suppliers, providing customer service, and tracking orders. ERP can also include application modules for the finance and human resources aspects of a business and may include specific vertical application modules for certain vertical businesses (i.e. Utilities, Petrochemicals etc. etc.). Typically, an ERP system uses or is integrated with a relational database or directory. Deployment of an ERP system can involve considerable business process analysis, employee retraining, and new work procedures

ERP automates the tasks involved in performing a business process such as order fulfillment, which involves taking an order from a customer, shipping it and billing for it. With ERP, when a customer service representative takes an order from a customer, he or she has all the information necessary to complete the order (the customer's credit rating and order history, the company's inventory levels and the shipping dock's trucking schedule). Everyone else in the company sees the same computer screen and has access to the single database that holds the customer's new order. When one department finishes with the order it is automatically routed via the ERP system to the next department. To find out where the order is at any point, one need only log into the ERP system and track it down. With luck, the order process moves rapidly through the organization, and customers get their orders faster and with fewer errors than before. ERP can apply that same value add to the other major business processes, such as employee benefits or financial reporting.

The ERP concept has its roots in the manufacturing automation and "just in time" delivery advances of the 1970s. Because all the functions share the underlying databases, information must be entered only once. For example, when a new employee is hired, the computerized records of his or her pay rate, benefits, retirement account, office location and phone number, and so on are available to human resource managers, financial managers, program managers, telecommunications managers and others who need the information. ERP systems also provide the kind of information that agencies expect to obtain from decision support systems or executive information systems: reports on revenue and expenditure trends, project schedules, hiring and retention, and other resource issues.

There's a downside to the benefit of ERP systems. As packaged or commercial, off-the-shelf (COTS) software, ERP systems are inflexible. Adopters have a choice of modifying their processes to match the software or modifying the software to fit the companies' processes.

The data from the ERP system must be combined with data from external systems for analysis purposes. Users with heavy analysis needs should include the cost of a data warehouse in the ERP budget. Integrators should expect to do quite a bit of work to make it run well. Refreshing all the ERP data in a big corporate data warehouse daily is difficult, and ERP systems do a poor job of indicating which information has changed from day to day, making selective warehouse updates tough. One expensive solution is custom programming. The upshot is that the wise will check all their data analysis needs before signing off on the budget.

ERP can also include customer relationship management or CRM, and supply chain management or SCM.

CONTACT RELATIONSHIP MANAGEMENT (CRM)

The importance of Customer Relationship Management (CRM) systems is well understood. Business today is highly customer-centric, where enterprises have to Engage and respond to customers with a unified voice across all touch-points. To build brand loyalty and to retain customers, companies must interact with customers in a consistent, personalized manner. Directory and CRM processes have become the beating heart of the enterprise, because without customers, you don't have a business. However, e-business is unleashing some important structural changes to the economy, including how businesses interact with each other. Just as the demand chain requires CRM, the supply chain requires Partner Relationship Management (PRM) systems. Defined by a set of flexible enterprise processes, PRM focuses on managing how partners engage each other. These could be collaborative processes, such as product design, as well as supplier relationships. Without effective PRM and CRM, no enterprise can expect to have an efficient value chain.

CRM is an information industry term for methodologies, software, and usually Internet capabilities that help an enterprise manage customer relationships in an organized way. For example, an enterprise might build a database about its customers that described relationships in sufficient detail so that management, salespeople, people providing service, and perhaps the customer directly could access information, match customer needs with product plans and offerings, remind customers of service requirements, know what other products a customer had purchased, and so forth. This is a very useful for planning purposes. Most industry analysts agree that CRM covers the following areas: Helping an enterprise to enable its marketing departments to identify and target their best customers, manage marketing campaigns with clear goals and objectives, and generate quality leads for the sales team. Assisting the organization to improve telesales, account, and sales management by optimizing information shared by multiple employees, and streamlining existing processes (for example, taking orders using mobile devices). Allowing the formation of individualized relationships with customers, with the aim of improving customer satisfaction and maximizing profits; identifying the most profitable customers and providing them the highest level of service. Providing employees with the information and processes necessary to know their customers, understand their needs, and effectively build relationships between the company, its customer base, and distribution partners.

Information systems automatically entered into my information systems." A variety of data exchange approaches have been employed to achieve that wish. Common elements among these approaches include:

- Data communications: networks and protocols to move bytes between companies

- Data formats: agreements on the structure and content of messages exchanged between companies

- Security: measures to assure the privacy, authenticity, and integrity of messages and means to support nonrepudiation

- Reliability and tracking: mechanisms to assure the delivery of messages and to capture a persistent record of communications progress.

The quest for intercompany data exchange dates back more than 20 years. In that time, much has changed. Early efforts focused on centralized data standards (e.g., X12 and EDIFACT) and the use of Value-Added Networks (VANs) for data communications. These approaches, known as traditional Electronic Data Interchange (EDI) continue to be used today. The standardization efforts associated with EDI attempt to reach broad-scale syntactic and semantic agreement on the data exchanged among companies (e.g., purchase orders, shipping notices, invoices, etc.). Third-party VANs that control communications address security and communications reliability concerns. More recently, the widespread availability of directory services has changed this process

Directory enabled CRM encompasses three distinct areas

- Sales force automation (SFA): Critical functions such as lead/ account management, contact management, quote management, forecasting, sales administration. Key infrastructure requirements are mobile synchronization and integrated product configuration. SFA tools are designed to improve field sales productivity.

- Customer Service and Support (CSS): Internal help desk and traditional inbound call-center support for customer inquiries, now evolved into the "customer interaction center" (CIC), using multiple channels (Web, phone/fax, face-to-face, kiosk, etc). Key infrastructure requirements include computer telephony integration (CTI), high volume processing capability, and reliability.

- Enterprise marketing automation (EMA): The execution side of campaign and lead management. Demographic analysis, variable segmentation, and predictive modeling occur on the analytical (Business Intelligence) side and are CPU intensive. The intent of EMA applications is to improve marketing campaign efficiencies.

Analytical CRM comprises all activities that analyze data about an enterprise's customers, presenting it so business decisions can be made quickly and easily. CRM analytics can be considered a fusion of directory services and online analytical processing (OLAP) and may employ data mining. Companies seeking new and faster ways to interact with customers look to directory services and analytics to turn data collected about customers into useful information.

CRM analytics can provide

- Customer segmentation groupings (at its simplest, dividing customers into those most and least likely to repurchase a product);

- Profitability analysis (which customers lead to the most profit over time);

- Personalization (the ability to market to individual customers based on the data collected about them);

- Event monitoring (for example, when a customer reaches a certain dollar volume of purchases);

- What-if scenarios (how likely is a customer or customer category that bought one product to buy a similar one);

- Predictive modeling: (for example, comparing various product development plans in terms of likely future success, given the customer knowledge base).

Data collection and analysis is viewed as a continuing and iterative process. Ideally, business decisions are refined over time, based on feedback from earlier analysis and decisions.

Potential benefits of CRM analytics lead to better and more productive customer relations in terms of sales and service, as well as improved supply chain management (lower inventory and speedier delivery), resulting in lower costs and more competitive pricing. One of the major challenges is how to integrate the CRM analytical software with existing legacy systems.

SUPPLY CHAIN PLANNING (SCM)

Adaptation is a natural condition in all aspects of life. From living organisms to businesses, survival often depends on the ability to adapt. In today's rapidly changing marketplace, adaptation is no longer optional; it is mandatory. The Internet and the ubiquity of information technology are requiring businesses to possess the flexibility to continually change and adapt to their environment. That's where adaptive supply chain networks come into play. Over the past few years, analysis of successful manufacturing and retail companies shows that in today's hyper-competitive business environment, supply chain efficiency is a necessary condition for survival. However, as we approach an age of super efficiency, adaptive supply chain networks, which have redundancies built in to withstand unpredictable shocks, are replacing traditional supply chains. Adaptive supply chain networks possess the flexibility to continually morph and respond to the environment in near real-time without compromising on operational and financial efficiencies. These networks seamlessly connect supply, planning, manufacturing, and distribution operations to critical enterprise applications and provide near real-time visibility across the supply network, thereby enabling rapid decision-making and optimal execution.

SCM is the oversight of materials, information, and finances as they move in a process from supplier to manufacturer to wholesaler to retailer to consumer. Supply chain management is the combination of demand planning, supply planning, and demand fulfillment and it involves coordinating and integrating these flows both within and among companies. It is said that the ultimate goal of any effective supply chain management system is to reduce inventory and save time (with the assumption that products are available when needed). As a solution for successful supply chain management, sophisticated software systems with Web interfaces are competing with Web-based application service providers (application service providers—ASP's) who promise to provide part or all of the SCM service for companies who rent their service.

Supply chain management flows can be divided into three main flows:

- The product flow
- The information flow

- The finances flow

The product flow includes the movement of goods from a supplier to a customer, as well as any customer returns or service needs. The information flow involves transmitting orders and updating the status of delivery. The financial flow consists of credit terms, payment schedules, and consignment and title ownership arrangements.

There are two main types of SCM software:

- planning applications
- Execution applications.

Planning applications use advanced algorithms to determine the best way to fill an order. Execution applications track the physical status of goods, the management of materials, and financial information involving all parties.

Some SCM applications are based on open data models that support the sharing of data both inside and outside the enterprise (this is called the extended enterprise, and includes key suppliers, manufacturers, and end customers of a specific company). This shared data may reside in diverse database systems, or data warehouse, at several different sites and companies.

By sharing this data "upstream" (with a company's suppliers) and "downstream" (with a company's clients), SCM applications have the potential to improve the time-to-market of products, reduce costs, and allow all parties in the supply chain to better manage current resources and plan for future needs.

Increasing numbers of companies are turning to Web sites and Web-based applications as part of the SCM solution. A number of major Web sites offer procurement marketplaces where manufacturers can trade and even make auction bids with suppliers.

Today, supply chains are becoming a key competitive weapon, and that means that they face a mounting array of challenges. They must move with ever-increasing speed. Supply customized, individually configured products. Promise and deliver with precision. And adapt quickly to shifts in demand, customer tastes, and economic conditions.

To succeed, the company has to find answers to some fundamental supply chain questions:

- How can it respond to changes in demand without carrying lots of inventory?

- How can it work with suppliers to change plans quickly?

- How can it maintain service while making more out of inventory, fixed capital, and transportation assets?

- How can it bring new products to market more quickly? And if they take off, how can it gear up?

- How can it shift to Internet-based selling and make sure that orders from the Web are processed through the rest of our systems and delivered to customers?

- How can it drive superior supply chain performance to provide selection and fast, dependable delivery—and stand out from the competition?

- How can it meet demand if preferred suppliers can't deliver?

Instead, the enterprise needs to create adaptive supply chain networks in which suppliers, manufacturers, distributors, and customers share information dynamically across the network. It needs to capture customer demand and share that information throughout the network. And the enterprise needs to coordinate planning and execution so that all partners in the network are working together seamlessly toward a common goal. To help companies create those adaptive supply chain networks,

Directory centric Supply Chain Management is a powerful, integrated approach that gives the enterprise the tools it need to manage its supply network from supply chain design to material sourcing and from forecasting demand to scheduling factories.

With directory enabled supply chain management, the company and its partners can capture and share customer demand information. Anticipate a shortage before it occurs and integrate a new supplier to avoid delay. Synchronize planning and execution. And have instant visibility into inventory levels, forecasts, production plans, and other key performance indicators so that you can adapt to changes using actual directory data rather than conjecture.

Directory enabled management can reach across organizational boundaries to build a truly adaptive supply chain network. And that can lead to reduced inventories, increased return on assets, improved quality, higher customer satisfaction, and the kind of speed and responsiveness your company needs to thrive in today's economy.

Supply Chain Planning

- Supply Chain Design: directory enabled supply chain management provides a centralized overview of the entire supply chain and key performance indicators, which helps you identify weak links and potential improvements. And it supports strategic planning by enabling a company to test various scenarios and perform what-if analyses to determine how changes in the market or customer demand can be cost-effectively and profitably addressed by the supply chain. These design capabilities help you to adapt to changing market conditions quickly and easily.

Collaborative Demand and Supply Planning

- Directory enabled supply chain management helps a company match demand to supply profitably. Demand planning tools let a company take into account historical demand data, causal factors, marketing events, market intelligence, and sales objectives—and enable the entire supply chain network to work from a single, accurate forecast. Supply planning tools allow you to create an overall supply plan that takes into account materials management, production, distribution and transportation requirements and constraints—and then share that plan with all members of the supply chain network. Overall, these demand and supply planning capabilities help you reduce the amount of material in the supply chain while maintaining high levels of customer service.

Supply Chain Execution

- Materials Management: Using a metadirectory a company can share accurate inventory and procurement order information to ensure that the materials required for manufacturing are available in the right place at the right time. It can perform plan-driven procurement, inventory management, and invoicing, and you can create a complete feedback loop between demand and supply to increase responsiveness across all areas of supply chain planning. Overall, the solution's materials management tools help you reduce raw material spend, procurement costs, safety stocks, and raw material and finished goods inventory.

Collaborative Manufacturing

- A metadirectory enables the company to share information with partners to coordinate production, and enable everyone to work together to increase both responsiveness and efficiency. You can support all production processes: engineer-to-order, configure-to order, make-to-order, and make-to-stock. You can create a continuous information flow across engineering, planning, and execution. And you can optimize production schedules across the supply chain, taking into account material and capacity constraints, as well as information from other planning areas like demand and supply planning.

- Collaborative Fulfillment: Using a common directory the company and its partners can intelligently commit to delivery dates in real time and fulfill orders from all channels on time. For example, a global available-to-promise shared directory lets the company locate finished products, components, and machine capacities in a matter of seconds. It can also manage the flow of products through your sales channels and match supply to market demand, reassign supply and demand to meet shifts in customer demand, and manage transportation and warehousing to provide on-time, low-cost delivery.

Supply Chain Coordination

- Supply Chain Event Management: The supply chain event management directory solution monitors the execution of supply chain events—the relevant milestones of a process like the goods issue of a pallet or the departure of a truck and permits the company to flag any problems that come up. In many cases, the solution can handle problems automatically using standard operating procedures. If problems do require attention, directory enabled supply chain management lets you collaborate with partners to implement solutions and use historical event data to learn and adapt to changing conditions.

- Performance Management: With a performance management directory the enterprise can define, select, and monitor key performance indicators like costs and assets and use them to gain an integrated, comprehensive view of performance across the supply chain. On a day-to-day level, directory enabled supply chain management provides constant surveillance of key performance measurements and automatically generates an alert if there is a deviation from plan. When there is a problem, directory enabled supply chain management works with both business Intelligence and data warehousing solutions and data analysis solution, so you can evaluate a range of possible actions rapidly and accurately. And on a strategic level, directory enabled supply chain management gives the company the feedback needed for true closed-loop supply chain management and continuous improvement.

Supply Chain Networking

- Private Exchange: a supply chain directory can enable an online marketplace to bring companies suppliers, partners, and customers together online in a secure environment where confidentiality is protected and information-sharing among partners is guaranteed. Through the exchange, the company or group can manage relationships with participants and give them 24x7 flexibility to track order status, view pricing scenarios, check inventory levels, track shipping status, inquire into the status of product returns, review their order histories—and collaborate on demand and supply management, procurement, fulfillment, event management, and product design.

- Enterprise Portal: With directory enabled supply chain management, the company can use Web-based portal tools to integrate third-party systems into your supply chain network and let employees collaborate with coworkers, business partners, and customers. The portal gives users personalized access to the wide range of information, applications, and services they need to do their jobs. It uses role-based technology to deliver information to users based on their individual responsibilities within the supply chain network. With the portal, you can provide information access regardless of participants' IT infrastructure, company size, or location, creating a communication structure that spans all supply chain processes.

- Mobile Supply Chain Management: With directory enabled supply chain management, users throughout the supply chain network can plan, execute, and monitor activity using mobile and remote devices. Users can perform mobile data entry and automate many data-capture activities in plants and warehouses to reduce errors and increase efficiency. And decision makers can gather information and act, whether they are on the road, working in a remote facility, or virtually anywhere a directory or unified messaging solution can interact with.

To create an adaptive supply chain network, companies must advance through specific stages. The time it takes to evolve through the different stages will vary depending on the degree of technology, the process maturity, and the characteristics of the industry. However, once the network operations begin to streamline, benefits will become visible almost immediately. The three key stages to the evolution are integrated, collaborative, and adaptive

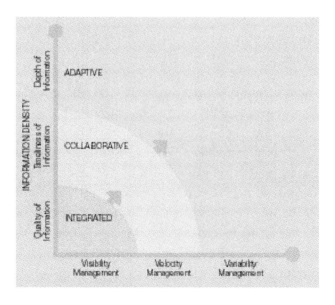

HUMAN RESOURCES (HRMS)

A specific subset of ERP systems HR applications focus on the needs of the human capital. HRMS systems help companies create a team-based organizational structure by enabling them to define competency-based teams, assign members to that team, and assess gaps in the skill sets of those team members.

Human Capital Management (HCM) enables organizations to improve business results and increase workforce performance by leveraging technology and applications within and beyond the enterprise. HCM already includes HRMS, Collaborative Applications, Workforce Analytics (WFA), Portal Solutions, and more. HRMS systems will permit:

- Manage and mobilize a unified, global workforce

- Connect people, processes, and systems

- Align workforce contribution with business objectives

Directories employed in conjunction with HRMS systems enable the following advances

Ubiquitous access to improve employee effectiveness and efficiency via directory enabled web applications. This means working from anywhere and at anytime. The size, format, and footprint of directory enabled technology deliverables will move from departmental desktop devices operating under the full control of the user organization to a mixture of hand-held pocket-sized integrated devices and wireless linkages that provide needed access on a real time basis to centralized processing and data storage capabilities. Instant access to all needed knowledge and to essential meaningful data will be a keystone for the successful enterprise.

Provide analytics and decision trees. Directory based expert systems will "walk" managers through every step of a decision about people issues. The information the manager receives from the directory at each step in the decision process will vary depending upon his or her answers to previous questions and will provide the manager with estimates of the risks associated with each alternative. These analytical systems will provide "predictor" algorithms that help anticipate and forecast possible problems such as turnover, recruitment, pay, and employee relations down to the individual employee level. What-if scenarios will provide virtual reality simulations that will enable managers to try out ideas and test different courses of action to make better people decisions.

Role based smart self-service—self-service expanding to communicate through smart phones and handheld personal data assistants (PDAs). Much of the new web self-service will reduce the need for call centers and most employees' self-service will be entirely web-based. In addition, natural language speech recognition enables intuitive application to be implemented, and while speech recognition is in the early stages of acceptance, it will be a factor in 21st century self-service. For both employee and manager, self-service will have to be more intuitive than ever. This will include push and pull technology; directory content that is filtered and relevant for the person in the role/s they are performing and event driven as well.

HR systems in the 21st century will enable employees to perform optimally by providing knowledgeable content that has been filtered based on the employee's role/s in the organization. The vendors of the future will provide not only the transactional systems necessary for this infrastructure, but the metadirectory will become the "aggregators" of content for their customers—and provide a wide range of hosting as the demand for better, faster, and cheaper technology support prevails.

Leading practice companies recognize that in a knowledge-intensive, innovate-or-die world, HR's role cannot be limited to doing the administrative stuff of hiring, firing, and employee-related paperwork.

HR has to do more. It has to become a full-fledged business partner/ advisor, not just an employee advocate.

First, HR has a strategic role to play in aligning human resource planning with the business strategy, particularly as we move to the highly adaptive, virtual, networked organization of organizations. What should the business keep in-house? What should it outsource? What skills and competencies are vital to execution of the business strategy, and which can, and should, be performed by the non-core staff? What must organizations do to address the social and psychology consequences of an impermanent project-oriented work environment? What support systems are needed to help employees shift from team to team and project to project efficiently and effectively? What are the implications of a multigenerational workforce? How can generational conflicts be avoided or, at least, mitigated? How can a company leverage the benefits of directory-enabled systems while simultaneously avoiding creating a privacy crisis? HR & directory professionals have a critical role to play in helping their companies find answers to these and similar questions. Second, HR has the job of acquiring and/or building a policy and systems infrastructure that can support the new organization's need for rapid response, global integration, and total flexibility.

ENTERPRISE INFORMATION INTEGRATION

Enterprise Information Integration (EII) is now a market separate from Enterprise Application Integration (EAI) and Extract-Transform-Load (ETL) solutions. The main reason that users now recognize a distinct need to integrate information across the enterprise is that the overall pool of proprietary enterprise information as distinct from information associated with specific packaged applications, directories, or data mining sources is now a key e-Business differentiator. The ability to leverage information from a wide variety of storage types, environments, applications, databases, and files via enterprise portals allows enterprises to deliver major value-add simultaneously to employees, partners, and customers. Enterprise integration has been discussed since the early days of computers in industry in general and in the manufacturing industry in particular directories finally enable this integration. CIM stands for operation integration and support of communication in manufacturing by means of information technology. In spite of the different understandings of the scope of CIM it has always stood for integration through efficient communication and information sharing across at least parts of the enterprise. Integration, which essentially consists of providing the right information, at the right time, at the right place.

Integration has also to be seen as a never-ending process. Over time both the internal and the external environment will change and the enterprise must react to these changes and adapt its operation accordingly. This requires up-to-date and integrated knowledge of both environments.

With this understanding the different needs in enterprise integration can be described:

- Provide the right information at the right time: requires explicit knowledge of both the information needed and created by the different activities in the enterprise operation. Knowledge, which has to be structured in the form of a dynamic model of the enterprise operation or workflow. A model, which describes the process dynamics as well as their functionalities and allows What-If analysis on both the static structure and the dynamic behavior of these processes.

- Provide the right information at the right place: requires information sharing systems and integration platforms capable of handling information transaction across heterogeneous environments. These environments are: those comprising heterogeneous hardware, different operating systems and monolithic software applications (legacy systems) and those crossing organizational boundaries and link the operation of different organizations on a temporal basis and with short set up times and limited time horizon (extended and virtual enterprises).

- Up-date the information in real time to reflect the actual state of the enterprise operation: requires not only the up-date of the operational data (information created during the operation), but adapting to environmental changes as well. Changes, which may originate from new customer demands, new technology, new legislation or new paradigms of the society at large. Changes which may require modification of the operational processes, reallocation or shift of responsibilities and authorities in the enterprise organization or even questioning the overall scope and goals of the enterprise (strategic planning).

These needs can be satisfied in a general sense through the use of:

- A model of the intra and inter enterprise operation and

- An IT infrastructure-enabling model based decision support and operation control and monitoring.

However, current information technology does not yet provide a complete solution for enterprise modeling and its use in the day-to-day operation by the operational staff is still limited. In addition, application of existing enterprise integration technologies has been hampered by a lack of business justification, a plethora of seemingly conflicting solutions and terminology, and by an insufficient understanding of the technology by the end-user community. These barriers inhibit, or at least delay, the use of relevant methods and tools in the industry, especially in small-to-medium-sized enterprises.

On the other hand the need for enterprise engineering and enterprise integration is intensifying through the increasing emphasis on agile operation in globally extended or virtual enterprises. To form and dissolve partnerships rapidly, and to integrate business discourse internationally requires not only intra but inter enterprise integration. These mostly short term co-operation require easy access and use of information on enterprise operations by the co-operating partners in order to assess potential contributions and to integrate those into the operation of the virtual enterprise.

14

Message Ques and Transaction Processors

The distinction between middleware solutions can sometime be blurred. A Metadirectory can be thought of as a specialized form of Message Oriented Middleware that routes messages and acts on operations according to the LDAP protocol. As a result no text on Metadirectory is complete without a section on Messaging and Message Oriented Middleware solutions.

What are Transactions

Transactions are a means to guarantee that database (or back-end) transactions are completed accurately and that they takeon all the "ACID" properties of an enterprise transaction:
• Atomicity—changes that a transaction makes to a database are made permanent, otherwise, all changes are rolled-back
• Consistency—a successful transaction transforms a database from a previous valid state to a new valid state
• Isolation—changes that a transaction makes to a database are not visible to other operations until the transaction completes its work
• Durability—changes that a transaction makes to a database survive future system or media failures

A distributed transaction is a transaction that updates multiple resource managers (such as databases) in a coordinated manner. In contrast, a local transaction begins and commits the transaction to a single resource manager that internally coordinates the transaction management on a single homogeneous system. The two-phase commit protocol is a method of coordinating a single transaction across two or more distributed systems with two or more transaction resource managers. It guarantees data integrity by ensuring that transactional updates are committed in all of the participating databases. If not, they are fully rolledback out of all the databases, reverting to the state prior to the start of the transaction. In other words, either all the participating databases are updated, or none of them are updated.

What is Messaging?
Messaging is a mechanism that allows programs to communicate with one another. There are many messaging technologies:

- TCP/IP sockets (including LDAP sockets)
- pipes
- files
- shared memory

Messaging is an import aspect of your distributed development. It provides two aspects: distributed, high-volume message communication and asynchronous notification. When used efficiently, messaging can become the entire backbone of a system. Good messaging systems provide guaranteed or certified delivery of all messages ensuring the success of messages through network or power failures. Messaging systems also provide transactional sessions. A transacted session allows a client to send or receive multiple messages as a single unit. Essentially, this is similar to buffering a few messages until they need to be processed. Guaranteed delivery order is the ability for a messaging server to guarantee that the order in which the messages were sent will be the order in which they arrive. These technologies and features are just the tip of the iceburg.

A Message Que Provides

- reliable messaging
- transactional sessions that buffer messages
- guaranteed delivery order of messages
- multiple messaging domain support

Messaging is generally considered to be any mechanism that allows two or more programs to communicate with one another. Messaging is typically based around the concept of a message, which is the content of a single transmission between two programs. Messaging provides programs a way of sending and receiving messages between one another. Using the general description provided here, there exists many different types of messaging systems in the world. Anything that allows a packet to be transmitted between two entities could be considered a messaging product. This would include TCP/IP sockets (network transmissions), piped output and input (routing the output of one program into the input of a second), files (one program storing a message in a file while a second program later reads the file), and shared memory (one program storing a message in a shared memory space while a second program later reads the memory) are all examples of messaging. Using this general description, you can also consider databases, hard drives, flash memory and LDAP directories a type of messaging service, too!

Message-Oriented Middleware (MOM) is used to refer to an infrastructure that supports messaging.

Typical MOM architectures define:

- message structure

- how to send/receive messages
- scaling guidelines

Message-Oriented Middleware has been in existence for a couple decades. It took on more popular forms during the mid-1980's when MOM providers created architectures that could behave similarly on a variety of platforms. They made large inroads into bridging the gap between the many platforms that existed for mainframes and personal computers. Today, there are 100's of companies that consider themselves to be middleware firms. Even though there is a lot of competition and variety that exists for MOM products, they all tend to fall into one of three categories: publish/subscribe, point-to-point, and request-reply.

POINT-TO-POINT

Point-to-Point (PTP) messaging was originally the term designated for machine to machine communications. It was the typical technique used to have two individual entities communicate directly. The PTP domain is really any system where only one consumer will ever process any individual message. Even though this implies only a single consumer of a message, it does not mean that there can't be multiple consumers on a single queue. It's just that the multiple consumers will not consume the same messages.

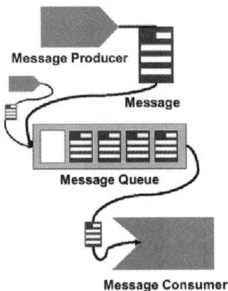

- Point-to-point messaging uses queues.

- Producers and consumers are decoupled from one another.

- Multiple producers and consumers can share a single queue

The PTP domain allows one client (called a producer) to send messages to another client (called a receiver). A client in a PTP system sends messages directly to another client. This messaging can be one-way or two-way. Many systems have clients that can only send or receive messages, but not both. This is a one-way relationship. If a client can send and receive messages, it is considered a two-way relationship. Many producers can serialize messages to multiple receivers in a queue. When using a PTP queue, multiple producers can place messages onto the queue. The queue serializes the messages into a linear order. Multiple receivers can take messages off of the queue, but the messages typically come off in a first-in, first-out (FIFO) order. This means that the oldest message on the queue is the first one to be taken off. A message can also only be delivered to a single receiver.

PUBLISH/SUBSCRIBE

The Publish/Subscribe (Pub/Sub) domain is used as the information propagation system for a distributed environment. The Pub/Sub domain is any system where at least one client receives a message. It does not guarantee, however, that more than one client consumes a message. There are various rules that can be applied in a Pub/Sub system that determine which clients receive a message. A Pub/Sub system can implement a variety of techniques to support the propagation of data. One technique is to allow for durable subscribers. A durable subscriber is any client that must receive every message sent to a topic. A messaging server stores and tracks which clients have not receive which messages and ensure their proper delivery the next time a particular client becomes active. Using Pub/Sub technologies, messaging can become an essential piece of a distributed system.

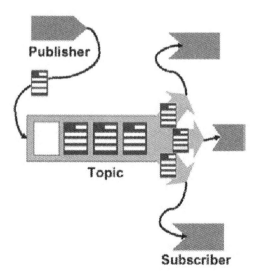

- Topics copy messages to all subscribers.

- Multiple publishers and subscribers can share a topic.

- Durable subscribers are clients that receive every message whether the client is active or inactive!

Message producers (called publishers), disseminate data to multiple consumers (called subscribers). Publish/Subscribe (pub/sub) is considered to be event-driven messaging. It is called event-driven because the messages produced by a publisher is usually triggered by some event or "happening" in the system. The consumers, who register for notification for messages produced by the publisher, receive the message when the producer decides to disseminate the data. This propagation of messages resembles a distributed event model where the message represents the event, the publisher is the event source, and the subscribers are the event listeners. Publishing and subscribing to a topic decouples producers from consumers. Having the publishers publish to a topic instead of directly to a list of subscribers decouples the publishers and subscribers. By doing this, the publishers no longer have to worry about the number of subscribers (if any) that need to receive the message. Also, by delegating the work of the message delivery to the MOM server (which manages the topic), the publisher does not have to worry about the delivery of guaranteed messages, fault tolerance of its production, load balancing, or other issues. Also, by decoupling a subscriber from the publisher, the subscriber does not have to concern itself with whether its publisher is active or not. As long as the MOM server is executing, the needs of both publishers and subscribers will be met.

REQUEST/REPLY

The Request/Reply domain has a program that sends a message and expects to receive a message in return.

This domain models:

- client/server computing
- distributed object computing
  - RMI
  - CORBA
  - DCOM

It is often typical to see this domain defined as a subset of the PTP or Pub/Sub domain. It is possible that in either PTP or Pub/Sub the receivers and subscribers of a message are required to generate a response for every message received. In this situation, the PTP and Pub/Sub domains are acting in the role of the Request/Reply domain.

The biggest benefit that MOM systems provide is an instant-messaging architecture upon which your system can be developed. MOM systems generally hide many of the aspects of inter-process communication away from the developer. These aspects, such as protocol details, keep-alives, message reconstruction, binary wire message format, delivery modes, etc., can be very time consuming and costly for a large-scale development project. MOM architectures provide an out-of-the-box solution for many of these problems. Robust systems provide support for a variety of protocols and platforms. The most popular systems support Sun Solaris, Microsoft Windows 95/NT, DEC OpenVMS, IBM MVS, and many others. The variety of network protocols that these systems support is just as extensive.

Many systems provide pre-built message formats and the capability for clients to create a custom message format. A message format could be as simple as a text based message, or as complicated as a fabrication of booleans, binary data, characters, text, dates, and numbers.

Most systems also provide guaranteed message delivery (GMD), also commonly called certified message delivery. A system that has GMD will "guarantee" the delivery of a message to its recipients despite network congestion, network failures, or even message server failures! Messages that contain content that must absolutely arrive at its destination can use GMD to ensure its delivery. MOM systems typically provide this benefit by storing the client's messages in a persistent store (usually a database) until the recipient of a message positively (or negatively in some products) responds to the receipt of a GMD message.

In addition to the above features, many MOM systems also provide support for dynamic routing of messages across the Internet or other WAN, load-balancing of message servers (so that one particular server isn't overwhelmed with messages), fault tolerance of message servers for 24/7 availability, and extensive configuration, management, and administration utilities.

MOM software falls into three categories that define which client receives a message:/

- Point-To-Point (PTP)
- Publish-Subscribe (Pub/Sub)
- Request-Reply (RR)

Message Oriented Middleware systems

- perform publish & subscribe messaging
- perform point-to-point messaging
- produce and consume messages of varying types
- filter messages based upon message selectors
- perform messaging in the context of a transaction

Systems built with MOM-based architectures generally have:

- messaging capability to multiple clients across heterogeneous systems

- increased level of scalability
- reduced risk
- shorter development time
- easy maintenance

The biggest benefit that MOM systems provide is an instant-messaging architecture upon which the system can be developed. MOM systems generally hide many of the aspects of inter-process communication away from the developer. These aspects, such as protocol details, keep-alives, message reconstruction, binary wire message format, delivery modes, etc., can be very time consuming and costly for a large-scale development project. MOM architectures provide an out-of-the-box solution for many of these problems.

In Summary: the Benefits of architectures incorporating MOM systems include:

- multi-protocol, multi-platform support
- user-defined message types
- guaranteed message delivery (GMD)
- load-balancing of messages
- fault tolerance of messaging servers
- cross-platform support
- GUI-based configuration and management

PART III

Directory Services Analysis/Architecture Methodology

Implementing a meta-directory involves collecting and replicating all existing user account attributes from the native information systems where they reside to a central directory where they are stored and managed. On the surface, this would seem a logical approach to managing disparate and scattered user privilege information. Unfortunately, this is not the case.

The meta-directory approach to managing user access information has proven to be highly problematic in many organizations. For one thing, reconciling user information across multiple systems tends to be a big challenge in most organizations. This is because there was no coordination initially in how an individual is universally identified across these systems. A single user often has multiple identities, or user names, within different systems and applications across the enterprise. Reconciling unconnected user information to create the meta-directory requires such a high degree of investigation and manual data scrubbing that many organizations find the task insurmountable. In the best of cases, meta-directory implementations for large organizations take a long time, typically 12-18 months.

In the following we propose a methodology for shortening that time-frame from 18 months to 4

Pohlman Metadirectory Methodology

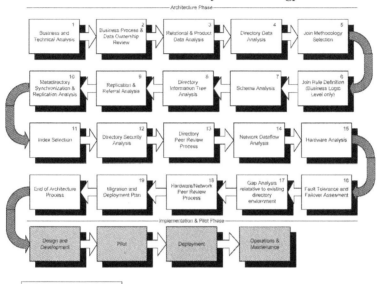

Legend

☐ Common to both Directory & Metadirectory Architectures

▨ Pilot and Deployment Phase (not part of Architecture Phase)

Pohlman Metadirectory Methodology

Step 1: Business Process and Technical Analysis

Step 2: Ownership Analysis

Step 3: Relational Data Analysis:

Step 4: Directory Data Analysis

Step 5: Join Methodology Selection

Step 5: Join Rule Definition (Business Logic Level only)

Step 6: Schema Analysis

Step 7: Directory Information Tree Analysis

Step 8: Replication & Referral Analysis

Step 9: Metadirectory Synchronization & Replication Analysis

Step 10: Index Selection

Step 11: Directory Security Analysis

Step 12: Directory Peer Review Process

Step 13: Network Dataflow Analysis

Step 14: Hardware Analysis

Step 15: Fault Tolerance and Failover Assesment

Step 16: Gap Analysis relative to existing directory environment

Step 17: Hardware/Network Peer Review Process

Step 18: Migration and Deployment Plan

Step 19: End of Directory Architecture Process

15

Business and Technical Analysis—Step 1

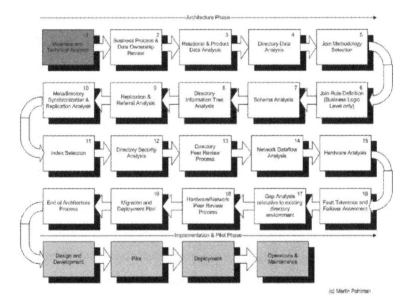

Business Process & Data Ownership Review — 2

Relational & Product Data Analysis — 3

Directory Data Analysis — 4

Join Methodology Selection — 5

Metadirectory Synchronization & Replication Analysis — 10

Replication & Referral Analysis — 9

Directory Information Tree Analysis — 8

Schema Analysis — 7

Join Rule Definition (Business Logic Level only) — 6

Index Selection — 11

Directory Security Analysis — 12

Directory Peer Review Process — 13

Network Dataflow Analysis — 14

Hardware Analysis — 15

End of Architecture Process

Migration and Deployment Plan — 19

Hardware/Network Peer Review Process — 18

Gap Analysis relative to existing directory environment — 17

Fault Tolerance and Failover Assessment — 16

Implementation & Pilot Phase

Design and Development

Pilot

Deployment

Operations & Maintenance

(c) Martin Pohlman

Initiate a Business Process Analysis of the system with a focus on the directory component. Directory systems have a direct and immediate impact on the business. From an information point of view, the solution to productive organizations is not how much information can be automated. The solution is what information is necessary to support the functional processes that make up the business, thus allowing for efficient operations. The directory must support the business plan, which lays out the processes that must be performed in order to accomplish the mission, and the individual roles. The directory schema and information tree must provide the common sheet of music so that each individual clearly knows how he or she fits into the organization and how he or she relates to others in the organization. In addition, the directory must provide each player, actor, and director the critical information needed to perform his or her individual roles. Each team member needs sufficient information on what is expected of him or her. If the directory and supporting system does not provide the essential information, confusion will result, and the mission of the entire organization will suffer.

Davenport & Short (1990) define business process as "a set of logically related tasks performed to achieve a defined business outcome." A process is "a structured, measured set of activities designed to produce a specified output for a particular customer or market. It implies a strong emphasis on how work is done within an organization" (Davenport 1993). In their view processes have two important characteristics:

- They have customers (internal or external)

- They cross organizational boundaries, i.e., they occur across or between organizational subunits.

One technique for identifying business processes in an organization is the value chain Processes are generally identified in terms of beginning and end points, interfaces, and organization units involved, particularly the customer unit. High Impact processes should have process owners.

- Processes may be defined based on three dimensions

- Entities: Processes take place between organizational entities. They could be Interorganizational (e.g. EDI), Interfunctional or Interpersonal (e.g. CSCW).

- Objects: Processes result in manipulation of objects. These objects could be Physical or Informational.

- Activities: Processes could involve two types of activities: Managerial (e.g. develop a budget) and Operational (e.g. fill a customer order).

One of the key elements of strategic planning for directory systems is the integration of directory systems planning with business planning (BP). This integration enables the directory to support business strategies more effectively. This extends existing results by examining the evolution of business process integration and the contingency variables that may influence business process integration. Directory services often follow an evolutionary pattern that can be defined in terms of movement through four types of BP-ISP integration: administrative integration to sequential integration to reciprocal integration to full integration. We choose to focus on the Directory service as the key enabler of BPR, which is considered as "radical change."

A strategic use of the directory is to challenge the assumptions inherent in the work processes that have existed before the introduction of directory services. The heart of reengineering is the notion of discontinuous thinking or recognizing and breaking away from the outdated rules and fundamental assumptions underlying operations. The business analysis phase should consider the following principals.

- Organize around outcomes, not tasks;

- Have those who use the output of the process perform the process;

- Subsume information processing work into the real work that produces the information;

- Treat geographically dispersed resources as though they were centralized;

- Link parallel activities instead of integrating their results;

- Put the decision point where the work is performed, and build control into the process;

- Capture information once and at the source.

Implementing a directory service requires taking a broader view of both IT and business activity, and of the relationships between them. The directory should be viewed as more than an automating or mechanizing force: to fundamentally reshape the way business is done.

Business activities should be viewed as more than a collection of individual or even functional tasks: in a process view for maximizing effectiveness. Directory services and BPR often have recursive relationship. The directories capabilities should support business processes, and business processes should be in terms of the capabilities the directory and supporting IT can provide.

The Directory team should initiate a Business Process Analysis of the system with a focus on the directory component. Business Process Reengineering often results from this effort. The first deliverable should be a process document detailing the movement of data through the system at a high level.

The Data flow diagram show the flow of data values from their sources in objects through the processes that transform them to their destination in other objects. Values can include input values, output values, and internal data stores. Control information is shown only in the form of control flows.

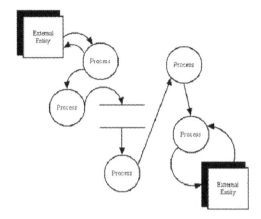

Next initiate a Technical Analysis of the existing infrastructure. The deliverable should be a document detailing the existing hardware and software system infrastructure including configuration data and existing deployment and development methodologies

Sizing involves making a rough estimate of the number of users and magnitude of the directory. This is important when deciding on a DIT and replication topology. The Usage parameters below should be considered minima. For example, a notable fast food chain has 550,000 employees world wide, 2 entries per person with a total object count of 1,100,000 but anticipates 2300 connections per second distributed among 14 Units due to the number of directory enabled applications and server distribution. This would classify the deployment as a Type III for scale, even though the number of users is less than a class III the number of objects classify it as a Type II

Usage	Connections/sec	DSA/slapd Instances in cluster	Number of Objects
TYPE I: DEPARTMENTAL	0-500	0-8	Less than 500,000

Usage	Connections/sec	DSA/slapd Instances in cluster	Number of Objects
Type II: Organization wide	500-2000	8-16	500,000 to 2,000,000
Type III: Enterprise wide	2000-8000	17-32	2,000,000 to 8,000,000
Type IV: Global/National	8000+	32+	8,000,000+

DELIVERABLES:

- Data Flow Diagram—High Level

- Infrastructure State Assessment

- Preliminary Directory Sizing

16

Ownership Analysis—Phase 2

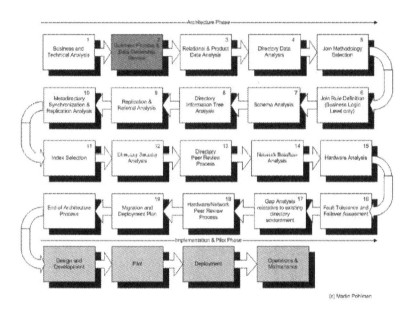

(c) Martin Pohlman

The European Commission's Directive on Data Protection went into effect in October, 1998, and prohibits the transfer of personal data to non-European Union nations that do not meet the European "adequacy" standard for privacy protection and entry self service. This can result in **criminal** penalties, including incarceration, for executives of non-European companies who do business within the European

Union and fail to properly handle the data of their European employees and business partners.

The European Commission's Directive on Data Protection can be addressed by conforming to the U.S. Department of Commerce Safe Harbor principals. In order to bridge the different privacy approaches and provide a streamlined means for U.S. organizations to comply with the Directive, the U.S. Department of Commerce in consultation with the European Commission developed a "safe harbor" framework. The safe harbor which was approved by the EU in July of 2000. The Safe Harbor principals are an important way for U.S. companies to avoid experiencing interruptions in their business dealings with the EU or facing prosecution by European authorities under European privacy laws. Certifying to the safe harbor will assure that EU organizations know that your company provides "adequate" privacy protection, as defined by the Directive.

The eight principals of the DOC safe harbor are:

- **Notice**—Organizations must inform individuals as to the purposes for which information about them is being collected and used, and the types of third parties to whom the organization may disclose information.

- **Choice**—Individuals must be provided the opportunity to "opt out" of allowing their information to be disclosed to a third party

- **Safe Harbor Sensitive Information Principle**—Individuals must opt in for sensitive personal information.

- **Onward Transfer**—Privacy protection must be maintained

- **Security**—Organizations must take precautions to protect personal information.

- **Data Integrity**—Organizations must take steps to ensure that data is accurate.

- **Access**—Organizations must provide individuals with access to correct, amend, or delete personal information.

- **Enforcement**—Organizations must define procedures and mechanisms for assuring compliance with the principles.

In addition, A statement of verification must either be signed by a corporate officer or an independent reviewer indicating that the organization's published privacy policy is accurate, comprehensive, prominently displayed, completely implemented, and in compliance with the safe harbor principles.

At this point it is important to initiate an independent 3rd party process ownership analysis. Data ownership refers to the person or organization that is responsible for making sure the data is up-to-date. As the architect plans data management, the architect needs to decide who you is able to write to the data. Some common strategies are:

- Allow read-only access to the directory for everyone except a small group of directory content managers.

- Allow a person's manager to write to some strategic subset of that person's information, such as contact information or job title.

- Allow an organization's administrator to create and manage entries for that organization. This effectively causes your enterprise's administrators to also be your directory content managers.

- Allow individual users to manage some strategic subset of information for themselves. This information might include a password, descriptive information and the roles within the organization, automobile license plate number, and contact information such as telephone numbers or office numbers.

- Create groups that define roles, such as Human Resources, Finance, or Accounting. Allow each of these roles to have read and/or write access only to the data, especially sensitive data, that is needed by the group, such as salary information, government identification number (in the US, social security number), and home phone numbers and address.

As the architect performs the analysis and determines who can write to the data, they may find that multiple individuals need to have write access to the same information. For example, they will want some information systems (IS) or directory management group to have write access to employee passwords. The architect may also want the employee themselves to have write access to their own passwords. While it is generally necessary to allow multiple people to have write access to the same information, this group should be kept small and easily identifiable. Doing so will more easily allow the architect to ensure your data's integrity.

Planning the directory's data is the most important aspect of the directory planning activities. Therefore, the project plan should budget plenty of time for data planning. The architect will spend the majority of their time surveying the enterprise to locate all the data stores where directory information is managed. As the team performs this survey, they should expect to find that some kinds of data are not well managed; some processes may be inefficient, inadequate, or nonexistent altogether; and some kinds of data that you expect to find are not available at all. All of these issues should be addressed before the team finishes the data-planning phase.

The data-planning activities should include:

- Determine what directory-enabled applications the enterprise wants to deploy and what their data needs are.

- Survey the enterprise and identify where the data comes from (such as NT or Netware directories, PBX systems, Human Resources databases, email systems, and so forth).

- Determine who needs access to the data pay attention to the enterprise's mission-critical applications. Find out if those applications can directly access and/or update the directory.

- For each piece of data, determine the location where it will be mastered.

- For each piece of data, determine who owns the data; that is, who is responsible for ensuring that the data is up-to-date.

- For each piece of data, determine the name of the attribute that the team will use to represent the data in the directory and the object class (the type of entry) that the data will be stored on.

If the project requires the import of data from other sources, develop a strategy for both bulk imports and incremental updates. As a part of this strategy, try to master any given piece of data in just a single location, and limit the number of applications that can change the data to as few as possible. Also, keep the number of people who can write to any given piece of data to a small, easily identifiable group. Doing this will help ensure the data's integrity while greatly reducing the enterprise's administrative overhead. Generally data planning should be driven by the applications that access your directory and the data needs of these applications. Some of the more common applications that you will use with your directory include:

- A directory browser application, such as an online telephone book. Decide what information (such as email addresses, telephone numbers, employee name, and so forth) you want your users to be able to obtain through the directory when doing telephone book lookups and make sure you put that kind of information into the directory.

- Email applications, especially email servers. Not all email servers will require the same types of information. All email servers require email addresses, user names, and some routing information to be available in the directory. Others, however, will require more advanced information such as the location on disk where a user's mailbox is stored, vacation notification information, and protocol information (IMAP versus POP, for example).

- Directory-enabled HR applications. These require more personal information such as government identification numbers, home addresses, home telephone numbers, birth dates, salary, and job title.

When planning directory data, plan not only what is required to be place in the directory today, but also try to determine what may be required to be included in the directory at some point in the future. While not strictly planning ahead can help you scale your directory service to take on larger roles in the enterprise.

Points to consider:

- What is required in the directory? That is, what is the immediate problem that is to be solved by deploying a directory service? What is immediately needed by the directory-enabled applications that will be used first?

- What is the long-term directory future? For example, the enterprise might use an accounting package that does not currently support LDAP, but which will be LDAP-enabled in the near future. The team should identify the data use by applications such as this and plan for the migration of the data into the directory when the technology becomes available.

- What might the enterprise want to someday store in the directory? This kind of planning helps to identify data stores (locations where information is managed) that might not otherwise become aware of.

Information that the team might want to include:

- contracts or client accounts
- payroll
- physical devices
- home contact information
- EDI data
- office contact information for the various sites within the enterprise

As the team determines who can write to the data, one may find that multiple individuals need to have write access to the same information. For example, one will want an information systems (IS) or directory management group to have write access to employee passwords. One may also want the employees themselves to have write access to their own passwords. While one generally must give multiple people write access to the same information, try to keep this group small and easy to identify. Keeping the group small helps ensure your data's integrity.

Common challenges?

- Finding owners for orphaned data.
- Gaining cooperation from data owners.
- Arbitrating disputed data ownership.
- Legal and privacy issues.
- Planning and implementing a meta-directory exposes major problems with business processes.

Data ownership should not be confused with database ownership

- The management of data as an enterprise asset

- Access requirements defined against content not platform

- Access requirements defined by data steward or functional manager

- User access rights administered by data steward

- Steward responsible for Accuracy, Reliability, Timeliness, Interoperability, Survivability

Once the processes are identified and owners are identified, initiate a data ownership analysis of the data as it passes through the defined process. It is important to separate data custody from data ownership at this phase. Any data generated by the process in question will have to have its resulting owner defined as well. In the event of ambiguous elements the Architect should first seek empowerment from a member of senior management and should this fail to materialize proceed on the assumption that incorrect judgment calls will be rectified with time

** Warning this is the most political component of the Directory Architecture Process **

DELIVERABLES:

- List of stakeholders in the directory deployment process

- Data & Process Ownership Statement/Position paper

- 2nd Level Dataflow Diagram at attribute level with transfer of custody and process elements included

17

Relational Data Analysis—Phase 3

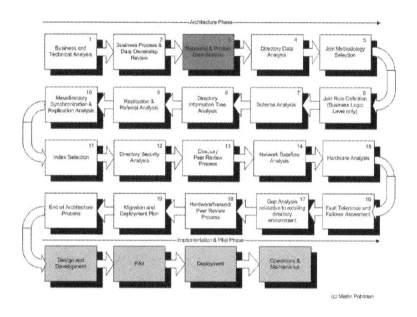

(c) Martin Pohlman

A Directory is a hybrid of a 3rd level normalized relational structure which can be expressed in a flat file referred to as an LDIF. In memory this is represented as a Binary Tree structure. When integrating a relational structure into a directory via a meta directory product several steps must be taken with respect to the relational structure to be integrated. While the skill of a DBA are not necessary, some database knowledge is necessary if one is to properly reflect the function of a database entry within a Directory. A "normalized" relational database in Third Normal Form (3NF) will be easily mapped into a directory by following the single primary key and mapping attributes into the appropriate directory entry.

In the event of a 3NF compliant relational database

Document the following:

- tables—lists the tables that exist
- columns—lists the columns for each table
- indexes—lists the keys and indexes for each table
- triggers—lists the summarize triggers for each table
- views—lists the view definitions

Document All Relationships and Joins

- One-to-One Relationships
- One-to-Many Relationships
- Many-to-Many Relationships

It may not be practical to preserve the structure of the data in the Directory. In an optimistic situation the following elements may be reproduced in the directory

- Data elements as attributes
- Tables as object classes
- Columns as individual entries within an object class
- Indexes as directory indexes
- Views as directory tree structures (not recommended)
- One to One relationships reflected in directory tree structure

- One to Many relationships reflected in the hierarchy of the directory tree

In the event the database deviates from the common Star or Snowflake normalized schema execute the following analysis

1st Examine the Database for Denormalization

A denormalized database may have several properties, including:

- Repetition of information.
- Inability to represent certain information.
- Loss of information.

Neophyte database designers (and professionals, on occasion) are prone to several common mistakes. Here are some common denormalized structures and suggestions of how to map the data into a directory.

Spreadsheet design. The database shouldn't resemble a single table of all sorts of business data, especially if it included a number of calculated values. Combining different types of data in one table defeats the whole purpose of using a relational database and makes mapping the data to a directory problematic. While storing calculated values can speed up query and report performance, databases generally calculate values on the fly so the data is always as current as possible. In this case the spreadsheet should be broken into a series of attributes, which will be mapped into the directory. Location of an attribute that can act as a primary key is essential in this instance

Too much data. The goal of a successfully designed database is to provide all of the information necessary for making decisions based on the data. There is an overwhelming desire, especially in neophytes, to encapsulate every possible nugget of data in the database. Too many fields in a form guarantee translation difficulties into a directory format. Plus this information increases the overall storage requirements for the database. Proper research can help identify what is essential, what might be useful in the future, and what is irrelevant.

Compound fields. Fields containing multiple discrete pieces of data lead to problems in searching, alphabetizing, and calculating those fields. It's much harder to get a report of customers by ZIP code when that value is buried in a field with the address, city, and state. If it's a distinct piece of data, make it a distinct field. Renormalize and map the resulting data to a unique directory attribute.

Missing keys. Every table needs some sort of key to identify individual records. make sure there is a distinct and unique key for each record in each table and if not, create one based on sequence numbers or date/time stamp. Then map the record into an object class.

Bad keys. A key has to be unique for each record. Existing database fields may appear to be good candidates for keys, but it is usually best to create an artificial key that is guaranteed to be unique. Phone numbers or Social Security Numbers seem like a great key for personnel records until you run into people who live in the same home or who have changed Social Security numbers due to family crisis. Again Date/time stamp is a neutral solution

Missing relations. If two tables are supposed to be related, there must be a field that relates the two databases. A well-designed table relationship is useless if the appropriate foreign keys are not added to the related tables (or if the linking table for a many-to-many relationship is not created). Simply map attributes if possible, This will have to be corrected by the DBA before proper mapping of schema elements can proceed

Unnecessary relationships. Just because every table can be linked to every other table does not mean that they have to be related. There is a temptation to relate tables that are logically unrelated just because you can. Reexamine the data and rate each element in order of relative importance, then commence mapping starting at the most important "key" and drilling down no more than three layers.

Incorrect relations. Creating relationships between tables does not require changes in each table. A one to many relationship requires the primary key from the "one" table to be inserted as a foreign key in the "many" table. It does not need a foreign key placed in the "one" table since the relationship is already established in the many table. In fact, this arrangement may yield incorrect query results. This must be corrected by the DBA before mapping can proceed

Duplicate field names. DBMS products prevent duplicate field names in a single table, but do not prevent duplicate names in different tables. While there is no programmatic reason to follow this practice, it becomes very difficult for humans to keep track of 15 relational tables where the primary key in each is called ID. It is much easier to write and debug queries if each field name is unique in the entire database. If possible ignore duplicate field names on mapping the data into attributes. This may require DBA or management intervention and business process review.

Cryptic field and table names. Even more frustrating than duplicate names are cryptic names. There is no reason to limit the length of a field or table name, so use as descriptive a name as possible. Writing queries and debugging are much easier when the focus is the logic and not what T1C1x means. Simply append the values with the "company prefix" and map each value into the directory

Embedded Business rules. Many businesses have strict rules that have nothing to do with program or database logic. Do not neglect these rules. The old adage of "garbage in, garbage out" applies since decisions made on incorrectly entered data may lead to erroneous query results and reporting. Note the rules and any omissions found for inclusion in stage 3.5.

Constraints. A very easy way to ensure that data are entered correctly is to use constraints. These can be implemented as checks to see if an entered value is within an approved list or range of choices. Constraints can also be implemented as masks that require phone numbers or ZIP codes to fit a specified format. These simply do not map to a directory and must be included manually

Referential integrity. Data records that participate in relationships need to be checked when they are created or deleted to ensure that they are not orphans. Deleting one record usually requires the deletion of that record in linked tables. Ensuring referential integrity involves making sure that table declarations ensure the existence of the appropriate relationships and that integrity checks are triggered when records are deleted. This will require extensive code in the join rule to emulate. Do not use the product specific referential integrity features as these have been known to degrade performance to unacceptable levels.

Database security. Almost all databases have methods to control access and user rights. For instance, end users of an invoice system probably should not have permission to create new tables or delete existing tables. Use the available security features of the directory server to prevent unauthorized access and control permissions of various users and classes of users.

International issues. As business becomes more global, keep in mind that there are a number of formats for business data other than those of the United States. Most databases understand the various European and American date, currency, and address formats. Fortunately the IETF has included internationalization within each RFC and this is not a problem

In summary, the basic elements of the redesign and attribute mapping process are:

- Defining the problem or objective

- Researching the current database

- Examine the data structures when crafting object classes and schema

- Document and when possible reflect relationships

- Attempt to reflect the database relationship in the schema when integrating views and reports

DELIVERABLES

- Relational Datasources Identified

- Existing 3NF Relational structure expressed in basic table layout

18

Directory Data Analysis—Phase 4

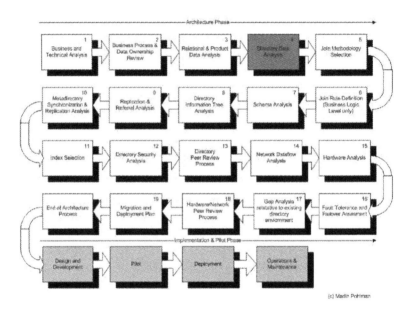

The challenges to enterprise directory deployment are not insignificant: In many cases, directory managers must find 'dirty' directory data, and end up mired in lengthy and unexpected information scrubbing exercises. Many customers find the cost and effort of creating a unique directory ID for users tougher than they initially thought. Disorganized directory management processes also can present an obstacle that managers must overcome. Finding authoritative sources for information amongst a myriad of sources and processes can be difficult. And political difficulties are always threat organizational units and divisions of a company must share the desire to create a unified directory if the project is to succeed.

To do proper directory data analysis one must understand how LDAP-compliant directories are deployed and utilized. In the network space, Directories serve three major roles: Authentication, Authorization and Personalization.

THE DIRECTORY AS AN AUTHENTICATION SOURCE

Using the Directory as an authentication source is a standard role since directories were designed around security concerns. Extremely granular, robust security mechanisms are available, allowing security down to the attribute level. Many Directory-enabled applications are available to extend directory security mechanisms to include a wide variety of authentication mechanisms, including PKI, biometrics, tokens, and other advanced forms of authentication.

Many portal deployments include a security framework that leverages a directory. The majorities of portal and application server products take advantage of the directory's security framework to allow multiple grades of authentication as well as distributed management and application authorization.

Databases are not, by default, as flexible with security. Most databases offer column-level security, but the advanced security solutions available with directories are far more flexible and granular.

THE DIRECTORY AS AN AUTHORIZATION SOURCE

Permissions and restrictions to resources are also a natural function of directories. Many security and identity management applications rely on directories to authorize users to resources or web-based applications. Many authentication servers incorporate policy-based authorization as a major component of their security architectures. Once security policies are established and configured, they do not change frequently. However, the frequency at which they are read remains high because the policies are constantly being checked to ensure security is properly enforced.

THE DIRECTORY FOR PERSONALIZATION

From e-mail systems to portals to policy-based security applications use the Directory as a repository for storing data related to the user. Since the directory maintains a record for each user, it makes sense to store user-specific data with the user. For example, names, addresses, telephone numbers and e-mail addresses are the most common type of personalized data found in a directory. This data is specific to the user, but often needed by many applications. When properly implemented this personalization can go much deeper to include many types of preferences (often referred to as profiling).

Among the benefits of using a directory are the hierarchical design, multi-value attribute support, extensible schema, and standard LDAP support and APIs. The need for speed and scalability also play well to the strength of directories. As opposed to systems designed on top of a RDBMS, directory enabled systems are able to achieve under 250 millisecond performance, with the directory responding to more than 2000 requests per second and upwards of 25 million directory lookups per day. The result is websites and portal servers with the ability to instantly personalize content, even under the most stressful situations.

DETERMINING DIRECTORY OR DATABASE

Taking these factors into account a decision needs to be made as to the storage of data in a Directory or RDBMS. Fortunately the two solutions are quite complementary.

Portal products are great examples of directories and databases working together. These products can be configured to rely on directories for authentication and maintenance of users and/or groups. However, these applications still utilize the RDBMS to store application-specific settings and entitlements, as well as data not suited for directories such as web pages, Java applets, BLOB data, and other information the portal needs to function.

Taking a closer look at the data and applications. The following questions are useful is determining suitability for inclusion in the directory:

- Is the data dynamic or relatively static?
- Does the data need to be distributed?
- Can the data be used by more than one application?
- Is the data multi-valued?
- Can your data or application take advantage of a hierarchical relationship?
- Do you need flexible security options?
- Do you need single sign-on?
- Do you need distributed or delegated administration capabilities?

As the analysis continues, determine if the data and/or the applications require the benefits of ACID transactions. While most directories offer some form of data integrity, such as referential integrity, the directory was never designed for transactional data. If the data changes frequently, then it probably doesn't belong in the directory. For example, one may want to keep ID's or account numbers in a directory because the data is relatively static. But one wouldn't store account balances in a directory because the number would likely change often.

Due to the loosely consistent nature of directories and the nature of multi-master replication, there may be times when a change made to a replica on Directory Server A will take some time to get replicated to Directory Server B. As such, an application reading from replica B could get a different result than an application reading from replica A if both are read immediately after the change is made to replica A. It is even possible that a different change can occur to the same data on replica B before the changes of replica A are made to replica B. The inconsistencies will, in time, correct themselves (conflict resolution can be handled via timestamps, changelog records, etc., and vary from vendor to vendor), but for accounting or finance applications, this is not suitable. The data must be committed and consistent. As such, finance and accounting data is best suited for a RDBMS.

Diirectory data should be relatively static such that its ratio or reads versus writes is relatively high. Since the data is unlikely to change, the probability of an event as mentioned above actually occuring is minimized. Furthermore, the nature of the data isn't such that it is dependant upon transactional level data integrity.

Many of these questions require a thorough understanding of the application and the data involved. Furthermore, consider the business requirements driving the project or application development. The business requirements will dictate the technology, not vice-versa. Directories and databases are complementary, not competitive, solutions. The more one understands the benefits and cost-savings one can gain from a directory, the better one can justify the implementation and migration to a directory-enabled network infrastructure

Identify each of the applications that touch or may touch the directory. Examine each application at the architecture level and identify the application level information sources. Interview the stakeholders and determine the business level information sources which correspond with the application level data. Questions to ask stakeholders are

- What directory applications and tools do you currently have deployed

- What directory applications and tools will you deploy and who will use them

- How will these applications be used (Interrogation, Update, Authentication, Extended)

- What processes are in place to get information into the directory applications.

- Where are the users located

- What will the interfaces looklike

- What other network appliances and network/OS level resources use the directory.

- What other application and infrastructure servers will be deployed.

Common Directory Applications Include

- Address Book

- Messaging and Collaboration Software

- Directory Server gateway

- Portal Servers

- Conference Room Locators

- Security—Single Sign On applications

- Help Desk

- Dynamic DNS and Router packages
- X.400 and X.500 legacy applications
- Wireless Gateway/Portals

Regardless of the different applications directories can support or the role they're playing, directories provide a common set of functions that most applications, and the directory itself, use in day-to-day operations. These basic functions are:

- Authentication and authorization
- Naming and locating network resources
- Administering and managing network resources
- Enabling applications

While no empirical model is ever perfect, these four functional categories are sufficient to define the range of directory-related activities in today's market. Although there is significant overlap and interdependence between the categories, in general each category represents a progression of sophistication that is dependent on the function of the previous category(s)."

Identify datasources. These can include

- Servers
- HR employee databases
- PBX systems
- NIS Systems
- Window NT and ADS Domains
- Flatfiles on desktops

When creating a Directory Data Matrix Ask:

- What are the required fields for all the identified LDAP directory applications

- Are there any additional fields that can be viewed by special users?

- Are there any hidden fields?

- Are you (or is the client) rewriting existing applications (recommend standards)

- Do the applications have the same views

- Are there fields in existing data sources that have not been identified as part of new applications but that could be useful?

- Is there non-people oriented information that could be useful if added to the directory?

- Where does this data come from

  - Where does this data currently exist

  - If there is more than one location, who owns the data (see 3.2 Ownership Analysis)

  - What is the authoritative source of the data

  - What processes need to change

  - What is the name for this data in the authoritative source

  - Do any IETF standards exist that would conflict or overlap with any current names

  - Do any products mandate a specific naming convention and can these names be incorporated.

Reviewing the previous step (Relational Data Analysis) determine what data belongs in the directory

- Data that is read often and written infrequently (e.g. 80/20 Rule)

- Data that can be expressed in attribute form

- Data that useful for more than one audience (no hash tables or mem maps)

- Data which is accessed from more than one location

- System information

  - Device Information such as printer location, type of printer, router configs.

  - Contact and Billing/EFT information for extranets such as EDI Map's, Supply Chain info, Identrus ID's, ECN Key Hash

  - User Prefrences such as webtop and thin client settings.

  - Resource Locations such as FTP servers, Web Servers, NIS data, DNS data, File System Info

Examples of data that should be represented by meta-directory Join's and not replicated into the directory

- Data that changes frequently. (e.g. Access Logs or Security Sign In Values)

- Large unstructured chunks of data which were designed for file systems, FTP server, Web Servers, Multi-Dimensional Matrix attributes or relational databases and complex stored procedures.

In the event these attributes are requested consider a Resource link, alias, referral or Join Rule to express this data outside the slapd (LDAP daemon) environment

Examples of Application Fields

- Employee Name
  - First Name
  - Last Name
  - Legal Name
  - X.509
- Employee Address
  - Home Address
  - Business Address
  - Cubical or Office
  - Floor
- Phone Number
  - Home
  - Business
  - Mobile
  - Pager
  - IM (AIM, ICQ, Netmeeting ID)

A broader paradigm of directory services than application-specific solutions

- Comprehensive, scalable methodologies to validate authenticity
- Association of specific validations with pre-specified authorizations
- Seamless, comprehensive interfaces to integrate all components of the enterprise

The term 'directory-enabled computing' defines the directory's role as a significant component of the enterprise computing infrastructure. That role will increase in focus as products mature and the industry consolidates. Organizations once were forced to deal with special-purpose directory technology that isolated information and increased the management burden. Now, however, they can begin to build an enterprise directory infrastructure around general-purpose products that can participate in an integrated enterprise directory infrastructure that reduces management overhead and supports a variety of applications. Customers must invest in and plan for that infrastructure now to take full advantage of these new roles as they mature. An individual company can realize benefits from moving from its many directories to a consolidated solution, clearly companies in an industry group should strive to achieve improved ROI. When e-business emerged as a primary driver for intranet and extranet architectures, however, the need to rationalize directory architecture reached critical mass. Companies need to simplify user and resource management internally while creating a scalable, secure, and manageable ebusiness infrastructure."

DELIVERABLES

- List of Directory inputs and outputs

- Directory Data Matrix

    1. Documents directory application fields

    2. Documents information sources

    3. Documents other directory data

Sample Directory Data Matrix (Excel Format)

	Directory Applications					Information Sources				Check field if Directory
Address Book	Application Server	ERP Systems	Portal Svr	Security	HR Dept	PBX Dept	Client Svcs	Network Adm	Server is Authoritative	

19

Join Methodology Selection—Phase 5 & 6

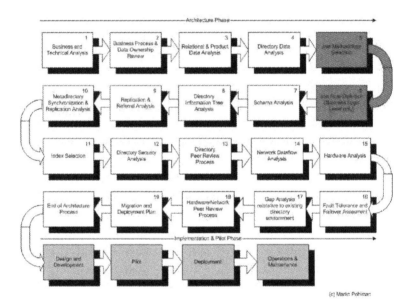

(c) Martin Pohlman

PHASE 5

The join methodology defines how the data sources interact with the master directory server. While the relationships are attribute based and the attribute may be pushed or polled based own ownership, there are instanced where new aggregates are created form multiple sources during the Join process. In order to determine the type and timing of the joins the business process drivers must be evaluated against the business requirements and the legal issues relation to data ownership. While the legal issues are covered in chapter 32, the immediate process drivers governing the join process outlined below must be addressed.

Process Drivers

1. User Account Integration: Single Sign on between multiple applications is often the most requested feature and Join selection should focus on simplifying the user experience

2. Messaging system integration: Integration of Groupware systems such as PhP groupware, NNTP & Lotus Notes/Domino with more traditional Mail systems such as SMTP, Exchange and Netscape Messaging Server is a driving force in Join systems

3. Systems integration: Integration of Proprietary OS directories, x.500 systems, ERP/SCP application sets, complementary systems such as EDI/EFT packages, Messaging/Groupware and Legacy systems

The diagram below illustrates the functions of a Metaview and Join engine in relation to the parsing engine (usually a Java or Perl interpreter) and the connector view.

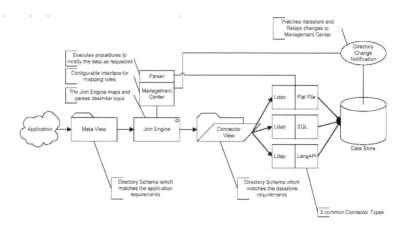

Common Meta Directory Features

- View: A Directory instance that acts as an intermediary between the raw data and the unified Metaview

- Meta view: a unified LDAP directory made up of both literal attributes and symbolic links to external systems.

- JoinEngine: A JoinEngine's function is to join information about persons and objects emanating from disparate enterprise data sources (Views) into a unified LDAP directory and then controlling the flow of information from the unified MetaView to external directories.

- Parser: A parser is a module that knows how to interpret and translate information from a byte stream into a structured information object where each piece of information is accessible by name and vice versa. A parser can (but need not) be bi-directional. This can take the form of Perl, Java, CPI, VB Script or a multitude of technologies

- Change Notification Service: Change Notification Service detects changes in the MetaView and in connected data sources and to provide change notification to the connected data sources that can accept notifications.

- Connector view: a directory instance made up parsed literal attributes and symbolic links to datastores

Functions of the View:

- Data aggregators

- Symbolic representations of external systems with restricted raw access

- Use specific data representations

Functions of the Metaview

- Principal repository of enterprise data and location information

- Central "root" switchboard for queries

- Point of reference for use specific Views

Functions of the Notification Service

- A listener service that queries multiple external sources with the following task list

- Incremental updates: External directories and databases are updated incrementally, as they are modified.

- Object creation: Objects in external directories and databases are created from within the MetaView.

- Object deletion: Objects can be deleted from the MetaView and from the external directory or database.

- Object modification: Objects can be modified in the MetaView to reflect modifications in the corresponding entry in the external directory or database.

Functions of a Join Engine

- Filtering: Filtering can be used to explicitly include or exclude entries within specific subtrees during synchronization.

- Join Rules: Join Rules are used to select the entries to be joined between Views and the MetaView. Search rules can be built using the Parser to refine selection criteria. Join rules are added in sequence to a rule set. Each rule in a set is applied to each entry until a single matching entry is found.

- DN Mapping Rules: DN mapping rules determine the name to use to create an entry in the destination view. When the JoinEngine is unable to join a source entry in the destination view, DN mappings rules are added in sequence to a rule set that is parsed until a valid rule is found. DN mapping rules can be grammar-based or invoke a Parser that builds the naming attribute.

Functions of the Parser

- A module that knows how to interpret and translate information from a byte stream into a structured information object where each piece of information is accessible by name and vice versa.

- Parsers execute **Procedural** code against data, massaging said data into the MetaView. Parsers come in a variety of flavors

  - LDAP Connector: An LDAP Connector is a direct connector where the data resides in an LDAP directory. An LDAP connector is effectively built in to the Directory Server when the Meta-Directory schema is added to the Directory Server configuration.

  - SQL Connector: The SQL Connector is a direct connector to data residing in a SQL-accessible database. Most Meta-Directories supports database connectors for Oracle, Sybase, Informix and MS SQL Server. The SQL Connector often uses a database trigger mechanism to detect and react to changes occurring in connected databases.

- Java (most often small psedo-object/classes, never complex)
- JavaScript
- Perl
- PerlScript
- VBScript
- Jscript
- REXX
- NETREXX
- LotusXSL
- BML
- C (never C++)
- CPI-C

Note: Use experience and common sense when selecting connectors. If this phase becomes a full development effort then the usefulness of this process is lost. Each join agreement should be represent able in a simple one-page flow chart.

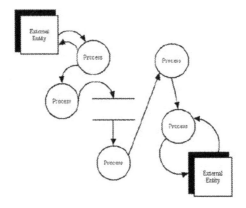

A standard Entity Relationship Diagram such as that shown above should be defined for each join.

DELIVERABLES—5:

- A list of Joins

- ERD—Entity Relationship Diagram

PHASE 6

In phase 5 each Process defined in the ERD cited above is detailed from a process perspective and a data flow diagram such as the one detailed below is added

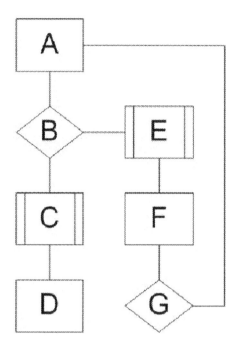

After which said diagram is translated to pseudo code with detailed conditions and procedures

```
Join 1

Process A  : Execute A
Condition B: IF Condition True then Process C Else GOTO
Process E
Process C  : Execute Process C
Process D  : END OF PROCESS
Process E  : Execute Process E
Process F  : Execute Process F
Condition G: If Condition False then Process A
```

DELIVERABLES—6:

- Data Flow Diagram

- Parser Pseudo Code for each Join

20

Schema Analysis—Phase 7

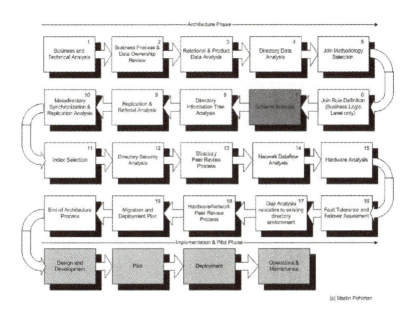

Step 1: Review the following IETF schemas RFCs at **http:// www.ietf.org**

RFC 1617	*Naming and Structuring Guidelines for X.500 Directory Pilots*	P. Barker, S. Kille, T. Lenggenhager
RFC 2798	*Definition of the inetOrgPerson LDAP Object Class*	M. Smith

RFC 2796	Definition of the inetOrgPerson LDAP Object Class	M. Smith
RFC 2377	Naming Plan for Internet Directory-Enabled Applications	A. Grimstad, R. Huber, S. Sataluri, M. Wahl
RFC 2218	A Common Schema for the Internet White Pages Service	T. Genovese, B. Jennings
RFC 1943	Building an X.500 Directory Service in the US	B. Jennings
RFC 1804	Schema Publishing in X.500 Directory	G. Mansfield, P. Rajeev, S. Raghavan, T. Howes
RFC 2252	Lightweight Directory Access Protocol (v3): Attribute Syntax Definitions	M. Wahl, A. Coulbeck, T. Howes, S. Kille
RFC 2713	Schema for Representing Java(tm) Objects in an LDAP Directory	V. Ryan, S. Seligman, R. Lee
RFC 2714	Schema for Representing CORBA Object References in an LDAP Directory	V. Ryan, S. Seligman, R. Lee
RFC 2739	Calendar Attributes for vCard and LDAP	T. Small, D. Hennessy, F. Dawson
RFC 2768	Network Policy and Services: A Report of a Workshop on Middleware	B. Aiken, J. Strassner, B. Carpenter, I. Foster, C. Lynch, J. Mambretti, R. Moore, B. Teitelbaum
RFC 2904	AAA Authorization Framework	J. Vollbrecht, P. Calhoun, S. Farrell, L. Gommans, G. Gross, B. de Bruijn, C. de Laat, M. Holdrege, D. Spence
RFC 2926	Conversion of LDAP Schemas to and from SLP Templates	J. Kempf, R. Moats, P. St. Pierre
RFC 2927	MIME Directory Profile for LDAP Schema	M. Wahl
RFC 2967	TISDAG—Technical Infrastructure for Swedish Directory Access Gateways	L. Daigle, R. Hedberg

RFC 2256	*LDAPv3 schema defined in X.520/X.521*	
RFC 3060	*Policy Core Information Model—Version 1 Specification*	B. Moore, E. Ellesson, J. Strassner, A. Westerinen

Step 2: Review the **http://www.dmtf.org/spec/denh.html** home page for Directory Enabled Network Schema's to determine if these apply to this instance of meta-directory

Step 3: Review the default schema provided with the Directory Product

Step 4: Review any product specific schemas

Step 5: Match application fields to Default Directory Schema if said fields exist as attributes.

Step 6: Match application fields to IETF RFC's or DMTF DEN Standards listed above extend the schema as listed in the RFC's and create said attributes if those do not already exist.

Step 7: Extend the information tree, schema and object model to include application specific fields as attributes inheriting from object-Class: top as a application specific custom object class.

To do list when matching application fields to existing schema's

• Identify the type of object the application field describes

• Select a similar object class from the default schema

• Select a similar attribute from the matching object class

• Transfer the application field and authoritative source to the new matrix if possible

• Create a list of unmatched fields

When extending the schema

• Provide a description of each new attribute and object class

• Describe operating procedures for administrators

- Describe update procedures for end users
- Define Attribute Types
  - bin, ces, cis, tel, dn, int
  - Single or Multivalue
- Define object class
  - Inheritance
  - Required attributes
  - Allowed Attributes
- Obtain OID numbers
  - X.500/ITU compatibility

Definitions Matrix

Directory Application					Directory Server Schema		IETF Schema	
Address Book	Siebel	Peoplesoft	Domino	Portal	Object Class	Attribute	Object Class	Attribute

Transfer Matrix

Application Field	Default/New Schema Attribute	Source

one can define the rules for the new object class and attributes in the matrix by following a convention of using italics for attributes that are allowed and normal type for attributes that are required. Use parentheticals under the objects to denote the superior object class and use square brackets next to each custom attribute to denote the data type

e.g.

---

mycompanyPerson [dn]
(inetOrgPerson)

Object naming conventions.

1. Never overlap existing native naming conventions within the directory server or meta-directory join engine

2. Never over look established IETF naming conventions, as other standards compliant servers will use these naming conventions as native.

3. Always prefix company specific "unique" object classes and attributes with an abbreviated company name such as using "mycompanyOrgPerson" for a company called My Company Inc.

4. When a vendor provides a GUI for modification of the slapd always take advantage of it if possible. Manual editing is a hazard, and while macho from a "hacker" perspective often creates more problems than it solves.

DELIVERABLES:

• Completed Definitions Matrix

- Completed Transfer Matrix
- List of private object classes

21

Directory Information Tree Analysis—Phase 8

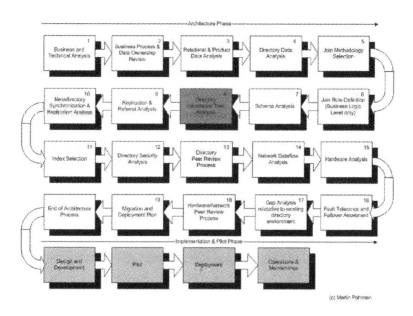

(c) Martin Pohlman

Steps involved in designing a directory tree hierarchy.

1. Select a directory suffix or suffixes for your tree

2. Diagram a directory tree design

3. Select branch points for your tree

4. Create sample entries on each branch point

5. Select unique relative distinguished names for your entries

Standards Related To Tree Design

RFC 1279	*X.500 and Domains*	S.E. Hardcastle-Kille
RFC 2377	*Naming Plan for Internet Directory-Enabled Applications*	A. Grimstad, R. Huber, S. Sataluri, M. Wahl

Directory objects are hierarchically organized in a single tree format known as the directory information tree (DIT) All objects are unique in this structure; even a copy of an object is considered a separate, unique object with all the same values for its properties as the original. To maintain object uniqueness, every object has a name. This name differentiates it from all other objects and is defined by its position in the tree. The distinguished name (DN) is the full identity of a unique object, as defined in the overall hierarchy.

Unfortunately there isn't a single global definition of what a tree should look like for every organization. The LDAP information model is flexible enough that you can define your own vision of the objects on your environment. This definition, called a schema, shows how objects are grouped together within the tree. The schema also defines the structure of individual objects in the directory.

Traditional x.500 Aligned Directory Model—Appropriate for Type I, II & III

```
DNS Aligned Directory Model—Appropriate for Type I, II & III
```

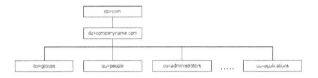

```
Domain Component Aligned Model—Appropriate for Type I, II &
III
```

A directory suffix identifies the root entry of a directory tree that is maintained by the directory server. It is possible to have multiple suffixes within a single Directory Server. This means you can have multiple root entries or directory trees within the meta directory Server

Within the slapd.ldbm.conf file three suffixes are often present depending on implementation

```
Suffix o=companyname.com
```

This is what the installation routine often provides

```
Suffix dc=hostname, dc=companyname, dc=com
```

This suffix identifies another directory tree in the server that is used internally to store information about itself and other instances of the server when initiating replication

```
Suffix o=VendorRoot
```

This is a directory known as the configuration directory. It holds information the server uses to operate and manage the directory. Only one configuration directory exists in an installation to support servers in the enterprise.

Next, Select Branch Points, Items to consider include

- X.500 coexistance

- Ease of Administration

- Replication or referrals

- Strategic use of views

EXAMPLE 21A BRANCHING TO SUPPORT X.500 COEXISTENCE

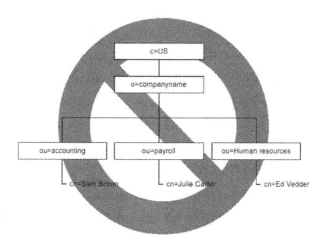

x.500 directory servers branch there directory trees to reflect organizations across the enterprise. If "companyname" had the organizational units of Accounting, Payroll and Human Resources the branch points would reflect those organizational units using the (ou) attribute.

In normal x.500 designs people within those entries would be identified by their common name or cn. This leads to future difficulties in issuing x.509's and establishing identity entries that follow a individual through the changes that often occur in the course of a career in a multi tier company.

The traditional x.500 method of creating branch points was to follow the country (c) designator with organization (o), organizational unit (ou) and then common name (cn). The main disadvantage of using organizationalUnits to match physical organizational structutres or departments is that they tend to change frequently. one cannot easily change the name of an organizationalUnit or an entry in an LDAP directory that has branch points below it. Its like trying to remove a directory from a file system that still has files below it. Before you can remove the directory, you have to remove everything below it. This is the same with LDAP but also applies to renaming entries. one can not rename an entry that has children below it. one must delete the entries first.

As a result the following structure is recommended. What we have done in the above model is to preserve this design while promoting a centralized People schema by the use of referrals. This is appropriate for Type I, II & III systems

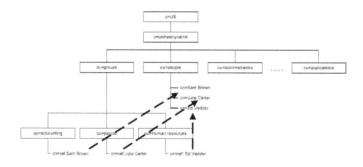

Branching to support x.500 coexistence with deployment flexibility

EXAMPLE 21B BRANCHING TO SUPPORT GEOGRAPHY

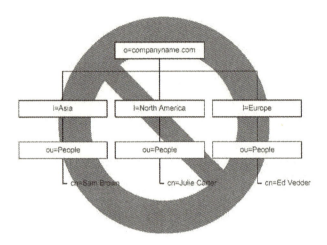

A common branching strategy is to branch the directory tree to support replication and/or referrals directly. The goal is to group the directory data together to make it easier to replicate an entire branch point to another server or provide a smart referral at a branch point that points to another server.

In the above example the strategy is to branch from root using the (l) location attribute and then create a People branch at each location using the organizationalUnit (ou) attribute. While this was perfectly acceptable in a straight directory schema bereft of a Meta directory component, a meta directory makes this into more of an artform

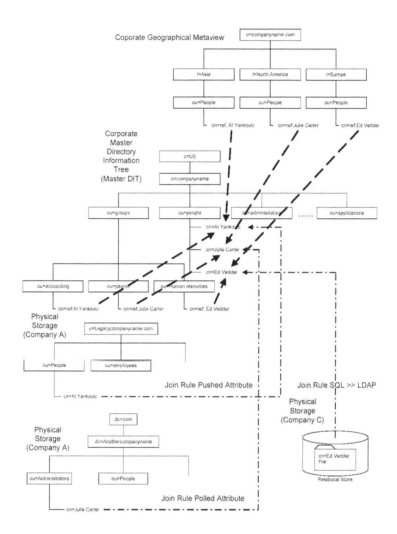

The example above illustrates the use of aliases to support geographical constraints within a DIT structure. This structure is Appropriate for Type I & II deployments, A Type III deployment can be supported but management of the alias structure becomes the logical limiting factor. Using this technique one can maintain geographic representation of an employee or contractor while properly expressing the individual within the global directory. Using this technique an individual can be expressed within an organization while not being bound to it for the life of the entry. This is important as the addition of an x.509 certificate binds the certificate to the relative distinguished name and cannot be changed without invalidating the certificate.

EXAMPLE 21C BRANCHING TO SUPPORT ADMINISTRATION

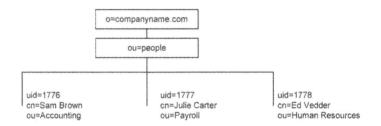

The most efficient solution is to put your directory data into a directory tree structure that does not have to be changed every time reorganization takes place, this structure scales across all deployment scales from I through Type IV with judicious use of aliasing. One can still use an attribute within the entry to describe what organizational Unit it belongs to. All an administrator needs to do is to update the attribute when the organizational Unit changes.

In the example above, all people related entries are put in the People branch using the organizational Unit (ou) attribute. People entries within the People branch use the (ou) attribute to identify which organizational Unit they belong to. If a person changes an organization an administrator simply needs to change to (ou) attribute value instead of moving the use to a different part of the tree.

A further enhancement is to have the organizations existing in a separate sub branch and have a series of *smart referrals* as entries in the organizational Unit (ou) attribute.

In this instance the people each have (ou) entries that refer to the group to which they belong. This is easily changed when the individuals position changes.

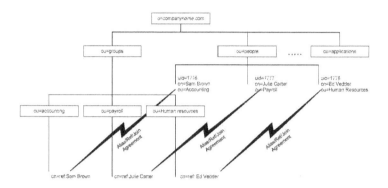

PEOPLE, ROLES, PLACES AND THINGS IN THE DIRECTORY TREE

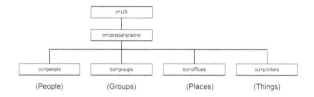

Consider entries in terms of people, places and things instead of thinking in terms of organizations or geography.

<u>People</u> are normally defined at the end of a branch in a directory. Consider putting all people in one logical branch point. This will save the administrator from moving the individual and reissuing a certificate every time the individual changes positions within the company or organization. Instead use the an attribute populated with a referral

within the entry to describe the organization where they work instead of using organizational branch points

<u>Roles</u> are made up of people with common interests, goals and environment. Consider using this branch point to represent the organizational structure keeping the amount of attributes stored in this branch very small and making best use of referrals and aliasing

<u>Places</u> are physical locations. Consider a tree design that is structured by places when you plan to replicate branches out to remote sites. Make clever use of views and the join engine process to abstract the replication process of frequently accessed individuals to remote, frequently accessed areas. Consider this in the paradigm of two overlapping structures one logical and one denoting physical data location when considering replication of data that is to be mastered in various locations.

<u>Things</u> are everything else from Printers to Routers. Some applications such as SNMP aware applications need to support and locate devices and servers in the environment.

BRANCHING RECOMMENDATIONS

- Be Consistent

  Some LDAP clients may be confused if the DN format is inconsistent across the directory tree. Example: If locality (l) is subordinate to organization (o) in one part of the tree make sure (l) is subordinate to organization (o) in all other parts of the tree

- Use traditional attributes to maintain interoperability

  Basing structures on RFC's such as 2377 and 1279 create the greatest likelihood of retaining interoperability with third party LDAP clients. Using IETF attributes recommendations also means the process of schema documentation is reduced to simple cut-n-paste or simply citing a reference. Which is desirable when it comes time to build the entries associated with the DN

- Try not to change the meanings of standard attributes

  Attribute names have meaning to align the attribute names with the type of entry they are representing. Example: don't use (l) to represent a country, organization, don't use (c) to represent an organizational unit

- Avoid branching based on organizational structure

  This creates a stability dependency between technology (application settings, custom code ect.) and business organization (intra company politics). Thus the business foundations are left vulnerable to the stream of change. This will set the project up to failure.

- When considering geography remember to utilize the metadirectory to abstract the locations in the master schema

- Consider people, Roles, places and things

DELIVERABLES

- DIT representing where attributes are stored including local mapped DIT

- Logical DIT which represents the master Metadirectory schema

- Common views which will be used to coordinate schema reconciliation between the two and server applications with specific DIT requirements

- Final Directory Sizing

Again sizing involves making an estimate of the number of users and magnitude of the directory. At this point the sizing is crucial as the schema, DIT and replication topology will become fixed for the remained of the process. Again usage parameters below should be considered minima. For example, a airline agency has 750,000 employees world wide, with a total entry count of 8,000,000 anticipating 1900 connections per second distributed among 15 directory instances. This would classify the deployment as a Type III for scale, even though the number of users is less than a class III the total number of entries classify it as a Type III.

Usage	Connections/sec	Directory (DSA or Slapd) Instances in cluster	Number of Objects
TYPE I: DEPARTMENTAL	0-500	0-8	Less than 500,000
Type II: Organization wide	500-2000	8-16	500,000 to 2,000,000
Type III: Enterprise wide	2000-8000	17-32	2,000,000 to 8,000,000
Type IV: Global/National	8000+	32+	8,000,000+

22

Replication & Referral Analysis—Phase 9

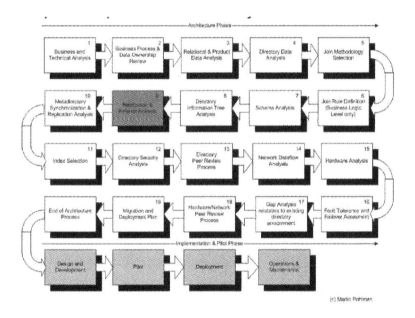

Objectives

- Identify design strategy goals
- Select directory server locations
- Map directory tree to directory servers

- Identify replication and referral paths
- Create replication agreements

Design Strategy Goals

- High Availability
- High Performance
- Load Balancing
- Local Management
- Scalability

Replication

Replication is the mechanism which directory automatically copies data from one directory server to another. Using replication, a Directory server can copy everything from the entire directory tree to individual directory entries. Replication enables several important benefits in the directory service. Each company approaches replication differently. Currently the IETF has a protocol extension in draft. Check **http://www.ietf.org/html.charters/ldup-charter.html** for more information. The draft-ietf-ldup-model-06.txt proposed by John Merrells, Ed Reed & Uppili Srinivasan is currently in its 6th draft incarnation.

Fault Tolerance

By replicating directory trees to multiple servers, an enterprise can ensure the directory service is available even if some hardware, software or network problem prevents your directory clients from accessing a given directory server instance.

High Performance

By replication directory entries to a location close to your users, you can vastly improve directory response time.

Load Balancing

By the directory tree across servers and using a Metadirectory Access Router, you can reduce the access load on any given machine, thereby improving server response time

Local Management

Replication allows the users to master data locally and replicate it to other directory servers across the enterprise. Referrals allow local management without the need to replicate the data. Referrals also permit aggregation of modify statements to suppliers and abstraction of users and Roles.

Scalability

Referrals permit scalability for large scale deployments

HA CLUSTER FOR 5 MILLION OR LESS.

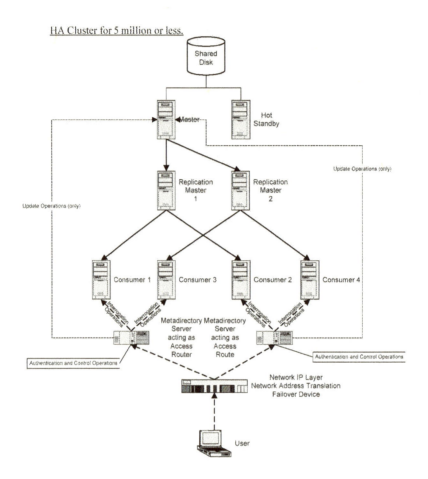

HA Cluster for 5 million or less.

Points about Design

1. No Single Point of Failure (Except network layer)

2. Scales up to 5 million person/objects

3. User can be LDAP-2 or LDAP-3 protocol and is abstracted from Consumer Bind's

4. Appropriate for Type I, II or some Type III

In this design replication is used to avoid a situation where the loss of a single server causes a loss of service. At minimum, the local directory tree should be replicated to at least one backup server.

In the preceding example, a single directory server is dedicated to being a supplier server. This server is responsible for maintaining all the directory data. Any requests to update information in the directory are handled by the supplier (master) server. This server offloads the task to two servers, which are tasked with storing and passing on the data on to four alternating consumer servers. If this seems like a waste of resources consider the ability to make backups from replication masters as opposed to Master servers which are continuously being bombarded by Update applications and the Consumer servers that are being hammered by Interrogation queries. Also the replication masters can be used as an additional level of back up provided the Metadirectory Server/Access Router configured with failover and promotion scripts.

- Given that each server in capable of 99% uptime w/an average of 1hour and 40 minutes down time per week.

- Given a average downtime/recovery of 16 minutes per server

- Given the odds of two servers failing simultaneously in a given week is 1 in 100 (16min out of 168 min for all 10 servers=(16/168)/10)

- Given the odds of two servers failing on the same tier (1 in 10 per simultaneous failure)

This is a three nines configuration (99.999 Uptime) when implemented without automated failover and promotion and becomes a traditional four nines (99.9999 Uptime) configuration when implemented with automated failover and promotion (assumed 1 in 10 chance of additional failure of software process). Five nines (99.99999 Uptime) is available with hardware redundancy (assumed additional 1 in 10 chance hardware HA will fail)

Characteristics

- User and group data storage
- Server configuration data storage
- User data is unique
- Down time must be minimal
- Under 5 million person/objects
- Master and Backup in a basic cluster
- Other components access consumers using directory failover

HIGH PERFORMANCE AND REPLICATION

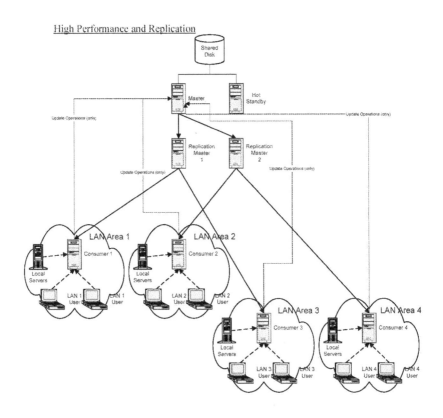

High Performance and Replication

Points about Design

1. Each LAN zone is isolated in the event of Network/Power failure

2. Scales up to 5 million person/objects

3. HA present in Master due to centralized write structure

4. Users must be LDAP-3 protocol or a Metadirectory Router at each location must be used to redirect updates to the Master

5. Appropriate for Type I, II or some Type III depending on volume

Replication for high performance by placing consumer directory servers in the same LAN as appropriate clients and servers is a logical decision for geographically separated locations. The example above shows replication a directory tree out to multiple consumer servers on multiple LANs. This allows clients and other servers to the LAN to be as close to the directory as possible. A decision can also be made to replicate only data needed on the LAN and use referrals to access non-LAN related data

Characteristics

- User and group data storage
- Server configuration data storage is by location/geography
- User data may differ based on Location
- Down time is isolated to a specific Network
- Under 5 million person/objects
- No cluster inherent in design, Failover and promotion of Replication Master is recovery method
- All Writes are directed to a single master

DEDICATED CONSUMERS FOR HIGH PERFORMANCE ON TARGETED APPLICATIONS

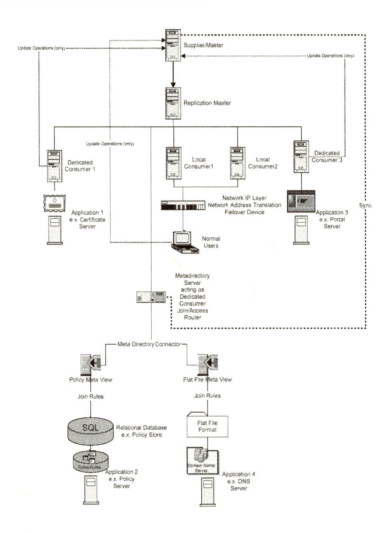

Points about Design

- Applications are isolated from the central directory and one another

- Scales up to 5 million person/objects

- Updates may be synched by use of replication agreements with each dedicated consumer assuming responsibility {custody} of new values until replication

- Schema's sub branches may differ

- Appropriate for Type I, II and Type III deployments

Another approach to high performance is the placing of dedicated directory servers or Join engines with appropriate clients and servers. The example above shows replicating a directory tree out to multiple consumer servers on multiple LAN's with some consumers being dedicated to a specific high usage application. This allows applications to be as close to the directory as possible, even co hosted. A decision can also be made to replicate only data needed on by the application and use referrals to access non-LAN related data.

Characteristics

- Schema reconciliation will be mandatory in the master metadirectory

- Server configuration data storage is by Application requirement

- User data may differ based on Application

- Down time is isolated to a specific Application

- Under 5 million person/objects

- No cluster inherent in design, Failover and promotion of Replication Master is recovery method

- All Writes are directed to a single master

LOAD BALANCING AND REPLICATION

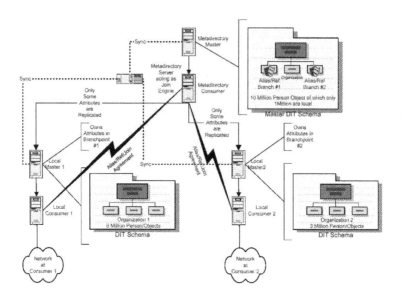

Points about Design

- Local Masters are quasi-independent domains

- Scales ABOVE 5 million person/objects

- Updates must be synched by use of replication agreements with each local master assuming responsibility {custody} of new values until replication

- Schema's sub branches WILL differ

- Scales up to most Type IV deployments

A Load Balancing Solution is similar to a Dedicated Consumer, High Availability or fault tolerant solution and high performance solution. Basically, the objective is to replicate when the server and/or network becomes overloaded either in terms of traffic of in the maximum number of person objects (usually around 5 Million).

Characteristics

- Schema reconciliation will be mandatory in the master metadirectory

- Server configuration data storage is by Organization

- User data WILL differ between organizations and some synchronization/join will be required

- Down time is isolated to a specific Organization/Local Master

- OVER 5 million person/objects

- No cluster inherent in design, Failover and promotion of local Replication Master is recovery method

- Writes are directed to the master local to the call

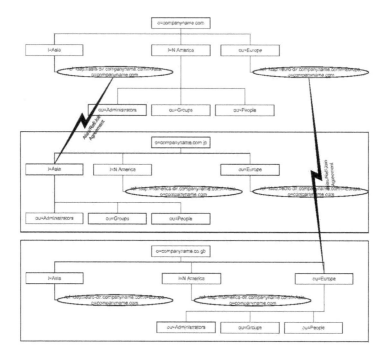

HA SOLUTION WITH RELATIONAL AGGREGATOR

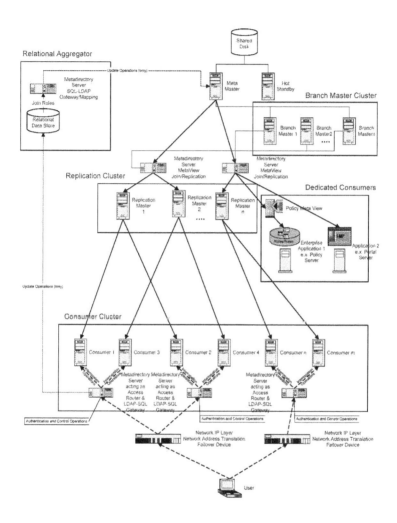

Consumer Cluster

- The Consumer Cluster permits the sustaining engineer to scale the system based on Interrogation and Authentication operations. The addition of a Metadirectory component at this level acts as an LDAP protocol router, interpreting and redirecting requests and introducing trigger operations which execute under specific conditions of the LDAP request

Replication Cluster

- The Replication Cluster offloads the processor intensive process of replication away from the Metadirectory Master. The Replication cluster scales linearly based on the size of the Consumer Cluster and the number of modifications per unit time that have to be sent.

Dedicated Consumers

- The dedicated consumers are use specific. Each Consumer serves a service or server. Dedicated consumers should be reserved for applications that require immediate access and a short response time or those applications that require an excessive ratio of Update Operations

Branch Master Cluster

- The Branch Master Cluster enables the directory server to scale above the 5-7 million mark. Each branch master owns a portion of the data and is linked via a join rule/referral to the primary master. One reason for this partition is the segmentation of data based on Update application ratio or for legal reasons when local information laws require a greater level of control.

Relational Aggregator

The relational aggregator acts as a reservoir or impedance matching element for Update operations. The design of the Aggregator should mirror that of the Metadirectory structure itself with a strict Primary Key mirroring the uid and table structure in the form of linked databases with standardized schemas in third normalized form

Points about Design

* Scales to Type IV on all criteria
* Updated may be delayed due to volume and tuning

SELECT DIRECTORY SERVER LOCATIONS

When applying the methodology, create a map of the user's network topology and list pertinent information such as data rates and user population. In the diagram the customer is an international bank (GenericBank.com). one can see how mapping their topology, user population and connection speed to each site will shape the final design and influences which of the afore mentioned Solution templates are applied.

Using a map like this then select where to put directory servers. The following questions can be used to further define the location selection:

* What are your major enterprise locations?
* How many directory users do you have at each site?

- How many mobile or remote users do you have at each site?

- What are your normal hours of business operation?

- What are the network links, speeds and utilizations?

- What is the support infrastructure at each location?

- What are your directory availability requirements at each site?

- How current does the directory data need to be at each site?

- What are the hours of operation?

- What is the average number of queries per second at each location?

- Do you have any older services (e.g. x.500, x.400) at these locations that also need Directory services?

- Do you have applications at these locations that require directory services?

- Do you need a directory server at each location, given the total cost of ownership?

MAP DIRECTORY TREE TO DIRECTORY SERVERS

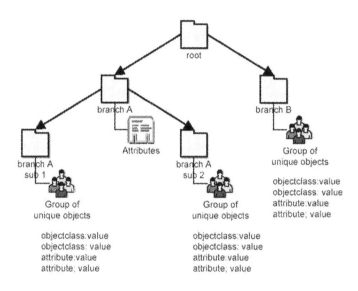

The next step in completing the directory tree design in anticipation of the replication and referral strategy is to start with the network topology diagram listed above and mapping the tree design into the network topology.

At this point the Architect needs to decide whether the complete tree or a portion of the tree design belongs in each directory server. In small directory designs composed of 5 million person/entries or less the entire tree will be replicated throughout the enterprise. In larger systems or systems where availability is at issue either due to usage or available bandwidth constraints the use of referrals, aliasing and join rules to point to different branches of the tree in different servers. A large enterprise that requires millions of entries may need to distribute those entries over several servers and use referrals to point to different branches of the tree

The architect must determine local management requirements for each directory server. Legal requirements such as European Union Privacy laws may require that European Union companies physically maintain ownership of the data on employees. In this case it becomes a prerequisite that the people entries be split into different branches do that the branches can be managed locally.

There are many factors within a company that determine the final tree design, schema, replication, referral and Join strategy. Many enterprise metadirectory structures undergo periodic revision as the use of the service expands.

Mapping Process

1. Start mapping the preliminary directory tree design onto each directory server.

   - Decide whether the entire tree or a portion of the tree belongs in each directory server

   - What applications at each site require directory services?

   - What resources do these applications need access to?

   - How many users at each site require directory services?

   - What resources do these users need access to

   - How would applications or users be affected if they had to access directory services from a remote site with a slow or down link

   - Determine the local management issues

2. Are there any local management issues?

   - What branches or entries need to be managed locally?

   - Will these branches or entries be available to the entire enterprise?

- Do these branches or entries need to be replicated to each site? Can Referrals or Meta Join Rules be used

- What is the native data format to the directory entry

- How will these branches or entries get updated?

- Does the original tree need to be redesigned to accommodate local management?

3. **Redesign the directory tree, if necessary, to accommodate local management**

- Is it necessary to branch to support local management?

- Does each location warrant its own suffix?

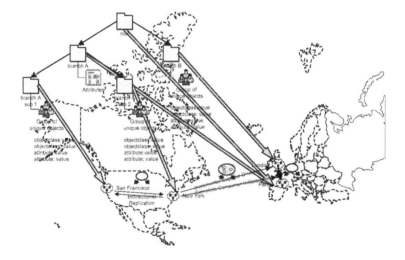

The database is the basic unit you use for tasks such as replication, indexing, performing backups, and restoring data. LDAP Directory Servers store all data in a single database. With a Metadirectory based solution, the architect has the option of separating the directory into manageable chunks and assign them to separate directory instances. These databases can then be distributed among a number of servers, reducing the workload for each server. The architect can then craft replication, indexing and back-up strategies specific to each locations unique need.

Distributing the data allows the architect to scale the directory across multiple servers without physically containing those directory entries on each server in your enterprise. A distributed directory can thus hold a much larger number of entries than would be possible with a single server.

In addition, the architect can configure the directory to hide the distributing details from the user. As far as users and applications are concerned, there is simply a single directory that answers their directory queries.

Questions to ask

- What are your normal hours of business operations?
- How would you characterize support at each location?
- What are your directory availability requirements at each site?

- Do you have applications at these locations that require directory services?

- How will these applications access the directory?

- What fail-over mechanisms are in place if the server goes down?

- How current does directory data need to be at each site?

- Do you need a directory server at each location? Costs?

- What is the normal set of LDAP operations for each directory application?

- What applications and/or data stores need to write to the directory?

- Do these applications and/or data stores need to master data locally?

  - Sites that do not have applications or data stores that write to the directory probably have no need to master data locally.

  - Sites that have no data stores, but have applications that write to the directory, could write over the network.

REPLICATION STRATEGY

Partitioning the directory tree requires identification of both root and sub suffixes in the design. Directory data in the tree is stored in databases on the physical server. These databases must start with either a root suffix or with a sub suffix, which allows the architect to store different branches under a root suffix in multiple databases.

Rational

- Management

- Local Master: Ease of local management, It may be necessary to manage certain parts of the tree in different physical locations. In that case, the tree divided into partitions.

- Backup/Restore: Ease of backup and restore management. It may be necessary to frequently backup some data as opposed to other data that is more static.

- Performance

  - Availability: Another reason for partitioning the directory tree is for Availability to high use applications It may be necessary to locate information in regional proximity to applications that have non standard requirements.

  - Scalability: Partitioning the directory enables a directory server to expand beyond the limits imposed by the product used to implement the directory. Few directory servers scale beyond 5 million person/objects

- Replication

  - Branch Points: Branch points enable replication in increments that inflict a minimal load on the system and replicate rapidly changing data while relaxing replication schedule on more static data elements

  - Filter Content: Legally some data may not be able to be replicated. In other instanced local laws and business relationships may require data to be replicated to partner firms or even government authorities.

- Failover

  - Multiple masters: A common rational for replication is to distribute databases to multiple directory servers at each location to provide write and load balancing.

- Replica Hubs for Read Fail-Over: The creation of multiple replica hub Directory Servers at each location to provides read fail-over for all replica databases.

- Replica Consumers for Load Balancing: The creation of multiple replica consumer Directory Servers at each location to provides additional load balancing.

METAMASTERS AND METADIRECTORY ROUTING

Metamasters: With databases at each location. It is possible to distribute your master databases to multiple servers for performance reasons the the extent that management becomes a greater challenge. For simplicity it is recommended that, use one metamaster server to coordinate all of the databases. In smaller environments it is possible to use master servers to receive replicas from other locations and client query operations at the same time without a performance impact, however, the recommended architecture for high performance environments is to off-load replication to replica hubs while the master servers receive and maintain updates. Dual replica hubs are often used to provide read fail-over with each replica hub being fed from two masters. Each replica hub receives databases from other replica hubs in the network and is responsible for cascading those databases to other locations as needed.

Metadirectory Routing: It is often possible to use the Metadirectory to do protocol level routing and provide the fail-over logic introducing the capability of doing fail-over with the application. This becomes complicated when it includes applications that write to the Root tree. It will be necessary to identify all of the replication paths between the local master servers and the replica hub servers for each master database. Each master database should be replicated to multiple replica hubs from both master servers. This ensures full fail-over capabilities. The more databases exist, the more replication paths exist. The more replication paths are required, the more administration and management is required. This is the cost incurred by flexible replication!

DELIVERABLES

- Document Local Master Requirements

- Create a Network Directory Map

  The map will:

  1. Define ownership of attributes

  2. Highlight where directory services are required within the network.

  3. Connect directory branch points with network locations

  4. Define replication, referral & join agreements between branches

  5. Identify Major Data Center Locations

  6. Identify Total Number of Directory Users

  7. Identify Directory Applications

  8. Identify Directory Data Stores

  9. Identify Network Links, Speed, and Utilization

- Define and build Metastructures defined within the directory map

  1. Consumer Cluster

  2. Replication Cluster

  3. Dedicated Consumers

  4. Branch Master Cluster

  5. Relational Aggregator

23

Integrating Entity & Attribute Flow into Directory Design—Phase 10

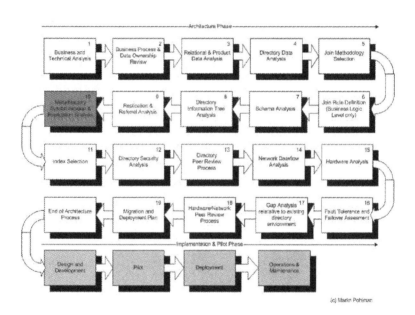

(c) Marlin Pohlman

SYNCHRONIZATION AGENTS

The Join Engine controls the interactions between a connected directory and the metadirectory. It contains the procedures required to handle object creation and deletion, property integrity and versioning. It resolves attribute ownership in the event of conflict. These Join Engine

397

instructions are embodied in the metadirectory as the Synchronization or Management Agents. These are specialized objects containing the configuration parameters, control scripts, transformation rules, attribute ownership and flow rules that define how a connected directory will be integrated with the metadirectory.

The Synchronization Agents manage the relationships between connected directories and the metadirectory's connector namespace at both the object and attribute level. They reside on the Join Engine server and are connected directory-specific. That is, the internal configuration of the synchronization agents is different for each connected directory.

THE SYNCHRONIZATION CYCLE

The Synchronization Agent is a directory object and service that sets up directory synchronization. It defines how the synchronization is performed, and it performs the synchronization. A control script directs three separate phases of synchronization agent operation: the discovery, synchronization and update phases. These phases are illustrated below.

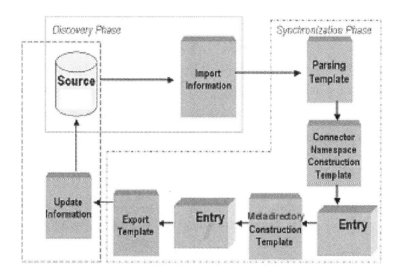

Management Agent Synchronization Phases

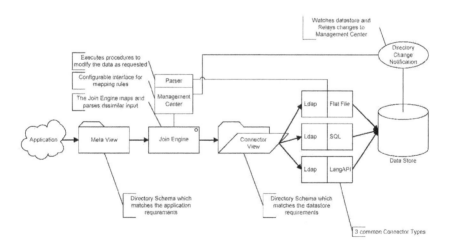

The discovery and update phase typically share code to bind to a connected directory and read and write directory information. The synchronization phase is the real heart of the Metadirectory. The synchronization phase uses import and export templates and attribute flow rules (which are stored as properties of the object) to determine the extent and scope of changes that must be applied to both the connected directory and the metadirectory

Restating the component roles:

Connector View: A Directory instance that acts as an intermediary between the raw data and the unified Metaview

Meta view: a unified LDAP directory made up of both literal attributes and symbolic links to external systems.

Join Engine: A Join Engine's function is to join information about persons and objects emanating from disparate enterprise data sources (Views) into a unified LDAP directory and then controlling the flow of information from the unified MetaView to external directories.

Parser: A parser is a module that knows how to interpret and translate information from a byte stream into a structured information object where each piece of information is accessible by name and vice versa. A parser can (but need not) be bi-directional. This can take the form of Perl, Java, CPI, VB Script or a multitude of technologies

Change Notification Service: Change Notification Service detects changes in the Meta View and in connected data sources and to provide change notification to the connected data sources that can accept notifications. The Change Notification Service polls the Changelog/ LCUP agent and notifies the Management Center of changes to the Join Engine not through the Join Engine call back mechanism. The service reads its configuration from the Management Center.

THE JOIN ENGINE

The join engine establishes a link between a metadirectory object and a specific connector space object. In linking the metadirectory object to the connector space object, the join indirectly also links it to the connected directory. Objects can be joined automatically according to predefined join criteria, or interactively by the architect.

A variety of join options is necessary for two reasons. First, there may be connected directories with entries preferably not merged in a common metadirectory object. Second, there may be no sure way of knowing when a metadirectory entry and a particular connector space entry describe the same object. For example, there may be several Marlin Pohlmans in an organization, (not likely but it happens) each represented in a different connected directory. One person may appear in those directories under several names, such as Marlin Pohlman, M. Pohlman, Mpohlman or Pohlman, Marlin B. Some degree of intervention is often required to resolve these kinds of ambiguities. But it is also true that in many cases there is no ambiguity. one can simply match entries based on a name or other attribute (employee number, for example).

A *Join Action* lets the architect define an automated batch join, based on predetermined join criteria, and execute it at will. a batch join is normally used when the implementer first brings a new connected directory into the metadirectory Inevitably you will be left with exceptions—those connected directory entries that fall between the cracks of the join criteria. They are left un-joined and remain *disconnectors* rather than *connectors*. one can then use stand-alone connector application to deal with these exceptions, by searching the metadirectory for a match, or by creating a new metadirectory object corresponding to the disconnector. But new objects may appear in the connected directory at any time. These also may have to be joined to metadirectory objects.

The Join Engine supports the following actions:

- Incremental updates. Allows the external data repositories to be updated incrementally as they are modified.

- Object creation. Allows objects to be created in the Meta View, and in the Connector Views data repositories connected to the Join Engine.

- Object deletion. Allows objects to be deleted from the Meta View and subsequently from the Connector Views data repositories from which they originated or to which they are connected.

- Object modification. Allows objects to be modified in the Meta View, and reflects the modifications in the corresponding entry in any number of external data repositories.

Important:

- **Join Engine needs to know where the "physical" Connector-View is located**

- **Join Engine automatically creates scripts based on Data Server Type and SQL Table**

Join rules. These enable you to specify rules for joining entries between the Meta View and Connector View.

Distinguished Name (DN) mapping rules. These enable you to specify how to transform DN's when mapping entries between a Connector View and Meta View.

Attribute flow. This enables you to map attributes between a Connector View and the Meta View.

Among the complicating factors are:

- There may be no exact metadirectory equivalent of certain connected directory attributes.

- The connected directory information may be in a different format than that required by the metadirectory.

- It may take more than one attribute within the connected directory to match a metadirectory attribute (and *vice-versa*).

- Additional metadirectory attribute information will almost certainly be necessary to ensure that the object is unique within the whole metadirectory.

- The connected directory may contain objects that you do not want to import into the metadirectory (and *vice-versa*).

Constructed attributes. These enable you to create attributes in entries stored in the Meta View or Connector View by combining and manipulating entry information.

Filters. These enable you to exclude entries from a Connector View or the Meta View by a subtree or a specific entry in a subtree.

When the Join Engine synchronizes one view with another, it uses these configurations to determine the correct join and data flow.

Integrate Entity & Attribute Flow into Directory Design

- Review and Expand Given Directory Design Matrix

- Integrate Entity Flow into Directory Design Matrix

- Integrate Attribute Flow into Directory Design Matrix

- Review Directory Design Matrix

- Select a Directory Connector

- Expand Directory Design Matrix

- Review Directory Tree Hierarchy

Select a Connector Type: The following are some common connector types and common terminology used to describe

- Direct Connector
  - LDAP v3 compliant
  - SQL Database
- Universal Connector (Procedural Custom Code aka: an Assembly line)
  - Perl
  - Java
  - C
  - Transaction Processor (BEA, MQ)
- Indirect Connector (Vendor Supplied Established Script or Executable)
  - Lotus Notes
  - Microsoft Exchange
  - cc:Mail, NT
  - Custom

Steps involved in integrating an Entity Flow into Directory Design

1. Identify Initial Population
2. Identify Entity Owner
3. Select a ConnectorView to Initialize MetaView
4. Identify Entity Flow
5. Identify Filter Configurations
6. Identify ConnectorView Attributes
7. Add Attribute Flow Data
8. Identify Constructed Attributes

9. Extend Directory Schema

10. Verify Install System Requirements

11. Install Parser

12. Prepare MetaView and ConnectorView Directories

13. Install the Meta-Directory Management Center

14. Install the JoinEngine and Create a New MetaView

15. Create Extended Schema

16. Add Custom Attribute Indexes

17. Add ConnectorView Suffix

18. Import ConnectorView Data

19. Configure Directory Server for Meta-Directory Operation

20. Enable Directory Server Changelog/LCUP agent or Transaction Processor

21. Load Meta-Directory Schema

22. Add Meta-Directory Attribute Indexes

23. Add Meta-Directory Configuration Directory Suffix

24. Create Meta-Directory Configuration Object in Product Database

Create from Meta Connector within Join Engine context

- A JoinEngine needs to know where the "physical" Connector-View is located

- A JoinEngine needs to know how to authenticate with the Data Server

- A JoinEngine needs to know where the ConnectorView is located in the tree

- A JoinEngine needs to know what operations to perform when changes occur

Fundamental Questions to Ask:

- Any entries or branches to ignore?
- What uniquely joins source and destination entries, and when?
- Replicate source Entries if no destination entry to join to?
- What source attributes do you want to flow, and when?
- Do any attributes need to be built?

RULES & JOIN RULES

Rules

- Rules are defined and cataloged into Rule Sets.
- Rules are applied to the Connector Views and Connector View through the Join Engine.

From the rule information entered into the User Interface, the Join Engine builds an LDAP query to search the target. If an entry matching the search criteria is found, link information is written into both the source and target entries.

Join Rule

- Which ConnectorView entry links to which Meta View entry?
- Link information is the heart of the joining process

Rule Definition

- Select MetaView or ConnectorView: Where will editor get list of available attributes for making the rule?

- MetaView Token Assignment: What attributes need to be split up into separate tokens (variables) for use in the rule?

Rule Selection Criteria

- When do you want rule the rule to be applied?
- Describe the
- Join Filter/Query
- What string will be used to search for matches?

Filters can be set up to prevent subtrees and/or entries from replicating between a MetaView and a ConnectorView.

Filters

- Which entries or subtrees should not flow?

From the information entered into the User Interface, the Join Engine constructs an attribute that is not explicitly stated. This placeholder variable is referred to as a constructed Attribute

ATTRIBUTE & ATTRIBUTE FLOW

Constructed Attributes

- Do any attributes need to be built?
- Constructed attributes are built in a target entry from pieces of information collected from a source entry.

From the rule information entered into the User Interface, the Join Engine composes a DN within the target for the replicated entry. When a Join Rule search fails, DN Mapping is performed to create the entry and link it.

LDAP Directory to Directory DN Mapping

- Where does the entry appear in the tree?

Attribute Flow

- Which attribute values flow?

- Attribute Flow Rules identify the attributes to move from source to target

CHANGE NOTIFICATION SERVICE

While most vendor implementations abstract this process from the end user it often proves helpful to understand how a change notification service works.

The Change log in its current form is proprietary and has absolutely no bearing on LDAP as a protocol.

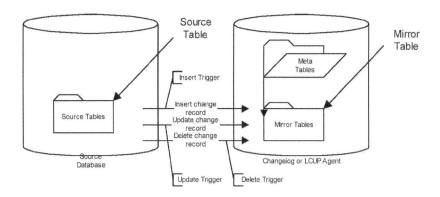

All tables monitored for changes have three triggers associated with them:

- Insert Trigger: Replicates all rows inserted on the table to the Changelog

- Update Trigger: Replicates the updated rows along with their old and new values to the Changelog thus two rows, one containing old values and the other new values are created for every row updated in the table.

- Delete Trigger: Moves all deleted rows to the Changelog.

In addition to populating the changelog, the triggers also often assign unique change numbers called *SynchPoints* to each change record.

OWNERSHIP

Ownership defines whether a particular entry is native to the system represented by the Connector View. Each entry contained within a Connector View is defined as either member or non-member. The set of member entries come from the source system as represented by the Connector View. The set of non-member entries have been replicated into the Connector View from a Meta View.

For each join between a Connector View and a Meta View there can be two possible configuration sets, a join set for native owned entries, and a second set for non-native entries. Default membership usually applies to the source entries but can be overwritten or assigned during the initial join to a MetaView.

In addition to entity ownership membership allows for additional differentiation of entries when this is necessary, as in the case of multiple Meta Views.

Connector View ownership and Connector View membership for a given entry are usually the same. To use membership requires additional link attributes, one each for the Connector View link and the Meta View link:

Important: The sole purpose of ownership is to confer delete privileges.

GENERAL SETTINGS

The majority of vendor Metadirectory implementations have the following general settings built into the product.

General Settings in the User Interface

- Ownership & Membership

- Capabilities

- Configuration to Connector View

- Configuration to Meta View

- Refresh Schedule

Configure Capabilities Settings
Used to set the following limitations on Connector Views and Meta Views:

- Addition
- Deletion
- Modification

Configure Configuration to Meta View Settings

- Assign already defined rule sets

Configure Configuration to Connector View Settings

- Assign already defined rule sets

Configure Refresh Schedule Settings

- Set schedule for refreshes

Process

1. Create a New Data Server
2. Create New ConnectorViews
3. Insert ConnectorViews into MetaView
4. Create Join Process Configuration Rules
5. Configure ConnectorView Settings
6. Refresh ConnectorView Status and Flow Attributes

Review Basic Troubleshooting Methodology

1. Verify MetaView—ConnectorView—Data Store Flow
2. Check Operational Status and Statistics
3. Track MetaView—ConnectorView Flow in Logs
4. Debug MetaView—ConnectorView Flow with Vendor Utilities
5. Debug Common Meta-Directory Problems
6. Debug JoinEngine Installation Problems
7. Debug Entity and Attribute Flow Problems

Create Join Process Configuration Rules

- Create Filter Configurations

- Create Constructed Attributes

- Create Join Rules

- Create DN Mapping Rules

- Create Attribute Flow Rules

PROTOCOL AWARE ROUTER/LDAP PROXY

When used as a Protocol Aware Router or LDAP Proxy a Metadirectory may decode, rewrite attributes, check security rules, encode, send request to ldap server, decode response, rewrite attributes, check other security rules, encode and send request back to the client. However, thr principal use of a Protocol Router is load balancing. There is no physical limit on the systems ability to load balance across N directory servers. However, as the amount of non-distribution work (like attribute renaming, setting operational limits, hiding data, etc.) goes up, throughput as a load balancer goes down. It is an added layer that provides additional functionality like security and filtering (caching features set aside for the sake of this example).

When used as a protocol router a Metadirectory provides three distinct feature sets:

1. Load Balancing

2. Firewall like Security Features

3. Client Inter-operability like schema mapping and referral following

This is accomplished by designing the schema such that Each connection to the metadirectory uses four Constructed attribute file descriptors: one for the client connection and one for the connection to the directory server; one for security and one for change management & notification

DELIVERABLES

• Entry condition spreadsheet

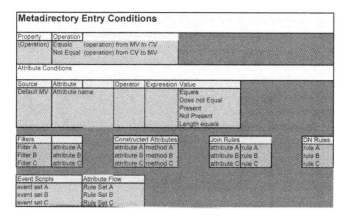

• Pseudocode for each join rule specified
  • Flow diagram

24

Index Selection—Phase 11

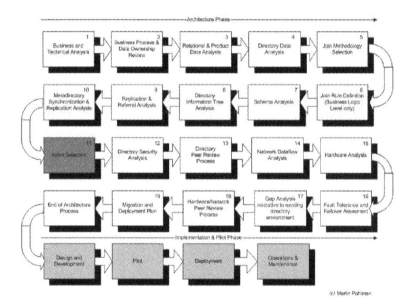

(c) Martin Pohlman

The majority of Metadirectory products on the market use some from of Index to speed searches.

Indexes have absolutely no bearing on LDAP as a protocol

Indexing is a proprietary approach the majority of Metadirectory vendors use to improve the performance of the Directory Server. The main goal of this section is to select the attributes to index and index types for each database at each location to improve read performance.

METADIRECTORY SERVER INDEXING

- Indexed searches are quicker and more efficient

- Indexing is the most important technique for improving read performance

Indexes are disk files that contain the IDs of entries in the database. The directory architect determines the specifications as to which attributes are indexed and what type indexes are used and the size of the index file often expressed as a percentage of the database size. Indexes significantly improve the performance of the server, however, creating, managing, and maintaining indexes impose an additional load on the server. Therefore, careful management of indexes and the attributes chosen for indexing is necessary.

INDEXED SEARCH DEFINED

Cursory Process Analysis

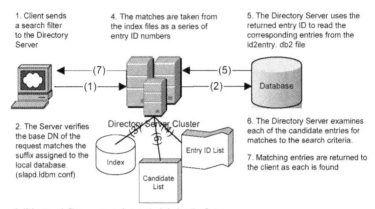

1. Client sends a search filter to the Directory Server

4. The matches are taken from the index files as a series of entry ID numbers

5. The Directory Server uses the returned entry ID to read the corresponding entries from the id2entry. db2 file

2. The Server verifies the base DN of the request matches the suffix assigned to the local database. (slapd.ldbm.conf)

6. The Directory Server examines each of the candidate entries for matches to the search criteria.

7. Matching entries are returned to the client as each is found

3. If the search filter corresponds to a single index, the Server reads that index and builds a list of possible matches If the search filter contains multiple criteria. the Server checks multiple indexes and builds a list of possible matches

In-depth Process Analysis

The directory server uses the following process when performing a search:

1. An LDAP client sends a search filter to the directory server/ metadirectory.

2. The directory server examines the incoming request to verify that the specified base DN matches a suffix assigned to the local database.

3. If they match, the directory server processes the request.

4. If they do not match, the directory server returns an error to the client indicating that the suffix does not match.

5. If the referral parameter is set, and V3 is supported the metadirectory also returns the LDAP URL where the client can attempt to pursue the request.

6. If the search filter criteria may be satisfied by a single index, then the server reads that index to generate a list of potential, or candidate, matches.

7. If an appropriate index is not found, the directory server generates a candidate list that includes all entries in the database.

8. If a search filter containing multiple criteria is used, the meta-directory consults multiple indexes and then combines the resulting lists of candidate entries.

9. The candidate matches are taken from the index files in the form of a series of entry ID numbers.

10. The returned entry ID numbers are used to read the corresponding entries from the id entry.

11. The server examines each of the candidate entries for matches to the search criteria.

12. Matching entries are returned to the client.

13. The search continues until all candidate entries are examined, or until one of the following limits is reached:

    - Size Limit: Specifies the maximum number of entries to return from a search operation. If this limit is reached, the slapd returns any entries it has located that match the search request, as well as an exceeded size limit error.

    - Time Limit: Specifies the maximum number of seconds for a search request. If this limit is reached, the server returns any entries that match the search request, as well as an exceeded time limit error.

    - Look Through Limit: Specifies the maximum number of entries that the directory server will check when seeking candidate entries in a search request. If this limit is reached, the server returns any entries it has located that match the request, as well as an exceeded size limit error.

The client may further restrict the number of returned entries by specifying lower values for the Size Limit and the Time limit parameters on the search request.

SEARCH PARAMETERS

1st Parameter: Base object for the search. Expressed as a DN.

2nd Parameter: Scope of the search. There are three scopes; sub tree, one level, and base. 3rd Parameter: Tells the server whether aliases should be de-referenced.

4th Parameter: The size limit in entries

5th Parameter: Time limit in seconds

6th Parameter: Boolean value that instructs the server to send either the attribute types or attribute values (but not both).

7th Parameter: The search filter. Six types of search filters with three Boolean operators are supported. The search filters are: equality, sub string, approximate, greater than or equal to, less than or equal to, and presence.

8th Parameter: A list of attributes to be returned for each matching entry.

Example: ldap://server.coradon.com:389/dc=coradon,dc=com?cn, phone?sub?(&(objectclass=person)(sn=*drennan*))

Search Filter: (&(objectclass=person)(sn=*drennan*))

COMMON TYPES OF INDEXES

• Presence

• Equality

- Approximate

- Substring

- Internationalization

- Browsing

Presence

Search for entries that contain this attribute.
Syntax: (AcctBalance=*)
The presence index (pres) is the simplest of the indexes. It lets you efficiently search the directory for entries that contain a specific attribute.

Equality

Search for entries that have an exact match for this attribute.
Syntax: (AcctBalance=0)
The equality index allows you to search for entries containing a specific attribute value. For example, an equality index on the cn attribute allows a user to perform a search for cn=Albert Yankovic.

Approximate

Searches for phonetic, or "sounds-like" matches using common pattern matching algorithms. Normally it is used only for string values such as commonName or givenName.
Syntax: (cn=~ Dave) this is supported ASCII only given regional and linguistic variances
The approximate index allows approximate or "sounds-like" searches. An entry may include the attribute value cn=Dave R. Jacoda. An approximate search would return this value for searches against cn~=Dave Jacoda, cn~=David, or cn~=Jacoda. Similarly, a search against l~=New Onerk (note the misspelling) would return entries including l=New York. Approximate indexes make little sense for attributes commonly containing numbers, such as telephone numbers.

Many commercial directory servers use a variation of the metaphone phonetic algorithm to perform this type of searching. Each value is treated as a sequence of words, and a phonetic code is generated for each word. Values entered on an approximate search are similarly translated into a sequence of phonetic codes. An entry is considered to match a query if both of the following are true:

- All of the query string codes are present in the codes generated in the entry string.

- All of the query string codes are specified in the same order as the entry string codes.

Substring

Searches for entries that contain a specified substring.
Syntax: (cn=*Lee*)
The substring index is resource expensive, but it allows efficient searching against substrings within entries. For example, searches of the form: cn=*derson would match the common names containing strings such as:

Arthur Anderson, Anderson Consulting, Steve Sanderson

Substring indexes make no sense for attributes such as passwords and photographs that do not contain readable strings.

Internationalization

The key to the Internationalization index is the linking of the local OID with the attributes to be indexed. The creation of an international index as a matching rule speeds up searches for information in international directories.

Internationalization index allows for searches that return entries sorted according to a specified collation order. Similar to regular indexes, except includes matching rule associating a locale (OID) with the attributes being indexed.

Browsing

A virtual list view index is particularly useful if a branch contains hundreds of entries.

The list view can be created on any branch point in the DIT. The browsing index speeds up the display of entries. The most common point is ou=people branch.

For those Metadirectory and directory products that are index based. When the directory server is installed two types of indexes are created automatically.

- System indexes: support Directory Server functionality by indexing (aci, changeNumbers, objectclass, entryDN)

- Default indexes: Improve the performance of the most common types of user directory searches by users and other servers.

Unused indexes do not require any resources

When index based directory products are installed, some indexes are created by default. default indexes are system indexes that you cannot remove. Indexes help to improve directory server performance. Directory-enabled servers also maintain a standard set of indexes in the directory. If those indexes are not used they do not require any resources

IDENTIFY INDEXES TO BE ADDED

There are two basic steps you must perform to successfully identify indexes for each database.

- Identify Application Search Filters:Identify the application search filters for each application that accesses directory data for each database. These filters reveal the types of searches applications perform on the directory and also the attributes that they search on.

- Select Attribute and Index Type: Select the attribute and index types for each database based on search filter

Requirements.

1. Identify both the types of searches applications are going to perform.

2. Identify the attributes that applications are going to regularly search on.

Index Analysis Process

1. Interview the applications developer

2. Analyze the audit log files and search filters

3. Break down the application object model searching mechanisms. The key is the isolation of search filters with the intent to index the more commonly used searches.

Audit Table

Location	Database		Directory Applications		LDAP Transactions				
Name	Name	Suffix	Directory Users	Directory Applications	Bind DN	Base DN	Operations	Filters (S)	Attributes (S)
			ex.Anonymous	ex.Address Book					
			ex.Authenticated	ex.Phone Book					
			ex.Administrator	ex.Locator					
			ex.Directory Manager						

This table allows you to identify search filters at each location, for each database, by each Application.

Pointers

- Maintain only indexes that will actually be used

- Consider adding indexes to increase application performance

- Avoid approximate indexes for numeric attributes

- Example: social security numbers

- Avoid substring indexes for attributes that do not contain readable strings

- Example: photographs and encrypted password

- Avoid maintaining indexes for attributes that are not commonly used in searches since this will increase overhead without improving performance

- Attributes that are not indexed can still be specified in search filters

- Consider how replication will affect the indexes you select for various instances of the Directory Server.

  - How often will the supplier server deal directly with client requests?

  - How about the replication master?

- Avoid reinitializing heavily indexed search servers, when a server is reinitialized it will refer LDAP operations, including searches, to its supplier which is very often a master charged with a heavy modify operational load and very few indexes.

- Remove indexes from servers in a modify only configuration

Review

- Review Default Indexes

- Identify Application Search Filters

- Identify Attributes to be Indexed

DELIVERABLES

- Index Audit Table

25

Directory Security Analysis—Phase 12

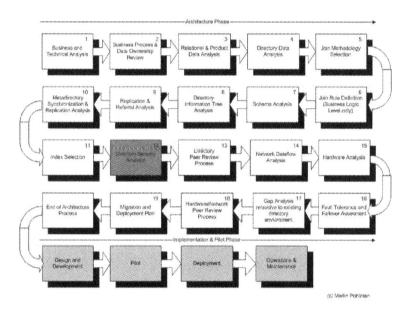

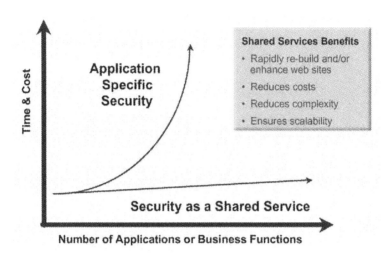

There are a number of areas covered by the term security. Authentication ensures that only trusted users have access to system resources. Authentication establishes the who of security. additionally security must establish what resources are available to what users. Authorization establishes the what of security. Confidentiality establishes visibility within security and is typically provided by encryption. Auditing and non-repudiation describe what happened in the past and additionally who performed these tasks, without any question or doubt. Before we can address how to secure the directory the we must define the systems associated with network security and explain how the directory impacts and is impacted by those systems.

There are a four areas that security encompasses:

- authentication
- authorization
- confidentiality
- auditing and non-repudiation

Authentication defines entities which are allowed access to a given system. Defining users in and of itself does not provide secure access but defines who wants access to a given resource.

Authorization defines resources and who may access them. Authorization defines the what of security. Authorization is to services and resources what authentication is to users. When we think of read, write, or execute access we an thinking of rights to a resource. Rights define operations which can be applied to any given resource. Rights typically include such operations as granting, denying, limiting, or in some way, controlling access.

Confidentiality is the ability to hide data or information controlling its visibility. Confidentiality encompasses the encryption of data and encrypting transmissions of data. A Directory Server relies heavily on secure socket layer, encryption and digital certificates to provide confidentiality.

Auditing is the process of tracking activities, access, and general use of system resources. Non-repudiation services provide undeniable evidence that a specific action occurred. Non-repudiation, at its most basic, is the ability to prove to an objective third party, after the fact, that a specific communication originated with, and was submitted by, a certain entity, or was delivered by a certain entity or to a certain entity. The two services, when used in concert, provide proof that a specific individual or entity performed a certain set of actions or operations.

PKI and x,509 certificates form the basis for implementation of these four areas

PKI PRIMER

PKI, Public key infrastructure is based on asymmetric keys. Each entity has two keys: one is called the public key (thus the term "public" key infrastructure) and is available to everyone, the other is called the private key and is known only to its owner. The strength of the PKI-based security services is dependent upon the security of the underlying cryptographic keys. Specifically, it requires protection of the private keys and the integrity of the public keys in delivery and storage.

The purpose of the public key infrastructure is to facilitate trusted electronic correspondence beyond those users with whom one could manually exchange public keys. Moreover, the infrastructure must be manageable and meet users' expectations regarding trust.

Essential to the creation of the trust is certification authorities or CAs. These certification authorities certify the association of a PKI entity, such as human beings, servers, or organizations with that entity's public key. Each certification results in a certificate from the issuing CA. In order for users to trust a certificate, a user needs to be assured that the public key bound to the certificate is the actual key of the person she or he claims to be. In other words, each CA must be a trusted entity.

A certificate is a digital document, formatted according to the X.509 standard, that contains an individual's name and his or her public key. It may also contain some other information as well, such as the individual's email address. Like any form of identification, a certificate is only as trustworthy as the authority and procedures that stand behind it. A certificate authority certifies, by digitally signing, for the authenticity and accuracy of the information in the certificate. Based on this trust, certificates allow parties who were previously unknown to each other to establish trust relationships and conduct secure communications. Below shows an example of a certificate.

```
Certificate
    Data
        Version: v3
        Serial Number
        01:43:10:00:01
        Signature Algorithm:MD5withRSA
```

```
Issuer:CN=MD-CA,OU=MC,O=Coradon, C=US
Validity
   Not Before: Wed March 24, 2001 12:00:00 AM
   Not After: Wed March 24, 2002 12:00:00 AM
Subject CN=Bryan Wright, OU=MC, O=Coradon, C=US
Subject Public Key Info:
   Algorithm:RSA
```

Inevitably, there will be cases where certificates need to be revoked. When a private key is known to be compromised or even when its compromise is only suspected, the certificate containing its associated public key must be revoked. There are other reasons for certificate revocation. One example would be severing of a relationship between a certificate owner and the organization with which the user was once associated. To inform users of such a compromised key, thus allowing them to identify and reject possibly fraudulent transactions, the certificate is placed on a certificate revocation list or CRL.

Distribution of certificates and certificate revocation lists is accomplished by storing them in a repository where certificate users can access them. The most commonly used repository is an LDAP based meta directory

How PKI works

Under normal, non-internet, circumstances data is sent between two parties. Where each party has the same key and can decipher the data. Such situations, where both parties use the same key to encrypt and decrypt the data, are termed symmetric key encryption. The problem with symmetric key encryption is that anyone can potentially see anything transmitted over the internet by intercepting its key as its being transferred. Using public key/private key encryption, the public key is freely available and can be transferred across the internet. Anyone who wishes can use the public key. Data is encrypted with the public key, but can only be decrypted with the private key which is held privately in secure storage. While the two keys are mathematically linked it is statistically impossible to generate the private key programatically, thus ensuring data security.

A simple case of how public key encryption technology works for a secure communication is illustrated in the figure below. It shows that Bryan encrypts the document using his own private key before sending it to Paul. When Paul receives the encrypted document, she decrypts the document using Bryan's public key in his certificate, which is certified by a certification authority and stored in a certificate repository. If Paul decrypts the document successfully, Paul knows it must have come from Bryan, since Bryan is the only person who has the private key that corresponds to the public key. Since the document is encrypted while in transit, the confidentiality of the message is preserved.

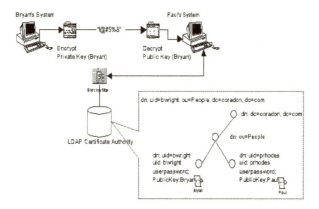

Deployment of PKI services has been somewhat slow largely because of the lack of PKI-ready applications. Some of the more common PKI-enabled applications include secure sockets layer or TLS, a widely endorsed Internet channel security technology and subset of Transport Layer Security RFC 2246 (see Appendix D); Secure Multipurpose Internet Mail Extensions or S/MIME; single sign-on or SSO; and object signing. Recently more applications such as virtual private network or VPN and certificate enrollment protocol or CEP are ready to take advantage of ever increasing use of the PKI.

Often companies deploy PKI for a single application. Then they discover they have other applications that can greatly benefit from PKI. Once the PKI is established like any other infrastructure, it can support multiple applications, thus spreading out costs.

X.509: DESIGNING FOR PKI AND SINGLE SIGN ON

Problems with Simple Name and Password schemes (e.g. the current status quo)

a. Weak authentication (clear text, guessable)

b. Difficult to remember -> easy to subvert policy (stickies, password sharing)

c. Expensive to administer (setup, change on each server)

d. No server authentication

LDAP provides an internet standard for directory access, including PKI. In LDAP based meta-directories data is:

a. arranged in a directory tree for access control.

b. configured to store certificate and CRL information

c. designed to allow retrieval of information

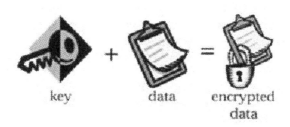

key   data   encrypted
data

Public/Private Key Pairs Public/Private Key Pairs

a. Public key/private key pairs are used to encrypt data.

b. Public keys are provided to everyone while private keys are kept hidden

Under normal, non-internet, circumstances data is sent between two parties. Where each party has the same key and can decipher the data. Such situations, where both parties use the same key to encrypt and decrypt the data, are termed symmetric key encryption. The problem with symmetric key encryption is that anyone can potentially see anything transmitted over the internet by intercepting its key as its being transferred. Using public key/private key encryption, the public key is freely available and can be transferred across the internet. Anyone who wishes can use the public key. Data is encrypted with the public key, but can only be decrypted with the private key which is held privately in secure storage. While the two keys are mathematically linked it is statistically impossible to generate the private key programatically, thus ensuring data security.

Typically someone wanting to send an encrypted message obtains a digital certificate from a trusted source known as a Certificate Authority or CA. The certificate authority issues a digital certificate containing the applicant's public key and identification information. The digital certificate is then encrypted by the certificate authority who's own public key is publicly available. The receiver of the message uses the certificate authority's public key to decode the digital certificate attached to the message, verifies it, then obtains the sender's public key and identification information held within the certificate. With this information, the recipient can send an encrypted reply which only the originator can decrypt.

Digital certificates provide a means to identify an organization or individual. A digital certificate, also called an authentication certificate, an X. 509 certificate, or a simple certificate allows you to confirm that a

message, connection, email, or other electronic communication originated from a given entity or individual. Digital certificates contain
information such as name, organization, location and other information about the entity the certificate was granted to as well as lifetime
information for the certificate itself. A digital certificate binds a public/
private key pair to a specific entity. Public/private key pairs are used in
verifying that a transmission or data came from a certain entity. Public/
private keys are used to digitally sign, encrypt or tag data such that it's
origin can be assured (signed), that it is useless to prying eyes
(encrypted) and/or that is has not been tampered with (tagged) during
transfer.

Digital certificates can be provided at a variety of levels based on how
well the requester has been identified. Level 1 certificates verify electronic mail addresses and contain little or no identification information. Level 1 certificates can be obtained typically free of charge. Level
2 certificates verify a user's name, address, social security number, and
other information against a credit bureau database. Level 2 certificates
must be securely transferred back to the original requestor. Level 3 and
4 certificates are available only to companies and corporations requiring similar company-level information.

Typically someone wanting to send an encrypted message obtains a
digital certificate from a trusted source known as a Certificate Authority or CA. The certificate authority issues a digital certificate containing the applicant's public key and identification information. The
digital certificate is then encrypted by the certificate authority who's
own public key is publicly available. The receiver of the message uses
the certificate authority's public key to decode the digital certificate
attached to the message, verifies it, then obtains the sender's public key
and identification information held within the certificate. With this
information, the recipient can send an encrypted reply which only the
originator can decrypt.

A certificate authorities(CA) is the digital equivalent of a passport organization. Certificate authorities are implicitly trusted and are responsible for validating the identity and credentials of the person or entity requesting a certificate. Once an entity has been validated, the certificate authority will generate and digitally sign a new certificate. This new certificate encapsulates the requester's identification information, such as name, organization, location. expiration date, generating a tamperproof, valid digital document.

x.509 Certificate Request and Response

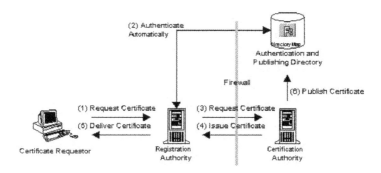

Each digital certificate is issued and signed by an authority. However, it's possible that you do not know the issuer of a certificate. Using certificate chains you can link a certificate back to its original source. If you trust the original source, you can potentially trust the intermediate source and the end certificate. It's up to the end user to decide how many levels of trust he/she will accept. It's possible that a certificate authority identified and verified the credentials of an intermediate authority, but that the intermediate authority abused that trust by issuing certificates to questionable entities. Most application Servers support specifying chains of up to three certificate authorities.

x.509 Certificate Publish and Remove

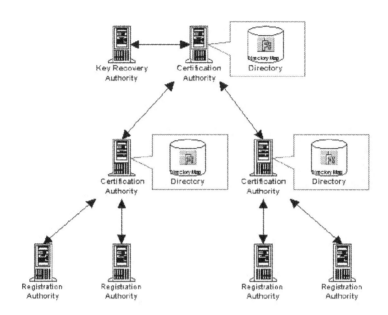

Within a LDAP based metadirectory two object classes play a principal role in the management of certificates and revocation lists relating to Public Key certificate authorities. These are the certificationAuthority and inetOrgPerson object classes. Within each object class key attribute values define what the key relationship is of each server and each individual

The certificationAuthority objectclass:

- cACertificate (required): defines the authority of the server in relation to other Certificate Authorities

- certificateRevocationList: a list of certificates to be revoked permissions

- authorityRevocationList: a list of active certificates whose credentals are to be challenged

- crossCertificatePair: a list of certificates who share trust relationships with the authority

The inetOrgPerson objectclass:

- userCertificate
- userSMimeCertificate
- userPKCS12

Here are some things to consider when creating a PKI enabled directory architecture:

- Which data is mastered where?
- Which servers consume the data?
- Which parts of the tree are replicated?
- Are there any referrals?
- Review topology decisions made earlier to ensure fit
- CAs must have write access to a directory to publish certificates and CRLs
- The security system may provide access as CN=Directory Manager
- Directory administrator may create special user with write access to PKI related components

NETWORK LEVEL SECURITY

The IPSec Working Group of the IETF has defined an open architecture and an open framework, known as "IPSec". IPSec is called a framework because it provides a stable, long lasting base for providing network layer security. It can accommodate today's cryptographic algorithms, and can also accommodate newer, more powerful algorithms as they become available. IPv6 implementations are required to support IPSec, and IPv4 implementations are strongly recommended to do so. In addition to providing the base security functions for the Internet, IPSec furnishes flexible building blocks from which robust, secure Virtual Private Networks can be constructed.

The IPSec Working Group has concentrated on defining protocols to address several major areas:

1. Data Origin Authentication verifies that each datagram was originated by the claimed sender

2. Data integrity verifies that the contents of the datagram were not changed in transit, either deliberately or due to random errors

3. Data confidentiality conceals the cleartext of a message, typically by using encryption

4. Replay protection assures that an attacker can not intercept a datagram and play it back at some later time

5. Automated management of cryptographic keys and security associations assures that Network Policy can be conveniently and accurately implemented throughout the extended network with little or no manual configuration. These functions make it possible for the Networks size to be scaled to whatever size a business requires.

The principal IPSec protocols are:

- **IP Authentication Header (AH)** provides data origin authentication, data integrity, and replay protection

- **IP Encapsulating Security Payload (ESP)** provides data confidentiality, data origin authentication, data integrity, and replay protection

- **Internet Security Association and Key Management Protocol (ISAKMP)** provide a method for automatically setting up security associations and managing their cryptographic keys.

Within the layered communications stack model, the Network layer is the lowest layer that can provide end-to-end security. Network-layer security protocols provide blanket protection for all upper-layer application data carried in the payload of an IP data gram, without requiring a user to modify the applications.
Authentication Header (AH)

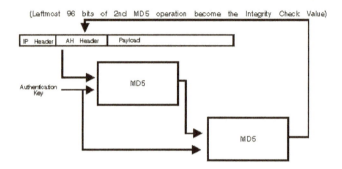

The IP Authentication Header provides connectionless (that is, per-packet) integrity and data origin authentication for IP datagrams, and also offers protection against replay. Data integrity is assured by the "checksum" generated by a message authentication code (for example, MD5); data origin authentication is assured by including a secret shared key in the data to be authenticated; and replay protection is provided by use of a sequence number field within the AH Header. In the IPSec vocabulary, these three distinct functions are lumped together and simply referred to by the name authentication.

The algorithms used by the AH protocol are known as hashed message authentication codes (HMAC). HMAC applies a conventional keyed message authentication code two times in succession: first to a secret key and the data, and then to the secret key and the output of the first round. Since the underlying message authentication code is MD5, this algorithm would be referred to as HMAC-MD5. The AH protocol also supports the use of HMAC-SHA. The mechanics are the same, but in this case, the Secure Hash Algorithm (SHA) is used as the base message authentication code rather than MD5.

AH protects the entire contents of an IP datagram except for certain fields in the IP header (called "mutable fields") that could normally be modified while the datagram is in transit(1). For purposes of calculating an integrity check value, the mutable fields are treated as if they contained all zeros.

AH can be applied in either of two modes: transport mode or tunnel mode.

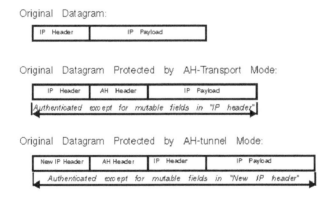

Transport mode

In transport mode, the original datagram's IP header is the outermost IP header, followed by the AH header, and then the payload of the original IP datagram. The entire original datagram, as well as the AH Header itself, is authenticated, and any change to any field (except for the mutable fields) can be detected. Note that all information in the datagram is in cleartext form, and therefore is subject to eavesdropping while it is in transit.

Tunnel mode

In tunnel mode, a new IP header is generated for use as the outer IP header of the resultant datagram. The source and destination address of the new header will generally differ from those used in the original header. The new header is then followed by the AH header, and then by the original datagrams in its entirety, both its IP header and the original payload. The entire datagram (new IP Header, AH Header, IP Header, and IP Payload) is protected by the AH protocol. Any change to any field (except the mutable fields) in the tunnel mode datagram can be detected. Note that all information in the datagram is in cleartext form, and therefore is subject to eavesdropping while it is in transit.

AH may be applied alone, in combination with ESP, or even nested within another instance of itself. With these combinations, authentication can be provided between a pair of communicating hosts, between a pair of communicating firewalls, or between a host and a firewall.

Encapsulating Security Payload (ESP)

The IP Encapsulating Security Payload provides data confidentiality (encryption), connectionless (that is per-packet) integrity, data origin authentication, and protection against replay. ESP always provides data confidentiality, and can also optionally provide data origin authentication, data integrity checking, and replay protection. Comparing ESP to AH, one sees that only ESP provides encryption, while either can provide authentication, integrity checking, and replay protection. ESP's encryption uses a symmetric shared key: that is, a shared key is used by both parties for encrypting and decrypting the data that is exchanged between them.

When ESP is used to provide authentication functions, it uses the same HMAC algorithms (HMAC-MD5 or HMAC-SHA) as are used by the AH protocol. However, the coverage is different:

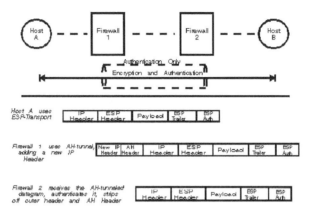

Transport mode

In transport mode, ESP's authentication functions protect only the original IP payload, but not the original IP header. (Recall that in transport mode, AH protected both the original IP Header and the IP Payload.)

In transport mode, the datagram's original IP header is also retained. Only the payload of the original IP datagram and the ESP Trailer are encrypted. Note that the IP Header itself is neither authenticated nor encrypted. Hence, the addressing information in the outer header is accessible to an attacker while the datagram is in transit.

Tunnel mode

In tunnel mode, ESP's authentication protects the original IP Header and the IP Payload, but not the New IP Header. (Recall that in tunnel mode, AH protected the New IP Header, the original IP Header, and the IP Payload.)

In tunnel mode, a new IP header is generated. The entire original IP datagram (both IP Header and IP Payload) and the ESP Trailer are encrypted. Because the original IP Header is encrypted, its contents are not accessible to an attacker while it is in transit. A common use of ESP tunnel mode, therefore, is to hide internal address information while a datagram is "tunneled" between two firewalls.

IPSec-based Solutions

ESP may be applied alone, in combination with AH, or even nested within another instance of itself. With these combinations, authentication can be provided between a pair of communicating hosts, between a pair of communicating firewalls, or between a host and a firewall.

Use of Transport and Tunnel Modes

AH and ESP can be used in transport mode or tunnel mode. IPSec's tunnel mode is an encapsulation technique modeled after "IP Encapsulation within IP" (RFC 2003). The key points to keep in mind are:

- Transport mode is normally used between the end points of a connection. For example, if secure communication is desired along all elements of a path from a client to a server, the client and server would use IPSec's transport mode.

- Tunnel mode is normally used between two machines when at least one of the machines is not an end point of the connection. For example, if secure communication is desired between two firewalls that are located between a client and a server, the firewalls would use IPSec's tunnel mode between themselves. Or if a remote host dialed in to its home network, it may want a secure path between itself and an entry gateway at its home network. Again, the remote host and the entry gateway would use IPSec's tunnel mode in this situation.

There are cases where it is desirable to use IPSec's transport and tunnel modes simultaneously—a capability called "nesting" or "bundling". For example, a path between a client and a server might pass through two firewalls. In this case, the client and server would use IPSec's transport mode, while the two firewalls would use IPSec's tunnel mode. Between the firewalls, both modes would be active:

Example: Host A uses ESP transport mode between itself and Host B.

- When the datagram created by Host A arrives at firewall 1, firewall 1 then applies AH tunnelmode to this datagram. That is, it adds a New IP Header, specifying itself as the source and firewall 2 as the destination, and it adds the AH Header.

- Since the outer header now has a destination of firewall 2, firewall 2 will process the incoming datagram. It will authenticate the inbound datagram, remove the outer header, and then remove the AH Header. At the end of this process, the original datagram launched by Host A will have been recovered.

- The original datagram will then be routed onward to Host B, who will process the ESP protocol to extract the underlying cleartext payload.

Notice that while traveling between the two firewalls, the original datagram was encapsulated: that is, it was carried inside the payload of the datagram with the new outer header. Different names are often given to this process: it is called tunneling, nesting, or encapsulation. All these terms are equivalent—they simply mean that an original IP datagram is being carried in the payload of another IP datagram. In theory, encapsulation can be applied iteratively, leading to nestings that are many levels deep. In practice, IPSec protocols require support for only two levels of nesting.

ISAKMP/Oakley

A Security Association (SA) contains all the relevant information that communicating systems need in order to execute the IPSec protocols, such as AH or ESP. For example, a Security Association will identify the cryptographic algorithm to be used, the keying information, the identities of the participating parties, etc. ISAKMP defines a standardized framework to support negotiation of Security Associations (SA), initial generation of all cryptographic keys, and subsequent refresh of these keys. Oakley is the mandatory key management protocol that is required to be used within the ISAKMP framework. ISAKMP supports automated negotiation of security associations, and automated generation and refresh of cryptographic keys. The ability to perform these functions with little or no manual configuration of machines will be a critical element as a encrypted network grows in size.

Secure exchange of keys is the most critical factor in establishing a secure communications environment—no matter how strong your authentication and encryption are, they are worthless if your key is compromised. Since the ISAKMP procedures deal with initializing the keys, they must be capable of running over links where no security can be assumed to exist—that is, they are used to "bootstrap" the IPSec protocols. Hence, the ISAKMP protocols use the most complex and processor-intensive operations in the IPSec protocol suite.

ISAKMP requires that all information exchanges must be both encrypted and authenticated: no one can eavesdrop on the keying material, and the keying material will be exchanged only among authenticated parties. In addition, the ISAKMP methods have been designed with the explicit goals of providing protection against several well-known exposures:

- Denial of Service: the messages are constructed with unique "cookies" that can be used to quickly identify and reject invalid messages without the need to execute processor-intensive cryptographic operations.

- Man-in-the-Middle: protection is provided against the common attacks such as deletion of messages, modification of messages, reflecting messages back to the sender, replaying of old messages, and redirection of messages to unintended recipients

- Perfect Forward Secrecy: compromise of past keys provides no useful clues for breaking any other key, whether it occurred before or after the compromised key. That is, each refreshed key will be derived without any dependence on predecessor keys.

ISAKMP has two phases:

Phase 1: This set of negotiation establishes a "master secret" from which all cryptographic keys will subsequently be derived for protecting the users' data traffic. In the most general case, public key cryptography is used to establish an ISAKMP security association between systems, and to establish the keys that will be used to protect the ISAKMP messages that will flow in the subsequent Phase 2 negotiations. Phase 1 is concerned only with establishing the protection suite for the ISAKMP messages themselves; but it does not establish any security associations or keys for protecting user data.

Phase 1 operations need only be done infrequently, and a single Phase 1 exchange can be used to support multiple subsequent Phase 2 exchanges. As a rule of thumb, Phase 1 negotiations are executed once a day or maybe once a week, while Phase 2 negotiations are executed once every few minutes.

Phase 2: A set of communicating systems negotiate the security associations and keys that will protect user data exchanges. Phase 2 ISAKMP messages are protected by the ISAKMP security association generated in Phase 1. Phase 2 negotiations generally occur more frequently than Phase 1: for example, a typical application of a Phase 2 negotiation is to refresh the cryptographic keys once every two to three minutes.

Implementation: Security Agents
Each server will utilize a security agent. The security policy enforcement agent named will be deployed. Then A second agent call "Secure Shell" will also be deployed on each server. Secure Shell allows encrypted access from one system to another through the use of shared keys. This is critical for administration and system management.

Each security agent require very little disk on the server between the two approximately 4 megabytes for software code. The secure shell will require additional space, less then 10 megabytes of disk space, for log storage. It is recommended that this be initially set at 20 megabytes. Each Security Agent process runs on a single CPU and occupies minimal overhead in the memory. The security agent consumes little CPU time until audit request or report retrieval is initiated. When the security agent first starts, it consumes 100% CPU while it gathers entropy to seed the pseudo random number generator for approximately 25 seconds. Once this is complete, the security agent system daemon is started which consumes some more time doing the same seed initialization. This second process will eventually die while the first one continues to run.

When an audit request is received, the security agent system daemon is started if it is not running. Then the security agent system daemon will run the audit. Auditing can consume various resources depending on what the audit is looking for. The security agent system daemon can and should be run at a lower priority.

An security agent system, after two full Audit cluster runs and a full set of pollet packages, consumes 3064 disk blocks (3MB). That is 1328 disk blocks (1.3MB) of report data.

When the Secure Shell daemon is started, the process will consume 100% CPU while it begins. The process should last no more than 2 seconds on an UltraSPARC processor. As remote clients access the daemon, the establishing of keys and seeding of encryption will consume additional CPU cycles but only for sub-second bursts of time.

SESSION LEVEL SECURITY

Figure 1: Logical—Security Basic LDAP Authentication over TLS/ TLS

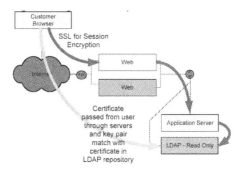

Figure 1 illustrates how a user can authenticate to an LDAP repository by presenting their user name and password. Their session from the browser to the application server is encrypted using 128-bit Secure Sockets Layer encryption from the Web server. This is single factor authentication based on "something you know."

Figure 2: Logical—Security LDAP Authentication with Certificate

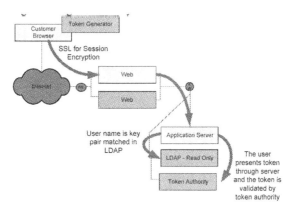

Figure 2 illustrates how a user can authenticate to an LDAP repository by presenting an x.509 certificate for stronger authentication and then potentially a user name and password. Once again, their session from the browser to the application server is encrypted using 128-bit Secure Sockets Layer encryption from the Web server. This form of authentication is considered stronger as it becomes dual factor authentication, "something you have" (a signed certificate even though it digitally stored) and "something you know" (username and password).

For reference the following ports are the established standard for TLS protocols.

Description	TCP Port	Aka
HTTP over TLS	443	HTTPS
SMTP over TLS	465	SSMTP
NNTP over TLS	563	SNNTP
LDAP over TLS	636	SLDAP
FTP over TLS	990	FTPS
POP3 over TLS	995	SPOP3

ACCESS CONTROL AND CLASS OF SERVICE

Having determined what the directory tree looks like, several factors influence how access control is implemented

- the directory applications and data stores that use the directory
- how the directory tree is distributed to multiple databases,
- how the databases are distributed to multiple locations
- how they are distributed to multiple servers at each location.

When planning access control one must recognized that each location contains a different set of users, applications, and data stores that all access the directory tree to either query or read information out of the tree or up date information in the tree.

Focusing on the application the architect must acknowledge that each of the applications have different entry points into the tree and each user has different entry points into the applications. What you the architect must do now is plan the security policies for the directory architecture. The architect must define how to protect the data in the tree, and how users get access to the tree, what parts of the tree, how applications update information, etc. This section focuses on how to control access to directory data using access control, in those products that include access control as a value add to the LDAP directory implementation.

An architecture requires the review of various user and application needs, development of a set of access control rules to help users and applications get proper access to the information in the directory tree. In an architecture evaluation users are divided into two general categories;

- General Users

General users are the general population users that use the directory. These users generally access the directory anonymously or without providing bind DN credentials.

- Special Users/Roles

Special Users are specific users or Roles of users which are represented by a generic role have special access control rights over multiple entries. For example, the role of directory administrators requires the right to be able to update information about any user in the directory, applications such as the Calendar need permissions to add or write profile settings for multiple users.

Steps to Define and Create Access Control Rules

1. **Review Directory Server Security Methods**: Review the various security methods available with the Directory Server in use that provide secure access to your directory.

2. **Define General User Access Control**: Define general user access control permissions for anonymous and authenticated users of your directory.

3. **Define Special User Access Control:** Define access control permissions for administrators and special users and/or Roles.

4. **Create Access Control Information (ACI) Statements**

Review Authentication Methods
One of the main security methods used in practically every directory architecture is authentication. This is where a user or application provides authentication credentials before gaining access to the directory.

Password Policies
Defines the criteria that a password must satisfy to be considered valid, for example, age, length, and syntax.

Encryption
Protects the privacy of information. When data is encrypted, it is scrambled in a way that only the recipient can understand.

There are a number of algorithms which are when providing security. Each algorithm was designed with a different purpose in mind. Speed of processing, level of security and algorithm complexity were all taken into account when encryption algorithms were first being designed. As a result a number of algorithms exist, each optimized for a different aspect of secure communications. RSA, developed in 1978 and named for its designers Ron Rivest, Adi Shamir, and A Leonard delman, is perhaps one of the most widely known and implemented encryption algorithms. RSA is based on the multiplicative combination of two large prime numbers to provide a public key/private key pair. DES, the Data Encryption Standard, works by taking a public key/private key pair and using it to to encrypt data by applying the key to a portion of data and then applying the output of the last round of encryption plus the key to the next portion of the data. RC2(Rivest cipher 2) and RC4(Rivest cipher 4) are similar standards to DES but are optimized for different applications such as streaming data. On average RC2 is 2x faster and RC4 10x faster then their DES counterparts. MD5 and SHA are not encryption standards but are used when data is sent in clear text but needs to be confirmed as unchanged upon receipt. Normally MD5 and SHA use a common known key to generate a signature or hash value which is applied to a message. On message receipt, the hashing algorithm is reapplied and the signature checked. If the signature matches, then the message can be guaranteed to be unchanged. Common key sources for MD5 and SHA including simply reading the first 512 or more bits of an agreed upon data source. Collectively, MD5, SHA and similar algorithms fall into the class of digital signature algorithms or DSAs.

Currently the United States regulates the sale and distribution of cryptography software to other nations. Due to this restriction, encryption can be obtained in two different strengths. The strength of an encryption algorithm is governed by the size of the keys it uses. Many software products come in two distinct and different flavors. The first is called exportable strength. Exportable strength products are limited to a length of 512-bits for certificates and public key's to a size of 40-bits. Domestic, or strong, encryption allows for a much higher level of security and is defined to be either 768 or 1023-bit certificates and 128-bit keys.

Just as a point of reference 56-bit encryption has more than 72 quadrillion, or 72,057,594,037,927,936, possible key pair combinations. A recent challenge, sponsored by RSA Inc., gave an encrypted message and offered $10, 000US to anyone who could decipher it. It took 4000 teams using thousands of computers 36 days to crack the code. An RSA official was quoted as saying the sun will be extinguished before the 128-bit challenge is cracked.

Review Access Control

Once a user or application is authenticated, the Directory Server controls access to the directory tree using a set of access control rules.

Account Inactivation

Disables a user account, group of accounts or an entire domain so that all authentication attempts are automatically rejected.

Signing with TLS

Maintains the integrity of information. If information is signed, the recipient can determine that it was not tampered with during transit.

The TLS/TLS protocol as defines in RFC 2246 uses a concept known as IP-tunneling to encrypt and decrypt packets. IP-tunneling is the process where packets of one protocol are encapsulated within packets of another protocol. In the case of TLS, packets which are tagged as secure are first routed through a network software layer which encrypts the given packet. The packet is then sent through the normal network stack to the remote host which in turn unwraps the secure packet and deciphers it. All of this takes place because your browser knows that any data sent over the HTTPS or LDAPS protocol must be secured in this fashion. It's important to note that tunneling and encryption do add overhead to a client connection and performance will be degraded when using a secure protocol.

Auditing

Allows you to determine if the security of your directory has been compromised. For example, the directory manager can audit the log files maintained by the directory.

There are several authentication methods available with a Directory Server. The two most common methods are anonymous access and simple password authentication.

Anonymous Access

Many Directory Servers allow you to set various anonymous access privileges in the directory to allow users to access directory data without having to authenticate.

Simple Password

One can setup Directory Server to require simple username and password authentication to access directory data.

Encrypted Password Authentication (SASL)

Enterprises are deploying strong authentication systems such as DCE and Kerberos V to provide a scalable authentication infrastructure for their users. There is often a need to integrate these services with enterprise directories based on the Lightweight Directory Access Protocol (LDAP). The Simple Authentication and Security Layer (SASL) is one such method for adding authentication support to connection-based protocols. LDAPv3 has adopted SASL as a standard way for multiple authentication protocols to be supported. After authentication, the server can grant additional privileges based on some site-specific policy. SASL grew out of the work on IMAP4, which includes the ability for mail clients and servers to negotiate the authentication mechanism they will use. The Network Working Group generalized the negotiation mechanism in IMAP4, creating an authentication abstraction layer that other protocols can use. SASL allows a client to request authentication from a server and negotiate the use of any registered authentication mechanism with only minimal knowledge of the underlying authentication system. There are currently four registered SASL authentication mechanisms: the Generic Security Services API, a generic programming interface designed to invoke security services; Kerberos Version 4; S/Key, an authentication protocol originally developed by Bellcore; and External, which allows clients and servers to use low-level encryption services like TLS and Ipsec. To use SASL, a protocol such as LDAP includes a command for identifying and authenticating a user to a server and for optionally negotiating protection of subsequent protocol interactions. If its use is negotiated, a security layer is inserted between the protocol and the connection. If use of a security layer is negotiated, it is applied to all subsequent data sent over the connection. The security layer takes effect immediately following the last response of the authentication exchange for data sent by the client and the completion indication for data sent by the server. Once the security layer is in effect, the protocol stream is processed by the security layer into buffers of cipher-text. Each buffer is transferred over the connection as a stream of octets prepended with a four octet field in network byte order that represents the length of the following buffer. The length of the cipher-text buffer must be no larger than the maximum size that was defined or negotiated by the other side.

Certificate-Based Authentication

CA involves using security certificates to bind to the directory. The directory prompts your users for a password when they first access it. However, rather than matching a password stored in the directory, the password opens the user's certificate database. If the user supplies the correct password, the directory client application obtains authentication information from the certificate database. The client application and the directory then use this information to identify the user by mapping the user's certificate to a directory DN. The directory allows or denies access based on the directory DN identified during this authentication process.

Simple Password Over TLS

When a secure connection is established between Directory Server and a client application using TLS or the Start TLS operation, the server can demand an extra level of authentication by requesting a password. In such cases, the password is not passed in clear over the wire.

Proxy Authentication

Proxy authentication is a special form of authentication because the user requesting access to the directory does not bind with its own DN but with a proxy DN. The proxy DN is an entity that has appropriate rights to perform the operation requested by the user. When you grant proxy rights to a person or an application, you grant the right to specify any DN as a proxy DN, with the exception of the Directory Manager DN. The proxy mechanism is very powerful. One of its main advantages is that the system can enable an LDAP application to use a single thread with a single bind to service multiple users making requests against the Directory Server. Instead of having to bind and authenticate for each user, the client application binds to the Directory Server using a proxy DN. The proxy DN is specified in the LDAP operation submitted by the client application. For example:

```
% ldapmodify -D "cn=bryan" -w password -y "cn=manager, dc=client-company, dc=com" -b "clientcompany.com" -f mods.ldif
```

This ldapmodify command gives a user named Bryan the permissions of the manager entry (cn=manager) to apply the modifications in the mods.ldif file. Note that he does not need to provide the password for the manager.

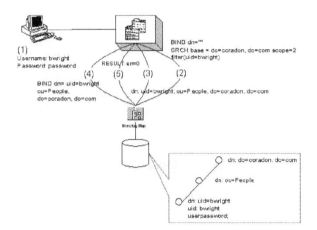

Most LDAP clients hide the bindDN from the user because DNs are often long strings that are hard to remember and type correctly.

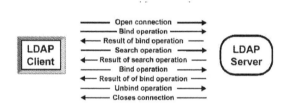

```
conn=45 fd=28 slot=28 connection from 206.230.49.199
conn=45 op=0 BIND dn="" method=128 version=3 conn=45 op=0
RESULT err=0 tag=97 nentries=0
conn=45 op=1 SRCH base="dc=coradon, dc=com" scope=2
filter="(uid=bwright)" conn=45 op=1 RESULT err=0 tag=97
nentries=0
conn=45 op=2 BIND dn="uid=bwright, ou=People, dc=coradon,
dc=com" method=128 version=3 conn=45 op=2 fd=28 RESULT
err=0 tag=97 nentries=0
conn=45 op=3 UNBIND
conn=45 op=3 fd=28 closed
```

This is an example of the handshaking and flow when a user authenticates. The lower section of the diagram is information that is recorded in the access log.

Access Control Overview

- **Where and/or what is the resource to be accessed?**
- **How can the resource be accessed?**
- **Who can and/or when can a resource be accessed?**

Access control is simply a mechanism that allows Directory Server administrators to control client access to various resources in the directory. Clients request access to resources, and Directory Servers allow or deny access to resources based on predefined rules. These rules are defined by Access Control Instruction (ACI) statements When a client requests access to a resource, the server evaluates all of the ACI statements it encounters in the directory tree path from the root entry to the requested resource before allowing or denying access to the resource. All of the ACI statements encountered in the path make up the Access Control List (ACL) for that resource. An ACI statement basically includes information on *who* can access a resource, *when* they can access a resource, *how* they can access a resource, *where* in the tree the rule applies, and *what* resource they can access. Resources can be any entry, or attribute of an entry, in the directory tree. Access control rules are placed directly in the directory tree using Access Control. Instruction (ACI) statements. The syntax for the ACI statement basically requires three inputs (target, permission, and bind rules). The flexibility and complexity in access control is the large number of combinations you can have for these three inputs.

In Brief

Who and When

A server can allow or deny access to a client based on the client's userdn, groupdn, etc. These are known as bind rules.

How

A server can set the allow or deny permissions to control how the clients access resources.

Where What

A server can allow or deny general access to all of the directory tree entries or specify a target, target attribute, targetattrfilter, or target filter within the directory. A target is a distinguished name within a directory;

A server can use any combination of bind rules, permissions, and targets to control client access to resources. This allows the architect to set up very complex security policies in the directory tree. This also means it can become a complex task!

Example 1—The iPlanet Directory Product

In the iPlanet product the Access Control is grafted into the slapd engine. The iPlanet product expresses Access Control within the directory in the following syntax.

```
aci:    (<target>)(version    3.0;acl"<name>";<permission><bind
rule>;)
```
where:

- `<target>` defines the object, attribute, or filter you are using to define what resource to control access to. The target can be a distinguished name, one or more attributes, and/or a single LDAP filter.

- `version 3.0` is a required string that identifies the ACL version.

- `acl "<name>"` is a name for the ACI. `<name>` can be any string that identifies the ACI. The ACI name is required.

- `<permission>` defines the actual access rights and whether they are to be allowed or denied.

- `<bind rules>` identify the circumstances under which the directory login must occur in order for the ACI to take effect.

In the iPlanet product the ACI statement is placed in the directory tree and defines the rules for that branch of the tree. Normally, most of the ACI statements are located at the top of the tree, but they can be placed anywhere in the tree depending on the desired action.

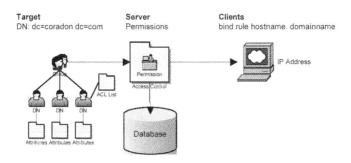

Anonymous access can be configured for the directory such that anyone can access the directory without providing bind credentials. That is, clients do not need to provide a bindDN or password to gain access. When a bindDN and password are not provided, the server assumes a null bindDN and a null password, and the access that it allows or denies is dependent upon the permissions that you have set up for anonymous access. If you are going to use an LDAP product that requires anonymous access, then you should carefully consider what pieces of directory data are required by that product and make sure to allow anonymous access only to those pieces of data. anonymous access rules are important because they are inherited by anyone who authenticates to the directory server.

Conceptually, directory authentication can be thought of as logging into the directory. LDAP directory servers, however, usually refer to this operation as binding to the directory. Generally, bind operations consist of providing the equivalent of a user ID and a password. However, in the case of an LDAP directory, the user ID is actually a distinguished name. The distinguished name used to access the directory is referred to as the bindDN. It is generally true that the bindDN corresponds to the name of an entry in the directory, although this is not always the case. When you bind as the root DN, for example, there is no corresponding directory entry. Also, the bindDN most frequently corresponds to an entry that represents a person, but again this is also not always true. Some directory administrators find it useful to bind as a directory branch point rather than as a person. The only real requirement is that the bindDN and the corresponding password must somehow be known to the directory. This means that the entry represented by the bindDN must use an object class structure that allows the userPassword attribute.

Example 2—The Microsoft Directory Approach

The Microsoft directory approach centers on a geographical centric domain. The *domain* is a collection of network objects, including organizational units, user accounts, groups, and computers, all of which share a common directory database with respect to security. In the Microsoft world security is server centric. In the Microsoft design domains form the core unit of logical structure, and play an essential role in security. Grouping objects into one or more domains allows the Microsoft network to reflect the way the company is organized, at least geographically.

As a result of the geographical limit imposed by the server based security model larger organizations will contain multiple domains, in which case the hierarchy of domains is called a domain tree, by most Microsoft professional. The first domain is the *root* domain, the *parent* to domains created beneath it, which are then called *child* domains. To support large organizations, domain trees must be linked together into an arrangement reffered to as a *forest,* by Microsoft professionals.

An active directory domain identifies a security authority and forms a security boundary with consistent internal policies and explicit security relationships to other domains. The administrator of a domain has rights to set policies within that domain only. This is necessary in large enterprises, because different administrators create and manage different domains in the organization.

In the Microsoft approach, an *organizational unit* (OU) is used as a container to organize objects into logical administrative groups within a domain. The organizational unit contains objects such as user accounts, groups, computers, printers, applications, file shares, and other OUs.

In the Microsoft approach, an *object* contains attributes about an individual item, such as a particular user, computer, or hardware.

Differences to remember when selecting Microsoft Active Directory

- The Active Directory domain is the smallest unit of partitioning and replication. It is not possible to subdivide an Active Directory domain into smaller, more manageable components.

- It is not possible to replicate just a portion of a domain's objects to another Active Directory domain controller, such as a single OU or part of the domain hierarchy. The entire domain must be replicated to all domain controllers.

- Each Active Directory domain controller can hold only a single domain replica.

- Adding or deleting a domain replica is not a simple operation but requires reassigning all file system trustees on the NT domain controller.

ACI'S AND ARCHITECTURE POLICY

The first step is to define how your general users access the directory both anonymously and when they authenticate (self) with the directory. A basic decision you need to make regarding your security policy is how users will generally access the directory. In short, will you allow anonymous access, or will you require every person who uses your directory to bind to the directory? If anonymous access is allowed, it is usually allowed only for read, search, and compare privileges (not for write, add, delete, or selfwrite). Also, access is usually limited to a subset of attributes that contain information generally useful across the enterprise, such as person names, telephone numbers, email addresses, and so forth. Anonymous access should never be allowed for more sensitive data such as government identification numbers (social security numbers in the United States), home phone numbers and addresses, salary information, and so forth.

There are several key points to consider here:
Anonymous access provides the easiest form of access to your directory. However, anonymous access does not allow you to track who is performing what kinds of searches; you only can track that someone is performing searches. Also, remember that anonymous access means anyone can access the data. Therefore, if you attempt to block a specific user or group of users from seeing some kinds of directory data but you have allowed anonymous access to that data, then those users can still access the data simply by binding to the directory anonymously.

Also remember some LDAP clients/applications require anonymous access for directory lookups. Normally it is good to allow search (s), read (r), and compare (c) privileges for anonymous access or no access at all. Be sure to consider the requirements of your directory applications. Some directory applications require anonymous access to function properly. One may also want to work with the legal department to help determine which attributes can be accessed anonymously.

One can specify self-authenticated access by reviewing each attribute associated with an authenticated user and deciding what privileges the user has on their directory entry when they bind to the directory. One may want to provide read privileges to attributes that don't have anonymous access or write privileges to attributes that the user has control over.

USE OF ROOTDN AND DIRECTORY MANAGER

Directory Manager (called *Root DN* in previous releases of the Directory Server) is a privileged user defined in the server's configuration settings that has universal access to the directory, regardless of the access control rules set in the directory. One authenticate as the Directory Manager by providing the appropriate bind DN and bind password similar to normal user authentication. The server automatically detects that this is the Directory Manager and authenticates using the internally stored password and grants total access. One may want to use Directory Manager to set up the server initially and then use a special group defined in the directory to administer your directory.

One frequently used option is to set up a special directory administrators group in the directory tree and add your administrators to that group. Then set up an ACI rule at the root of the tree that grants all the same privileges as Directory Manager to the special directory administrators group. This allows you to track who added or modified an entry and when. The server automatically appends to every directory entry the creator's name (`creatorsname`), when the entry was created (`createtimestamp`), the modifier's name (`modifiersname`), and when the entry was modified (`modifytimestamp`).

Step one, identify the access privileges for the special users and/or Roles in the directory data matrix. One can use the following letters to indicated the access privilege:

- Read (r) indicates whether directory data may be read.

- Write (w) indicates whether attributes may be added, modified, or deleted.

- Add (a) indicates whether the user or application can create entries.

- Delete (d) indicates whether entries can be deleted.

- Search (s) indicates whether the directory data can be searched for. Users must have Search and Read rights in order to view the data returned as part of a search operation.

- Compare (c) indicates whether the data may be used in comparison operations. With compare rights, the directory returns a yes or no in response to an inquiry, but the user cannot see the value of the entry or attribute.

- Selfwrite (f) indicates whether people can add or delete themselves from a group. This right is used only for group management.

The next step after defining your users and Roles in the matrix is to create Access Control Instructions (ACI) for each of those users and Roles. There may be several approaches to creating ACI statements for your directory. This approach is access centric and can be easily applied to Role Based Security systems.

The following four steps will help you create your ACI statements for each user and/or group in this approach:

1. Define to whom (who) and when the rule applies. the first step in creating an ACI statement is to define who the rule is applied to and possibly when the rule applies and the authenti-

cation method required. Basically, you define the bind rule first, since you already know what users and Roles you have from the matrix.

2. Define what attributes the rule applies to. The second step is to define what attributes the rule applies to or what attributes in the directory tree the user and/or group has access to.

3. Define where in the tree the rule applies: This is the first portion of the target syntax and defines where in the directory tree the rule is applied. All directory entries below this point are affected by this rule. One can obtain this information from the branch points defined in the matrix.

4. Define how the rule applies (permissions): The final step is to define how the rule applies or how the server applies it. The goal when defining any rule is to write the rule so that the permission keyword in the rule is *allow* and not *deny*. One want to avoid explicit denies if possible. Once a server encounters a deny rule, that rule takes precedence over any allow rule.

Example 4a iPlanet Directory Servers ACI

The iPlanet product expresses the ACI structure as listed below

```
aci: (<target>)(version 3.0; acl"<name>";
<permission><bind rule>;)
```

Using this syntax there are several options when defining a bind rule for your ACI statements. The following is the general syntax of a bind rule:

```
<keyword>="<expression>" or <keyword>!="<expression>";
```

The following are some examples to consider when defining bind rules for the iPlanet Directory Products:

`(userdn="ldap:///anyone")`
This rule is true for anonymous access.

`(userdn="ldap:///all"`
This rule is true for all authenticated users.

`(userdn="ldap:///self")`
This rule is true for self-authenticated users accessing their own entry.

`(userdn="ldap:///parent")`
This rule is true for all child entries below the bind DN.

`(userdn!="ldap:///uid=*,ou=People,o=Coradon.com")`
This rule is true for any bind DN except for those binding with the above DN. Note: wildcards can be used on the DN except for the suffix in the iPlanet product.

`(userdn="ldap:///o=Coradon.com??sub?(|(ou=Engineer-`
`ing)(ou=Exec))")`
This rule is true for any client that has either of these attributes in their entry.

`(groupdn="ldap:///cn=Costcenter    Managers,ou=Roles,o=Cora-`
`don.com")`
This rule is true for any bind DN that matches the manager attribute dn value.

`(userdnattr="Manager")`
The bind rule is true if the bind DN is the same as the value set for the manager attribute of the targeted entry. This is useful for, for example, allowing a user's manager to manage employees' password attribute.
This rule is true for any bind DN that matches the group attribute dn value.

`(groupdnattr="owner")`
The bind rule is true if the bind DN is a member of the group identified by the owner attribute of the targeted entry. This is useful, for example, for allowing a a group of people to manage employees' password attribute.

```
(ip="107.212.143.*" or dns="*.coradon.com")
```
This rule is true if the client binds with either an IP address that falls
with 107.212.143 or has a DNS name that ends in coradon.com.

Next Define What Attributes the Rule Applies

```
aci:  (<target>)(version 3.0; acl"<name>";  <permission><bind
rule>;)
(target="ldap:///<distinguished        name>")(targetattr="
<attribute>[ ||
<attribute>]")[(targetfilter="<search filter>")]
(targetattr="*")
(targetattr="userPassword")
(targetattr!="userPassword || coradon*|| home*")
(targetfilter="(ou=accounting)")
(targetfilter="(|(ou=accounting)(ou=engineering))")
```

Next define the permission set

```
aci:  (<target>)(version 3.0; acl"<name>";  <permission><bind
rule>;)
```
allow | deny (<rights>)

read—directory data may be read

write—attributes may be added, modified, or deleted

add—user or application can create entries

delete—entries can be deleted

search—directory data can be searched for

compare—data may be used in comparison operations

selfwrite—people can add or delete themselves from a group

proxy—new

all—keyword for all permissions

allow (read, search, compare)

deny (add, delete)

The last step in designing the security policy is to evaluate the Access Control List (ACL) by ordering the list of ACI statements from top to bottom to align with the directory tree design.

1. Select an attribute from the sample entry that you want to evaluate.

2. Use that attribute to read through each ACI in the path from the bottom to the top of the tree.

3. Evaluate the access rights for each ACI statement.

DELIVERABLES

- Directory Security Policy

26

Directory Peer Review Process—Phase 13

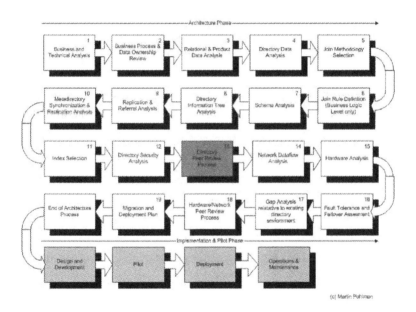

(c) Martin Pohlman

THE MODEL

The model proposed consists of the primary client and one other prominent ranking stakeholder acting as the co-editors and a group of other stakeholders and coworkers acting as the consultant panel.

The internal peer review in the past has been secretive (because only the Editor can see the whole process), narrow (because each article is usually reviewed by only one, two or three people) and somewhat arbitrary (because the choice of reviewers is limited by the Editor's knowledge and the time constraints of the potential reviewers).

The new model to be tested attempts to address some of these theoretical weaknesses. The procedure integrates peer review with the electronic publication process, allowing rapid publication after rigorous peer review. It preserves the chief virtue of the traditional peer review system (expert appraisal before publication), but brings a new openness to the procedure that we hope will enhance its accuracy and fairness.

In this model, peer review and editorial decision making are conducted under the eyes of the authors and a consultant panel. The client and one other prominent stakeholder (e.g. Security or Network infrastructure director) continue to carry the traditional responsibility of ensuring that the article is comprehensively reviewed; the extra participants may provide broader perspectives, catch other errors in the design, correct deficiencies in the reviews and smooth potential biases.

The openness of the dialogue is a more democratic model of peer review, which might improve the architects satisfaction with the procedure. All participants are better informed about the impact of their comments and the shape of the process as a whole (no longer is the Editor the only participant with a proper overview). This requires the architect to make decisions out in the open, which might be unnerving, but the hoped-for gains are better advice, demonstrated accountability and, ultimately, an improved service to readers through providing better articles.

DELIVERABLES

- Process Improvement

27

Network Dataflow Analysis—Phase 14

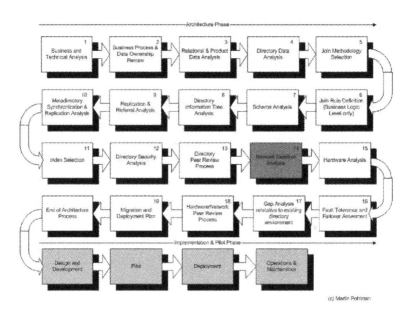

CAPACITY PLANNING

How we determine which computers to use falls into the realm of Capacity Planning. Capacity planning is the art of determining how many computers, and of what variety are required to serve a given need. Capacity planning, is without a doubt, more an art than a science and there are few hard and fast rules. In this section we will examine the factors involved in capacity planning and provide baseline numbers and guidelines for making appropriate planning decisions.

There are many factors affecting capacity:

- client application mix(Java vs. http)

- available memory

- generated traffic

- performance packs

- security

- directory usage

- bandwidth requirements

BANDWIDTH

- pure programmatic server operates at 125-150% of a mixed client server

- on average 56k/s=7-10 simultaneous connects

- netstat –s or –e for information on network performance.

  Bandwidth can be a major bottleneck in server performance. One can have a gigabyte of main memory and still The Directory Server will appear to perform poorly because your network simply cannot serve packets fast enough. As a rule you can assume that every 56k of bandwidth can serve 7-10 clients. This means that using a 10mb network connection, a server can serve appropriately 10mb/56kb=~ 20*7=140 at the low end, and 20*10 or 200 at the high end clients.

NUMBER OF PROCESSES

Another of the configurable parameters is the number of processes in use by each instance of the metadirectory proxy server. Most metadirectory Proxy Servers are built on the process mob architecture, with some amount of threaded code within each process.

Setting this value too low will result in connections being lost, with no record at the proxy server. Setting this value too high will utilize more memory than is needed, and will reduce the memory available to the other proxy instances installed on the machine.

The optimum number of processes to run is not a trivial number to calculate, and depends upon some characteristics of the traffic load seen over time.

Ideally, the value for the number of processes to run is based on the formula:

NUM processes=NUM requests/sec x NUM sec/request/process

The *Transfer Time* value from the Extended 2 Log Format show the amount of time it took to complete that request. If that value were 2 seconds, then it would take a minimum of 40 processes to handle the desired load (20 connections per second times 2 seconds per request). Any value lower than 40 would not be able to sustain the desired throughput.

This also does not accommodate error conditions. Errors usually take much longer to process than do normal requests. To calculate the number of processes consumed by handling errors, use the formula:

NUM processes$_{bad}$=NUM requests$_{bad}$/sec x NUM sec/request$_{bad}$/process

If there is a single bad request every ten seconds (and with a dedicated user interface for TGAOL, this number is probably high), and each bad request took 60 seconds to complete (which isn't unusual in situations where server timeouts are occurring), you'll get 6 additional processes used to handle errors (0.1 x 60).

Therefore, the number of processes to configure should be a minimum of 46, and a value 10-20% higher is not unreasonable at all to accommodate.

SECURITY

Security has a major impact on Directory Server performance. A Directory Server, when configured to use the TLS/TLS feature, must encrypt and decrypt incoming and outgoing packets. The encrypt/decrypt process significantly impacts performance. One can assume that for every secure client, The Directory Server can process 3 non-secure clients or approximately a 33% decline in performance using domestic encryption. Stronger levels of encryption will require additional CPU cycles further reducing performance.

OPERATING SYSTEM PERFORMANCE

On any operating system we would like to monitor:

- virtual memory
- CPU usage
- network performance of the OS
- disk IO

Windows NT/2000/XP

Windows NT 2000 and XP provide several tools for examining operating system performance. The Performance Monitor tool, found under Start programs/Administrative Tools/Performance Monitor, supports tracking CPU usage, memory, thread and a host of other information. The Network Monitor can monitor:

- percentage of network utilization

- frames & bytes/second
- capture information for later review

The Network Monitor allows administrators to examine networking information including bytes sent and general network utilization.

Unix

There are a number of tools, common to many Unix platforms, for monitoring performance:

- netstat [-i|-I] interface—show net statistics
- top—display CPU information
- vmstat—show virtual memory statistics

Solaris

There are Solaris-specific tools for examining system performance:

- perfmeter, stdperfmeter—graphical display of system statistics
- iostat—display IO statistics

Linux

Linux tools for performance monitoring include:

- xcpustate—graphical display of cpu info
- asload, ascpu—graphical display of system load

TUNING

In order to tune your directory performance you must determine appropriate test metrics and baseline performance. Once you have a testable environment, one in which you can repeat the same test and get the same or similar results, you can begin the process of stressing your application to determine bottlenecks and improve performance.

The best way examine application performance is through the use of custom tests and simulations. Tests which mimic how your expect your system to perform under actual load conditions.

There are a number of factors involved with directory tuning:

- average expected number users
- peak number of users
- expected throughput in operations/second
- peak throughput
- expected growth

A good test mix covers both peak and off-peak throughput requirements and supports collection of performance statistics. It's also important to have tests at different levels in the architecture, providing unit as well as integration level testing. When developing test suites make sure that your tests include the ability to analyze small system changes and that they can be rerun in order to perform regression analysis.

The best way to model performance is by developing custom test suites that:

- perform peak and off-peak testing
- collect statistics on throughput
- allow for single change retesting
- can be used with profiling tools

Always re-run your test after each small system change.

Establish a baseline by examining:

- average/peak network traffic
- average/peak CPU usage

- average/peak memory usage

PROFILING

In order to improve directory performance you need the ability to profile where your directory is spending its time. Specifically we would like to know which operations are invoked most often, where IO takes place and how long that IO takes. Additionally we would like to know where memory is allocated, and how calls impact performance. A good application profiler will be able to address many of these questions.

There are a number of tools which can be used for profiling and monitoring. When profiling you want to examine:

- peak and off-peak values
- CPU usage
- memory usage
- network performance

SCALABILITY

- A single machine can only do a limited amount of work.

- When business grows beyond the capability of a single machine, a system that expands multiple machines is needed.

When business grows beyond the available equipment, you are not at a dead end, but you do need to take into account how to maintain the integrity of your transactions and underlying data in an environment in which many machines could be processing related requests. It is no small trick to find a way to make sure that this will all work, no matter how many machines are doing your task.

Further subdividing your task also can help, but then you face problems with complexity of deployment. Who will maintain your system, when every machine is running some different but necessary part of your application? If not thought through, your administration costs can grow faster than your business.

MAINTAINABILITY

- Most systems are built before all the requirements are defined.

- Most target markets for business applications are constantly changing and the infrastructure, which supports them, must be equally flexible.

The solution includes:

- keeping business logic in reusable components

- removing directory & database access from the user interface

As an architect you should be familiar with Object Oriented Analysis & Design. Many individuals have a passing familiarity with it. If so, you know that requirements for a piece of software will continue to trickle in right up to the day that your software is made obsolete by a new product.

Currently, the strategy to handle this issue is that code should be built in small reusable components. In this way, if some government regulation changes some piece of business logic, only a small amount of your application will have to change. If some new application needs to be built to generate a new report, based on the same data and calculations, no new back-end needs to be written. If the structure of your database has to change, the user software can remain unaffected. These selling points of OOAD are especially important in the field of distributed software. Distributed applications are not a brand new idea. We have had them for a few decades now. As our needs became more sophisticated, various types of operations became routine parts of building such behemoths. These tasks are the ones listed above. Commercial solutions to most of these tasks appeared, and came into common use. Many large projects developed by respectable companies had to be abandoned because some of the above were handled so poorly that the code never worked correctly. In recent years this has been less of an issue. Still, an incredible number of man-hours have been spent re-inventing these very complicated wheels.

28

Hardware Analysis—Phase 15

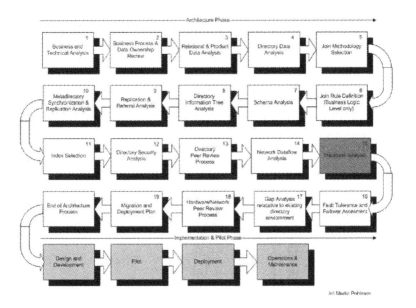

Directories add an additional element of complexity to capacity planning. The vast majority of installations will discover that their database server runs out of capacity before there application server. Often a application server will appear to be performing poorly when in fact most of the time is spent waiting for directory calls. directory capacity planning is a complete art unto itself, but as a rule the directory server should be a separate machine from your application server and should be 3 to 4 times more powerful in turns of raw performance, disk performance and memory. A good indicator that your directory is a bot-tleneck is that you cannot get your application CPU performance above %80 to %85 percent.

MEMORY

How much memory is enough?

- 256 MB is considered a minimum
- use 80-85% of available RAM

192 to 256mb of main memory per CPU. Since each connection to Directory Server requires a thread and each thread requires memory it stands to reason that more memory equals more threads.

Java Memory Management: Using Java based directory servers

Due to the overwhelming support of LDAP in Java both by indepen-dent developers (e.g. Innosoft's JDAP) and by native Java Classes included by Sun Microsystems (e.g. JNDI Appendix E). LDAP Meta-directory products are often designed and implemented in Java. LDAP Directory Servers and Metadirectory components written in Java often take the form of Servlets. As a result any discussion of Java based direc-tory server memory management must address the constraints of the servlet.

Servlet

A servlet is an independent thread of control that runs in the context of a server. The server acts as the "environment" in which the servlet lives. A server controls the life cycle, security, and execution of the servlets running within it's environment. This means that the server is respon-sible for the creation, access, and destruction of the servlet. The server also acts as the mechanism that clients and servlets use to pass data between one another. This role allows the server to control client's access to and from the servlet. This access control is the reason a servlet has the same security of the server it is run on (as in a trusted 3rd party vendor.) Essentially, the server behaves as a broker, being a "middleman" for the requests and responses generated. Since the servlet is a server side program, it has access to all of the resources available on that particular server. This includes databases, transaction monitors, files, directory structures, naming services, other servers, and other servlets! The servlet uses all of the resources available at its "fingertips" to generate a dynamic response to give back to the client. The response given back to the client is dynamic because the data being pulled from the resources on the server is non-deterministic and unpredictable. Since the servlet has access to every resource, there are some security issues that must be considered. Servlet developers have to be cautious to not author a malicious servlet that disrupts or destroys a system resource. Servlets differ from applets in that servlets do not run in a web browser or with a graphical user interface. Instead, servlets interact with the servlet container running the web server through requests and responses. The servlet has access to many server-side resources. These resources include, but not limited to, databases, transaction servers, file systems, naming services, application servers, messaging services, and directory services.

Directory Servers, Memory and the Java Virtual Machine

A good rule of thumb with respect to memory is "More is Better". This holds especially true with a LDAP Directory Server. One can specify the amount of memory the a Java based directory server uses at start time via the –ms and –mx parameters to the Java Virtual machine. Note that if you are using a JVM other then that provided by Sun these parameters may differ. The –ms parameter to controls the minimum heap size and –mx the maximum. The larger the heap the more threads that can be executing at a given moment allowing the directory to perform more useful work. The Java 2 JDKs have much better garbage collecting facilities then the JDK1 JDKs. Practically, this means that you should use as large a heap size as possible without causing your system to "swap" pages to disk (some implementations actually allocate as much as twice the heap size specified to support the copying half space). If you are booting your directory server and you see that your allocated "virtual" memory is more than your RAM can handle, you should lower your heap. Typically, use 80-85% of available RAM not taken by the operating system or other processes for your JVM running directory server. When the JVM runs out of memory in the heap, all execution in the JVM stops while a Garbage Collection (GC) algorithm goes through memory and frees space that is no longer required by an application. This is an obvious performance hit because your application must wait while GC happens. No server-side work can be done during GC. The JDK 1.1. x implementations used a mark and sweep mechanism were objects where marked free and reclaimed during GC. JDK1.2. x implementations use least recently used algorithms(LRU) to better manage memory. The garbage collectors in HotSpot, Jview and JDK1.2 manage their heap size more efficiently than the previous versions.

When monitoring garbage collection look for:

- leaks
- every growing heap size

One can make minor adjustments to the heap size that impact this issue.

TPS

Transactions Per Second

- Transactions per second(TPS) is a measure of performance.
- Peak TPS is often 2-3x normal performance or more.

Transactions per second is typically used to measure the performance of a directory server or a application server/directory combination. The higher the count the better the performance. When determining capacity we need to determine our expected TPS requirements. Capacity planners will need to work with developers and web designers to help understand what an appropriate expected TPS requirement is. Within the context of directory server we will consider both operations per second and all support services such as indexing, referrals and aliasing.

Transactions per second ratings help developers and planners alike determine how a given configuration of a directory server may perform. In this example we assume that a given installation of directory server will need to handle 1000 simultaneous connections and that new requests arrive at about 20 second intervals. Given 1000 concurrent connections each of which generates a new operation every 20 seconds we can expect an average of 50 operations per second. However, peak transaction requirements are much more useful then average. Typically, a 2-3x increase in average operations per second is a reasonable expectation for peak TPS. Using a 3X expectation of peak TPS, we see that directory server will need to handle approximately 150 operations per second in order to support our original requirements.

A TPS Example

Computing required transactions per second:

- Assuming 1000 simultaneous connections

- New requests every 20 seconds

- 1000/20=50tps(average)

What about peak?

- Assume 2-3x increase

- 1000/(20/2)=100tps

- 1000(20/3)=150tps

Windows NT Baseline			HP-UX on PA-RISC		
CPU	Memory	TPS	CPU	Memory	TPS
1x450mhz	1gb	49tps	1x160mhz	1gb	18tps
2x450mhz	1gb	74tps	2x240mhz	1.5gb	55tps
4x450mhz	1gb	100tps	4x240mhz	2gb	87tps
			6x240mhz	2gb	108tps

What kind of machine is required for 1000 sim users at 50tps with peaks of 150tps?

- 2x450mhz Windows NT Server gives 74tps
- 74x2=~ 150tps.
- therefore a cluster of 2 NT servers should be acceptable

We can apply the baseline numbers to determine an appropriate configuration of Directory Server to handle a given load. Using the earlier figures of 1000 concurrent users each making requests every 20 seconds we find a peak load of 150tps. Using the baseline figures we can see that a Windows NT machine handles approximately 74 transactions per second and as such a directory cluster of two such machines should provide acceptable performance.

If we assume that security is required and given our earlier assumptions that security causes a 33-50% performance decrease we can refigure our estimates. Assuming domestic security, at a decrease of 33%, we see that a 3 node cluster should provide sufficient performance.

MANAGING THREADS

When should the thread count be increased? Use profiling and monitoring to identify this situation.

- when the directory is rejecting requests and CPU is not running at 100%
- when directory requests are blocking

One need to very careful when manipulating the number of execution threads in the a directory server that permits thread management. Many factors control how many threads a directory server can actually take advantage of. CPU, memory, swap and heap size all interact making manipulating thread counts difficult. In most cases the best indicator of how your application will benefit by increasing the thread count is your application. Before you make any changes profile your application. Then make a minor change, adding 10% or increasing the count by 2-3 and then re-profile to determine if your change had a positive effect. Consider the following example:

Assume that:

n=executeThreadCount (number of threads) and k=number of CPUs

The following scenarios are possible:

1. If (n < k) this results in an under utilized CPU, we need to increase the thread count.
2. If (n==k) that is theoretically ideal, but the CPUs are under utilized, we need to add more threads
3. If (n > k) by a "moderate amount of threads". This is practically ideal, resulting in a moderate amount of context switching and a high CPU utilization rate. Tune the "moderate amount of threads" and compare performance results.

4. If (n > k) by "many threads". This could lead to significant performance degradation as it results in too much context switching, so reduce the number of threads.

For example, if you have 4 processors, then 4 threads can concurrently be running. One would want the execute threads to be 4+(the number of blocked threads). Thread count is very application dependent. For instance, how long the application might block on threads, which can invalidate the above formula.

Steps To Updating Thread Count

- establish baseline performance

- manipulate a single application variable

- increase count slightly

- re-establish baseline performance numbers

There is no better way to determine the impact of changing the directory server thread count then actually testing your directory applications under load using a utility such as Mercury or DirectoryMark. An iterative test process where you determine timing and performance information, manipulate a facet of the system and then re-determine performance is always the best approach. When tuning, change only a single application or Directory Server variable at one time. Changing more they one parameter for a given test makes understanding performance impacts very difficult.

ONE OR MANY MACHINES ONE OR MANY MACHINES

As a general rule it is better to have many individual machines rather then one multi-CPU machine. When determining capacity its important to examine the one or many machines question. Experience shows that Directory Server performs better in a clustered environment. Clusters have a number of benefits over multi-cpu machines, redundancy being only one such benefit. While a single. multi-cpu machine, may perform better individually a cluster of machines will scale better and be more reliable. For these reasons, and may others, clusters are most likely a better application architecture.

A cluster:

- is redundant

- can be incrementally updated(easy to add machines, hard to add CPUs)

- has better price/performance (small machines are inexpensive)

There are a number of additional impacts on capacity and performance. When determining the capacity of the directory server is running on other applications need to be considered. For optimal performance the directory should not have to contend with other applications on the same platform. Obviously, a directory server running on a machine providing database services will not perform as well as a directory on its own machine. Its also important to property tune the machine running the directory. Threads counts, heap size and other parameters can either improve or decrease directory performance. Clustering is another area where significant capacity can be gained. Studies have shown that adding a second machine to a cluster can increases performance up to 95%. Thus a two machine cluster can perform at as much as 195% of the capacity of a single, similarly configured, machine.

There are many other considerations when examining capacity:

- will the server be doing anything else

- is the Directory Server properly tuned

- is clustering configured

- is the application well tuned

DELIVERABLES

- Network Dataflow Diagram

29

Fault Tolerance and Failover
Assesment—Phase 16

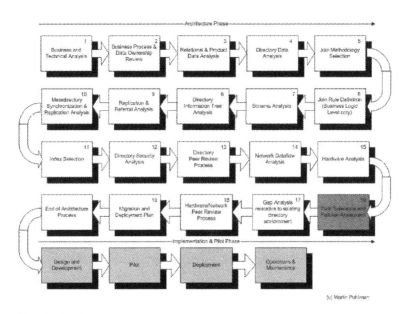

High Availability

HIGH AVAILABILITY

24-7 Availability is needed by applications such as:

- ATM Banking

- stock & commodities trading
- e-commerce
- law-enforcement
- call center reporting
- travel reservations
- fire-arms background checks
- military communications

High availability, also called fault tolerance, is needed by any system where the cost of being down is unacceptable. Systems that require consistent operation and 100% availability to their users are called fault tolerant. Fault tolerance is a feature of many aspects of a computer system. Fault tolerance is implemented in the hardware, operating systems, and software that run on these machines. The levels of tolerance that a system can have can vary wildly. From a system that has a simple RAID drive to a fully clustered directory system, there is a variety of configurations that you can use. directory provides high availability through its clustering features.

CLUSTERING

Clustering is a group of Servers that act in a coordinated way to provide access to clustered services. Clustering is a group of Servers that coordinate with one another to provide clients access to the services provided by the entire cluster. These services may be a superset of the services provided by a single Server instance. A cluster can exist on one or more computers as long as there is more than one instance that is executing. The cluster provides an encapsulated interface to the services of the cluster. The cluster appears as a single instance to clients whether those clients are web-based or Java-based. By replicating the services provided on a single instance, an enterprise system achieves a failsafe environment and a scalable one. High availability is achieved through the replication of services so that when one service fails, a second service can resume operation where the first left off. Scalability is achieved through balancing the load of incoming requests across the servers in the clusters. If there are four instances in a cluster and four requests enter the cluster, scalability can be achieved through the balancing of those four requests evenly across the cluster instances.

Clustering provides:

- a failsafe environment
- scalability through load balancing requests

A cluster configuration requires:

- all servers to be located on the same LAN
- all servers to be reachable via IP multicast
- all servers use static IP addresses
- all servers have access to a shared file system
- all Directory Servers on a single tier are the same LDAP version

To participate in a tier each participating Directory Server must:

- use the same IP multicast address
- have a unique IP address
- listen on the same TCP/IP port
- listen on the same TLS/TLS port

Cluster Shared Directory Structure
A cluster directory system can be divided into three types

- a global directory accessible to all application servers in all clusters

- a per-cluster directory accessible to all application servers in a single cluster

- a per-server directory accessible to a single application server in a single directory

Instance Clusters

A instance only cluster, is simple and efficient. In an instance only cluster, the directory instances all initialize themselves from a common properties file that contains registration entries for a variety of instances. For each registration entry in the directory. properties file, each directory instance will initialize a memory replica. After boot, all of the directory server instances will have their own memory instance of the same server running within their virtual machine. When a client makes a directory requests Depending upon the technique used to gain access to the cluster, the logic in the initial access technique determines the exact directory server instance which should handle the request. In a instance only scenario, it does not matter which directory instance is selected for the incoming request since each of the server instances have identical versions of each program executing.

With in-memory state replication, a database is not required to achieve clustering with session objects. Rather, a configuration using a front end cluster proxy is required. The cluster proxy provides client routing information, which tracks which clients are using which sessions and on which server. Each time a client request is sent for the cluster, it is first routed through the cluster proxy which forwards the request to a server that has the client's session. Subsequent requests that filter through the cluster proxy will be routed to the same directory server instance if session data is associated with the client.

Multi homing

A multi-homed machine is a machine with multiple IP addresses.

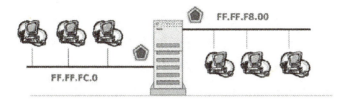

A multihomed machine:

- can run a different directory instance bound to each IP address
- can be used to configure a cluster on a single machine

A multi homed machine is one where multiple IP addresses are all bound to a single machine. A multi-homed machine may have more then one network card or simply multiple IP addresses bound to a single network card. In either case, a machine with more then one IP address is considered to be multi-homed. Multi-homed machines can be configured to run multiple instances of a Directory Server, each bound to a specific IP address and in this way can simulate clustering.

In order to get multi-homing to work on a single machine, the operating system must allow you to configure multiple IP addresses for a single machine. The Directory will refer to these operating system IP addresses at boot time based upon the value of the operating system property. The IP addresses for the actual server must refer to the physical machine that Directory Server will be running on—a directory server cannot try binding to an IP address specified on a different machine. Under Windows NT you can specify an IP address using the Networking utility in the Control Panel. On Solaris, Linux or other Unix variants you normally use the ifconfig utility.

One can configure a multiple IP addresses for a given network adapter, such as an ethernet card, in Windows NT by selecting the Network control panel utility. This utility provides the necessary interface for configuring all networking aspects of a single machine operating on a TCP/IP, NT, or other network. Under the Protocols tab, there should be a "TCP/IP Protocol" option that you can configure. One can configure a variety of TCP/IP parameters including DNS servers, IP addresses, gateways, IP forwarding, DHCP, and others. Additional IP addresses can be specified by selecting the "Advanced" button. An "Advanced IP Addressing" dialog box will appear where you can add additional IP addresses.

One can configure IP addresses on Unix systems ifconfig command. The ifconfig command operates on interfaces, which are usually adapters to a particular network interface card. The ifconfig command is typically found in /sbin or /usr/sbin. It provides a number of features for manipulating and viewing the characteristics of a network interface such as an ethernet card or other network adapter. See the Unix man pages for a complete description of the ifconfig command.

Please note that there is a different syntax for listing IP addresses than what is used for adding IP addresses.

SNMP

The Simple Network Management Protocol (SNMP) is a protocol for managing distributed devices. Examples of devices include:

- bridges
- routers
- servers
- printers

The Simple Network Management Protocol (SNMP) was designed to be an easily implemented, basic network management tool that could be used to meet network management needs. SNMP has become the dominant standardized network management scheme in use today.

The SNMP set of standards provides a framework for the definition of management information along with a protocol for the exchange of that information.

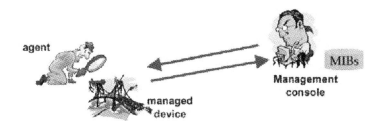

SNMP Architecture

- SNMP works by monitoring devices through software known as agents.

- Agents report information on demand(polling) or automatically(traps).

The SNMP model assumes the existence of managers and agents. A manager is a software program responsible for monitoring and managing all or part of a set of SNMP enabled devices. An agent is a software module, running within a managed device, responsible for maintaining local state information. Agents deliver that information to a manager using the SNMP protocol. Agents implement a strict API set and function by collecting data and sending that data in response to a request, or asynchronously when an unusual event occurs. Information exchange, between agents and managers, can be initiated by the manager (via polling) or by the agent (via a trap). The network manager makes virtual connections to the SNMP agent which executes on a remote network device, and sends information to the requestor regarding the device's status. In order for a manager to make requests of an agent and to interpret the responses and unsolicited traps that it receives, it uses a database which describes the information available from the agent. The database is referred to as the SNMP Management Information Base (MIB). There is a standard set of statistical and control values defined for hardware elements on a network, each of which is described with its own MIB. For example industry standard devices such as routers, bridges and similar devices are all defined my industry standard MIBs. SNMP also allows the addition of private MIBs which are particular to a new device which the industry has not yet recognized as a standard device

SNMP Polling

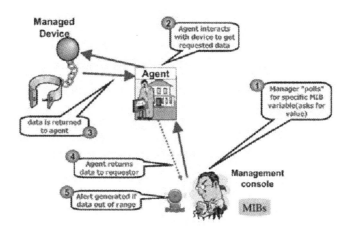

Polling works as follows: A manager program periodically requests a specific MIB variable from a network device. When data is returned by the remove SNMP agent it is compared with what are considered "normal" range values for that variable. What is normal is determined either a System Administrator or via predefined values stored in the MIB for the managed device. For values outside the normal range an alert is generated. Alerts can be email, ringing bells or some other mechanism which tells a System Administrator that special action needs to be taken.

SNMP Traps

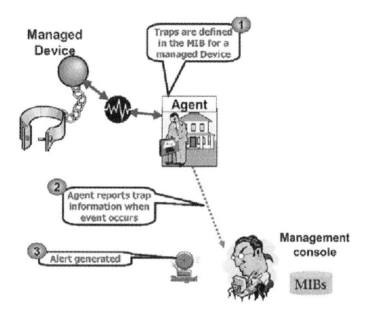

Traps are asynchronous events generated by a remote agent and set to any management program which has been defined to receive them. An agent generates a trap by determining, via some internal mechanism, that an error condition that a management program should be aware of has occurred. Traps are defined within the MIB for the device. Standard traps exist for standard devices, ie such as route down for a router or disk full for a disk device. Many trap types exist for managed devices. Management programs make sense of traps by applying information stored in the trap to MIBs defined in their MIB database. Unexpected traps, those that are not recognized as matching any MIB, are dropped. Recognized traps cause an alert to be generated in much the same way as polling.

Why provide an SNMP link to SNMP-compliant management systems? The main reason is that WLS is part of an overall organization or business solution. It is not the only application that will be running on your network. Integrating LDAP with SNMP allows you to effectively manage all of your large-scale applications using the SNMP-compliant network management tool of your choice. Since most of the management platforms support SNMP today, directory server SNMP Agent can be integrated into virtually every management framework. Examples of such systems include HP OpenView, IBM Tivoli, Sun Domain/SunNet/Site Manager, and CA Unicenter.

SNMP manageability of Directory Server provides the following benefits:

- Enables you to move towards a single management console and thus provide integrated systems management of WebLogic Server based applications.

- Enables you to connect WebLogic Server to popular management systems such as HP OpenView, Sun SunNet Manager, and IBM NetView. This makes managing WebLogic Server more effective by providing a whole-system perspective instead of piecemeal solutions.

- Enables you to preserve your standard-based, compliant (SNMP-capable) management frameworks.

- Enables you to benefit from the experience of the large community of SNMP users.

- Enables providers of management applications to customize them for Directory Server customers.

The directory server SNMP agent will enable you to remotely monitor the status of your server or server cluster. It will report statistics including the availability of your server, the number of connections, and the average queue length. UDP ports 161 and 162 are the default ports reserved for SNMP. The agent listens for requests and replies to them over port 161 and reports asynchronous traps on port 162, unless it is instructed to use different ports.

Any directory server under consideration should support four basic SNMP traps as a minimum.

- server restart
- server shutdown
- server down
- server up

DNS Round Robining

DNS round-robining is a network feature that allows clients to access multiple machines through a single IP address.

DNS round-robining is a feature of the DNS naming service that allows a system administrator to configure a single host name that maps to multiple machines. DNS will automatically load balance incoming requests for the DNS name across all of the servers configured to the host name. This is a feature of DNS and has to be configured through the network DNS administration utility.

Round Robining Alternative

A client application can bypass DNS round-robining by using a multi-IP URL.

An alternative method of specifying the initial point of contact with the cluster is to supply a comma-delimited list of DNS Server names or IP addresses. If DNS round-robining is not available in your system, you can use the multi-IP URL to make initial contact with the cluster. The cluster will be aware that the URL is a multi-IP URL and automatically decide which server instance should handle your request.

Cluster Proxy

A Proxy Server:

- forwards requests to other machines
- can be used as a level of indirection and security
- can be used to load balance a system

A proxy server is a piece of software that accepts a request on behalf of a client and forwards the request onto a machine that satisfy the request. The proxy server typically maintains some sort of mapping mechanism to determine which type of client requests get forwarded to which servers. A proxy server decouples clients from the server that provides the implementation for the client. This level of indirection gives administrators and architects a level of security and the ability to reconfigure the backend network without impacting existing clients. A proxy server can also be used to load balance a system of servers on the backend. If there are multiple processing servers that all perform the same tasks, a proxy server can vary the server that it forwards requests to, essentially giving your system a greater level of scalability.

A Cluster Proxy incoming requests to from a instance to another instance or cluster. The proxy will take any incoming request and forward the request to a specified recipient. The recipient will process the request and send any response back to the proxy servlet. The proxy servlet ensures that the response is returned to the originating client. One will want to use this servlet when you have a configuration of multiple clusters where different clusters have different responsibilities in the system.

The cluster proxy provides client routing information, which tracks which clients are using which sessions and on which directory server. Each time a client request is sent for the cluster, it is first routed through the cluster proxy which forwards the request to a directory server that has the client's session. Subsequent requests that filter through the cluster proxy will be routed to the same directory server instance if session data is associated with the client.

With in-memory replication client sessions are not accessible by all server instances in the cluster. Rather, when a session is first created, that session is called the primary session. A backup session object is created on another server instance. In the event of a failure of the primary session object, the secondary session object will be promoted to the primary object for all future requests. When a fail over situation occurs, another backup session object will be created. This is ideal since the replication of object data only has to occur between the primary and secondary objects (rather than the entire cluster). So, whenever the proxy receives multiple operations from a client, the proxy ensures that subsequent operations are forwarded to the directory server containing the primary session objects.

IP Multicast

IP Multicast is a range of the IP bandwidth where a message can be broadcasted a single time and received by multiple machines. Servers in a cluster are all configured on a single IP Multicast address (in addition to their per-server IP address). All communication messages occur on the IP multicast address that each of the servers monitors.

Directory Replica & Replica Aware Stub

Serviceable stubs contain a replica handler that encapsulates load-balancing and fail-over logic.

The replica handler can use different balancing algorithms:

- random
- round-robin
- weight-based
- code-level, parameter-based routing

In this instance the replica acts as an association that a stub makes with a single directory instance. Therefore, a replica handler is the logic that a stub performs to make an association with a single directory instance. Since a stub can perform direct communication with a invoking Server, the stub can vary its balancing algorithms in a variety of ways. Since the stub is bypassing the DNS round robining, router, and any proxy plug-ins, the stub can control the logic for changing servers programmatically, too.

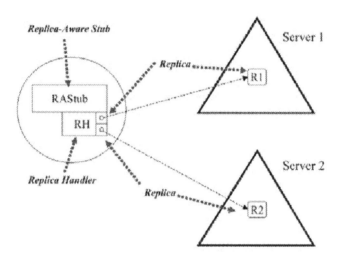

1. Client calls a method on the stub.

2. The stub calls replica-handler to choose replica (which maps to a directory server).

3. The stub sends the LDAP command to the replica (which sends reply to Replica Handler).

    a. If no exception occurs, stub returns successfully.

    b. If an exception occurs, stub calls replica-handler to choose another replica. The replica-handler either returns another replica or re-throws an exception.

```
When a failure occurs, the stub first decides whether the
exception warrants a retry, based on two conditions:

a.  If the exception indicates that its cause may be a
    failure to reach the directory server.

b.  If the exception indicates that it's safe to retry,
    which is indicated when the failure occurred before
    the operation was carried out, or the operation
    requested returned an error.
```

As a result, since a client application uses a stub that is performing load balancing and fail over logic, the client will have to be prepared to handle stub failures. After all, if the stub now contains the balancing and fail over logic (rather than a proxy or DNS round robining), the client will see intermittent behavior if the stub fails.

ALGORITHM SUMMARIES

Random Balancing Algorithm

The random balancing algorithm randomly chooses a server instance each time the replica handler chooses a replica. The random balancing algorithm is fast and simple, but susceptible to statistical irregularities. If speed is critical to your clustered application, the random balancing algorithm should be a consideration.

- The replica handler chooses a replica at random.

- Each replica is given the same weight (ie, there is no preference given).

- Simple and fast, but susceptible to statistical irregularities.

Round-Robin Balancing Algorithm

The round-robin balancing algorithm weights each server instance equally so that each directory instance will receive the exact same number of requests. The round-robin algorithm is also fast and not susceptible to the statistical irregularities seen by the random balancing algorithm.

- The replica handler cycles evenly through replicas.

- Each replica is given the same weight forcing equal distribution.

- Simple, fast, and not susceptible to statistical irregularities.

Weight Based Balancing Algorithm

The weight-based balancing algorithm is a round-robin implementation where certain directory instances have a greater weight factor than other directory instances. The number of requests routed to a particular server is based upon a ratio determined by the value assigned to each server. This implies that if server1 has a weight of 50 and server2 has a weight of 25, server1 will receive twice as many requests as server2. This algorithm should be used if you want to take into account performance variances in different servers. Be careful, however, the weight-based algorithm has a longer computational time than the other algorithms.

- Each server is given a relative weight between 1 and 100.

- The replica handle is more likely to choose a heavier server in its cycling.

- Simple and not susceptible to statistical irregularities.

Parameter Routing Approach

A Java programmer can develop a call router that chooses the server in the cluster based upon the values of the parameters passed into different methods. Since a remote object or EJB is composed of many methods (each having multiple parameters), the call router can route requests based upon the values passed in to any method!

A developer can associate a call router with a stub that:

- can programmatically choose a directory server based upon operation input parameters

- returns an ordered list of servers for the directory replica handler to try

- can default to the existing balancing algorithm

DELIVERABLES

- Directory Fault Tolerance Assessment

- Directory Fail over Strategy

30

Bringing it all together—Phase 17, 18 & 19

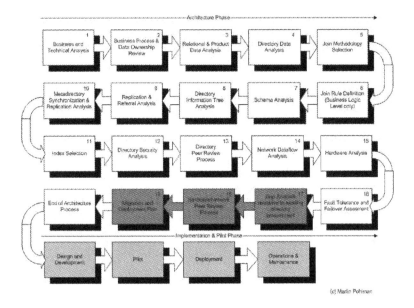

(c) Martin Pohlman

The following 3 phases are team oriented and collaborative in nature. While they are part of the methodology they are not documentable in the same fashion the previous 16 phases. Traditional team building and group dynamic techniques should be employed

PHASE 17—GAP ANALYSIS

Gap Analysis is all about evaluating and improving business performance. A gap is a space or opening—in management terms it is the space between where you are and where you want to be. The purpose of a gap analysis is to help you determine how much of the system you currently have in place. This will help you determine how far you have to go.

When you do a gap analysis please bear in mind a gap analysis which just lists deficiencies in very brief form (for example: "complete", "in progress", "incomplete") will not be very helpful. These types of gap analyses are oriented more to giving a score than giving you helpful advice for implementing the system

PHASE 18—PEER REVIEW

Peer review is an organized method for evaluating work which is used by scientists and engineers to certify the correctness of procedures, establish the plausibility of results, and allocation of resources. Peer Review can be a highly valuable experience if the peer review team is efficient, cost-effective and provides valuable feedback. The Peer review should include coordination between Architectural and Implementation documents and procedures as well as a basic code review for any joins or non-commercial code.

PHASE 19—MIGRATION AND DEPLOYMENT

Migration and deployment procedures are as unique to a business as fingerprints are to the individuals within the company. Every migration strategy should have a test, staging and deployment process with critical systems being shielded during migration. Directory replicas may be promoted to master to facilitate a smooth transition. Virtual Directories may be used to redirect traffic and maintain existing operations while new systems are put in place. Metadirectory may be used to create logical aggregates of existing systems to serve new applications while maintaining current dataflows. A Unique strategy and approach is required for each environment in each deployment.

PART IV

Other Perspectives

31

Directories from a Relational Perspective

CHARACTERISTICS OF AN LDAP-COMPLIANT DIRECTORY

The Directory is perhaps the most misused piece of network infrastructure in an enterprise. From application protocol to file system, many companies have misconceptions regarding the function of the directory:

A. Extremely fast Read Operations—Directories are tuned for higher read performance because the nature of the data in the directory is more commonly read than written or updated.

B. Relatively Static Data—The data most commonly stored in the directory is not frequently subjected to change or modification.

C. Distributed—The directory, and henceforth the data it stores, is distributed in nature.

D. Hierarchical—The directory is capable of storing objects in a hierarchical fashion for organization and relationship.

E. Object-Oriented—The directory represents elements and objects. Objects are created from object classes, which represent a collection of attributes.

F. Standard Schema—Directories utilize a standard schema that is available to all applications making use of the directory.

G. Multi-valued attributes—Directory attributes can be single or multi-valued.

H. Multi-Master replication—Most leading directories offer multi-master replication, allowing writes and updates to occur on multiple servers. Therefore, even if servers are unable to communicate for periods of time, operations can still occur locally and then be sent to other replicas once communication is restored.

Additionally, if the Directory is LDAP compliant, the directory will interpret and respond to LDAP queries and requests from any LDAP-enabled application. LDAP is a protocol supported and maintained by the Internet Engineering Task Force. The LDAP standard also encompasses schema definitions, the LDIF file exchange format, and definitions for some object based classes.

CHARACTERISTICS OF A RELATIONAL SYSTEM

The Relational Database also possesses a set of characteristics relatively common across all relational systems including:

A. Write Intensive Operations—The relational system is frequently written to and is often used in transaction-oriented applications.

B. Data in Flux or Historical Data—The relational system is designed to handle frequently changing data. Alternatively, a relational system can also store vast amounts of historical data which can later be anaylzed or "mined."

C. Application-Specific Schema—The relational system is configured on a per-application basis and a unique schema exists to support each application.

D. Complex Data Models—The Relational nature of the relational system makes it suitable for handling sophisticated, complex data models that require many tables, foreign key values, complex join operations, etc.

E. Data Integrity—The relational system features many components designed to ensure data integrity and. This includes rollback operations, referential integrity, and transaction-oriented operations.

F. ACID transactions—Atomic, Consistent, Isolation, and Durable. The transaction either commits (such that all actions are completed) or it aborts (all actions are reversed or not performed).

   • Atomic—Atomic transactions consist of grouping of changes to tables or rows such that all or none of the changes take place. A rollback operation can reverse all the actions of the atomic transaction.

   • Consistent—Transactions operate on a consistent view of the data. When the transaction is completed, the data is left in a consistent state.

   • Isolation—Transactions run isolated from other transactions. So if transactions are running concurrently, the effects of transaction A are invisible to transaction B, and vice-versa, until the transaction is completed.

   • Durable—Upon commitment of the transaction, its changes are guaranteed. Until the transaction commits, none of its actions are durable or persistent. If the system crashes prior to a commit, the effects of the transaction will be rolled back.

LDAP directories can be deployed as applications on top of Relational databases. The LDAP specification does not define the underlying data store for the directory, so each vendor is left to choose an underlying database. There are many challenges, possible limitations, and performance implications that may be associated with such an approach. Mapping the LDAP hierarchy, supporting extensible schema, translating queries to SQL, and supporting multi-valued attributes are just some of the challenges faced by these solutions. However, the fact most relational system vendors have embraced LDAP and directory technology demonstrates that the directory does indeed have a unique position in the enterprise, working alongside the relational system to solve business problems.

DIRECTORY VERSUS DATABASE?

A common misconception is that directories exist to somehow replace traditional relational databases (RDBMS). However, directories and databases complement one another. Directories and databases serve different purposes and each is optimized for suitability to their respective tasks.

Directories are optimized for reading rather than writing. This makes the directory an ideal place to store information that does not change frequently. Directories lend themselves well to query and lookup operations. Directories are hierarchical, allowing for distributed administration. Directories are designed for easy replication and distribution. Finally, directories incorporate standard schemas that can be extended, replicated, and distributed.

Relational databases are designed to be transactional. They provide no standard schema. Administration and storage are centralized. Databases provide repositories for storage of historical, general-purpose data and provide query functionality for reporting and analysis (using

Structured Query Language). Databases are relational, not hierarchical and they are not object-oriented in nature.

The same user object implemented in a relational database will have a different structure than the same user object implemented in a directory. For example, data representing the user will be spread across one or more tables instead of existing within individual entries in a directory. Furthermore, the data will be structured slightly differently, to accommodate different data structures and access protocols that can be used in a database implementation compared to the directory implementation. Relationships to other objects, rather than containment of objects, is one of the main differences between a relational database implementation and a directory implementation

So when deciding which pieces of data to store in the directory versus a relational system, evaluate the strengths and weaknesses of each system and their suitability to the task. The directory is the ideal data store for frequently read information that needs to be distributed.

Furthermore, the directory offers powerful, yet flexible security services that go beyond simple passwords. The authentication and authorization services available via the directory enable you to provide single sign-on, PKI, digital certificates, biometrics, tokens, and other advanced forms of security services.

WHAT IS A DIRECTORY SERVICE?

An organized listing of data or information, the directory with which most companies are familiar is the telephone book. The white pages directory provides a easy way to store, organize, and search for telephone numbers and addresses of people and businesses in your community. Desktop computers also store data in directories (or folders). The Windows directory, for example, contains files related to the Windows operating system. Underneath the Windows directory is a System folder, which contains files related to the operations of the operating system (such as DLLs). So the file system directory allows the user to create a hierarchy of folders to logically organize and manage files.

A directory service stores information about a network and the resources available on the network and makes this information available to users, devices, applications or anything else that requests the information. The directory commonly stores information about users, servers, printers, and other network devices. Directory entries are represented as objects. Objects contain information that identifies and characterizes the entry they represent.

Directory service design allows for a hierarchical arrangement of network resources. This design is referred to as the Directory Information Tree. The tree is actually inverted, starting with the ROOT at the top and then branching out. The tree can be made up of either container or leaf objects.

A container object is analogous to a folder or branch because it can store other objects beneath it. Container objects are commonly used to organize the directory. For example, if there is a company with offices in New York and Chicago, it may wish to use two container objects, one for each city, to organize the structure of your tree to reflect that of your geography. Container objects may contain additional containers, or subcontainers, to further divide and organize the tree.

A leaf object represents an actual network entry such as a user, group, printer, server, etc. Leaf objects don't necessarily represent something physical. Rather, they represent organized units of data stored in the directory. For example, a leaf object may represent rules or policies used by a particular application or device.

The directory itself is governed by certain rules that define the type of data it can store, the syntax of that data, and the objects the directory can contain. These rules are collectively referred to as the directory schema. The schema rules can be divided into two sets of definitions—object classes and attributes.

- User information. Including identity-related data, as well as profile information.

- Object class definitions define the type of objects the directory can store and the attributes the object can have.

- Attribute definitions define the structure of an attribute including syntax and constraints. The attribute value is the actual content or data.

One of the prime benefits of directories is schema extensibility. This allows for easy modification of the directory to meet the needs of your applications or business requirements. For example, Novell's directory schema is easily extended through its support for all leading interfaces and programming languages, and on most popular servers.

Applications need access to user information and attributes in the directory. Directory-enabled applications can make use of the directory to store user information and so that users can move freely from desk to desk (and to laptop and handheld) without worrying about configuration details.

What Isn't a Directory Service

Based on the broad definition of a directory, many rudimentary user stores appear to have the fundamental building blocks of a directory service. The best approach is to examine the taxonomy of a directory service by examining differences between a full-service directory and the rudimentary user lookup and authentication stores in use in many of today's applications.

While simplified directory stores, such as domains, relational database tables, or flat files, can provide authentication services, these architectures generally lack the sophistication to store meaningful user data and securely share that data with other applications or resources across the network and the Internet. These systems are designed for specialized uses and limited user counts, using proprietary databases that lack the scalability to handle millions of users. And because these systems are designed for specific applications, they are often unable to interoperate with the corporate directory, leaving network customers with a plethora of usernames and passwords to manage. Finally, because these systems lack an open, extensible schema they are unable to expand and adapt to the needs of the customer's business.

In database systems, the challenge of Referential Integrity is usually addressed with transactions that ensure all updates occur successfully or are rolled back as a unit. Unfortunately, most directory services and application programming interfaces do not support transactions. This means that identity management solutions must find other ways—such as using log-based, desired state mechanisms that continue to request changes until confirmed—to ensure that all repositories eventually reflect changes.

DATABASE STRUCTURE

- A *field* is the most basic structural unit of a database. It is a container for a piece of data. In most cases, only a single logical piece of data fits in each field.

- A *key* is a field that contains a unique identifier for each row in a data table. Even though each individual record represents a separate piece of data, some of those records may look identical. A key provides a completely unambiguous way to distinguish between distinct records, and more importantly, serves as a pointer to a particular record in the table. In many cases, data table keys are constructed by simply adding an additional field to function as the key.

- A set of fields describing a larger unit is normally called a *record* or a *row*. The fields in a record provide a complete description of each item in a collection. A record is a unique instance of data about an object or event.

- A *table* is the formal name given to the group of records that contain the elements of the collection. A table normally represents a distinct object (business clients or library books), or an event (product orders or stock prices).

- A *database* is basically a collection of tables. It also often includes forms for entering data, rules for checking and validating data that has been entered, and the format for creating informative reports from the data in the database.

- Relationships and Joins

ONE-TO-ONE RELATIONSHIPS

Two tables are related in a one-to-one (1–1) relationship if, for every row in the first table, there is at most one row in the second table. True one-to-one relationships seldom occur in the real world. This type of relationship is often created to get around some limitation of the database management software rather than to model a real-world situation.

- One-to-Many Relationships:

  Two tables are related in a one-to-many (1–M) relationship if for every row in the first table, there can be zero, one, or many rows in the second table, but for every row in the second table there is exactly one row in the first table.

- Many-to-Many Relationships:

  Two tables are related in a many-to-many (M–M) relationship when for every row in the first table, there can be many rows in the second table, and for every row in the second table, there can be many rows in the first table. Many-to-many relationships can't be directly modeled in relational database programs

NORMAL FORMS

The Normal Forms are based on relations rather than tables. A relation is a special type of table that has the following attributes:

1. They describe one entity.

2. They have no duplicate rows; hence there is always a primary key.

3. The columns are unordered.

4. The rows are unordered.

First Normal Form

First Normal Form (1NF) says that all column values must be atomic

SECOND NORMAL FORM

A table is said to be in Second Normal Form (2NF), if it is in 1NF and every non-key column is fully dependent on the (entire) primary key. (Put another way, tables should only store data relating to one "thing" (or entity) and that entity should be described by its primary key.)

THIRD NORMAL FORM

A table is said to be in Third Normal Form (3NF), if it is in 2NF and if all non-key columns are mutually independent. An obvious example of a dependency is a calculated column. Dependencies cause problems when you add, update, or delete records.

Form Anomalies

An Anomaly is simply an error or inconsistency in the database. A poorly designed database runs the risk of introducing numerous anomalies. There are three types of anomalies:

• **Insertion**—an anomaly that occurs during the insertion of a record. For example, the insertion of a new row causes a calculated total field stored in another table to report the wrong total.

• **Deletion**—an anomaly that occurs during the deletion of a record. For example, the deletion of a row in the database deletes more information than you wished to delete.

• **Update**—an anomaly that occurs during the updating of a record. For example, updating a description column for a single part in an inventory database requires you to make a change to thousands of rows.

Integrity Rules

Primary and Foreign Keys

The relational model defines several integrity rules that, while not part of the definition of the Normal Forms are nonetheless a necessary part of any relational database. There are two types of integrity rules: general and database-specific.

General Integrity Rules

The relational model specifies two general integrity rules. They are referred to as general rules, because they apply to all databases. They are: entity integrity and referential integrity.

Referential Integrity

The referential integrity rule says that the database must not contain any unmatched foreign key values. This implies that:

• A row may not be added to a table with a foreign key unless the referenced value exists in the referenced table.

- If the value in a table that's referenced by a foreign key is changed (or the entire row is deleted), the rows in the table with the foreign key must not be "orphaned."

In general, there are three options available when a referenced primary key value changes or a row is deleted. The options are:

1. Disallow. The change is completely disallowed.

2. Cascade. For updates, the change is cascaded to all dependent tables. For deletions, the rows in all dependent tables are deleted.

3. Nullify. For deletions, the dependent foreign key values are set to Null.

Take some time to learn the business (or other system) you are trying to model. This will usually involve sitting down and meeting with the people who will be using the system and asking them lots of questions.

On paper, write out a basic mission statement for the system. For example, you might write something like "This system will be used to take orders from customers and track orders for accounting and inventory purposes." In addition, list out the requirements of the system. These requirements will guide you in creating the database schema and business rules. For example, create a list that includes entries such as "Must be able to track customer address for subsequent direct mail."

Start to rough out (on paper) the data entry forms. (If rules come to mind as you lay out the tables, add them to the list of requirements outlined in step 2.) The specific approach you take will be guided by the state of any existing system.

- If this system was never before computerized, take the existing paper-based system and rough out the table design based on these forms. It's very likely that these forms will be non-normalized.

- If the database will be converted from an existing computerized system, use its tables as a starting point. Remember, however, that it's very likely that the existing schema will be non-normalized. It's much easier to normalize the database *now* rather than later. Print out the existing schema, table by table, and the existing data entry forms to use in the design process.

- If you are *really* starting from scratch (e.g., for a brand new business), then rough out on paper what forms you envision filling out.

Based on the forms, you created, rough out your tables on paper. If normalization doesn't come naturally (or from experience), you can start by creating one huge, non-normalized table per form that you will later normalize. If you're comfortable with normalization theory, try and keep it in mind as you create your tables, remembering that each table should describe a single entity.

Look at your existing paper or computerized reports. (If you're starting from scratch, rough out the types of reports you'd like to see on paper.) For existing systems that aren't currently meeting the user needs, it's likely that key reports are missing. Create them now on paper.

Take the roughed-out reports and make sure that the tables include this data. If information is not being collected, add it to the existing tables or create new ones.

On paper, add several rows to each roughed-out table. Use real data if at all possible.
Start the normalization process.

- First, identify candidate keys for every table and using the candidates, choose the primary key. Remember to choose a primary key that is minimal, stable, simple, and familiar. Every table must have a primary key! Make sure that the primary key will guard against all present *and* future duplicate entries.

Note foreign keys, adding them if necessary to related tables. Draw relationships between the tables, noting if they are one-to-one or one-to-many. If they are many-to-many, then create linking tables.

- Determine whether the tables are in First Normal Form. Are all fields atomic? Are there any repeating Roles? Decompose if necessary to meet 1NF.

- Determine whether the tables are in Second Normal Form. Does each table describe a single entity? Are all non-key columns fully dependent on the primary key? Put another way, does the primary key imply all of the other columns in each table? Decompose to meet 2NF. If the table has a composite primary key, then the decomposition should, in general, be guided by breaking the key apart and putting all columns pertaining to each component of the primary key in their own tables.

- Determine if the tables are in Third Normal Form. Are there any computed columns? Are there any mutually dependent non-key columns? Remove computed columns. Eliminate mutual dependent columns by breaking out lookup tables.

Using the normalized tables, refine the relationships between the tables.
Create the tables using a database program and add sample data to the tables.

Create prototype queries, forms, and reports. While creating these objects, design deficiencies should become obvious. Refine the design as needed.

Bring the client back in. Have them evaluate your forms and reports. Are their needs met? If not, refine the design. Remember to re-normalize if necessary.

- Go back to the table design and add business rules. (e.g. Stored Procedures)

- Create the final forms, reports, and queries. Develop the application. Refine the design as necessary.

- Have the users test the system. Refine the design as needed.

- Deliver the final system.

A nice guide on how to design relational databases that leads to simpler (to implement) applications and to more maintainable systems is the set of rules that define the three normal forms:

- All column values are atomic

- All column values depends on the value of the primary key

- No column value depends on the value of any other column except the primary key.

Normalization theory gives us the concept of normal forms to assist in achieving the optimum structure. The normal forms are a linear progression of rules that you apply to your database, with each higher normal form achieving a better, more efficient design. The normal forms are:

Third Normal Form (3NF), or simply it is "normalized". A normalized database generally improves performance, lowers storage requirements, and makes it easier to change the application to add new features. Remember, most software projects change it's requirements during it's development, so the time spend normalizing a database will actually mean less development time.

The relational model dictates that each row in a table be unique. If you allow duplicate rows in a table, then there's no way to uniquely address a given row via programming

32

Directories from an Object Oriented Design Perspective

OBJECT-ORIENTED INFORMATION MODELING

An object-oriented information model is a means of using object-oriented techniques to design a set of classes and relationships to represent the different objects in a managed environment. An information model is fundamentally different than a data model or a schema:

- **Data model**—A concrete representation of the characteristics of a set of related objects in terms appropriate to a specific data storage and access technology

- **Schema**—A set of data models that describe a set of related objects to be managed

- **Information model**—A *technology-independent* specification of the characteristics of a set of objects, and their relationships to other objects in a managed environment, with no reference to storage methods, access protocols, or specific type of repositories

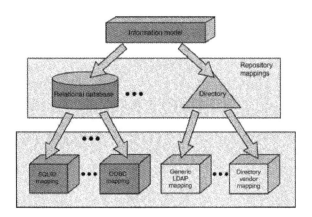

The primary purpose of the information model is to define a single universal representation of the data and objects to be managed that is independent of any specific storage technology and access protocol. The information model is used to define the appropriate objects in the environment that are to be managed and to show how they relate to each other.

Because the nature of the objects and the data describing these objects is different, it is therefore reasonable to expect that different data stores will be required to represent these objects and their interrelationships. The advantage of the information model is to be capable of representing how these different types of data and objects relate to each other in a single consistent manner without being biased by the capabilities of any one particular repository. Put another way, the information model specifies a logical repository that describes the objects and data to be managed. The logical repository maps into a set of physical data repositories. The specific set of data repositories to be used depends on the needs of the applications using the repositories. This enables the developer to choose the appropriate data store(s) and protocol(s) to use for a given application.

Applications have different needs, requiring different data stores. Requiring the creation of mappings from the (single) information model to each type of data store that is being used. In general, these mappings will be different because each type of repository uses a specific type of storage technology that uses one or more particular access protocols. This makes one schema different from another. For example, a directory schema is fundamentally different than a relational database schema. However, all schemata so derived can be related to each other because they are all derived from a universal information model.

An object-oriented information model uses object-oriented techniques to model information about a particular set of objects that exist in a managed environment. The key difference in an information model is that, in addition to describing the characteristics of entities, it also describes their behavior and interaction with each other. These latter two concepts may not be able to be captured in all repositories. Thus, the information model prescribes a means for relating different types of information, regardless of the type of data store that is being used. It is up to the developer to choose the right type of repository and other auxiliary tools to implement all facets of the information model if the repository itself is not capable of implementing the data and relationships in the information model.

OBJECT ORIENTED PROGRAMMING

There are many definitions of an object, An object has state, behavior, and identity; the structure and behavior of similar objects are defined in their common class; the terms instance and object are interchangeable. An object represents an individual, identifiable item, unit, or entity, either real or abstract, with a well-defined role in the problem domain. Anything with a crisply defined boundary and anything to which a concept an idea or notion we share that applies to certain objects in our awareness defines can also be considered an object. In short, an object is an abstraction of a set of real-world things.

A x.500 or LDAP enabled system may be considered an object oriented database in that an object oriented databases may be characterized as database systems that integrate tightly with a language with object-oriented features. In this definition slapd and x.500 DSAs qualify as they are based on active client model with language independent interface.

As such OO analysis and design (OOAD) methodology is an effective guide to applying LDAP aware tools to business problems. OO analysis is OO design of an application or interface in terms of objects, classes, clusters, frameworks and system interactions. While the details of OO methodology are beyond the scope of this text. The impact OO methodologies have had on the formation of directory services cannot be under stated. Many of the traditional OO techniques are directly applicable to directory analysis and design and many of those similarities have been incorporated in the methodology defined in the preceding chapters.

Representative Object Oriented Techniques Include:

- Full Lifecycle Object-Oriented Testing (FLOOT) methodology
- UML Lifecycle
- Hierarchical Object-Oriented Analysis (HOORA)
- OOHCI Methods for interactive systems design
- Rational Unified Process
- The Booch Method
- Coad and Yourdon
- Martin and Odell
- Rumbaugh

- Shlaer and Mellor
- Wirfs-Brock

DISTRIBUTED OBJECT TECHNOLOGY

Distributed object technology makes object oriented programming even more powerful and efficient by making use of the objects that are available on different systems connected on a heterogeneous network, in addition to the locally defined objects. Wide range of hardware platforms and variety of operating systems can be inter-connected at the software level and deliver a more robust and comprehensive solution for today's Internet driven businesses. Internet itself plays an important role as a backbone for this technology. As the scope of the application code is not restricted to single source, platform or language, maximum attention must be paid to the security of the applications. The objective of this paper is to give a brief introduction to distributed object technology and an overview of security features available in Microsoft.NET and CORBA. The paper explains the architecture of .NET and covers some of its key security concepts like Security Policy, Code Access Security, Role Based Security, Verification and Stackwalk. It also explains CORBA and its security concepts like CORBA Security Services, Security Specifications, Security Policy, Domain Access Policy and Delegation. The paper concludes by explaining the way in which some key security concerns are addressed in .NET and CORBA.

Distributed computing brings together the power of different hardware platforms and operating systems to deliver high performance applications. Object oriented programming modularizes the software development and improves the optimum usage of system resources.

Distributed object technology is the combination of these two technologies that complements each other's features and provides the scalable platform to develop efficient and faster applications. Following are some of the most important objectives of this technology providing framework of standard services and libraries

Most important methods that can be used in various kinds of development environments must be readily available for usage. A set of guidelines should be provided which describe the interfaces to these kinds of services and libraries. More importantly this kind framework should be easily extendable i.e. adding more services and libraries should be possible.

- Platform independence: An application should be able to use the objects developed and available on different kinds of platforms. Code developed using this technology should work on all kinds of platforms.

- Hardware independence: Application should work on different kinds of hardware platforms. Integration of objects available on different kinds of hardware platforms should be possible.

- Language interoperability/independence: Developers should be able to use a programming language of their choice, selection based on the ability of the language to perform different tasks. Methods developed in one programming language should be exportable to other programming languages.

Thus, distributed object technology seamlessly integrates different modules of software developed in more than one programming language and residing on systems of various platforms and architecture.

Security Perspective
Security is an essential requirement at different stages of an application developed using this technology, because:

- Application is depending on the code from the systems connected over the network (could be Internet also). Authenticity and integrity of the code must be verified before allowing access to protected resources. Network transfer should not compromise the data sensitivity.

- Application is developed in different programming languages, so exposures like buffer overflows must be considered very carefully.

- Each module of the application may require varying degree of access to system resources and hence resource access should be granted in a very controlled manner.

Following are the examples of the distributed object technology platforms available today:

- Microsoft.NET

- CORBA

- Java JINI & RMI

- DCE

CORBA

CORBA, the Common Object Request Broker Architecture was defined by the Object Management Group (OMG), specifies how software objects distributed over a network can work together without regard to client and server operating systems and programming languages.

CORBA is a complete distributed object platform. It extends applications across networks, languages, component boundaries, and operating systems. A CORBA Object Request Broker (ORB) connects a client application with the objects it wishes to use. The client application does not need to know whether the object resides on the same computer or on a remote computer elsewhere on the network. The client application needs to know only two pieces of information: the object's name and how to use the object's interface. The ORB takes care of the details of locating the object, routing the request, and returning the result.

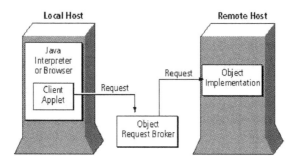

HISTORY

As CORBA grew, three influential trends were taking shape:

1. The software development community realized the importance of object-oriented programming techniques, even though they'd been around for the better part of two decades.

2. Industry leaders-including were advocating new application models based on small, task-specific components. Because they are smaller than general-purpose applications, components are easier to write and update. Developers can, conveniently and cheaply, upgrade only those parts of their software that are out of date, and users don't have to purchase new versions of the entire package. Also, small components can be distributed over a network more easily than their monolithic ancestors. With component architectures comes the promise of a cross-platform future where components running on different systems work together seamlessly.

3. Just after the release of CORBA 2.0 in early 1995, the Java programming language burst forth, as if to validate the con-

cepts underlying the vision of an object-oriented, component-based future. Java provided an object-oriented development environment for producing small software components that could run on any operating system with a Java virtual machine. And the components could be used over the Internet, which by then was surging in popularity.

CORBA fits the component-based and Internet-based approaches to building and using software. It defines a way to divide application logic among objects distributed over a network, some on clients, others on a variety of servers. It also defines a way for those objects to communicate and use each other's services. CORBA supplements Java with a rich set of services that includes introspection, dynamic discovery, transactions, security, naming, and more. CORBA links the Java mobile code environment and the world of interoperable objects.

FEATURES AND BENEFITS

CORBA defines an object-oriented approach to creating software components that one can reuse and share between applications. Each object encapsulates the details of its inner workings and presents a well-defined interface, reducing application complexity. The CORBA approach also reduces development costs, because once an object is implemented and tested, it can be used over and over again. CORBA's platform independence lets one run and invoke the object from any platform; one can run an object from the platform that makes the most sense for that object. CORBA's language independence lets one reuse existing code and leverage your existing programming skills.

Choice. CORBA is based on an open, published specification. It is implemented on and supported by numerous hardware and operating system platforms. CORBA Java objects are portable. one can build objects on one platform and deploy them on any other supported platform.

Interoperability. CORBA objects are fully interoperable because they communicate using the Internet Inter-ORB Protocol (IIOP). An enterprise IT organization need consider only its functional needs when selecting an ORB, CORBA services, and software objects, even when they are developed by different vendors. In addition, software bridges enable communications between CORBA objects and objects developed using Microsoft's DCOM technology.

Modularity. CORBA objects interact via interfaces. Because interface and implementation are separate, developers can modify objects without breaking other parts of the application. Changing an object's implementation does not affect other objects or applications because that object's interface stays the same.

Compatibility. CORBA protects your investment in existing systems. one can encapsulate a legacy application, module, or entry point in a CORBA IDL wrapper that defines an interface to the legacy code. This object wrapper makes the legacy code interoperable with other objects in a distributed computing environment.

Security. CORBA provides security features such as encryption, authentication, and authorization to protect data and to control user access to objects and their service

.NET

.NET is developed by Microsoft. .NET framework provides a platform to develop web services, distributed web based applications and windows applications using distributed object technology. .NET is directory centric with the objects methods and properties being expressed in the Active Directory component of the Microsoft operating system Following concepts helps in understanding .NET architecture:

Managed code

Managed code is the code developed in a programming language that is targeted for Common Language Runtime at compilation time. Any other code is unmanaged code.

Not all programming languages are capable of producing managed code. Languages that can produce managed code include C++ with managed extensions, C#, Visual basic and Jscript. Managed code can exploit complete functionality of the Common Language Runtime. It can efficiently manage the resources required for execution or make use of the latest CPU instruction set. More importantly, while executing a managed code, Common Language Runtime enforces the security policy. Executing an unmanaged code on Common Language Runtime bypasses the entire security policy. Managed code is not targeted to specific hardware platform or operating system i.e. the executable will not be in x86 native language or any x-bit operating system native language. It is in Microsoft Intermediate Language (MSIL). MSIL plays an important role in security of .NET framework.

Metadata

Metadata is the data generated by the compiler and placed inside the managed code, that describes various methods implemented, object instances and types declared. Common Language Runtime performs metadata validation before executing any code as part of its verification. Verification is a security management feature of Common Language Runtime.

Assembly

Assembly is a group of one or more files that can be executed (as managed code) together to perform certain task or execute an application itself. Assembly is the fundamental building block at which security is enforced i.e. permissions are requested and granted. Each assembly comes with a manifest that describes the contents of the assembly, controls what types and resources are exposed outside the assembly and what are the other assemblies that are required to execute this.

Microsoft.NET architecture

.NET is comprised of two main components.

- Common Language Runtime (CLR)
- NET framework class library

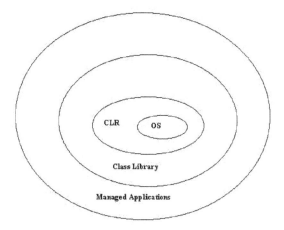

Common Language Runtime is the heart of .NET framework. This is the agent software running on the operating system. Common Language Runtime isolates the managed code from the operating system. While executing the code, Common Language Runtime translates the managed code into machine language. Common Language Runtime is capable of executing both managed code and unmanaged code. However, Common Language Runtime will not offer its complete functionality to unmanaged code. Besides executing the code that is targeted for Common Language Runtime, it also offers different services like:

- Thread execution
- Memory Management

- Just In Time (JIT) Compilation
- Security Management
- Code safety verification

Class library offers commonly used services to be readily used into the code built by developers. This library is object oriented and contains various types, classes and methods. Some of the example methods are file access, database operations and string manipulations. Security is built into the code using the classes provided by this library. Classes that provide similar functionality are grouped into namespaces. Some of the namespaces related to security are

- System.Security
- System.Security.Permissions
- System.Security.Principal
- System.Security.Policy
- System.Security.Cryptography

The fundamental building block of an application is assembly. An application may consist of many assemblies. An assembly will be loaded into an application domain before running an application. Each assembly is loaded into a separate application domain. Common Language Runtime provides complete isolation among the application domains. Multiple application domains can safely run under the same process.

.NET security is governed by a security policy, which may be defined as a set of rules that can be configured. This policy decides whether a particular code or user can access a protected resource or not. Some of the resources that can be protected are files, environment variables, clipboard, user interface and registry settings. Access to resources is controlled based on the origin of the code, the user executing the code or both.

The security manager in the Common Language Runtime maps the evidence to the security policy that is configured on the system. After successful mapping, the security manager determines the allowed permissions to that assembly. A class in the Class Library called Systems.Security. SecurityManager provides this mapping functionality.

Security policy is comprised of three elements:

- Code groups
- Named permission sets
- Policy assemblies

Security Mechanisms in Microsoft.NET Security in .NET is offered through various mechanisms. Some of the key mechanisms are;

- Verification
- Code Access Security
- Role based Security
- Stackwalk.

Verification

When an assembly is executed the Common Language Runtime validates the Microsoft Intermediate Language and verifies metadata that is part of the code. Verification is the first security check performed by Common Language Runtime. Before running the code, Common Language Runtime checks that Microsoft Intermediate Language is type safe. A code is considered to be type safe only when it accesses its types in well-defined and allowable ways according to Microsoft Intermediate Language grammar. In other words, interaction between types should always be through publicly exposed contracts (set of rules that define how to access a type). In addition to this, Common Language Runtime also checks for correct usage of exception handling and stack overflow. If the code is found to be not type safe, then a security exception is raised and execution stops at once. Common Language Runtime also verifies the metadata by examining the metadata tokens. All these tokens should index correctly into their type tables. If it is a string table, it checks that the tokens are not pointing at strings that are longer than their buffer size to avoid any possible buffer overflow. If the code passes verification, then the Microsoft Intermediate Language is translated into native language of the system using a Just in time compiler. If the assembly is completely loaded from local system, then verification happens as part of just in time compilation.

Role based Security

.NET allows developers to implement role based security in the application. These roles are not the same roles, which the operating system offers. These are very specific to the application and defined within the application only. Permissions are granted based on the Identity and Principal. Identity of a user can be established through authentication, which can be done using the native operating system or through an authentication service like Passport. Principal contains the Identity and the authorization roles the user has. There are three types of Principals:

- Generic Principals: These are defined in the application only.

- Windows Principals: They represent the NT users and their roles.

- Custom Principals: These are special kind of principals that are custom made for the application.

Similar to code access security, role based security is also implemented using the objects and classes provided by the Class Library. It is also possible to make use of Windows Roles inside the application. Information obtained from code access security and role based security are used to grant permissions according to the security policy defined on the system.

Identification and authentication

Distributed object technology allows clients to access objects or services available remotely. It is very important to establish the identity of clients through proper authentication mechanisms, before granting access.

.NET allows the usage of various kinds of user authentication mechanisms like native operating system or Passport service. Developers can implement their own authentication mechanisms within the application. By comparison CORBA Security services provide interfaces, which can be used to provide authentication. External security services can also be integrated with CORBA using interceptors

Access Control Comparison

Various objects and services access system resources and application resources differently. Control mechanisms that are used to protect critical resources should be scalable and flexible.

Four levels of security policy in .NET offers fine grained access control. A group of systems can be managed by defining enterprise policy. Access control can be further restricted on individual systems using Machine Policy or User Policy.

By comparison domain access policy in CORBA can be used to define access control for similar type of objects. Any number of objects can be made domain members and an object can be made member of multiple domains.

Authorization

Access to critical resources may be required for some legitimate users. Mechanisms to define authority and make access decisions based on the authority are required.

Role based security in .NET grants special permissions to access resources without allowing unauthorized access and disclosure. These roles can be completely specific to the application or operating system (Windows NT) roles.

By comparison privilege attributes in CORBA in the form of roles or group membership can be used to define authority.

JNDI

The Java Naming and Directory Interface is an API for accessing different naming and directory services uniformly.

This is a major step forward because:

- different services use vastly different naming schemes
- Java applications will be able to navigate across databases, files, directories, objects, and networks seamlessly

JNDI comes with two interfaces: the Application Programming Interface (API) and the Service Provider Interface (SPI). Application developers use the API in an application to access a naming or directory service.

By providing a well designed, object-oriented interface to accessing naming and directory services, Java programmers will not have to be bogged down by the details and idiosyncrasies involved with accessing a native library of one of these services. There already has been broad support given for JNDI and there are already at least 10 service providers who have provided implementations according to the SPI specification.

JNDI Structure

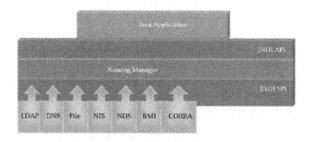

There exists a variety of naming and directory services in production today. These include services such as Lightweight Directory Access Protocol (LDAP), Domain Name Service (DNS), Network Information Service (NIS), Remote Method Invocation (RMI), and many others. Using the JNDI SPI, service providers for these industry naming and directory services provide a mapping from JNDI to their particular service. Java applications can then use the JNDI API to access any individual service uniformly. Access to the service is provided via a Naming Manager.

A complete list of existing service providers and an archive of their JAR files can be located at **http://java.sun.com/products/jndi**

A naming service provides a method for mapping identifiers to entities or objects.

A binding is the association of an atomic name with an object. With DNS, we give familiar names such as **www.amazon.com** to objects such as IP addresses with the value 204. 165.216.210.

A namespace is a set of all names in a naming system in which the names remain unique. A file directory is a sample namespace. Inside that particular directory, no two files can have the same name. However, two files in different directories (namespaces) can have the same name.

A compound name is a name in the namespace of a single naming system. It is a sequence of zero or more atomic names composed according to the naming convention of that naming system. An absolute path in a file system is an example of a compound name. If we use the file path c:\temp\myfile. txt, we can see that this compound name is made up of a root directory (c:\), a temp directory, and a file. The compound name combines the three objects together to form a single name.

A composite name is a name that spans multiple naming systems. A URL is a basic example of a composite name. If you access **http://www.trgi.com/training**, you are accessing the HTTP service on our host machine which has a different naming system than if you had used file:///c:\\temp\\myfile. txt.

The combination of a directory object inside of another directory object automatically provides a hierarchical format to the data that you store. The directory service can use the nesting of the objects within one another to form a compound name that can make the directory service dual as a naming service.

Also, since the objects that can be stored in a directory service can be of nearly any type or structure, you can serialize your Java objects and store them directly in the directory service. The objects could then be reused across multiple applications in your enterprise to accomplish various tasks.

In JNDI A principal is an entity that can authenticate into a system. Most of the time, the principal of a security system is the user running the application, but other principals can exist: a background process or other resource perhaps.

JNDI is:

- a Java API for accessing naming and directory servers
- built as a layer over DNS, LDAP, etc.

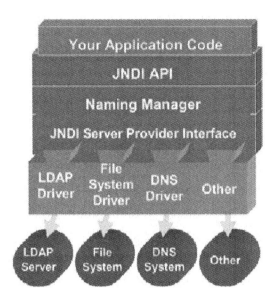

Naming and directory servers are used to hierarchically structure items that need to be made available to distributed programs. Naming and directory servers provide lookup, search, and binding features to their clients. Clients can navigate the trees and contexts of a naming or directory service in search of the object they require. There are a variety of different naming and directory servers available. JNDI is an API and a standard that Java programs use to access existing naming or directory servers. JNDI is not a naming or directory server! It is merely the mapping. Different naming and directory servers store objects in various ways. Client programs connection to the naming server and download various Java objects that they will need to use.

Use JNDI to store Java objects that contain directory based configuration information that can be used across the enterprise.

J2EE

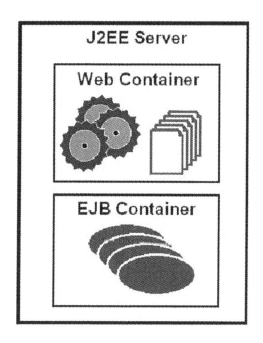

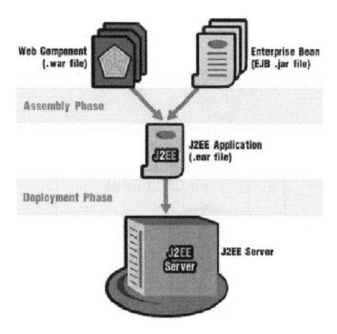

Enterprise beans can be configured to permit access only to users with the appropriate level of authorization.

- Defining roles
- Defining method permissions
- Security role references
- Realm

DCE

DCE Distributed Computing Environment, is a similar technology to CORBA. It is older than CORBA, but more stable and scalable. Not only does it offer the basic RPC mechanisms and IDL stub compilers needed to create distributed applications, but it also offers security & authentication through Kerberos. Unlike CORBA, it is not a ground-up redesign of the principles of distributed computing, is rather a tightly integrated package of existing technologies. Powerful in true large-scale, enterprise-class applications. DCE is the package of choice for large object oriented deployments.

DCE is developed and maintained by the Open Systems Foundation (OSF). The DCE is a specifically defined set of integrated system services designed to provide interoperability for heterogeneous networked environments.

DCE has requirements for the ITU x.500 standard to supply directory services. In this requirement there is a requirement to implement and support the Remote Operations Service (ROSE) and Association Control Service Element (ACSE). Incorporated with its use of directory services is the concept of cells which represent nodes and platforms in the directory. DCE enables cells to be managed by the directory.

DATAMINING

Though not object oriented, data mining techniques may be expressed as object methods where the data is the target of the method. Data mining is the descendant and arguably the successor of statistics as it is currently practiced. One of the most intriguing uses of directories is the creation of data marts & data mining.

Data mining, by its simplest definition, automates the detection of relevant patterns in a database. For data mining to impact a business, it needs to have relevance to the underlying business process. Data mining is part of a much larger series of steps that takes place between a company and its customers. The way in which data mining impacts a business depends on the business process, not the data mining process. The issue that must be addressed is that the results of data mining are different from other data-driven business processes. In most standard interactions with customer data, nearly all of the results presented to the user are things that they knew existed in the database already. Data mining, on the other hand, extracts information from a database that the user did not know existed. Relationships between variables and customer behaviors that are non-intuitive are the jewels that data mining hopes to find. And because the user does not know beforehand what the data mining process has discovered, it is a much bigger leap to take the output of the system and translate it into a solution to a business problem

Statistics and data mining have the same goal, which is to build models accounting for the relations binding the description of a situation (in the form of a certain number of descriptive variables) to a result (or a judgment) concerning this description (the predicted variable). The advantage of having such a model is twofold:

- the model is descriptive and explanatory: it clarifies the situation in telling the implementer where to look which of the descriptive variables are significant to determine the result, and what their relations are between each other and to the predicted variable.

- The model is predictive: if you have a new situation, described by the variables on which you based your model, you can run the model on these variables to obtain an estimate of the result to expect.

A concrete example is then exposed and the resulting role of statistics in the activity of the directory can hardly be overestimated. In addition to the application of datamining techniques to directories which is a common application of existing OLAP (Online Analytical Processing) Directories can be used to enhance non rule-based datamining techniques.

Neural Networks

DARPA Neural Network Study (1988, AFCEA International Press, p. 60): a neural network is a system composed of many simple processing elements operating in parallel whose function is determined by network structure, connection strengths, and the processing performed at computing elements or nodes.

Neural networks are a series of software synapses used to create a prediction model by clustering information into natural groups and then predicting into which groups new records will fall. The first phase in the neural network process is a training phase against a subset of the data where the neural network "learns." Once trained, the model is validated against other subsets of the databases and its predictive accuracy is determined. This combination of training and validation is performed many times until the predictive accuracy does not improve with additional training

Neural networks can be easily expressed in a directory format. The resulting applications are considerably faster at back propagation than relational structures.

Genetic Algorithms

A genetic algorithm is an optimization technique based loosely on the principles of natural selection. A random set or generation of solutions is created and their performance is measured. The genetic algorithm processes this generation into subsequent generations of solutions by biasing future generations on prior performances, by sharing information between solutions, and by random transformations of prior solutions

Benefits

Genetic algorithms have proved to be an effective method for searching a high-dimensional input space for an optimal subset of features distinguishing between true-positive and false-positive detections.

Genetic Algorithms have a great deal of benefits Genetic Algorithms produce explainable results Genetic Algorithms easy to apply the results because they take the form of parameters in the fitness function Genetic Algorithms handle a wide range of data types and Genetic Algorithms integrate well with Neural Nets

However limitations are present Genetic Algorithms difficulty in encoding may problems into logical chromosome form Genetic Algorithms have no guarantee of optimality, solutions may become centered on local optima, Or converge on a solution so rapidly that a critical juncture is missed Genetic Algorithms is computationally intensive: This is especially true when the fitness function comprises multiple functions on the training set however a few commercial applications are available.

Like neural networks the use of directories to cache data used by Genetic Algorithms yields a significant gain in performance on the read cycle of the process once the solutions become centered on local optima.

Simulated Annealing:
(Neural Networks with some aspects of Genetic Algorithms)

This process is pattered after the annealing process metals undergo during the tempering process. Annealing deviates from a standard neural network in that the weight factors of the neural links are continually varied in a manner similar to Genetic systems to optimize the network. Simulated annealing is a Monte Carlo approach for minimizing multivariate functions. In this process the simulated annealing process lowers the temperature by slow stages until the system statistically freezes and no further changes occur. At this point the data may be expressed in directory format with significant benefits being realized from the speed gained from the data being maintained in cache.

To apply simulated annealing, the system is initialized with a particular configuration. A new configuration is constructed by imposing a random displacement. If the statistical energy of this new state is lower than that of the previous one, the change is accepted unconditionally and the system is updated. If the energy is greater, the new configuration is accepted probabilistically. This is the Metropolis step and requires the directory to be reindexed as the Metropolis step updates the data, as the Metropolis step is the fundamental procedure of simulated annealing. This procedure allows the system to move consistently towards lower statistical energy states, yet still `jump' out of local minima due to the probabilistic acceptance of some upward moves. If the statistical temperature is decreased logarithmically, simulated annealing guarantees an optimal solution.

33

Directories from an integration Perspective

From an integration perspective two initiatives define the future of directory services from an interoperability perspective DSMLv2 defines the format and syntax for application directory interactions. DEN defines the future of directories from a network perspective enabling distributed architectures which span corporations, operating systems and supply chains creating a unified platform for electronic commerce.

DEN DIRECTORY ENABLED NETWORKING

As Internet develops, it becomes more complex to manage a network. The information about the nodes, or devices, attached to a network is stored in a special purpose database called directory. Directory service is the physically distributed, logically centralized repository of infrequently changing data that is used to manage a computing environment.

As an integration approach, writing APIs doesn't work due to the fact that a given API is usually a reflection of the internal functionality of the application. This requires the developer to have access to and be familiar with the operation of the application to be integrated and each time that the applications being integrated change, the APIs would have to change.

DEN solves this by defining a standard way to represent information. By using techniques such as DSMLv2, developers can encode their data as represented in DEN and can ship it to another application on a different platform. That application can then decode the DEN data and use it directly in its own interface.

- The administrator needs to learn only one application.

- APIs don't have to be built only to break with each change of each application.

- Data can be reused and shared between applications, which enables best-of-breed applications to work together seamlessly.

DEN therefore enables different vendors to build different network elements and applications that can communicate with each other. This enables various types of systems as well as network elements to be equal partners in implementing and reacting to decisions made throughout the networked environment.

DEN, Directory Enabled Networks, are networks where users and applications interact in a controlled way with network elements and network services to provide predictable and repeatable services to users, while also strengthening security and simplifying provisioning and management of network resources.

Initiated by Cisco and Microsoft, DEN initiative is supported widely in the industry area by many companies. The information model and base schema of DEN are derived from CIM and X.500, plus some new concepts. The model structure is object-oriented modeling. DEN uses LDAP to access, manage, and manipulate directory information

Directory-enabled networking is not a product or even a technology. Rather, it is a *philosophy* that uses the Directory-Enabled Networks (DEN) specification to bind services available in the network to clients using the network. The DEN specification enables applications to leverage the capabilities of the network as well as better support the needs of the applications using it.

DEN is in reality two things:

1. A specification of an object-oriented information model that models network elements and services as part of a managed environment in a repository-independent fashion

2. A mapping of this information to a form that is suitable for implementation in a directory that uses LDAP or X.500 as its access protocol

A directory enabled network is a network where user profiles, applications and network services are integrated through a common information model that stores network state and exposes network information. This information then enables bandwidth utilization to be optimized; it enables policy-based management; it provides a single point of administration of all network resources; and all this serves to lower total cost of ownership, and improves the services that end-users can rely on regardless of their physical location.

Rapid Internet growth over past years has created the need for more robust, scalable and secure directory services. DEN provides a new paradigm for using directory services where the directory is an authoritative, distributed, intelligent repository of information for services and applications.

In DEN, users, applications, and services can be abstracted through profiles. A profile is a template of attributes and behaviors that describe an object or a set of objects. Profiles provide a higher level of abstraction for important system components, while still providing the ability to model and operate on the fundamental objects. Profiles just tell the system what needs to be done.

DEN enables the network manager to configure the entire network so that the bandwidth and latency allocations for the organization's application portfolio can be dynamically managed in the most effective manner for the entire organization. The allocation of these two critical resources is done on a global basis taking into consideration all of the needs of the enterprise. DENs also rationalize the day-to-day management of the entire enterprise network. For example, configuration control is centrally located. Thus, if the company's routers need an upgrade to their firmware, a DEN-based application can keep track of the installation process, providing progress reports and proof that all of the upgrades have been performed. A DEN also enables a user to correlate the different characteristics of each individual database repository in such a way that different applications can effectively use relevant data from anywhere in the organization, regardless of its physical format. It separates the logical properties of abstract concepts such as security, bandwidth allocation, latency guarantee, quality of service demands, etc., from the physical components of the enterprise network. DENs have two main components: the Directory and the Policy Server.

A directory in this context is a mechanism to store and retrieve information about cross-referenced data. Directory Enabled Networking correlates all LAN directories and integrates them into a single centralized logical entity using a metadirectory or virtual directory. It also provides automatic-mapping mechanisms to switch back and forth between different data formats. DEN formally separates parts of the network into separate entities, such as the Policy Server, the Directory Server, the Application Server and anything else that would benefit from logical and/or physical separation.

Policy Server

The desire to allocate resources according to the business rules of the company is a critical requirement. The DEN policy server enforces a continuum of policies, each optimized. The Policy Server helps companies enforce sophisticated policies. For example, a business rule may prohibit shipping code over the public Internet. Thus, even though a user successfully authenticates over a dialup line, the policy will correctly deny authorization to connect to a code server because the system recognizes that the user is connecting over the public Internet. The key technology used is DEN's concepts of services and policies, and the capability to link them to users as well as devices. DEN is also able to control the management and provisioning of network devices through the use of policies. The business community wanted a way to map service-level agreements and business rules to a common set of policies. These policies would control the allocation of network resources based on user, subnet, time-of-day, or other appropriate factors. Most importantly, they ensure that services are implemented in a hardware-independent way. Of course, this cannot be done without a standard information model.

In a distributed networking environment, simply managing individual devices is no longer sufficient. Network administrators need to define and manage policies to control the network and its resources in a distributed, yet logically centralized, manner. Directories are simply databases; they are not designed to collect information from multiple sources and then make a policy decision.

In DEN policies define what resources a given resource consumer can use in the context of a given application or service. Technically, a policy is a rule that instructs a network node on how to manage requests for network resources. It is essentially a mechanism for encoding business objectives concerning the proper use of scarce resources.

DEN specification defines schema and an information model for representing network element and service information and relationships gathered from the network using existing protocols and other sources of network information. An access protocol is also included to store and retrieve information.

It develops a corporate directory service for storing network element and service information. It also defines an extensible information model representing the structural, behavioral and functional relationships between objects in the schema. LDAP access protocol is used to access, manage and manipulate directory information.

DEN Information Model

DEN Information Model

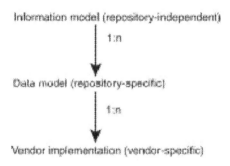

An information model is an abstraction of knowledge. The DEN information model structures the knowledge about users, applications, networks, and how they interact into multiple knowledge domains to enable different people to use it. This structure is object-oriented modeling.

The DEN information model consists of three parts:

- Six base class hierarchies that form the basic framework that represents network elements and services;

- An extensible schema based on inheritance and aggregation for modeling application-specific properties and information;

- Simple mechanisms for establishing relationships among object instances.

The primary purpose of DEN is to separate the specification and representation of network elements and services from implementation details. A secondary purpose is to provide an extensible framework to represent vendor-specific functionality and implementation mechanisms by vendor-specific subclasses.

CIM

The Common Information Model (CIM) is an object-oriented conceptual model for the information required to manage many common aspects of complex computer systems defined by the DMTF. CIM is an object-oriented information model that describes how a system and its components may be managed. CIM is defined by the Distributed Management Task Force (DMTF). CIM is part of an industry-wide initiative for enabling enterprise management of devices and applications. The goal of CIM is the presentation of a consistent view of the managed environment, independent of the various protocols and data formats supported by those devices and applications. Many network infrastructure and management software providers have accepted CIM as an information model for enterprise management tools.

Common models are focused sets of classes, attributes, methods, and relationships that extend particular concepts in the core model. For example, the core model generically defines a service. The network model refines this concept to describe different types of services that are specific to networking, such as the forwarding and routing of traffic.

The seven common models are these:

- **System**—Defines key system components, such as computer system, operating system, file, and the relationships required to assemble them.

- **Device**—Defines how to realize physical devices in hardware and how to model connections between devices such as storage devices, media, sensors, printers, and power supplies.

- **Application**—Defines how to manage software installation within a system.

- **Network**—Defines refinement of the logical element class hierarchies to model network elements and services.

- **Physical**—Defines physical organization, containment structure, and compositions of devices and device interconnections.

- **User**—Models users, groups, and organizations, and shows how these objects interact with other components of a managed system.

- **Policy**—Builds on the original policy model proposed by DEN and provides a generic structure for representing and defining policy rules, conditions, and actions. It also specializes this to represent the specific requirement of QoS policy rules, conditions, and actions.

The combination of the core model and one or more common models provides the basis for a CIM- or DEN-compliant schema that can be bound to a specific application.

CIM is a layered information model, meaning that it consists of a set of submodels that build on and refine the knowledge present in outer, more generic layers. Specifically, a set of common abstractions and functions are defined in the core model. These are then enhanced through the definition of submodels that are layered on, or use, the information in this core model. One of these layers is the network model, which came from DEN.

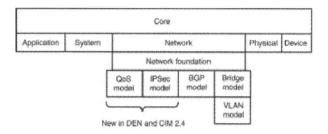

CIM consists of a core model, which is used to define concepts in the information model that apply to all areas of management. It is comprised of a set of classes, attributes, methods, and relationships that describe common concepts for managing systems and system components. The core model is the foundation for the class inheritance and relationship hierarchies, and is the basis for all common and extension models.

CIM and X.500

The DEN schema incorporates concepts from both CIM and X.500. CIM provides a rich framework, including representation of products, systems, applications, and components that can be managed. The concepts defined by CIM are used for supporting the network element and services modeling in DEN.

Six base class hierarchies form the root for DEN's representation of network elements and services. These are

- Network Device
- Network Protocol
- Network Media
- Profile, Policy

- Network Service

Applications take a pivotal role refining the DEN classes into more specific subclasses to represent the desired additional functionality accommodate application-specific needs.

Once network elements are bootstrapped into the system, they will then exchange a set of queries and responses with information about themselves. Four different types of information are necessary to model the structural information of network elements and services:

- Intrinsic. Information essential to representing a particular element or service

- Configurable. Information that controls the operation of a device, or helps determines how that device or service operates

- Operational. Information that controls how a device or service interacts with its surrounding environment

- Contextual. Information defining how the device or service relates to other components in a larger, network-wide context.

Relationships

The DEN information model consists of both a data model and a relationship model. The data model is represented by the schema. The relationship model describes how different objects in the schema are related to one another. There are three main types of relationships: links, associations, and aggregations.

A link is physical or conceptual relationship between two object instances. The relationship can be defined as an ordered tuple or an instance of an association.

An association is a group of links with a common structure and set of semantics. An association can be modeled as a class with its own attributes and methods.

An aggregation is a special type of association. It represents a relationship where some objects are "a-part-of" another object. Aggregation has additional semantics, such as transitivity, anti-symmetricity, separability, and property propagation.

DEN Base Schema

The schema of a directory defines the set of objects that can be created in that directory and the set of attributes that can be used to describe those objects.

The DEN schema consists of abstract base classes from which all other network-specific classes are derived. The base classes are refined by specialization from the basic model for representing network elements, services, consumers, etc

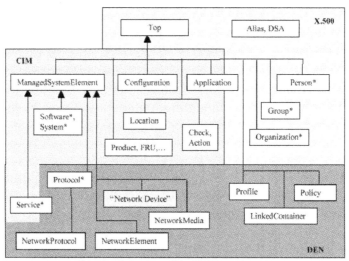

Functional structure of the DEN base classes. .

This image shows the functional structure of the DEN base classes, with key classes defined by CIM, X.500, and DEN listed separately.

DEN is the aggregation of concepts from CIM and X.500 specification and a collection of new ideas to model network elements and services.

Base Classes Derived from X.500

- **Top**: Root of the directory tree.

- **Person**: Generic concept of a person, an employee, a person with a residence. DEN uses it as a client to bind network services to, or as owner/administrator of a device or a service.

- **Group**: Providing grouping constructs for users as well as devices.

- **Organization**: Business entity to which devices and services belong.

- **Application**: X.500 defines the ApplicationProcess and ApplicationEntity classes. DEN adds information so that these classes can be associated with network elements and services.

- **Alias, DSA**: Necessary entities for proper directory operation.

Base Classes Derived from CIM

- **Product, FRU, etc**: A collection of classes that represent a product and replaceable parts of a product. Included for completeness.

- **ManagedSystemElement**: Base class for any system or system component that should be managed.

- **Configuration**: Modeling the configuration and provisioning of network elements and services.

- **Service**: Definition, management and delivery of network services.

- **Software**: General notation of software.

- **System**: Realizing the concept of a logical network element.

- **Location**: Specifying the address and location of a physical element.

- **Check** and **Action**: Used by DEN to augment notions of configuration and reboot of network devices.

- **Application**: CIM adds the concept that an application is used to support a particular business function.

New DEN Classes

- **NetworkService**: Root of the network service hierarchy.

- **NetworkProtocol**: Root of all network protocol classes.

- **Enhancements to PhysicalPackage and Card**: Extensions and enhancements to include the functionality required by network devices.

- **NetworkElement**: Logical aspects of a network element.

New DEN concepts

- **Policy**: Rule instructing a network node on how to manage requests for network resources.

- **Profile**: Template of attributes and behaviors that describe an object or a set of objects.

- **NetworkMedia**: Associating the particular media of a given interface with services that are running on it.

- **LinkedContainer**: Container class implementing a forward link.

In summary DEN is two things:

- An extension of the information model defined in CIM that describes the physical and logical characteristics of network elements and services, as well as policies that control the provisioning and management of network elements and services

- A mapping of information to a format that can be stored in a directory that uses (L)DAP as its access protocol

The schemata for network integration defined in the DEN and CIM specifications are complementary. CIM is primarily concerned with the management of individual components in the context of an enterprise. DEN is primarily concerned with providing more detail about the networking components of a system

DEN AND VIRTUAL DIRECTORIES

The DEN standardization effort offers the opportunity to have a single source of information and encourages storage of data in a standard format to enable interoperability and Independent Software Vendor innovation. A large amount of standardization work has been done in the area of standardizing the LDAP schemas that will be used to provide these services. However, other crucial areas like security, replication, and triggers have been left unstandardized. This is unfortunate because it will leave users with poor interoperability among different LDAP servers since they will require the use of non-standard features. It will also make DEN applications hard to port from one LDAP server to another. Furthermore, existing approaches to adding trigger functionality to existing systems require either:

1. Modification to system internals (e.g., adding either a full-fledged trigger system or associating plug-ins with directory commands),

2. Knowledge of proprietary log formats

3. Periodic polling of database state (expensive).

Implementing DEN functionality almost always requires a Virtual Directory to act as a trigger gateway. A virtual directory does not solve the security portability problems that result from the lack of security or operation standardization, but it does work with the existing heterogeneous security features in a portable way, so it makes the problems no worse.

Virtual Directories can be used for a wide variety of DEN functions, since many DEN applications require monitoring some resource and then either alerting a user or pushing data to some application. Virtual Directories can also be used to audit LDAP updates. LDAP currently lacks facilities to perform standard integrity checks like referential integrity and range constraints that relational databases provide. Given the extremely weak integrity checking available for LDAP updates, A Virtual Directories ability to provide much stronger checking is quite valuable. Clearly, such checks will be crucial if a LDAP server is to be used to provide a single source of needed data.

Both Microsoft and Cisco plan to add triggering capabilities to Active Directory for DEN, but the capabilities do no exist yet. Novell does not appear to have triggering capabilities associated with their LDAP products.

DSMLV2

The most common approach to managing DEN enabled applications and devices is to adopt a metadirectory approach. In this scenario, the LDAP directory still becomes the central user profile data repository, but many existing user directories and databases are left intact. To update and synchronize the many databases and directories in the enterprise that contain user information, the metadirectory employs connectors. With this approach, when a change is made to a user profile, the meta-directory translates the data and then pushes down the translated data to each and every directory, in a format that the directory understands. Realizing the importance of this functionality, all the major directory vendors have rolled out or announced metadirectory capabilities for their LDAP directories. Historically, this approach has been limited by the proprietary nature of each directory and connector implementation. Recently, the Directory Services Markup Language

(DSML) initiative has offered promise to the meta-directory approach, by attempting to standardize the format for passing data between disparate database systems.

DSML seeks to put interoperability problems of DEN into the past tense. While directories are the best tools for managing the meta-data about resources XML is the best way to describe application/resource data. DSML is the markup language that provides the missing piece that allows these two to work together, and provides a common ground for all XML-based applications to make better use of directories. The brainchild of the DSML Working Group—which consists of leading directory vendors Bowstreet, Microsoft, Novell, the Sun/Netscape Alliance, IBM, and Oracle—it was unleashed at the close of 1999 as an attempt to solve the interoperability issue. Directory Services Markup Language (DSML) has been heralded in industry press as a key component to the future of e-commerce and Web-based applications that link businesses and business processes together. Some examples of such business-to-business and business to customer applications include those in the area of supply chain management (SCM) or customer service, where someone in one company might use a Web interface to order items or to find out inventory levels on a vendor's products. Information in a variety of directories may need to be furnished in order to display the correct information to an end user.

Directory Service Markup Language is a vocabulary and schema (a structured framework) for describing the structure and content of directory services information in an XML Document. Directory information can then be easily used by any application that makes use of XML, including browsers and e-commerce applications—enabling frictionless e-commerce.

DSML was created to standardize the way directory services information is represented in XML. With a recognized standard, applications can be written to make use of DSML and capture the scalability, replication, security and management strengths of directory services.

The DSML specification defines an open, extensible, standards-based format for publishing directory schemata and interchanging directory contents based on the Extensible Markup Language (XML), which is one key to understanding its usefulness.

In the DSML specification, the related XML schema defines types of information found in today's network and enterprise directories. It then defines a common XML document format that should be used to display the contents of each directory.

DSMLv2 fosters a new computing approach in which XML-enabled applications leverage business functionality and services, managed in directories and delivered via the Web. DSMLv2 will enable customers to use directory information from, and exchange directory information with, their customers and partners, regardless of the specific directories at the remote DSMLv2 also fosters a new computing approach in which XML-enabled applications leverage business functionality and services, managed in directories and delivered via the Web. Directories enable corporate computing resources—including information and users—to be dynamically and securely matched over networks. By mixing that capability with XML, highly intelligent extranets can enable customized applications to be created "on the fly" with minimal programming.

The protocol defines an XML-based interchange syntax, or vocabulary (a set of markup tag) that supports directory operations. This syntax includes a specified XML namespace, document structure, directory-entry definition tags, directory-schema definition tags, and application and document profiles.

The protocol works across a variety of Internet protocols—including HTTP and SMTP, in addition to Lightweight Directory Access Protocol (LDAP) 3—using XML as a universal translator. Because of this,

DSMLv2 can access directories in cases where Internet firewalls screen out LDAP requests. It can also be used for nondirectory-based applications, such as e-commerce transactions.

The Directory Services Markup Language version 2.0 (DSMLv2) is an XML application that provides a method for expressing directory queries, updates, and the results of these operations. Whereas DSML version 1 provided a means for representing directory contents XML documents, DSML version 2 with bindings such as the Simple Object Access Protocol (SOAP) which defines the use of XML and HTTP to access services, objects, and servers in a platform-independent manner.

DSMLv2 is designed as a programming protocol SOAP Request/ Response Binding, allows for directories to be manipulated via XML. DSMLv2 focuses on extending the reach of LDAP directories. Therefore, as in DSMLv1, the design approach is not to abstract the capabilities of LDAP directories as they exist today, but instead to faithfully represent LDAP directories in XML. The difference is that DSMLv1 represented the state of a directory while DSMLv2 represents the operations that an LDAP directory can perform and the results of such operations. Therefore the design approach for DSMLv2 is to express LDAP requests and responses as XML document fragments To further clarify the distinction the. DSMLv2 is an XML data definition specification which can be transported within SOAP.

DSMLv1 represented the *state* of a directory while DSMLv2 represents the *operations* that an LDAP directory can perform and the results of such operations providing a method for expressing directory queries and updates (and the results of these operations) as XML documents. DSMLv2 documents can be used in a variety of ways. For instance, they can be written to files in order to be consumed and produced by programs, or they can be transported over HTTP to and from a server that interprets and generates them.

DSMLv2 lets the schema and data of a particular directory communicate with an application, supplying the knowledge of the directory schema that LDAP needs to retrieve information from it. DSML offers a standardized method to access data stored in an LDAP repository. The objective is to eliminate the need to install specialized applications and clients on workstations to manage the infrastructure

DSMLv2 functionality is motivated by scenarios including:

- A smart cell phone or PDA needs to access directory information but does not contain an LDAP client.

- A program needs to access a directory through a firewall, but the firewall is not allowed to pass LDAP protocol traffic because it isn't capable of auditing such traffic.

- A programmer is writing an application using XML programming tools and techniques, and the application needs to access a directory.

Featured addressed by DSMLv2 include:

- Mapping of LDAP functions to DSML to enable directory access, and read and write operations over HTTP for firewall traversal and directory-enablement of Web applications;

- Publishing the hierarchical directory information of a DSML-enabled directory service;

- Identifying and profiling the source of DSML-encoded directory schemata and entries;

- Translating directory elements and attributes between DSML and legacy file formats;

- Defining mechanisms for DSML-enabled directories to dynamically extend their schemata in response to new directory elements and attributes contained in incoming DSML documents;

- Defining access controls applicable to elements and attributes in exported directory schemata, elements, and attributes;

- Signing and encrypting DSML-encoded directory schemata and entries to ensure that unauthorized parties don't modify them.

The tracking of users and their applications would be dynamically invoked processes, as the users appear or leave the network. User relationships could be managed by yet another, higher, policy entity. It would be impractical to implement all this as a single, huge application, but it is realistic as a set of interacting applets, all keyed from a singular directory-based data set.

DSML Leverages LDAP. LDAP provides a means for accessing directory information. DSML provides the means for reading and understanding directory content. Without the DSML standard, developers who want to use directory policy and profile information must write code for each directory they want to support. Many use LDAP access protocols to generate LDIFF or XML documents that can drive customization within applications such as electronic commerce. But such proprietary solutions impede inter-company integration, making it expensive and time-consuming to build and manage such systems as supply chain management and distribution channel management. With a DSML standard, any XML-based application will be able to leverage directory information expressed as XML. DSMLv2 focuses on extending the reach of LDAP directories. Therefore, as in DSMLv1, the design approach is not to abstract the capabilities of LDAP directories, as they exist today, but instead to faithfully represent LDAP directories in XML.

The design approach for DSMLv2 is to express LDAP requests and responses as XML document fragments. For the most part DSMLv2 is a systematic translation of LDAP's ASN.1 grammar (defined by RFC 2251) into XML-Schema. Thus, when a DSMLv2 element name matches an identifier in LDAP's ASN.1 grammar, the named element means the same thing in DSMLv2 and in LDAP. Except where noted otherwise, the DSMLv2 grammar follows the same rules as the LDAP grammar, even if those rules are not explicitly expressed in the DSMLv2 schema—for example, a DSMLv2 AttributeDescription can contain only those characters allowed by LDAP.

There are two types of DSMLv2 document: the *request* document and the *response* document. In a DSMLv2-based interaction between a client and a server there is a pairing of requests and responses: For each request document submitted by the client there is one response document produced by the server. The structure of the request and response documents depends on the specification of a *binding* of DSMLv2 to some underlying protocol.

DSMLv2 is defined in terms of a set of XML fragments that are used as payloads in a binding. A binding defines how the DSMLv2 XML fragments are sent as requests and responses in the context of a specific transport such as SOAP, SMTP, or a simple data file.

DSMLv2 defines two normative bindings:

- A SOAP request/response binding;

- A file binding that serves as the DSMLv2 analog of LDIF

The simple correspondence between LDAP and DSMLv2 has compelling advantages. However there are a few places where it makes sense for DSMLv2 to diverge from LDAP:

- An LDAP application associates a security principal with an LDAP connection by issuing a Bind request or, in the SASL Bind case, by issuing as many successive Bind requests as needed to complete the authentication. A DSMLv2 document can be transported via a variety of mechanisms, so the document itself is not used to authenticate the requestor. DSMLv2 includes an

Authentication request that may be used to associate a security principal with a collection of DSMLv2 operations.

- LDAP does not include a method of grouping operations to be expressed in a single request. DSMLv2 allows multiple LDAP operations to be expressed in one request document, and by specifying a simple positional correspondence between individual requests within a request document and individual responses within a response document.

- In LDAP, a single search request typically generates multiple responses, closed by a *searchResultDone* response. To enable the positional correspondence between requests and responses DSMLv2 provides for a binding to wrap the complete set of related search responses into a single *searchResponse* element containing the individual LDAP responses to a search request.

- The systematic translation of RFC 2251 results in a redundant level of nested element, the *LDAPMessage*. DSMLv2 eliminates this extra level.

- Defaulting works more naturally in XML documents than in ASN.1 structures, so DSMLv2 uses defaulting in a few places where LDAP doesn't. In DSMLv2 the string-valued elements *matchedDN* and *errorMessage* (from *LDAPResult* in LDAP) and *attributes* (from *SearchRequest* in LDAP) are optional, and when absent are treated as the empty string. The *sizeLimit*, *timeLimit*, and *typesOnly* elements (from *SearchRequest* in LDAP) default to 0, 0, and FALSE respectively.

From an integration perspective, the future of directories is entwined with DEN and XML in the next chapter we will discuss the future form a business perspective and how Virtual Directories enable DEN compliant systems.

34
The Future of Directories

Directories are databases that are optimized for reads, and that contain key institutional and personal data for use by a wide variety of applications. Directories need ways to describe the sequence of fields in the database (a schema), the names of the fields (a namespace) and the contents of the fields (attribute values). Directories also need indices into the database (identifiers).

Directories are the operational linchpin of almost all middleware services. They can contain critical customization information for people, processes, resources and groups. By placing such information in a common storage area, diverse applications from diverse locations can access a consistent and comprehensive source for current values of key data. A common theme across most Intranet/Extranet applications is the need for directory information about user, system, and organizational objects. The application's requirements can be described very simply: they need to find out who a user is, what they trying to do, whether there allowed to do it, and how the company wants it done. In technical terms, these requirements are called authentication, certification, access control, profiling, policy representation, and policy or business rule enforcement. Most of the information to support such requirements should be stored in an enterprise directory; this consolidation of data creates legal and procedural issues both with respect to existing laws and in the area of Mergers, Acquisitions and Divestitures.

Confronted with directory synchronization issues, messaging users and vendors have understood the importance of directories all along. NOS vendors have also gotten the message. Banyan provided the StreetTalk directory with VINES (and later NetWare and NT) as an early proof of what could be done at the enterprise NOS level. Novell came next, with NetWare Directory Systems (NDS). Netscape galvanized the industry in 1996 with its concept of a secure, standards-based, and modular Intranet applications infrastructure supported by LDAP, DNS, and X.509 security at the directory level. Soon, Microsoft stepped into the fray, pushing the Active Directory as an integral component of the planned NT 5.0 release. To see vendors of Banyan, Microsoft, Netscape, and Novell's stature focus on the directory issue to this extent has raised IS awareness.

While the lightweight directory access protocol (LDAP) standard succeeded in opening proprietary directories to many applications, its role will become more limited as XML-based documents become the preferred interface for information exchange between applications and directory services. Meta-directories and Virtual directories will make it easier for large organizations to combine identity information and offer more useful views of this data to applications

VIRTUAL DIRECTORIES

Virtual directories add a valuable layer of security and flexibility that directories themselves do not hold. A key element of this integration is to know who users are, what their role is and what privileges they have. Unlike a metadirectory a virtual directory solution, provides access to the existing data sources without moving the data out of the original repository. A Virtual Directory can logically represent information from a number of disparate directories, databases, and other data repositories in a virtual directory tree. Various users and applications can get different views of the information, based on their access rights. Features like namespace conversion and schema adaptations provide customers with a flexible solution that can continually grow and change to support various demands from current and future applications and demands for security and privacy without changing the underlying architecture and design of data stores like databases and directories.

The Virtual Directories or directory proxy acts as a middleware between an LDAP Directory server and a client. The main purpose of a Virtual Directories is to transfer data (requests, responses) from one to the other, while at the same time providing the use of configurable modules that allow data to be manipulated during the transfer. The benefit of using this approach is that the process is not restricted by standard LDAP design and operation. User-defined criteria allow the programmer to modify search requests sent to the directory server, and similarly, allow for LDAP responses to be changed before being delivered to the client.

A Virtual Directory is capable of:

- Caching returned LDAP data for efficiency and faster lookups

- "Rolling over" to other LDAP servers, in case of server timeouts

- Ability to keep track of timed-out servers, and to check them again at specified intervals

- Enabling the use of user-defined modules to implement additional features

- Ability to communicate over secure connections with an LDAP server

- Triggering operations based on data received

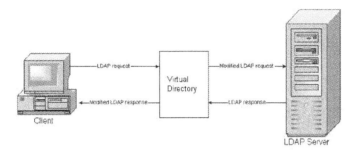

Triggers are a well-known technique for databases. A user specifies an event (or pattern of events) of interest that the system is to monitor for, a condition to check (which may always be true), and an action to take. When the event is detected and the condition holds true, the system performs the action. The novelty of a virtual directory is its support for failed triggers, necessary to cope with the weak transactions of LDAP, and the use of a proxy to provide trigger support. Previous techniques to adding triggers detected events either by adding event detection into the core database engine and/or by using pre-processors on database code to signal events.

Virtual Directories forms secure connections to the LDAP server and often caches data for performance. Building upon this model allows given requests from the client to be changed, and supplied responses from LDAP to be modified according to the custom configuration model.

On of the failings of the current protocol is the absence of a method to invoke stored procedures. As a result LDAP directories do not have active database functionality (i.e., triggers). However, triggers are nec-essary for monitoring changes to directories and taking appropriate actions, just as they are for databases. For instance, when a high-level security policy is changed in a LDAP server, changes to a variety of routers throughout the network must be made to implement the changed policy. These changes should be made automatically by the system to increase reliability as well as administrator productivity. Such functionality is crucial to take full advantage of proposals like the Directory Enabled Network (DEN) initiative cited in prior chapters.

Most virtual directories with triggered events follow the standard Event-Condition-Action (ECA) model. Triggers are specified to fire when a directory entry is affected, that is read or written, by an operation. Users specify an Event to monitor for, a Condition to check, and an Action to perform if the event occurs and the condition holds. They specify these by instantiating a C++ or Java Trigger object and then registering it with the system. Each specified event monitors the progress of an LDAP operation; examples being before a LDAP modify or after a LDAP delete. The condition is the conjunction of a number of parts that must be satisfied by the entry affected by the operation. For example, the condition might specify that the affected entry must be of a particular type and must involve the modification of certain attributes.

Due to the fact that a virtual directory aggregates and maps information into an LDAP directory service rather than physically storing actual information elements in the directory, providing a virtual mapping of source data into an LDAP namespace. Virtual directories are the most promising solution for the following legal and organizational issues defining the future of the directory

USA PATRIOT ACT OF 2001

"Uniting and Strengthening America by Providing Appropriate Tools Required to Intercept and Obstruct Terrorism Act of 2001" or USAPA was signed into law on October 26, 2001, five weeks from its initial introduction. It passed overwhelmingly with a vote of 357-66 in the House of Representatives and 98-1 in the Senate. Proponents of the Law praise it as a necessary step in the government's fight to protect Americans and in the American's right to feel safe from terrorism.

Opponents criticize it as being government friendly, socialist, and too invasive. On the surface the majority of the USAPA makes modifications of varying degrees to many preexisting laws regarding immigration, surveillance, victim compensation, money laundering, and intelligence gathering and sharing. At its heart the USAPA grants additional powers to law enforcement and intelligence agencies, both international and domestic, while removing many of the obstacles that were formerly in place.

Directories can be viewed as target system of this piece of legislation as The Act clarifies that pen/trap orders may be used to collect all non-content information used in transmitting and receiving electronic communications. That means they can monitor things like the to and from lines of an email header, but they cannot look into an email and view the contents without additional authority this makes the directory a key enforcement technology. In the case where a pen/trap order is issued for a public service provider, it is specified that the provider must conduct the installation, monitoring, data gathering, and removal of the device. In the rare cases where this is not possible, the courts can allow law enforcement officials to conduct the installation, operation, and removal of the device, but they are bound by additional restrictions. They must provide the following information to the court under seal within 30 days:

1. The identity of the officers who installed or accessed the device;

2. The date/time the device was installed, accessed and removed;

3. The configuration of the device at the time is was installed, and any modifications made to it;

4. The information collected by the device

The Act allows victims of computer attacks to authorize law enforcement or "persons acting under the color of law" to monitor trespassers on their computer systems. The owner/operator of the computer system must authorize the interception of the trespasser's communications. In addition, law enforcement must have reasonable grounds to suspect the contents of the intercepted communications will be relevant to the investigation. Law enforcement can only intercept the communications sent or received by the trespasser making the directory BIND operation the key to this nonrepudiation of identity

The Act gives the courts permission to compel assistance from any communications provider in the United States whose assistance is appropriate to further an investigation. This includes directory managers and any individual with administrative authority within the enterprise. This act allows federal investigators to execute the same search warrant on any downstream communication provider, regardless of which state it was operating in. The direct impact of this on directory servers is that the access and change logs must be afforded special consideration by the directory manager. The Act also states that, if the provider requests, law enforcement must provide a written or electronic certification that the order applies to the provider.

Section 203 grants government agencies a much greater ability to share investigative information across what used to be barriers in jurisdiction. It states that law enforcement, with knowledge obtained by "…electronic communication, or evidence derived there from, may disclose such contents to any other Federal law enforcement, intelligence, protective, immigration, national defense, or national security official as such the Act allows courts to authorize the use of pen/traps in other districts, so long as the issuing court has jurisdiction over the crime being investigated, this could be interpreted to include BIND records maintained within the access logs of the software. The Act grants investigators who have previously obtained an applicable search warrant to compel records outside of the district in which the court was located. This amendment to law expires December 31, 2005. The Act expands the definition of "protected computer" to include those outside the borders of the United States, so long as they affect inter-state or foreign commerce or communications of the United States from this one may conclude that directories and metadirectory shared across national boarders fall under this provision. The Act also specifically grants the ability to prosecute foreign hackers in US courts.

With regard to directory enabled EDI systems. The act expands significantly the data that can be subpoenaed from a service provider. Now they can specifically request information regarding session connect times and durations, the assigned IP Address of the session, as well as the means and source of payment. This allows law enforcement to more accurately tie an actor to a crime and the directory is key in this process.

Section 105 orders the expansion of the nation's electronic crime task force "for the purpose of preventing, detecting, and investigating various forms of electronic crimes, including potential terrorist attacks against critical infrastructure and financial payment systems." This expansion will mean the creation of many new jobs in directory services as the act also requires Attorneys General to establish regional forensic laboratories to be used to investigate and prosecute computer crime. These laboratories are also to be used to provide training and forensic capabilities to local law enforcement agencies and personnel this will make directory literacy a key skill set for law enforcement.

HIPPA HEALTH INSURANCE PORTABILITY AND ACCOUNTABILITY ACT OF 1996

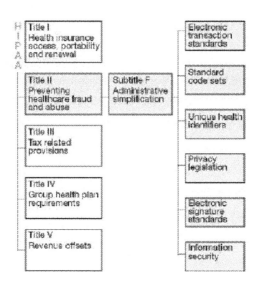

Recognizing the need for national standards for the protection of patient records, President Clinton and Congress enacted the Health Insurance Portability and Accountability Act of 1996 (HIPAA). HIPAA was enacted with the intent to reduce healthcare fraud and abuse, ensure security and privacy of health information, assure portability, and enforce health information standards.

This information, if used inappropriately, can not only result in embarrassment or alienation to the individual, it can also result in financial difficulties and even job loss. Within the supplementary information of the final HIPAA rule, The Department of Health and Human Services sites several cases in which improperly disclosed health information had adverse effects on the individual whom the information pertained to. Among those cases was a banker, in 1994, who sat on a county health board and gained access to patient information. Using this information, he called in several mortgages of individuals suffering from cancer. Another sited case involved a candidate running for Congress who had her medical information released to the media.

The HIPAA legislation provided Congress three years to pass comprehensive health privacy legislation. If legislation had not been passed by the deadline of August 21, 1999, HIPAA provided the Department of Health and Human Services (HHS) with the authority to develop the privacy and security regulations. With guidance from the principles and polices contained within HIPAA legislation, the HHS released proposed regulations in October of 1999. A comment period followed the publishing of the proposed regulation in which the HHS received more than 52,000 comments. Due to an oversight by the Clinton administration and a re-opening of the comment period by the Bush administration, the effective date for the final privacy regulation has not been

Although this law is not comprehensive in its mandate to protect medical information, it does provide a sound basis for a 'defense in depth' approach. Several items have been identified and/or mandated to ensure the security of this information. They have been grouped into four categories. The first three include administrative procedures, physical safeguards and technical security to ensure availability, confidentiality and integrity of the data. The fourth category includes additional technical security measures to ensure the reliability of transmitted data.

By using message authentication, a company can provide a level of assurance through validation of a sender's message. An important primary step is to assign user specific network IDs and passwords. This is a basic element of defense in depth. Using unique user IDs as part of the authorization process serves as an additional hurdle for intruders before they can access your network.

Generally, employees should be strongly warned against sharing accounts and passwords. Companies should also limit or even prohibit users from giving send-as permissions in the e-mail system. If an employee is granted permissions to another user's mailbox, by default they have the ability to send messages posing as the other party.

Assigning a range of TCP/IP addresses for specific departments or building floors can help towards validating a sender's message. If the sender's IP address does not reside within the pre-determined range of addresses, it could be an indication of a security issue.

When using FTP for communications on a UNIX platform, an encryption package should be used. This also helps to satisfy the above-mentioned Integrity Control requirement of HIPAA. A authentication tool such as the *tcpdump* program, which reads network traffic. It can be set to monitor specifically indicated values, such as unauthorized traffic on a specific port. The logs should be monitored and backed-up on a regular basis.

Administrative procedures relate to the establishment of processes and procedures that must be documented and implemented by all regulated entities. They have been defined as the following twelve areas:

1. Certification of computer systems and networks, internally or by external party, to ensure they comply with security standards.

2. 'Chain of Trust' agreements between organizations that share health information to ensure the protection of this data when it is passed between parties.

3. Contingency plans to prevent loss and provide for data recovery in case of an emergency or disaster. Includes a review of data and application to determine criticality, backup procedures, disaster recovery plans and a process for testing and revising procedures.

4. Formal data processing procedures covering routine as well as non-routine handling of health information, including the receipt, storage, manipulation, and disposal of information.

5. Access control procedures covering the granting of varying levels of access to health information, including the authorization, establishment and modification of access.

6. Internal audit procedures providing for the periodic review of file access, systems logons, and other security events in order to detect security violations.

7. Personnel security, including such activities as supervision of maintenance personnel by a knowledgeable and authorized person, retaining of access authorization records and the training of personnel in proper security procedures/policies.

8. Proper security configuration management that covers documentation, hardware and software installation/modification and testing, testing of security features and virus scanning to ensure modifications do not contribute or cause a security weakness.

9. Incident handling procedures for responding to and reporting all levels of security incidents.

10. Security management process that oversees the creation, administration and modification of policies to ensure prevention, detection and proper handling of any security breaches.

11. Employee termination procedures documenting the steps necessary to ensure security when an individual is no longer authorized to access patient information.

There are a number of items covered by the HIPAA Technical Security Mechanisms Rule but in general, it can be divided into three subject areas:

- data authentication
- data encryption
- external network protection.

If a covered entity transmits protected health information (PHI) over a network, it must have the following security mechanisms in place:

- Integrity controls
- Message authentication
- Alarm
- Audit trail
- Entity authentication
- Event reporting

If the provider communicates with others via a network, it must also utilize one of the following implementation features:

- Access controls
- Encryption

Standard Transaction

Standard means a set of rules for a set of codes, data elements, transactions, or identifiers promulgated either by an organization accredited by the American National Standards Institute or HHS for the electronic transmission of health information.

Transaction means the exchange of information between two parties to carry out financial and administrative activities related to health care. It includes the following:

(1) Health claims or equivalent encounter information.
(2) Health care payment and remittance advice.
(3) Coordination of benefits.

(4) Health claims status.

(5) Enrollment and disenrollment in a health plan.

(6) Eligibility for a health plan.

(7) Health plan premium payments.

(8) Referral certification and authorization.

(9) First report of injury.

(10) Health claims attachments.

(11) Other transactions as the Secretary may prescribe by regulation.

Business Partner is defined as a person to whom a covered entity discloses protected health information so that the person can carry out, assist with the performance of, or perform on behalf of, a function or activity for the covered entity.

Technology security represents the third category involved in ensuring the availability, confidentiality and integrity of data. Technology security relates to the software controls and protocols that are responsible for processing and storing protected data. These areas include:

1. Access controls that restrict access only to entities with a business need. Types of access controls will include roll-based, user-based or context-based access.

2. Audit controls that provide for the recording and examining of system and security activities to provide a means of identifying suspicious activity.

3. Data authentication mechanisms to ensure that data within an organization has not been altered or destroyed in an unauthorized manner.

4. Entity authentication mechanisms to ensure the identification of the entity, such as passwords, biometrics, PINs, modem callbacks and automatic logoffs.

The fourth category involves technology security utilized in the transmission of medical information to ensure that data can not be accessed by unauthorized third parties. The areas of concern within the transmission of data are:

1. Data authentication to ensure data is not altered during the transmission of protected data from one entity to another.

2. External protection to minimize the possibility of intruders gaining access through communication ports.

3. Encryption technology to ensure that if data is intercepted it is not easily accessed or understood.

The regulations have been written in such a way that it remains technology neutral. Each entity will be required to assess and implement technology that it believes will reasonably satisfy the requirements of the legislature. This stance also allows for the adoption of newer and more secure technology as it becomes available.

Of key note to directory users is that HIPAA requires medical records to be held for six years or more. During that time, several practitioners and other medical staff will need access to those records. By constructing an audit trail, a company can monitor the access activity of specific medical files.

Log files are the mechanism by which to record audit trails. This is an essential consideration to the directory manager. Properly documenting logs in this way is crucial for corrective and/or legal action, as it reveals the sequence of events of the incident in question.

A directory administrator should consider the following:

• Enabling Event Auditing is done within the directory application. Various events to consider monitoring are: authentication, creation/deletion of sensitive information, access rights administration, and any additional actions that might affect the security of the system.

- Save the directory logs on a separate system or disk on a regular basis.

- Use a third party monitoring and filtering tool. There are several to choose from and they vary in scope and price.

If a company does business in the health care environment, the first step is to determine whether the business is affected by HIPAA.

There are two groups defined by HIPAA that must comply with the regulation. They are defined as a Covered Entity and a Business Partner.

- Covered entities must comply with all aspects of HIPAA and it is towards these organizations that the legislation is directed.

- Business partners would be required to comply with HIPAA through individual contracts with each covered entity. The purpose of these contracts would be to extend the "sphere of privacy" coverage that exists for the primary health care organization on to the business partner's organization. A business partner, is not directly accountable to HIPAA. It is the covered entity through the contract that will impose HIPAA compliance on the organization.

The fact that a company does business in the health care environment does not in itself mandate HIPAA compliance. It depends on how the company interacts with the covered entity. It must comply with HIPAA (through a contract with each individual covered entity) if it stores or process protected health information.

Who has to comply with HIPAA:

- Health Care Plan consisting of: provider that serves more than 50 participants and is administered by someone other than the

employer; health insurance issuer; health maintenance organization; and most all other types of health care plan providers. See
public law 104-191 for complete details.

- Health Care Clearinghouses, public or private that processes
  health information.

- Health Care Provider of medical or other health services and
  any other person furnishing health care services or supplies.

The HIPAA legislation sets forth civil and federal penalties for the misuse of patient information by covered entities. Civil penalties include a
$100 per person per incident fine with maximums of $25,000 per person for each standard within a single year for all health plans, providers
and clearinghouses. Covering the same three groups, federal penalties
of up to $50,000 and one year imprisonment could be levied for
knowingly obtaining or disclosing protected information. A stiffer pen-
alty of up to $100,000 and five years imprisonment could result if the
misuse is under false pretense; and up to $250,000 and 10 years of
imprisonment for obtaining or disclosing protected information with
the intent to sell, transfer, or use for personal or commercial gain or to
cause malicious harm. The HIPAA legislation supersedes all current
state laws that contradict this legislation by providing less stringent
requirements. State laws that provide for stronger security and privacy
will still apply. The penalties stated above do not affect other federal
penalties imposed by other federal legislation

Other information of note

- The Privacy Act of 1974, PL 93-579.

- Computer Security Act of 1987, PL 100-235.

- National Security Decision Directive Number 145, National
  Policy on Telecommunications and Automated Information
  Systems Security.

- DoD Directive 5200.28, Security Requirements for Automated Information Systems.

- Department of Defense Trusted Computer System Evaluation Criteria.

GLBA—GRAMM LEACH BLILEY ACT OF 1999

Gramm Leach Bliley Act of 1999 (referred here as GLBA or the Act) and also known as the Financial Services Modernization Act of 1999. The Act requires banks to develop privacy notices and give their customers the option to prohibit the banks from sharing their customer information with non affiliated third parties. The Act also requires financial institutions to have a comprehensive written information security program in place by July 1, 2001. This has a direct impact on directory implementers and directory managers which will become evident upon explanation of the act.

Potential supervisory authorities include

- Office of the Comptroller of the Currency (OCC),

- The Federal Reserve System (Fed),

- The Federal Deposit Insurance Corporation (FDIC)

- The Office of Thrift Supervision (OTS)

The Fed, OTS, OCC and FDIC published a joint final rule entitled "Interagency Guidelines Establishing Standards for Safeguarding Customer Information". By attaching the guidelines as an appendix to their safety and soundness regulations, the agencies made it clear that complying with the guidelines, or the failure to do so, would affect the safety and soundness of the institution. Since all four agencies agreed on a common terminology and interpretation of the Act with only slight differences.

The following key terms and phrases used throughout the Act.

- Customers and consumers
- Customer information
- Customer Information System
- Nonpublic personal information
- Service provider

The guidelines define the difference between a consumer and a customer. Under the Privacy Rule, a customer is a consumer who has established a continuing relationship with an institution under which the institution provided one or more financial products or services to the consumer to be used primarily for personal, family or household purposes. Customer does not include a business, nor does it include a consumer who has not established an ongoing relationship with a financial institution (e.g., an individual who merely uses an institution's ATM or applies for a loan). See sections 3(h) and (i) of the Privacy Rule. It is very important to remember that the GLBA does not apply to business entities.

Customer information is defined as "any records containing nonpublic personal information, as defined in section .3(n) of the Privacy Rule for each Agency, about a customer." Since the GLBA refers to the protection of customer records and information, the guidelines uses customer information to refer to both information and records.

Nonpublic personally identifiable information is defined as personally identifiable financial information that is not available publicly and is either created or contains nonpublic personal information. Examples of nonpublic personally identifiable information would be lists containing such information as loan balances or overdraft information. While a list of public personal information would only contain such things as name, address, phone number and other publicly available types of account information (such as mortgages) held at the bank.

Customer information system is defined to be "any methods used to access, collect, store, use, transmit, protect, or dispose of customer information."

A service provider is defined as any person or entity that maintains, processes, or otherwise is permitted access to customer information through its provision of services directly to the client or the bank.

Each financial institution is responsible for assessing, managing and controlling the risk to their customers' information. First and foremost, the Act requires the bank to design an information security program that adequately protects customer information based on the complexity and scope of the bank's activity. For example given the inherent risks of the Internet, banks that have Internet banking capabilities have a much higher potential risk to customer information than a traditional bricks and mortar bank.

Each institution must consider the following eight factors when designing their information security program. While they do not have to implement every suggestion, they need to adopt the appropriate ones for their bank's size and complexity.

The eight factors for protecting customer information are:

- Access control
- Physical security at locations where customer information is stored
- Encryption of electronic customer information (especially in transit)
- Implement a change management process for customer information system modifications

- Dual control, segregation of duties and employee background checks for employees with access to customer information

- Monitoring systems and procedures to detect any actual or attempted attacks or intrusions on customer information systems

- Develop an incident response program for how to handle attempted and actual unauthorized access to customer information

- Disaster recovery program for the protection against destruction of customer information due to physical hazards and technical failures

Taking the above into account the directory, as both data repository and authentication database is a key component in the enforcement and implementation of the GLBA statutes, Care should be taken in the data analysis and ownership phases of the metadirectory implementation. Encryption of data and proper ACL placement as well as accurate use of delegated management and role-based security are essential to proper implementation of GLBA requirements.

DOC SAFE HARBOR

While the United States and the European Union share the goal of enhancing privacy protection for their citizens, the United States takes a different approach to privacy from that taken by the European Union. The United States uses a sectoral approach that relies on a mix of legislation, regulation, and self regulation. The European Union, however, relies on comprehensive legislation that, for example, requires creation of government data protection agencies, registration of databases, including directories, with those agencies, and in some instances prior approval before personal data processing may begin. As a result of these different privacy approaches, the Directive could have significantly hampered the ability of U.S. companies to engage in many trans-Atlantic transactions

The U.S. and European Union (EU) have historically taken differing approaches to protecting the privacy of their citizens and the free movement of personal data. The EU has moved toward comprehensive legislation with the adoption of the Directive on Data Protection (Directive 95/46/EC), while the U.S. relies on an approach based heavily on industry and self regulation, combining some federal and state legislation where needed.

Directive 95/46/EC prohibits the transfer of personal data from EU members to non EU nations except in those cases where the non EU nation has complied with the European "adequacy" standard for privacy protection. As a nation, the U.S.'s current approach to privacy protection is not considered to be adequate by European standards.

Recognizing the potential impact on trade with EU member nations, the U.S. Department of Commerce negotiated with the EU to develop the safe harbor provisions, which provide individual U.S. organizations with clear mechanisms for addressing this situation. Under the safe harbor provisions, organizations are provided a means by which they can assert adequate privacy practices, thus avoiding potential interruptions in flow of critical business data or the potential prosecution by European authorities under European privacy laws.

The European Commission's Directive on Data Protection (Directive 95/46/EC) went into effect in October 1998. The Directive enables the free movement of personal data between the 15 European Union member states by harmonizing national data protection laws. The differences between the national data protection laws of the various member states were seen as an obstacle that could seriously impede the future growth of the information society.

The Directive is designed to protect privacy of individuals by legislating the manner in which personal data is processed, where processing includes operations such as collection, storage, disclosure, etc. Personal data is limited to information that relates to any identified person (e.g., names, birth dates, unique identifiers, pictures, addresses, etc.) as well as information that could reasonably lead to the identification of an unknown person.

The Directive places obligations on all data controllers (i.e., individuals determining the purposes and means of processing) to collect personal data only for specified, legitimate purposes and to use it accordingly. This is of direct concern to implementers of directory systems, which not only maintain personal data but also regulate access to that data. Data controllers are advised to keep data in a form, which permits identification of individuals for, no longer than it is necessary. Under the Directive, data subjects have the right to access their personal data, the right to know where the data originated, the right to have inaccurate data rectified, a right of recourse in the event of unlawful processing and the right to withhold permission to use their data in certain circumstances. This makes employee self service of a directory system a mandate for any company working under the European union jurisdiction or the DOC safe harbor framework. Sensitive data, such as an individual's ethnic or racial origin, political or religious beliefs, trade union membership or data concerning medical history or sexual orientation, can only be processed with the explicit consent of the individual making these fields optional and not allowed to be pre-populated by an HR application or provisioning system. Situations were there is a critical public interest is considered exceptions, however, alternative safeguards must be established.

In order to ensure the continued protection of personal data, the Directive prohibits the transfer of such data to non European Union nations that do not meet the European "adequacy" standard for privacy protection. This restricts the type of replication agreements and metadirectory joins that can be used to connect international directory systems. Certain limited exceptions are supported by the Directive where the individual has given their unambiguous consent for the transfer or where the transfer is in response to actions taken by the individual (e.g., job application) or if the transfer is perceived as protecting the vital interests of the individual. Transfers can also be allowed in cases where contractual provisions have been developed that bind the receiver of the data to providing the same safeguards as enumerated within the Directive. Properly implemented metadirectory systems can be used to facilitate compliance with this directive.

A Safe Harbor: Program Overview

Implications of the EU Directive for multinational organizations could be significant, resulting in the disruption of business operations. Concerned about the potential impact on U.S.—EU trade, which in 1999 amounted to $350 billion, the U.S. Department of Commerce, in consultation with the European Commission, has established a "safe harbor" framework for U.S. organizations. Under this agreement, U.S. companies can continue to receive personal data from all 15 EU member states, as long as they subscribe to a set of privacy principles associated with the safe harbor provision. The safe harbor principles were developed to more closely reflect the U.S. approach to privacy while also meeting the European Commission adequacy standards.

The safe harbor provisions were approved by the EU in July, 2000 and went into effect in the U.S. in November 1, 2000. This program is applicable to any U.S. organization receiving or storing personally identifiable data about citizens from any of the European Union countries. In order to participate organizations will need to either adopt or modify current data protection practices so they are compliant the seven safe harbor principles. Then, on an annual basis, the organization will be required to self certify to the Department of Commerce that it agrees to adhere to the safe harbor requirements. The organization's published privacy policy must also state that it adheres to the safe harbor privacy principles. A list of the safe harbor organizations will be maintained by the Department of Commerce at their website (**www.export.gov/safeharbor**).

Enforcement will rely heavily on private sector self-regulation, with approved government agencies providing back up through the enforcement of federal and state laws prohibiting unfair and deceptive acts. In order for the safe harbor provisions to be successful, organizations failing to comply with self-regulation must be actionable by approved government bodies. The Federal Trade Commission and the Department of Transportation have both pledged to enforce actions against organizations failing to live up to claims of compliance. For example, the Federal Trade Commission Act makes it illegal in the U.S. to make representations to consumers or to commit deceptive acts that are likely to mislead reasonable consumers. As such, the FTC has the ability to seek civil penalties up to $12,000 per day for violations and instances of misrepresentation by organizations failing to abide by prior stated commitments to the safe harbor privacy principles.

At this point in time, only those organizations falling under the jurisdiction of the FTC or U.S. air carriers and ticket agents subject to the jurisdiction of the DOT may participate in the safe harbor program. This currently excludes the financial services and telecommunications sectors. Discussions specifically regarding financial services have been placed on hold pending guidance regarding the implementation of the Gramm-Leach-Bliley Act of 1999. It is expected that additional government agencies will agree to enforce the program provisions thus opening the program to other industries.

Participation in the safe harbor is completely voluntary. Organizations may choose to explore other alternatives such as negotiating directly with European authorities regarding the transfer of information. Organizations can also chose to change business processes such that personal data is processed within EU member state borders or made anonymous either by stripping relevant fields or through aggregation. The safe harbor principles are thought to offer a more flexible and simpler means of demonstrating compliance, which will particularly benefit small to medium enterprises.

Safe Harbor Principles

Compliant privacy policies must address the seven safe harbor privacy principles as well as any relevant points covered in the safe harbor frequently asked questions (FAQs). In addition, the privacy policy must document actual and planned information handling practices, and clearly state that the organization is compliant with the safe harbor privacy principles.

The FAQs provide guidance for implementing the privacy provisions with respect to specific industries or types of data. In addition, exceptions to the provisions are discussed. For instance, the FAQs address journalistic exceptions, the issue of secondary liability, and requirements for handling data such as human resources information, travel information, and information relating to the development of pharmaceutical and medical products. Other FAQs provide elaboration on meeting particular aspects of the safe harbor principles such as verification and enforcement.

A high level overview of the safe harbor principles is as follows:

- **Notice**—Organizations must inform individuals as to the purposes for which information about them is being collected and used, and the types of third parties to whom the organization may disclose information. Individuals must be informed how they can contact the organization with inquires or complaints as well as the choices they have with respect to limiting the use and disclosure of information about them.

- **Choice**—Individuals must be provided the opportunity to "opt out" of allowing their information to be disclosed to a third party or to be used for a purpose incompatible with the purpose for which it was originally collected.

- **Safe Harbor Sensitive Information Principle**—For sensitive personal information, such as that specifying medical conditions, racial or ethnic origin, political opinions, religious beliefs, or sexual orientation, individuals must explicitly "opt in" before such information can be disclosed to a third party or be used in a manner other than for which it was originally collected.

- **Onward Transfer**—Prior to disclosing information to a third party, the organization must ensure that the third party provides the same level of privacy protection as required by the safe harbor principles. Having done this, the organization will not be held responsible should the third party process the data in a manner contrary to the safe harbor privacy principles.

- **Security**—Organizations must take reasonable precautions to protect personal information from loss, misuse and unauthorized access, disclosure, alteration and destruction.

- **Data Integrity**—Organizations must take reasonable steps to ensure that data is accurate, complete, current, relevant, and reliable for its intended use.

- **Access**—Organizations must provide individuals with access to personal information collected about them. Individuals must be allowed to correct, amend, or delete such information if it is inaccurate. Exceptions to this principle may be allowed where the burden or expense of providing such access is considered disproportionate to the risks to the individual's privacy.

- **Enforcement**—Organizations must define procedures and mechanisms for assuring compliance with the principles. These mechanisms must also include a means by which complaints and disputes raised will be investigated and resolved, and obligations whereby sanctions will be applied should the organization fail to be compliant.

A statement of verification must either be signed by a corporate officer or an independent reviewer indicating that the organization's published privacy policy is accurate, comprehensive, prominently displayed, completely implemented, and in compliance with the safe harbor principles. Coradon Consulting Inc. provides this service in regard to provisioning, directory and metadirectory services. Its website can be found at **http://www.coradon.com**.

Organizations must also clearly advertise how complaints from individuals who feel their privacy may have been violated will be investigated and resolved. Organizations can choose to engage a third party dispute resolution mechanism by complying with one of the private sector seal programs being developed by entities such as BBBOnline, Truste, AICPA WebTrust, and the Direct Marketing Association.

Organizations may also choose to cooperate with either U.S. government supervisory authorities or data protection authorities located in Europe. Regardless of the dispute resolution system chosen, the safe harbor provisions require that potential sanctions applied through the system must be severe enough to ensure compliance by the organization. For instance, they should include public notification of findings of non-compliance as well as possible suspension from the safe harbor program in some cases.

Organizations may choose to withdraw from the program at any time by notifying the Department of Commerce. Failure to comply with safe harbor provisions without officially withdrawing from the program could be interrupted as a misrepresentation with respect to asserted compliance. Such misrepresentations could be actionable under the False Statements Act (18 U.S.C. 1001).

Private Sector Seal Programs

Truste, a non profit organization which currently licenses its existing seal to approximately 2,000 Web sites, announced on November 1, 2000 that they would be launching a safe harbor certification program. Under the program Truste would certify that an organization's data gathering and handling practices and policies are in compliance with safe harbor provisions. A quarterly monitoring program will be implemented to support enforcement of the provisions and ensure ongoing compliance. As an additional service, Truste will handle dispute resolution for organization's participating under its certification program. The dispute resolution can cover both online and offline cases. Such private sector seal programs are welcomed and supported by the Department of Commerce. Additional information about the Truste program and a model compliant privacy statement can be found at their website **http://www.truste.com**. Similar programs are under development by BBBOnline, AICPA WebTrust, and the Direct Marketing Association.

While increased reliance on the Internet has allowed for significant growth in international e-commerce, conducting business around the globe introduces many issues that are not solved strictly by technology. In order to successfully maximize international e-commerce opportunities, organizations must be sensitive to the differences within specific countries with respect to consumer protection and privacy laws.

The European Commission Directive on Data Protection is of particular interest to organizations seeking to conduct business within any of the 15 European Union member states. In an effort to protect the personal information of European Union citizens, the directive legislates that personal information may only be transferred to non European Union nations where the receiving nation has implemented privacy protections deemed adequate under the provisions of the directive. U.S. companies choosing to comply with the safe harbor provisions would be allowed to continue to receive and handle personal information regarding citizens from European Union nations.

To date, adoption of the Safe Harbor provisions has been slow. As of January 5, 2001 only 12 companies have joined the safe harbor program. In an effort to raise awareness about the program and encourage participation, the Department of Commerce is partnering with the Software and Information Association (SIIA), the U.S. Council for International Business, and Morrison & Foerster to offer the Safe Harbor Business Implementation Forum. The forum is being offered early this spring in California, Washington D.C., New York, and Dallas. The focus of the event is to raise awareness among industry representatives regarding the new U.S.-EU Safe Harbor agreement and provide guidance for developing corporate data privacy policies. For more information see **http://www.trensreport.net/events/calendar/events.asp**

MERGERS, ACQUISITIONS AND DIVESTITURES.

Mergers, Acquisitions and Divestitures represent a complex challenge in the blending or separation of corporate directories. Added to this is the special challenge for today's information-economy enterprises, where IT resources are tightly integrated with business processes, and success depends on secure, reliable connectivity. Many questions arise when the boundaries of an organization are redefined.

- How will the directory of an acquired operation be merged with that of its new parent?

- How will its removal from a former parent affect the performance and security of both systems?

- How will different platforms, protocols, hardware combinations, naming conventions, and security policies be merged together seamlessly?

- How do you transform your directories without interfering with the day-to-day operations of all the organizations involved?

According to Business Layers, M&A specialist Seth Deutsch, This type of due diligence process, where integation is a sepreate phase produces the following aggregate outcomes:

- Only 23 percent of all acquisitions earn at leas the cost of capital;

- In Ex Post (before the merger analysis), the purchasing company's stock rises in only 30 percent of all cases;

- In acquired companies, while in Ex Post analysis, their stock rises initially in more than 65 percent of the cases, 47 percent of key executives leave within the first year of the completed transaction, and 75 percent leave within the first three years;

- Synergies, which ranks as one of the most ill-designed ways to predict and/or evaluate the success of M&A, fail to realize their perceived affects in more than 70 percent of the cases after two years;

- In the first four to eight months of the integration phase (see Figure 1), productivity has been recorded as being reducded by up to 50 percent;

- The average financial performance of newly merged companies is graded by their managers as a C-.

It is clear that the pure strategy of acquisitions and divestitures is not realizing the types of results its proponents profer, and the majority of times Acquisitions and Divestitures is reaching the point of failure in the integration phase. Before going deeper into the specifics of the process and the data, It is important to examine what executuves have identified as issues with regard to integration.

According to Deutsch, a record number of mergers and acquisitions were staged in 1999 totaling more than $3.4 trillion in capital invested—but fewer than half of these of failed to deliver the success and value thought to be inherent to the deal itself. In the year 2000 and 2001 the number of Mergers, Acquisitions and Divestitures had been slowing down for various economic reasons, some qualitative and other quantitative, but to a large extent companies have not been able to integrate acquired or merged units in a way that leads to value building growth. Directory mismanagement is a key symptom integration deficiency and can be leveraged to increase value in the M&A process. In most of the cases cited the transactions were executed on paper, but not executed in practice. Organizations are shedding non-core, non-integrated and mismanaged units. The technical and cost implications of divestitures can add up if all of the associated assets relative to the divested tangible and intangible assets are not accounted for and reconciled in a timely and efficient manner. According to Deutsch, The trends and perception that mergers and acquisitions (M&A) create value for shareholders and stakeholders has led to a 377% increase in M&A activity since 1997. Clearly, Mergers, Acquisitions and Divestitures have become one of the most important methods of reallocating resources, achieving strategic growth and building long-term value—at least that is the premise under which Mergers, Acquisitions and Divestitures take place. The delivery and execution of the mergers and acquisitions has certainly not lived up to expectations more often due to lack of integration at the data and system levels.

Booz, Allen and Hamilton conducted a research study revealed that 51.3 percent of M&A transactions executed resulted in the cannibalization of shareholder value, while 48.7 percent resulted in positive gains over a two year period (Albert J. Viscio, John R. Harbison, Amy Asin and Richard P. Vitaro, 1999). Other studies have shown that in all, M&A activity fails in more than 60 percent of the cases wherein it is executed as a pattern of strategic growth—and wherein 55 percent of those failures are reported in the "integration" phase. When coupling the extraordinary failure rate of M&A with its staggering growth rate, it becomes clear that global organizations are not taking the right steps to ensure success. As a hard fact, the failure rate accounted for $2.04 trillion, or almost 4 percent of the United State's Gross National Product, in transaction costs alone (not including the soft costs unreported in trying to achieve integration, market share and/or customer share lost, et cetera). Clearly there is room for improvement.

The room for improvement lies in the real methodologies and processes used to evaluate deals that have a real impact on organizations, employees, shareholders and all constituents tied to the deal being made. There are many reasons within these methodologies of deal making that point to failure—yet no one, to date, has put together a comprehensive and holistic view that considers all soft assets along with process and technology to create value.

Speed and execution can be addresses simultaneously if the right steps are taken very early on. This is extremely important for companies that approach MD&A activites as essential to growth and will pursue multiple opportunites in a given year and over a span of time. Speed and execution are addressed by putting a platform, team, and process into place that are treated as reusable objectds within an organization. Speed and execution are also realized when directory integration is introduced very early into the process; thus, when the deal is done, it is really a matter of turning on the light, not building the infrastrucutre to deliver electricity to the merger organizations. The MD&A directory methodology is based on a staggered, iterative process that describes the integration based on directory technology and related systems, data, and is utilized at the beginning of the due diligence. Thus, the platform is always being used and is always part of the process; this enables the MD&A directory team to gather experience throughout all points of intersection, and leads to greater ability to move quickly and efficiently. It also eliminates the type of down time and ineffeciency often realized in the first six months following an acquisition, and therefore had a positive multiplier affect in realizing returns on capital employed, positive gains in shareholder value, and positive expasion with regard to both customer and market share.

Use and Philosophy of Information Technology:

- What types of technology platforms and architecture currently exist?
- Is there a planned investment in IT or any directory related initiativcs?
- Is there schema and hardware compatibility?
- Which business systems are in use and which are still on the books but no longer in use?
- Which business systems are in development?
- Is there compatibility of business systems, and if so to what extent?
- How is directory technology being used to leverage staff experience, knowledge, and increase productivity?
- How is the mobile computing handled?
- What inter directory communication systems exist?
- Is the overlap and synergy in communications systems or will there be need for consolidation, reconciliation and integration?
- What skill levels exist within current software applications?
- With which products, suites and programs?
- How is the IT department serviced and staffed?
- What is the current level of directory service and support, and what will the new company need?
- What are the current issues or concerns with IT, in general?

- What major legacy systems and applications exist?

Information Transfer Between and Among Individuals:

- Is communication between and among individuals and departments typically formal or informal? Are directories shared across departments?

- Are instructions, feedback and communication given primarily in writing or in person?

- To ensure fast and effective transfer of information, what types of regularly scheduled meetings exist throughout the organization?

- Are the meetings effective in attaining their goals or are they perceived more as obligatory time constraints?

Organizational Information Transfer:

- How readily is directory information (about financial, HR, operating performance, and so on) disseminated throughout the organization?

- What is routinely communicated or held back?

- To what extent do employees and managers believe that they have access to important information?

- What types of organization wide communication channels, programs and media exist?

Human Capital:

- How is the human resources (HR) department positioned in the organization—as a strategic business partner? An administrative unit?

- To what extent are HR systems directory enabled

- How able is HR to affect significant change in the organization?

- How are reward programs designed to motivate desired types of behavior and align them with business objectives?

- What is the data stewardship strategy, Who is authorative?

- How are benefits provided?

- What level of internal customer service or employee self-service is provided to employees?

- What is the general orientation of the company to its employees?

- Does the data demonstrate that HR data is treated as a valued resource? How?

Enable

Communication:

- Users should be able to use directories to generate ad hoc lists easily, including lists generated by role; by cost center; by organization; by title; by application; by project; and by combinations of these and other attributes.

- New companies also have multiple e-mail systems and communication devices. Directory consolidation is essential to enable communication quickly from an IT perspective.

Prepare for the Future: Mergers, divestitures and acquisitions will happen repeatedly in the life of the corporation. It is essential that companies integrate quickly to prepare for their next phase of growth. If companies cannot realize operational synergies through integration they will realize financial pressure quickly as they continue to acquire or will have to back away from strategic targets because of ongoing negative financial implications. Integrate to prepare for the next deal.

Executing mergers and acquisitions is not easy, and has not proven to be successful for most companies. Failure resides in two intertwined areas: the failure to execute a successful process, and the failure to gather and analyze the right types of value. Central to this process is the directory which serves as the center post for all IT systems and applications

Appendix

Vendor List

Directory Services Vendors
Critical Path: **http://www.cp.net/**
Data Connection: **http://www.dataconnection.com/**
IBM/Lotus IBM SecureWay Directory: **http://www-3.ibm.com/software/network/directory/**
Sun ONE/iPlanet: **http://www.iplanet.com/**
Microsoft: **http://www.microsoft.com/ms.htm**
Mirapoint **http://www.mirapoint.com/**
Novell: **http://www.novell.com/**
Opennetwork Technologies: **http://www.opennetwork.com/**
Oracle: **http://www.oracle.com/**
Siemens: **http://www.siemens.com/**
Syntegra: **http://www.syntegra.com/**

Virtual Directory Vendors
MaXware International: **http://www.maxware.com/**
Radiant Logic: **http://main.radiantlogic.com/RLISite/**
Schlumberger: **http://www.slb.com/**

Directory Manipulation Product Vendors
Bowstreet: **http://www.bowstreet.com/**
Calendra: **http://www.calendra.com/us/home/index.htm**
Metamerge: **http://www.metamerge.com**
Oblix: **http://www.oblix.com/**

Provisioning Software Vendors

Access360: **http://www.access360.com**

BMC Software: **http://www.bmc.com/**

Business Layers: **http://www.businesslayers.com/**

Waveset: **http://www.waveset.com/**

Thor Technologies: **http://www.thortech.com**

Capabilities Statement

CORADON CONSULTING INC.
Directory, Metadirectory & Provisioning Specialists

Capabilities Statement

Capability Statement

Our group has over 12 years of experience designing, implementing and integrating Active Directory, LDAP & x.500 Directory, Metadirectory and Provisioning system architectures. Our clients include Citibank, AXA Financial Services, GE Equity, Alliance Capital, Bank of New York and the US Department of Defense. We have acted as subcontractors for Netscape, iPlanet, Sun Professional Services, IBM, Lotus Development, Schlumberger and BEA Systems.

Services Include:
- Directory Architecture Methodology
- Directory DOC Safe Harbor Audit & Certification
- 3rd Party Architecture and Implementation Audit
- Directory services for Mergers, Divestitures and Aquisitions

Using the **Pohlman Metadirectory Methodology** described in our book **LDAP Metadirectory Provisioning Methodology**, our team can design systems to scale to tens of millions of directory entries.

There are times a corporation will require a second opinion regarding a existing deployment, architecture, proposal, statement of work or professional services engagement. As a non-bias 3rd party we are positioned to provide an objective viewpoint regarding progress, cost, architecture, RFP, and general health of a engagement or deployment.

In addition, our team drawing on a wealth of international experience offers directory audits for compliance with
- *USA Patriot Act of 2001*
- HIPPA Health Insurance Portability Accountability Act
- GLBA—Gramm Leach Bliley Act
- DOC Safe Harbor
- Anti Trust Legislation

CORADON CONSULTING INC.

7966 East 41st Unit 11
Tulsa, Ok 74145

Phone: 918-633-7798
Alt: 918-746-1914
Fax: 281-966-1863
Email: mpohlman@coradon.com

(Email for a quote)

Biography

Marlin Pohlman has over 14 years experience in x.500 and LDAP based directory structures. As a former Sr. Managing Principal for Netscape professional services Mr. Pohlman lead the directory server implementation for companies such as Ford Motor Co, The Automotive Industry Action Group, Home Depot, Citigroup, AXA Insurance, Bank of NY, Alliance capital, GE Equity, Federal Express and the US Department of Defense Credit card issuance system. Dr. Pohlman was an original contributor to the IETF ASID group and implemented the worlds 2nd implementation of RFC 1777 for Sanlam insurance, in Cape Town, South Africa. The directory structure implemented in

Sydney Australia, for the 2000 Olympics held the record for the largest non x.500 meta directory implementation in a client server environment. Dr. Pohlman received his MBA from Lexington and his Ph.D. in computer science from Trinity. His thesis was "Scaling Factors in Very Large, High Availability Directory Architectures." Special thanks to Ivan Henley, Assoc. editor

0-595-26726-2